The State
after Communism

The State after Communism

Governance in the New Russia

Edited by
Timothy J. Colton and Stephen Holmes

ROWMAN & LITTLEFIELD PUBLISHERS, INC.
Lanham • Boulder • New York • Toronto • Oxford

ROWMAN & LITTLEFIELD PUBLISHERS, INC.

Published in the United States of America
by Rowman & Littlefield Publishers, Inc.
A wholly owned subsidary of The Rowman & Littlefield Publishing Group, Inc.
4501 Forbes Boulevard, Suite 200, Lanham, Maryland 20706
www.rowmanlittlefield.com

P.O. Box 317, Oxford OX2 9RU, UK

British Library Cataloguing in Publication Information Available

Library of Congress Cataloguing-in-Publication Data

The state after communism : governance in the new Russia / edited by
Timothy J. Colton and Stephen Holmes.
    p. cm.
    Includes bibliographical references and index.
    ISBN-13: 978-0-7425-3941-9 (cloth : alk. paper)
    ISBN-10: 0-7425-3941-5 (cloth : alk. paper)
    ISBN-13: 978-0-7425-3942-6 (pbk. : alk. paper)
    ISBN-10: 0-7425-3942-3 (pbk. : alk. paper)
    1. Russia (Federation)—Politics and government—1991– 2. Post-communism—
Russia (Federation)   I. Colton, Timothy J., 1947–   II. Holmes, Stephen, 1948–
   JN6695.S737 2006
   320.947—dc22

                               2006009571

Printed in the United States of America

♾™ The paper used in this publication meets the minimum requirements of American
National Standard for Information Sciences—Permanence of Paper for Printed Library
Materials, ANSI/NISO Z39.48–1992.

Contents

Figures

Tables

Chapter One

Introduction: Governance and Postcommunist Politics

Timothy J. Colton

Stephen Holmes and I undertook this volume, and the collaborative project underlying it, because we sensed that something surprising and intellectually challenging was happening to and with the state in the several dozen Eurasian and East European countries where communist regimes crumbled at the turn of the 1990s. This puzzling phenomenon most caught our eye in Russia, the birthplace of the single-party Leninist dictatorship, and so we selected it as our empirical laboratory.[1] Its experience, our preliminary conversations convinced us, was not only of inherent interest but would afford general lessons for the comparative study of social and political change.

RUSSIA'S PUZZLING STATE

Western specialists on the Soviet system were in their day preoccupied with the state and with the apparatus of the Communist Party sitting at its core. It would never have entered their heads to ignore the top-down governing structures that penetrated, monitored, and guided every sphere of life. Not coincidentally, the title of the best-selling textbook on the politics of the USSR, by Merle Fainsod, was *How Russia Is Ruled*.[2] After communism's collapse, a bottom-up research agenda for Russia and its neighbors suddenly seemed apt. The hegemonic party was in its grave; a self-declared democrat, Boris Yeltsin, was in the Kremlin; political competition had been introduced; and subjects

1

had been turned into citizens. Foreign and indigenous scholars were dazzled by all manner of opportunities for delving into previously closed or secondary realms. There was an explosion of work on such matters as public opinion, voting choice and electoral cleavages, party development, civil society, and the emergence of a business class.[3] Of special relevance to continent-spanning and multiethnic Russia, again for the best of reasons, was the knot of issues associated with regional and municipal government, minority nationalism, and federalism.[4] Governance, the central state, the federal ministries, and public policy were the odd men out.[5]

A bias toward grassroots research and relative indifference toward the state resonated with the larger literature on regime change. The canonic works on democratization in the late twentieth century, which had plenty to say about the doings of state officials in the phase of breakdown of authoritarian rule, banished them to the margins once the "transition" to a more democratic political system had gathered momentum. In their panoramic essay on democratization in Latin America and southern Europe, for example, Guillermo O'Donnell and Philippe C. Schmitter wrote at length about the tug of war between hard-liners and soft-liners in the bureaucracy and armed forces on the eve of and during the course of negotiations with opposition groups over opening up the old regime. Governmental officials then fade out of the picture, dislodged by themes like round tables and pact making, the resurrection of civil society, and founding elections. The possibility of "selective repression, manipulation, and cooptation by those still in control of the state apparatus" did not become a reality.[6] In a more recent tour of the horizon, Juan J. Linz and Alfred Stepan acknowledged the topicality of "stateness" to democratic transition and consolidation. Unfortunately, they reduced stateness to the issue of national boundaries and citizenship and proffered little about bureaucracy or state actors' influence over events, active and passive, in other respects.[7]

Given the twin legacies of tsarist and Soviet tyranny and Sovietologists' fixation on the party-state, it is profoundly ironic that students of present-day Russia would need to hear the injunction to "bring the state back in" that rang out two decades ago among scholars of other parts of the globe where the state was traditionally a far less awesome player.[8] But hear it they must, if their work is to hold up an accurate mirror to postcommunist politics and to engage other social scientists.

What exactly is it about the state after communism that warrants our attention? Anna Grzymala-Busse and Pauline Jones Luong have observed that the prevailing view of the communist state as a towering "behemoth" tempted anticommunist critics and then successor governments at the outset to be more concerned with dismantling state institutions than with building them. The task of postcommunist rulers, however, is to construct a serviceable state that politicians can harness to fulfillment of society's requirements and yearnings. This building effort, Grzymala-Busse and Jones Luong reasoned, will tell political scientists a great deal "about how the state becomes—that is, how it comes into being and into action in the modern era."[9]

In framing *The State after Communism*, we came at the problem from the same overall direction but not quite the same angle of attack. Whereas democratic politics and market economics may be thought of as the inverse of practices under Soviet-style communism (authoritarian mobilization and the command economy), inversion does not apply as neatly to the state. States are indeed pivotal in the post-Soviet and postcommunist space, but they did not so much have to be conjured into being as to be *rebuilt and reprogrammed* to render them responsive, innovative, and effective tools of governance in a democratized political order.

Using Max Weber's not yet improved-upon definition of the state as a compulsory association that dominates a territory through monopoly of the legitimate use of force,[10] state structures existed on a massive scale on Russian and Soviet soil before 1991. Their personnel, physical assets, and sovereign authority passed into the hands of the governments that juridically succeeded the USSR. What is most fascinating about this institutional inheritance is how poorly it appears to have operated in the milieu into which it was transplanted.

A wave of violent criminality in the early Yeltsin years was the first trend that awakened scholars to the value of a decently run state in postcommunist Russia. The critique soon widened out to a much more all-embracing front. Scholars, us included, took to summarizing the travails of Russian government with the image of the "weak state." The catchphrase had already achieved considerable vogue in comparative politics by the 1980s, as analysts "started labeling states, especially modern national states, 'stronger' or 'weaker' according to how closely they approximated the ideal type of centralized and fully rationalized Weberian bureaucracy, supposedly able to work its will efficiently and without social opposition."[11] Taking contemporary Russia's measure by this yardstick, a host of analysts concluded that they were beholding virtually the epitome of the weak and dysfunctional state. On the ground in Russia, the apparent weakness of the state, Stephen Holmes put in print in 1997, had spawned an unexpected crisis of governance that was throwing into disrepute what remained of the democratic ideals in whose name communism had been overthrown: "The problem liberal reformers face is no longer censorship and the command economy . . . but something quite new: an incoherent state tenuously connected to a demoralized society."[12] In the same spirit, Mark R. Beissinger and Crawford Young pointed up "the massive failure of the state to live up to its own pretensions," drawing a comparison between postcommunist Eurasia and postcolonial Africa on this score, while the Russian sociologist Vadim Volkov characterized the state as mired in "deep functional crisis."[13]

Intriguingly, Russian politicians have not cared to dispute this diagnosis. Vladimir Putin, Russia's second president, explicitly endorsed it as he climbed to power in 1999–2000. Putin likened the Russian state to a broken-down jalopy. "The state machine," he said ruefully, "has gotten out of hand, and its motor, the executive branch, rattles and wheezes as soon as you try to get it into motion. Clerks shuffle paper without getting things done and have almost forgotten the meaning of official discipline."[14] Once installed as president, Putin saluted the "strong state" as Russia's salvation and pledged to bring it about, implicitly chiding Yeltsin for not doing the job on his watch: "My position is absolutely clear: only a strong or . . . if someone does not like the word 'strong,' let us say an effective state and a democratic state will be up to defending civil, political, and economic freedoms and able to create the conditions for social well-being and for our motherland to thrive."[15]

This statist rhetoric did not originate with Putin, whose well-known past in the security services presumably biases him toward it. The more democratically attuned Yeltsin, his ticket to the top a populist crusade against the heavy-handed Soviet state, routinely resorted to similar phrases, sometimes expatiating on them in graphic terms.[16] He named his maiden state-of-the-country address to parliament in 1994 "On the Strengthening of the Russian State." Describing the edifice of state as "weak" (*slaboye*), he sketched the same link to a devaluing of the post-Soviet reform course that Western scholars were starting to discern:

> We must confess openly that democratic principles and the organizations of government are more and more being discredited. There is being formed a negative image of democracy as a weak and amorphous system of power that gives little to the majority of people and defends above all its own corporate interests. Russian society has attained freedom, but does not yet feel democracy as a system of state power that is both strong and wholly accountable before the nation.[17]

In his 1997 message, billed as "Order in the State, Order in the Country," the president swore that governmental paralysis had hobbled economic, social, and legal advances:

> This has been discussed over and over again. Programs have been assembled and instructions have been issued, but [reform] continues to skid. The conclusion is clear: the big obstacle to the development of a new economic system and a new political system is the ineffectiveness of government, the absence of appropriate order in the work of the state apparatus. In other words, even when we build we do it slowly, chaotically, without discipline, and with extraordinary wastefulness.[18]

Holding forth to legislators the final time, in 1999, Yeltsin complained vehemently that the demands of his previous edicts had gone unmet and reminded his audience, "Problems of state building have been the leitmotif of all [my] presidential addresses."[19]

A close reading of these utterances hints at some of the complexities lurking in the political and academic discourse about state capacity. Skeptical voices in the scholarly literature on governance have long been cool to posing too rigid and apolitical a polarity between weak and strong states and have cautioned that state behavior and capacity must always be evaluated with respect to tangible purposes. They are on firm ground in insisting that the questions "How weak?" "How strong?" and "How capacious?" can be meaningfully answered only relative to the actual political *ends* pursued through state means.[20] It is eminently possible for a state to be feeble in some regards and formidable in some others.[21] It is also possible that the perception of the state's strength or weakness will itself be subject to manipulation for political purposes. Public officials may under certain conditions want to exaggerate state strength; under others, they may find it expedient to feign impotence in order to deflect annoying demands.

In the case at hand, today's Russia has not descended to the level of the "failed states," "collapsed states," and "shadow states" in which Africa abounds. Under Yeltsin and more so under Putin, state officials have asserted far greater sway over the instruments of naked coercion. Except in Chechnya, they have not tolerated the warlords and private armies that have cropped up in several other ex-Soviet countries.[22] There are certain things they do inadequately and grudgingly, but maintaining rudimentary physical control of their territory is not one of them.

In commenting on the state over which he presided, Yeltsin could refer in one breath to its weak and amorphous character and in the next to a bureaucracy that was somehow adept at protecting its corporate interests. Russia's state, in his judgment, was flaccid and unresponsive when it came to executing the collective will of society and its political representatives and yet quite nicely set up to collect rents on behalf of the individuals staffing it. This dualism threaded through Yeltsin's pronouncements. While castigating the state hierarchy for being a balky tool for him and his leadership colleagues, he repeatedly commented on the upward creep in the numbers of state employees and on the copious prerogatives they had amassed since 1991. In 1999 he pointed out how inventive state administrators were crafting "feeding systems" through such devices as off-budget slush funds, arbitrary fines, and trading in confiscated property. "One of the most serious defects in the setup of the organs of the state," he continued, "is the concentration in the same hands of regulatory, licensing, and checking functions, which creates fertile ground for abuses and corruption."[23]

The disinterestedness of Yeltsin's motives in volunteering these revelations may be questioned. He glossed over subtleties in describing the state's disorders—declining to mention, for one, that some of the new desks in the federal bureaucracy were there due to a transfer of welfare functions performed in the Soviet system by state-owned enterprises, rather than to scheming and empire building on the bureaucrats' part. And, like most domestic political actors, Yeltsin was loath to accept any of the blame for the state's disorders, while at the same time commenting scathingly on everyone else's eagerness to pass the buck.[24] Where, the woman or man on the street might fairly have wondered in listening to the lament, was Russia's elected president, so lavishly outfitted with constitutional powers, when such horrors were being perpetrated? How complicit were he and his political allies in them? Would different people at the helm have bred a different outcome, or was the design of executive institutions and not the people inhabiting them the culprit? How much of the fault lay with the legislative and judicial branches of government?

Our aim in the present collection is to explore the workings and dynamics of the postcommunist state through the tracing of specific aspects of its activity in the Russian Federation. We perceive this institutional construct as puzzling for a series of reasons. Prime among them is that what many think of as the abnormally weak Russian state is the descendant of a Soviet state that in its prime was generally considered abnormally strong. As Charles H. Fairbanks Jr. has remarked, "the quick transformation of an overly strong state into a very weak state [is] the key transition development that we did not foresee."[25]

To be sure, careful scholarship on the Soviet state has established that it was not without its infirmities. It was sapped of energy and élan over the years, and was infested with patron–client networks and turf wars.[26] It was more proficient at coercion and punishment than at fine-grained problem management, relying, in the idiom of Charles E. Lindblom, on blunt administrative thumbs rather than supple fingers.[27] The fact remains, though, that under the communists the state deployed vast resources to accomplish ambitious objectives, and this their heirs had difficulty doing with any consistency.

The Soviet state did not, of course, yield the stage to the post-Soviet Russian state overnight or without turbulence. Mikhail Gorbachev's quixotic attempt to save the Soviet system by reforming it from within had the unintended consequence of making the state weaker, producing by 1990–1991 the political equivalent of a bank run, as officials and citizens dissociated themselves from what increasingly looked like failing structures.[28] For many of those who brought down the communist regime, though, it was an article of faith that state malaise was no worse than one of the death pangs of communism and that normal governance would quickly ensue under the auspices of a democratic regime.

One background reason it did not, Holmes and I conjectured as our research group began work, is the appropriation of Soviet-era institutions by post-Soviet governments as fragments—fragments all originally spun off by an ideological, one-party dictatorship, headquartered in Moscow, that was dead and buried and that had never made any provision for their separate existence. Entities such as the government ministries, the Federal Security Service, the Procuracy, the Academy of Sciences, and the several state television stations were orphans of the Communist Party. Now cast adrift in search of a mission, they did not appear well suited by personnel endowment, structure, or administrative culture to serve democracy or free-market capitalism and did not quite know what their own interests were, beyond bare survival. Successor governments, for their part, were ill equipped to coordinate them or so much as to keep dependable track of these bureaucratic asteroids' whereabouts and actions. In short, we see here more than a morning-after effect of the dissolution of the Soviet dictatorship and the messiness of the interregnum. The syndrome has been robust enough to persist year after year despite what ostensibly was ample motivation to redress it.

The state in communism's wake is not coterminous with the replacement political regime and should not be conflated with it. Russia's regime since the Soviet implosion has been a hybrid mix of autocratic and democratic strands, with the former gradually gaining on the latter.[29] All the same, the pathologies of the state machinery were as vexing to leaders in the relatively liberal atmosphere of the early and mid-1990s as they were in the relatively illiberal times before and especially after the transfer of supreme power from Yeltsin to the more authoritarian Putin. Nor can the infirm state be interpreted as a straightforward expression of national mores and culture, a connection country specialists might naturally wish to make. Russia's heritage, Putin has correctly said, predisposes it in the diametrically opposite direction: "A strong state for Russians is not an anomaly, not something that must be fought against, but on the contrary is the source and guarantor of order, the initiator and main driving force of all change."[30] If that is so, then the chronic distemper of the past decade cries out for explanation.

Cross-national macrohistorical perspectives, along the avenue pioneered by Charles Tilly, may be of some utility in unraveling the mystery of the postcommunist state, provided they are deployed with discernment. Tilly tied the rise of modern states in Western Europe to the military imperative, depicting them as chiefly an inadvertent byproduct of dynastic rulers' efforts to form rule-sanctioned "protection rackets" that would prepare for, pay for, and wage wars.[31] This insight from centuries past may perhaps be transferable today to late industrializers laboring to erect a state from scratch, and in a modified way to the Soviet Union itself, which had a mammoth military-industrial complex and sought economic autarchy and insulation from global capitalism. Unamended, these ideas do not give us a lot of leverage over post-Soviet conditions. The Russian Federation, like nearly all of the USSR's heirs, faced few significant external threats to its security in the 1990s, now that the Cold War was over. Moscow did fight two internal wars in the North Caucasus republic of Chechnya. In defiance of Tilly's narrow logic, these occasioned some of the shoddiest institutional performances of the decade and, despite the generals' humiliations, did not spur military or statewide reforms.[32]

An enduring merit of Tilly's work is that it sensitizes us to the international context in which states function and develop. During the Cold War, as he points out, the United States and the Soviet Union bulked up the security and military forces of allied and client governments, relieving them of the responsibility both to defend themselves and to confer with society, thereby perhaps arriving at the kinds of bargains that mature into consultative governance.[33] For Russia, post-Cold War decompression may conceivably account for some fraction of its new institutional laxity. It is amazing on the face of it, nonetheless, that leaders who took power in 1991 because their predecessors were overwhelmed by internal social demands, and not primarily because of jousting with outside powers, were not then able to work out social compacts, downsize a bloated army, and funnel a peace dividend to welfare programs starved of funds under the Soviets. Whatever they did or did not do domestically, all postcommunist governments, as Grzymala-Busse and Jones Luong note, have had to abandon the quest for military superiority and economic autarchy and have been subjected to incessant pressure to conform to the expectations of foreign governments and supranational bodies as to institutional design, financial soundness, treatment of minorities, and numerous other criteria.[34]

STATE CAPACITY

One of the two principal foci of our book is state capacity in the new Russia, which we take to encompass the relative ability of constituted authorities to recognize societal problems, fashion cogent responses to them, and effectively deliver corrective action, both in reaction to urgent crises and through planning ahead and steering social change.

State capacity is usefully thought of along two dimensions instead of as an undifferentiated whole. The first is what Michael Mann in his magisterial overview of the genesis and evolution of states dubs their "infrastructural power"—"the institutional capacity of a central state . . . to penetrate its territories and logistically implement decisions."[35] Examples of infrastructural capacity are systems for policing the national territory, guarding its borders, subordinating local to national interests, facilitating internal communication and trade, garnering statistical and cartographic information, and extracting revenues from inhabitants and nonstate organizations. Infrastructural capacity and the carving out of "state spaces," as James C. Scott calls them, are a prerequisite for doing all the other things states do, for better or for worse.[36] These remaining functions we unite under the heading "distributive power," rewording Michael Mann but retaining his meaning.[37] Distributive capacity is the capability to supply public goods in the form of government services, promotion of socioeconomic development, regulation of socially costly private acts, and transfers of income and wealth. Examples would be provision of schools, contract enforcement in the courts, subsidies or tax breaks for businesses, depositor's insurance, inspection of food handlers, pollution controls, and old-age pensions.

The most illuminating studies of state capacity dwell on resource flows and the accretion of expertise and skills, a sense of corporate purpose and pride, and practical coordinating mechanisms among policy makers and administrators. This is typically an incremental and painstaking process, although it can be accelerated by capability-elevating emergencies such as, in American history, a surfeit of elderly Civil War veterans or the Great Depression of the 1930s.[38] By the same token, state capacity can be thwarted or can atrophy in an excessively permissive environment. A well-covered instance is the petroleum-rich societies where governments, lulled by the oil bonanza of the 1970s, grew reliant on windfall revenues, did not ready themselves for price fluctuations, and liquidated administrative assets. The Saudi Arabian kingdom ceased to levy almost all domestic taxes; this rash act triggered "elimination of the government's main source of information about the economy" and "undermined base-line ideas about citizenship," putting social stability in peril by the time the boom ended.[39] In Latin America, military coups and severe conflicts in the civilian leadership have been recurrent drains on state capacity: "Competence tends to suffer during transitions both to and from military rule. Islands of competence nurtured for decades can be destroyed during a few months by presidents engaged in chaotic struggles to defend themselves against overthrow."[40]

A revealing marker of capacity is the coherence of the state's actions. Here we concur in Peter B. Evans and Dietrich Rueschemeyer's claim, "It is particularly incumbent on those who take the state's role as a social actor seriously to raise the issue of corporate cohesiveness. Otherwise, what may be the most important single limitation on the possibility of effective state intervention remains unanalyzed."[41] States whose left hands, figuratively speaking, do not know what their right hands are doing may plausibly have appreciable micro-capacity and competence, issue by issue, yet be deficient in macro-capacity, if one surveys the full grid of problems simultaneously.

As we scoped out the project on Russian governance, we were struck by the abundance of anecdotal data about a state in disequilibrium, with capacity in many ways diminished from Soviet levels and desperately short of what was needed to service a politically empowered society. We had at our disposal a litany of reports flagging infrastructural shortfalls—porous borders; an army that made Chechnya a wasteland without managing to hunt down lightly armed bands of guerrillas; freelancing regional governors who, without becoming warlords, regularly thumbed their noses at Moscow; venal and bumbling police and customs officers; rampant tax evasion and yawning budget deficits, Russia's bounty of exportable minerals and fuels notwithstanding; a flight from the ruble into foreign currencies, money surrogates, and barter; and a financial meltdown in 1998 that devalued the currency fivefold and saw the treasury default on its sovereign debt.[42] The distributive capacity of the national government was under constant fire as well, accused of mishandling everything from teacher training to disaster relief. There were, moreover, credible indications of a remarkable incoherence to the state's conduct. Its symptoms were bureaucratic redundancy and confusion, dedication to contradictory missions, a lack of foresight and coordination, and a predilection for ad hoc and ad hominem decision making in the place of seamless and transparent laws. Here, too, political leaders echoed the assessment. "The executive branch," no less qualified a witness than President Yeltsin testified in 1997, "tends to act like a dispatcher or a fire brigade, even though its main responsibilities are to work out a strategic line, take timely decisions, and put them into effect. . . . The functions and powers of many agencies are shapeless and frequently duplicate one another."[43] "We cannot accept it as normal," he declared indignantly the next year, "when on one and the same problem high officials publicly articulate not only diverse but at times even contradictory positions. This situation is extremely dangerous for the state."[44] It was also extremely corrosive of any semblance of democracy, inasmuch as Russian citizens now had on paper the right to expect government to respond to their needs and interests with deeds and not mere words.

One of our goals in this volume is thus more fully to describe and to gauge the magnitude of state weakness and incoherence in post-Soviet Russia. We also seek to shed light on their roots. We shall try to outdo self-serving and politicized narratives of causality by sifting through the records of an array of facets of state capacity.

STATE–SOCIETY RELATIONS

The second major focus of our inquiry is state–society relations in the new Russia. Plainly, interactions between social and state actors can occur on many plateaus and come in countless forms and permutations. Attempts to generalize about them across countries and across political regimes have not been enormously fruitful, but they do furnish us with some good orienting questions.

Just as civics textbooks paint state structures in democracies as unswerving agents of the popular majority, Marxist analyses by and large see them as subservient to one social minority, the capitalist class. Studies of public administration refine the first approach by allowing for slippage in the implementation of policy objectives as directives wend their way through the bureaucracy.[45] Neo-Marxist scholars in turn have come up with the concept of "state autonomy" or "relative state autonomy," an arrangement whereby elected officials and bureaucrats in advanced capitalist societies have sufficient insulation from the short-term prescripts of big business to be able, allegedly, to take decisions that facilitate long-term capital accumulation and mute the class struggle.[46] Eric A. Nordlinger, not terribly persuasively, grafted the state-autonomy formula onto a pluralist mode of analysis.[47] Peering through a different lens at developing nations, Joel S. Migdal found them distinguished by "strong societies and weak states." As Migdal saw it, the fundamental fact of life for state elites in these countries is that they are constrained by entrenched private interests and informal practices, the consequence being "faltering efforts to get their populations to do what state policy makers want them to do."[48]

Since Russia possesses at the very best a semidemocracy nested in a semimarketized economy, we have been leery about mechanically evoking theories grounded in the experience of mature capitalist democracies. We have also tried to be cognizant of the intricacy of the relationship between governors and the governed. A state can be accountable to a thin elite stratum or to the majority of voters. Democratic government, especially, must to an extent be "unresponsive" to some of its constituents, assuming that they are making contradictory or unrealistic demands. Under the most benign of circumstances, the gap between political input and policy output will be more than bureaucratic slippage—it will reflect the painful tradeoffs involved in composing coherent policy out of democratic cacophony. As for relative state autonomy, any systematic account would have to distinguish between origins and results. The mere fact that a particular state serves bourgeois interests would not be an explanation of why such a state comes about or what sustains the bond.

Migdal's strong society/weak state paradigm is more appealing, but, again, stems from a very different social setting, this time largely preindustrial nations in the Third World. It suffers from the same penchant for overly tidy dichotomies that infuses too much of the literature about state capacity. There is no compelling reason in principle why a country could not have a weak society and a weak state or, for that matter, a strong society and a strong state: one's weakness does not inevitably imply the other's strength. The state–society interplay, as John A. Hall and G. John Ikenberry argue, is not a zero-sum game and may in fact prove to be advantageous to both:

> It is an error to equate the strength or autonomy of the state with the ability of state elites to ignore other social actors or to impose their will in any simple manner on society. If this were the case, totalitarian states, which seek to suppress the independence of other social actors, would be most capable of realizing state goals and of promoting larger social purposes. Such a conclusion is not justified: a deeper dimension of state power has more to do with the state's ability to work through and with other centres of power. The capacity of states to act rationally is furthered and not curtailed when the state co-ordinates other autonomous power sources.[49]

Evans pushes the point further to make the proposition that "joint projects" bridging the state–society divide are a developmental necessity and will do much to sculpt both kinds of actor. Social disorganization and apathy, he suggests, will make it harder for an effective state to take shape, while "The absence of a coherent state apparatus makes it less likely that civil society will organize itself beyond a loose web of local loyalties."[50] In fact, Joseph Stalin's regime, in its defeat of Nazi Germany—like Alexander I's vanquishing of the Napoleonic invasion in the nineteenth century—showed that it is feasible for a decidedly nondemocratic state to rally dispersed social talents for a common purpose. All the more dumbfounding, then, is the contrast with a post-Soviet Russian government whose army withdrew from Chechnya in 1996 after failing to win over the populace and subdue a few thousand rebels.

For formerly communist countries, one concrete idea about the state–society nexus has piqued the curiosity of researchers. That is the idea of "state capture"—the acquisition by potent economic actors of preponderant influence over the cells and subunits of government and ultimately over the organism in its entirety. The most thorough investigation, a World Bank paper on twenty-two countries by Joel S. Hellman, Geraint Jones, and Daniel Kaufman, defined state capture as "shaping the formation of the basic rules of the game (i.e., laws, rules, decrees, and regulations) through illicit and non-transparent private payments to public officials," in other words, through acts of corruption and collusion that go well beyond the purchase of petty favors.[51] Eleven countries ranked low on a multi-item index of state capture, and eleven, Russia prominently among them, ranked high. The impression left is not so unlike classic Marxist treatments of capitalist mastery of the state in Western societies.

There can be no doubt that well-situated economic actors wield disproportionate influence in postcommunist politics. But there are other bases for being skeptical a priori about the model of state capture. It presupposes a hard-and-fast differentiation between state and society, or power and wealth, that has arguably not yet occurred in a Russia where state and society alike are in an open-ended process of transformation and where there is tremendous fluidity and indeterminacy within each sector.[52] Hellman, Jones, and Kaufman themselves notice that the firms most aggressive in their quest for influence over officialdom have more insecure property rights than average. Also leaning against the notion of corporate unity among Russia's "oligarchs" are the cutthroat rivalry among them and their unscrupulousness in cutting deals with politicians prejudicial to their peers.[53] As for the targets of their predation, institutional inchoateness in the halls of Russian government would seem to have reached such heights in the 1990s that one can well ask whether anyone under the circumstances could have accomplished unitary control of "the state." And it remains an open question just who was acquiring control over whom. The portrait by Hellman et al. of the sale of government benefactions "à la carte" lends itself as feasibly to thinking of bureaucrats' unlawful feasting on commercial assets as vice versa, and whether that is true or not few entrepreneurs in Russia's in-between economy were able to make money without an endless chain of bureaucratic permissions and a stable of political benefactors. Without dropping the question of who influences the state, it may be wiser to pursue it in the postcommunist setting by disaggregating state capture and asking what kinds of relations exist between particular state agencies and particular private interests, looking for various forms of interaction and for the possible presence of multisided arrangements such as the "iron triangles"—involving bureaucratic subunits, legislative committees, and producer and consumer lobbies—that are so prominent in the literature on the policy process in Washington.[54]

As with state capacity, then, we have tried to unbundle state–society relations into tractable components rather than to proceed from grand claims about the whole. Our authors were tasked with looking for evidence in their chosen subject matter of insulation and/or engagement vis-à-vis social actors and under that rubric to be alert to the possibility of collusion, corrupt sellout of the public interest, or arrogant exploitation of private resources by state officials.

PLAN OF THE BOOK

State capacity and state–society relations are in the end related categories. For a state structure to have the ability to carry out most kinds of governmental work, it must be in a position to cooperate with and summon synergistic effort from social groups. For accountability to society to mean anything, the state must be able to accomplish its assignments, that is, it must have some measure of strength.

Ultimately, we are interested in the postcommunist state because we believe that it and its betterment are highly relevant to good government and to the resumption of progress toward democracy. Vladimir Putin also sees this relevance, but prescribes remedies that we fear will not really upgrade governance and will move the country further away from democracy. For Putin thus far, a stronger and more effective state is tantamount to a more disciplined but also a more inscrutable executive branch—as if a press blackout would make the bureaucracy less feckless. He also tends to leave the legislature, the courts, and the press out of the reckoning, as if they had little or nothing to contribute to solving the problems of governance.

Before getting into remedies, it behooves analysts to examine the roots and manifestations of a problem. Most of this book is devoted to precisely such an exercise. One by one, the authors, all of them charter participants in the project, consider aspects of state capacity and state–society relations. Through original empirical research, they address a common range of *questions*, without predetermined answers to those questions. Each chapter describes the basic events in a particular domain of state activity, considers the dynamics and breakpoints involved, assesses the key determinants of the pattern observed, and ponders the consequences. The balance of emphasis between the Yeltsin and Putin periods varies from chapter to chapter, yet every author pays at least some attention to both.

Three chapters spotlight selected pieces of Mann's infrastructural power. Gerald Easter writes about the ebbing and partial recovery of the Russian state's ability to tax economic activity, arguably the lifeblood of any modern government. Yoshiko Herrera examines Goskomstat, the main Russian statistical agency, and finds intricate changes in the government's ability to generate reliable measures of the fabric of its own society. The chapter by Kathryn Stoner-Weiss hones in on formal and informal sides of the federal dimension of state capacity in Russia, which divides power between central and regional government and complicates the already formidable obstacles to smooth governance. Four chapters take up the politics surrounding the distributive functions of the state. Linda Cook targets the bread-and-butter area of social policy, and in particular the provision of pensions to the population. Timothy Frye looks at attempts to regulate Russia's banks, which by anyone's standards were among the biggest winners in the redistribution of assets after communism. Daniel Treisman scrutinizes the policies governing currency exchange rates. Erika Weinthal and Pauline Jones Luong analyze energy policy, a realm where Russia has considerable natural assets but assets that in some other countries have obstructed rather than facilitated the growth of state capacity. Cook, Frye, Treisman, and Weinthal and Luong all view Russia in comparative context as experiencing severe problems generating coherent state action in the 1990s but also as making marked gains in recent years. In a final case study, Thomas Remington reviews trends in parliamentary oversight of the Russian bureaucracy, a subject of great pertinence to democratic theory and practice. Stephen Holmes in his concluding chapter summarizes our findings and weighs the implications for future efforts to build an effective liberal or illiberal state in the homeland of twentieth-century communism.

NOTES

1. Had time and resources permitted, we would have expanded the inquiry geographically. We may yet do so in the future.

2. Merle Faison, *How Russia Is Ruled* (Cambridge, MA: Harvard University Press, 1953 and 1963). An extensively revised edition was published as Jerry F. Hough and Merle Fainsod, *How the Soviet Union Is Governed* (Cambridge, MA: Harvard University Press, 1979). As Hough and Fainsod said (vii), "the mechanisms of control—and the degree to which they are successful—have been the central question of Soviet studies for three decades."

3. A sampling of the relevant works would include articles and books on public opinion by Raymond Duch, Theodore Gerber, James Gibson, Vicki Hesli, David Mason, Sarah Mendelson, Arthur Miller, William Reisinger, Stephen Whitefield, and William Zimmerman; on voting and parties by Laura Belin, Yitzhak Brudny, Timothy Colton, Steven Fish, Grigorii Golosov, Henry Hale, Stephen Hanson, Jerry Hough, Christopher Marsh, Michael McFaul, Robert Moser, Sarah Oates, Richard Rose, Richard Sakwa, Regina Smyth, Olga Shvetsova, Joshua Tucker, Michael Urban, and Stephen White; on civil society and political participation by Donna Bahry, Linda Cook, Stephen Crowley, Jane Dawson, Jeffrey Hahn, Marc Morjé Howard, Debra Javeline, Cynthia Kaplan, Oleg Kharkhordin, Valerie Sperling, and Marcia Weagle; and on new economic players by Anders Åslund, Timothy Frye, Thane Gustafson, Joel Hellman, David Hoffman, Caroline Humphrey, Juliet Johnson, David Lane, Peter Rutland, Vadim Volkov, Janine Wedel, and David Woodruff.

4. Representative authors here would be Katherine Burns, John Dunlop, Matthew Evangelista, Gerald Easter, Vladimir Gelman, Dmitry Gorenburg, Jeffrey Hahn, Yoshiko Herrera, Jeffrey Kahn, Peter Kirkow, Andrew Konitzer-Smirnov, Mary McAuley, Beth Mitchneck, Lynne Nelson, Peter Ordeshook, Robert Orttung, Nicolai Petro, Nikolai Petrov, Cameron Ross, Blair Ruble, Olga Shvetsova, Darrell Slider, Steven Solnick, Kathryn Stoner-Weiss, Daniel Treisman, Veljko Vujacic, Edward Walker, Gary Wilson, and John Young.

5. This neglect was not absolute. Most of the authors cited in notes 3 and 4 did address state building to some extent. And a few insightful book-length studies of Russia's central government have appeared—for example, George W. Breslauer, *Gorbachev and Yeltsin as Leaders* (Cambridge: Cambridge University Press, 2002); Eugene Huskey, *Presidential Power in Russia* (Armonk, NY: Sharpe, 1999); Thomas M. Nichols, *The Russian Presidency: Society and Politics in the Second Russian Republic* (New York:

St. Martin's, 1999); and Valerie Sperling, ed., *Building the Russian State: Institutional Crisis and the Quest for Democratic Governance* (Boulder, CO: Westview, 2000). Valerie Bunce, *Subversive Institutions: The Design and the Destruction of Socialism and the State* (Cambridge: Cambridge University Press, 1999), traces the effects of communist-era institutions on the breakup of the Soviet, Yugoslav, and Czechoslovak federations.

6. Guillermo O'Donnell and Philippe C. Schmitter, *Transitions from Authoritarian Rule: Tentative Conclusions about Uncertain Democracies* (Baltimore: Johns Hopkins University Press, 1986) (quotation at 55).

7. Juan J. Linz and Alfred Stepan, *Problems of Democratic Transition and Consolidation: Southern Europe, South America, and Post-Communist Europe* (Baltimore: Johns Hopkins University Press, 1996). They did bring up issues of state capacity and strength briefly in a section on economic privatization (436–39). The landmark piece on stateness, defining it more expansively than Linz and Stepan, is J. P. Nettl, "The State as a Conceptual Variable," first published in 1968 and reprinted in *The State: Critical Concepts*, vol. 1, ed. John A. Hall (London: Routledge, 1994), 9–36.

8. Peter B. Evans, Dietrich Rueschemeyer, and Theda Skocpol, eds., *Bringing the State Back In* (Cambridge: Cambridge University Press, 1985). Chapters of this book dealt with Taiwan, Sweden, Britain, the United States, Switzerland, Austria, Nigeria, and the southern cone of South America, but not with any then-communist country.

9. Anna Grzymala-Busse and Pauline Jones Luong, "Reconceptualizing the State: Lessons from Post-Communism," *Politics & Society* 30 (December 2002): 530.

10. Max Weber, "Politics as Vocation," in *From Max Weber: Essays in Sociology*, ed. Hans Gerth and C. Wright Mills (New York: Oxford University Press, 1958), 82–83.

11. Peter B. Evans, Dietrich Rueschemeyer, and Theda Skocpol, "On the Road toward a More Adequate Understanding of the State," in Evans, Rueschemeyer, and Skocpol, *Bringing the State Back In*, 351.

12. Stephen Holmes, "What Russia Teaches Us Now: How Weak States Threaten Freedom," *The American Prospect* 33 (July–August 1997): 31.

13. Mark R. Beissinger and Crawford Young, "Introduction: Comparing State Crises across Two Continents," in Beissinger and Young, eds., *Beyond State Crisis? Postcolonial Africa and Post-Soviet Eurasia in Comparative Perspective* (Washington, DC: Woodrow Wilson Center Press, 2002), 10; Vadim Volkov, "Who Is Strong When the State Is Weak? Violent Entrepreneurship in Russia's Emerging Markets," in Beissinger and Young, eds., *Beyond State Crisis? Postcolonial Africa and Post-Soviet Eurasia in Comparative Perspective*, 83.

14. "Otkrytoye pis'mo Vladimira Putina k rossiiskim izbiratelyam," *Izvestiya*, February 25, 2000, 4. See the discussion of Putin's presidential election campaign in Timothy J. Colton and Michael McFaul, *Popular Choice and Managed Democracy: The Russian Elections of 1999 and 2000* (Washington, DC: Brookings Institution Press, 2003), chap. 7.

15. "Vystupleniye V. V. Putina pri predstavlenii yezhegodnogo Poslaniya Prezidenta RF Federal'nomu Sobraniyu RF 8 iyulya 2000 g" (processed, unpaginated).

16. During the course of the Russian governance project, we were frequently reminded of this point by our Moscow colleagues Mikhail Krasnov and Georgii Satarov, who worked as aides to Yeltsin when many of the speeches cited here were drafted by his office.

17. "Poslaniye Prezidenta Rossiiskoi Federatsii Federal'nomu Sobraniyu, 'Ob ukreplenii rossiiskogo gosudarstva'" (Moscow, 1994), 14.

18. "Poslaniye Prezidenta Rossiiskoi Federatsii Federal'nomu Sobraniyu, 'Poryadok vo vlasti—poryadok v strane'" (Moscow, 1997), 22.

19. "Poslaniye Prezidenta RF ot 30 marta 1999 g" (processed, unpaginated).

20. "Explanation of the orientation of state policy requires some examination of the politics behind state action. To speak of the strong state suggests that politics can be taken out of the equation for some states and not for others. The action of the strong state depends as much on politics as does that of the weak one" (Peter Gourevitch, "The Second Image Reversed: The International Sources of Domestic Politics," first published 1978 and reprinted in Hall, *The State: Critical Concepts*; quotation at 222–23). Thorough critiques of sloppy thinking about state strength and weakness may be found in John A. Hall and G. John Ikenberry, *The State* (Milton Keynes: Open University Press, 1989), 12–14, and Robert W. Jackman, *Power without Force: The Political Capacity of Nation-States* (Ann Arbor: University of Michigan Press, 1993), chap. 3.

21. "One should not assume that any specific capability for an individual country is highly uniform across a large number of policy areas or over time.... Indeed, one should not assume without investigation that it is productive to speak of capabilities as general patterns of government action across a variety of policy areas" (R. Kent Weaver and Bert A. Rockman, "Assessing the Effects of Institutions," in *Do Institutions Matter? Government Capabilities in the United States and Abroad*, ed. Weaver and Rockman [Washington, DC: Brookings Institution Press, 1993], 6–7). Theda Skocpol has made the same point in a number of her writings.

22. This point is well made in William Reno, "Mafiya Troubles, Warlord Crises," in Beissinger and Young, *Beyond State Crisis*, 119–23. For examples of warlordism in Georgia, Azerbaijan, and Tajikistan, see Charles H. Fairbanks Jr., "Weak States and Private Armies," in Beissinger and Young, *Beyond State Crisis*, 129–59.

23. "Poslaniye Prezidenta" (1999).

24. For example, in one presidential address he observed that administrators often pressed for additional powers, "but when it comes time to do concrete work they shift from one difficult question to another and cite the incompleteness of our legislation and the shortage of resources" ("Poslaniye Prezidenta" [1997], 29).

25. Fairbanks, "Weak States and Private Armies," 129.

26. Patron–client networks are well documented from archival evidence in Gerald M. Easter, *Reconstructing the State: Personal Networks and Elite Identity in Soviet Russia* (Cambridge: Cambridge University Press, 2000). Older Kremlinological works derived entirely from public sources gave fainter hints of the same pattern. See, for example, Robert Conquest, *Power and Policy in the U.S.S.R.: The Study of Soviet Dynasties* (London: Macmillan, 1961).

27. Two works that apply Lindblom's thumbs–finger metaphor to Soviet government are Thane Gustafson, *Reform in Soviet Politics: Lessons of Recent Policies on Land and Water* (Cambridge: Cambridge University Press, 1981), and Timothy J. Colton, *Moscow: Governing the Soviet Metropolis* (Cambridge, MA: Harvard University Press, 1995). The source of the reference is Charles E. Lindblom, *Politics and Markets: The World's Political-Economic Systems* (New York: Basic, 1977), chap. 3.

28. See especially Steven L. Solnick, *Stealing the State: Control and Collapse in Soviet Institutions* (Cambridge, MA: Harvard University Press, 1998).

29. For discussion of hybrid regimes, with applications to Russia, see Michael McFaul, "The Fourth Wave of Democracy *and* Dictatorship: Noncooperative Transitions in the Postcommunist World," *World Politics* 54 (January 2002): 212–44; Larry Diamond, "Thinking about Hybrid Regimes," *Journal of Democracy* 13 (July 2002): 21–35; Steven Levitsky and Lucan Way, "The Rise of Competitive Authoritarianism," *Journal of Democracy* 13 (July 2002): 51–65; Larry Diamond and Marc F. Plattner, eds., *Democracy after Communism* (Baltimore: Johns Hopkins University Press, 2002); and Marina Ottaway, *Democracy Challenged: The Rise of Semi-Authoritarianism* (Washington, DC: Carnegie Endowment for International Peace, 2003).

30. Putin made this statement in a manifesto on "Russia at the Turn of the Millennium" posted a few days before Yeltsin made him acting president in December 1999. Quoted in Henry E. Hale, ed., *Russia's Electoral War of 1999–2000: The Russian Election Watch Compendium* (Cambridge, MA: Strengthening Democratic Institutions Project, John F. Kennedy School of Government, Harvard University), 115.

31. Charles Tilly, *Coercion, Capital, and European States, AD 990–1992* (Oxford: Blackwell, 1992). This book refines claims advanced in Tilly, ed., *The Formation of National States in Western Europe* (Princeton, NJ: Princeton University Press, 1975), and "War Making and State Making as Organized Crime," in Evans, Rueschemeyer, and Skocpol, *Bringing the State Back In*, 169–91.

32. On the army's ineptitude in the first war, when unmotivated Russian conscripts shirked risk and actually sold weapons to the Chechen fighters, see Anatol Lieven, *Chechnya: Tombstone of Russian Power* (New Haven, CT: Yale University Press, 1998). Another study has noted the successful building of military capacity in post-Soviet ethnic enclaves like Abkhazia (in Georgia), Transnistria (in Moldova), and Karabakh (in Azerbaijan). Charles King, "The Benefits of Ethnic War: Understanding Eurasia's Unrecognized States," *World Politics* 53 (July 2001): 524–52. But King also describes these mini-states as highly corrupt and in violation of the tenets of good governance in almost every civilian domain of policy.

33. Tilly, "War Making and State Making as Organized Crime," 186.

34. Grzymala-Busse and Jones Luong, "Reconceptualizing the State," 536. For an eloquent early statement of the same point, see Valerie Bunce and Mária Csanádi, "Uncertainty in the Transition: Post-Communism in Hungary," *East European Politics and Society* 7 (Spring 1993): 249–51.

35. Michael Mann, *The Sources of Social Power, vol. 2, The Rise of Classes and Nation-States* (Cambridge: Cambridge University Press, 1993), 59.

36. James C. Scott, *Seeing Like a State: How Certain Schemes to Improve the Human Condition Have Failed* (New Haven, CT: Yale University Press, 1998), 186.

37. Mann prefers the harsher phrase "despotic power," but interchanges it with "distributive power."

38. On the protection of veterans and needy mothers, which paved the way for the more ambitious expansion of government in the New Deal, See Theda Skocpol, *Protecting Soldiers and Mothers: The Political Origins of Social Policy in the United States* (Cambridge, MA: Harvard University Press, 1992).

39. Kiren Aziz Chaudhry, *The Price of Wealth: Economies and Institutions in the Middle East* (Ithaca, NY: Cornell University Press, 1997), 164–65. See also Terry Lynn Karl, *The Paradox of Plenty: Oil Booms and Petro-States* (Berkeley: University of California Press, 1997), and Jahangir Amuzegar, *Managing the Oil Wealth: OPEC's Windfalls and Pitfalls* (London: I. B., Tauris, 1999).

40. Barbara Geddes, *Politician's Dilemma: Building State Capacity in Latin America* (Berkeley: University of California Press, 1994), 23.

41. Peter B. Evans and Dietrich Rueschemeyer, "The State and Economic Transformation," in Evans, Rueschemeyer, and Skocpol, *Bringing the State Back In*, 59.

42. David Woodruff, *Money Unmade: Barter and the Fate of Russian Capitalism* (Ithaca, NY: Cornell University Press, 1999) is a fine study of one of the most glaring of these problems, the gutting of the Russian ruble.

43. "Poslaniye Prezidenta" (1997), 29.

44. "Poslaniye Prezidenta Rossiiskoi Federatsii Federal'nomy Sobraniyu, 'Obshchimi silami—k pod" emu Rossii" (Moscow, 1998), 28.

45. The literature is voluminous. Handy access points are still Anthony Downs, *Inside Bureaucracy* (Boston: Little, Brown, 1967), and Jeffrey L. Pressman and Aaron Wildavsky, *Implementation* (Berkeley: University of California Press, 1979).

46. See, for example, Nicos Poulantzas, *Political Power and Social Classes*, trans. Timothy O'Hagen (London: New Left Books, 1973); Bob Jessop, "Recent Theories of the Capitalist State," reprinted in Hall, *The State*, 81–103; and Claus Offe, "Structural Problems of the Capitalist State" in Hall, *The State*, 104–29.

47. Eric A. Nordlinger, *On the Autonomy of the Democratic State* (Cambridge, MA: Harvard University Press, 1981).

48. Joel S. Migdal, *Strong Societies and Weak States: State-Society Relations and State Capabilities in the Third World* (Princeton, NJ: Princeton University Press, 1988), 9. See also his *State in Society: Studying How States and Societies Transform and Constitute One Another* (Cambridge: Cambridge University Press, 2001). Casting a yet more expansive net, Jackman (*Power without Force*) identified "political capacity" in society's eyes as a universal problem. State actions, he said, will fail or succeed according to the legitimacy of the political system and the degree of uncoerced compliance officeholders can elicit. This useful insight is a reminder that the analytical categories scholars employ in the study of the state (in this instance state capacity and legitimacy, as an aspect of state–society relations) often overlap.

49. Hall and Ikenberry, *The State*, 95.

50. Peter B. Evans, *Embedded Autonomy: States and Industrial Transformation* (Princeton, NJ: Princeton University Press, 1995), 41.

51. Joel S. Hellman, Geraint Jones, and Daniel Kaufman, "'Seize the State, Seize the Day'": State Capture, Corruption, and Influence in Transition (Washington, DC: World Bank Institute Policy Research Working Paper no. 2444, September 2000), 2. The authors' source of information was a survey of business executives in the twenty-two countries. A similar argument was made in *Transition Report 1999: Ten Years of Transition* (London: European Bank for Reconstruction and Development, 1999), 116–17.

52. Grzymala-Busse and Jones Luong, "Reconceptualizing the State," 533–34, deftly make the point about blurry boundaries but underplay the point about inde-terminacy within the sectors. Yeltsin's homilies on misgovernment often bracketed state dysfunction with disarray on the societal side of the equation, as in a 1997 fusil-lade against corruption: "When 'free purchase and sale' spread to the adoption of laws, to the actions of bureaucrats, and to the decisions of the courts, this is not only immoral but lethal for society and state" ("Poslaniye Prezidenta" [1997], 18).

53. Consult Chrystia Freeland, *Sale of the Century: Russia's Wild Ride from Commu-nism to Capitalism* (New York: Crown, 2000), and David E. Hoffman, *The Oligarchs: Wealth and Power in the New Russia* (New York: PublicAffairs, 2002).

54. I am grateful to Thomas Remington for helping me to clarify this problem.

Chapter Two

Building Fiscal Capacity

Gerald Easter

Revenue extraction enhances state strength, and strong states extract more revenue. This truism is widely found in comparative scholarship on state building. This chapter investigates the process of building fiscal capacity in the postcommunist Russian state with a focus on the politics of tax collection. Difficulties with tax collection have been identified as a principal source of state weakness in postcommunist Russia. The postcommunist Russian state emerged amid fiscal crisis. To find a way out, a new tax regime was needed for the transition economy, but early efforts were undermined by political constraints, which eventually led to the fiscal collapse of the state. More recently, however, economic conditions have improved and the political constraints have been transformed. The result was a "Russian Tax Revolution," by which fiscal capacity was significantly enhanced in the postcommunist state.

The tax regime provides insight into the distributive and infrastructural components of postcommunist states by focusing attention on the state's ability to make claims upon society, to develop capacities to realize those claims, and to devise strategies to assure society's compliance. In Russia, in particular, it reveals how the postcommunist state continues to exploit economic concessions and coercive resources inherited from the old regime to undermine the development of legal and institutional mechanisms that would fundamentally redefine its relationship to society. The postcommunist Russian state remains only weakly constrained by society, while the tax regime itself has become an instrument of state coercion.

TAX COLLECTION AND THE POSTCOMMUNIST STATE

Coercion, Concessions, and Postcommunist State Building

Over the past decade, scholars have expressed a reversal of opinion on the nature and role of the state in postcommunist Russia. Early on it was presumed that the state was harmful for the development of postcommunist society and needed to be scaled back. But by the end of the 1990s, it was widely accepted that Russia's weakened state was to blame for distorting and undermining transition goals. This contradictory appraisal is reconciled by distinguishing between the claims and capabilities of the state. While the Russian state showed chronic inconsistency in performing the tasks of governance, it did not relinquish its claims on power resources inherited from the old regime.

Postcommunist states start out with a preponderance of power resources in relation to society. They possess an abundance of coercive, economic, and bureaucratic-legal resources, amassed by their communist predecessors. Postcommunist society, meanwhile, is lacking in organizational and economic resources and remains dependent on the state. This vast inheritance of power resources sets the postcommunist cases apart from other state-building experiences. It is less about the cultivation and accumulation of power resources from society and more about the readjustment and redistribution of power resources between state and society and within the state. The process entails the reconfiguration of existing power resources into new institutional forms for new purposes.

The development of the postcommunist Russian state was shaped by the politics of regime breakdown and the consolidation of a new order. The fall of communist regimes in Eastern Europe in 1989 stirred movement politics in Soviet society and exposed cleavages within the state elite. Some state cadres chose to remain loyal, others voiced criticism, and still others headed for the exit. Defecting cadres tried to take with them the power resources with which they were entrusted in the old regime. Thus, defecting cadres seized the opportunity to switch loyalty to Boris Yeltsin's rival "Russian state," in which they sought to make a proprietary claim on the valued resources of the collapsing Soviet state. The undoing of the USSR had less to do with social movements staging protests and more to do with state elites seeking better deals. As a result, the new Russian state was impaired by fragmentation of power resources in the early 1990s.[1] In some cases, the state's power resources were simply seized unilaterally, while in other cases, they were bargained away.

Russia's postcommunist transition did not benefit from elite consensus over institutional design and policy direction. Indeed, by the summer of 1992, Russia was experiencing a political crisis. At the top, executive–legislative relations were paralyzed by competing claims over policymaking. Meanwhile, center–regional relations were frayed by assertions of sovereignty by provincial governors and legislators. The crisis was finally resolved in the second half of 1993, when Yeltsin forcibly shut down the legislature and imposed a new constitution. The resulting division of institutional powers established a strong presidential system with limited institutional checks. While the new constitution settled the institutional struggle, it did not reconcile the still polarized elite. Intra-elite conflict marred the entire Yeltsin period.

According to the constitution, the power resources of the state were entrusted to the executive in general and to the president in particular. The president was charged with direct oversight of the state's coercive agencies and exercised personal discretion in the allocation of the command economy's valued assets.[2] Through the executive, the Russian state employed coercion without countervailing constraints and doled out economic resources as concessions that could be reclaimed. Institutional and legal checks on the state's claims to these power resources were only weakly developed. Coercion and concessions served as the sources of state strength in postcommunist Russia. Personal intervention by the president and his staff into decision making became a chronic feature of postcommunist politics. However, differences in political circumstances as well as leadership styles led to variation in the patterns of deployment of power resources by the postcommunist state.

Boris Yeltsin's tenure was marked by a protracted and destabilizing intra-elite conflict over the direction of the transition. In response, Yeltsin built alliances with regional and economic elites through the generous distribution of economic concessions. With notable exceptions, he displayed reluctance to employ coercion. Instead, Yeltsin preferred to assuage challengers through discrete bargains in which the central state temporarily ceded its claims on particular resources. This bargaining process facilitated the rise of newly empowered regional and economic elites. Under Yeltsin, the state resembled a medieval mosaic of competing political and economic fiefdoms, in which governing capabilities often appeared to be enfeebled. Postcommunist elites made attempts to consolidate their claims on power resources through formal agreements. But in granting concessions, Yeltsin did not give up the central state's ultimate claim on their use.

By the time Vladimir Putin succeeded Yeltsin, the political crises of the early transition were past. Putin's presidency benefited from a stable institutional framework. With patriotic credentials intact, the unassuming and pragmatic Putin was hardly the polarizing personality that Yeltsin had been. Instead, his presidency was shaped by the political fallout of the 1998 financial collapse of the state. The fiscal crisis focused attention on the inherent conflict of interest between deal-seeking elites and the governing capabilities of the central state.

Putin emphasized the need to rebuild the "vertical" structures of power, that is, to reclaim for the central state the power resources that had been claimed by regional and economic elites. He showed a greater willingness to deploy the coercive resources of the state against noncompliant elites. He did not abandon the practice of using economic concessions, but readily redistributed them on the basis of political favor. Putin sought to undo the individual bargains negotiated by his predecessor and steadfastly rejected offerings of a grand bargain put forth by the postcommunist elite.

Dilemmas of Tax Collection in the Transition Economy

The Soviet command economy provided an extreme response to the perennial state challenge of revenue extraction. Instead of adapting its extractive capabilities to fit the revenue base, the state remolded the base to fit its extractive capabilities. The command economy featured a narrow revenue base in which economic resources were concentrated into large state-managed units. Soviet society was among the most heavily taxed in the world. But the state did not have to locate, claim, and collect revenue from autonomous or dispersed economic actors. Rather the command economy was structured so that the state had direct access to economic resources. Over 90 percent of budgetary revenues were collected from state enterprises.[3] Throughout the postwar period, the Soviet tax regime kept the state budget operating in the black.[4]

In the 1980s, the Soviet state witnessed something that it had not experienced since World War II: budget deficits. In the final years of communist rule, the state's take from the profits tax steadily shrank: 1986—R129.8 billion, 1987—R127.4 billion, 1988—R119.6 billion, 1989—R115.5 billion.[5] By 1988, the budget was in the red. To meet expenses, the state's fiscal managers resorted to borrowing as internal debt increased from R11.7 billion in 1985 to R90.1 billion in 1988.[6] In addition, the state began to issue monetary credits to cover budgetary expenses, setting off an inflationary spiral. In the last year of communist rule, the economy's ruble supply increased by more than 70 percent.[7]

The Soviet state was in fiscal crisis. In response, the government initiated the first major changes in the tax system in five decades. But before the new system was operational, the economic crisis gave way to a political crisis. One of the decisive battles became the struggle between Gorbachev's Soviet government and Yeltsin's Russian government over the tax revenues. Yeltsin offered enterprise managers reduced tax rates and special deals in exchange for recognizing the authority of his Russian government's revenue claims.[8] The final blow came in late 1991, when the Russian government seized the Soviet revenue base. Deprived of income, Gorbachev acknowledged defeat and consigned the Soviet state to history. But in laying claim to the economic resources of the Soviet state, the new Russian state also inherited the fiscal crisis of the old regime: declining tax income, rising budget deficits, and increasing money supply.[9]

The Soviet tax system was designed to fit the command economy. But the introduction of radical economic reform required a fundamental redesign of the tax system. The radical reform package of stabilization, liberalization, and privatization contained hidden "fiscal traps," which subverted the flow of income to the state and exacerbated the fiscal crisis.[10] The first trap, the Tanzi effect, occurred early in the reform process as price liberalization fed inflation.[11] State coffers at first benefited from a brief surge in revenues, which quickly dropped off as inflation overtook and consumed the revenue base. Taxes were paid with devalued currency. Second, monetary stabilization limited the resources available for subsidies and investments in the state sector. For industrial firms, the decline in financial support was compounded by severed trade agreements and broken protective barriers. Firms responded by scaling back production. Economic contraction caused further erosion in the revenue base. A third trap emerged from privatization. As a private sector emerged, it became more difficult for the ill-equipped tax administration to monitor transactions and enforce revenue claims.

State fiscal capacity encompasses a bundle of policy and administration issues, including currency, credit, and budgets, while at the foundation is income. Given the institutional legacy of the command economy and the fiscal crisis of early transition, tax collection posed one of the biggest challenges for postcommunist state builders.

The decline and recovery of state revenues in the Russian state have been well chronicled. A clear correlation exists between general economic trends and the state's revenue yields. In the years leading to the 1998 fiscal crisis, the economy experienced an overall decline in industrial productive capacities and the profitability of firms. Since the collapse, the devalued ruble made domestic firms more competitive, leading to a steady increase in industrial productivity and profitable enterprises. Between 1995 and 1998, the number of firms declaring profits dropped from 86,889 to 70,238; in 1999, the number shot up to 89,238.[12] Heavily dependent on oil and gas exports, the state budget is highly sensitive to fluctuations in world energy markets. In 1998, the average price for a barrel of Urals crude dropped to less than $12 per barrel; in 2000, the average price was closer to $25 per barrel, and in 2004 the price was over $40 per barrel.[13] Table 2.1 shows that in the early and mid-1990s, the state revenue base was shrinking, but the subsequent revival of economic growth led to budget surpluses.

The early to mid-1990s marked a period of declining revenue extraction capacity. The rise in uncollected tax revenues grew dramatically during these

Table 2.1. Overview of Economic and Fiscal Indicators

A) Annual Percentage Changes in GDP from Previous Year (1992 equals 100%)

1992	1993	1994	1995	1996	1997	1998	1999	2000	2001	2002
100%	91.3%	87.3%	95.9%	96.6%	100.9%	95.1%	105%	109%	105%	104.3%

B) Consolidated Budget Deficit/Surplus as Percentage of GDP (center and regions)

1992	1993	1994	1995	1996	1997	1998	1999	2000	2001	2002
−25.6	−8.1	−11.8	−4.8	−7.8	−5.6	−3.6	−1.2	1.9	2.9	1.0

C) Federal Budget Deficit/Surplus as Percentage of GDP

1992	1993	1994	1995	1996	1997	1998	1999	2000	2001	2002
−28	−9.2	−12.1	−4.9	−7.4	−6	−3.2	−1.1	1.4	2.9	1.4

Source: *Natsional'nye scheta Rossi v 1993–2000 godakh* (Moscow: Goskomstat, 2001), 16, table 1.1; *Russian Economy: Trends and Outlooks, 2001* (Moscow: Institute for Economy in Transition, 2002), 72, table 4; *Russian Economy: Trends and Outlooks, 2002* (Moscow: Institute for Economy in Transition, 2002), 59, table 4; 157, table 1.

years: from \$3.3 billion in 1993, to \$12 billion in 1995, to \$31.3 billion in 1997.[14] Following the 1998 fiscal collapse, however, revenue extraction capabilities improved remarkably. These trends are indicated in table 2.2, which shows the particularly good showing of the federal budget following the 1998 fiscal collapse.

The inability of the central state to collect taxes efficiently from the transition economy was one of the main factors leading to the 1998 fiscal collapse. More recently, however, the central state has exceeded its tax collection goals and boasted budgetary surpluses. While the decline and recovery of tax revenue is directly related to overall economic performance, political factors have also mattered. The turnaround in state tax collection efforts coincides with changes

Table 2.2. Revenue Extraction in the Postcommunist Russian State

A) Tax Collection to Consolidated Budget as Percentage of GDP

1992	1993	1994	1995	1996	1997	1998	1999	2000	2001	2002
18.6	25.9	25.0	23.8	22.8	23.9	21.7	24.6	27.2	27.0	29.7

B) Tax Collection to Federal Budget as Percentage of GDP

1992	1993	1994	1995	1996	1997	1998	1999	2000	2001	2002
16.6	12.4	11.5	11.6	11.0	10.9	9.6	12.6	15	16.2	18.6

C) Central Revenue Take as a Percentage of All Tax Revenue Collected

1992	1993	1994	1995	1996	1997	1998	1999	2000	2001	2002
54.5	39.5	39	45.2	44.7	44.2	44.9	50.6	55	60	62.6

Source: *Russian Economy: Trends and Outlooks, 2002* (Moscow: Institute for the Economy in Transition, 2003), 59, table 4; *Russian Economy: Trends and Outlooks, 2001* (Moscow: Institute for the Economy in Transition, 2002), 72, table 4; *Russian Economy: Trends and Outlooks, 2002*, 59, table 4. *Finansy v Rossi, 2001*, 28, table 2.5; Lev Freinkman, Daniel Treisman, and Stepan Titov, *Subnational Budgeting in Russia* (Washington, DC: World Bank Technical Paper 452, 1999), 109.

in the tax policy process, the introduction of tax reform, the recentralization of fiscal-administrative process, and the improvement in tax compliance.

POLITICS OF BUILDING A NEW TAX REGIME

Competing Actors in the Tax Policy Process

In the postcommunist state, four groups of actors vied for influence in the making of a new tax regime. These groups were distinguished by their preferences for tax policy and administration as well as their views on the role of taxation in the transition economy (see table 2.3). They included: market rationalizers, corporate collaborators, fiscal federalists, and fiscal populists. Their distinguishing characteristics represent general group features and policy tendencies, while individual actors did not always conform to these ideal types.[15]

The first group, the market rationalizers, was composed mainly of economists, familiar with and supportive of the assumptions of neoliberal economics. They had little experience in politics and management, but instead emerged from policy research institutes. In the new state, they tended to occupy positions related to macroeconomic policymaking on the executive side,

Table 2.3. Competing Actors in the Tax Policy Process

Policy Orientation	Tax Policy	Tax Administration	Taxation Goals
Market Rationalizers	low rates simplified and uniform code	centralized structure coercive enforcement	stimulate macro-economic growth
Corporate Collaborators	low rates specialized and particularist code	decentralized structure administrative enforcement	industrial development (sector or individual)
Fiscal Federalists	high rates specialized and particularist code	decentralized structure administrative enforcement	regional economic autonomy (federal or individual)
Fiscal Populists	high rates simplified and uniform code	centralized structure coercive enforcement	economic redistribution

especially in the finance ministry and tax administration. The second group, corporate collaborators, represented the interests of the postcommunist indus-trial and financial elite. They included the old industrial management corps as well as the new financial elite. Their interests did not often coincide, inhibiting the formation of collective action. Those corporate leaders whose businesses were most profitable emerged as influential actors in tax policy. Their repre-sentatives were located across the political system, in government ministries, industrial lobbies, legislative committees, and ad hoc commissions. Under Yeltsin, individual corporate collaborators had key allies in the presidential administration.

The third group, fiscal federalists, represented the interests of regions. They included the newly empowered regional governors. Schooled in the command economy, they were accustomed to lobbying the center for economic resources. Like corporate collaborators, the fiscal federalists were internally divided and had difficulty organizing collectively against the center. A cleavage line ran between the richer regions, which were net donors to the state budget, and the poorer regions, which were net recipients. The upper house of parliament was for awhile their main institutional base; at least some regional governors had allies in the presidential administration. The fourth group, fiscal populists, included leftist political parties, trade unions, and noncompetitive enterprises. The fiscal populists were located mainly in the legislature, which gave them direct access to the policy process.

Extraordinary Politics and the New Tax Regime

In the fall of 1991, lifted by his victories over the Communist Party, Yeltsin enjoyed the confidence of the Russian Supreme Soviet, which granted him emergency powers to sort out the wreckage of the Soviet collapse. With the Supreme Soviet retreating temporally to the sidelines, the policymaking powers of the new state were entrusted to the person of Yeltsin, who acted officially as president and unofficially as prime minister. In choosing an economic policy, Yeltsin was presented with several options, which varied by pace and scope. He opted for the most radical. This decision was facilitated by favorable, though short-lived, political conditions. It marked a brief moment of "extraordinary politics" in postcommunist Russia, in which the political opposition had yet to mobilize against the new regime.[16]

Taking advantage of this situation, Yeltsin authorized Deputy Prime Minister Yegor Gaidar to draft a program for a swift transition to a market economy. However, radical reform threatened to subvert the flow of state revenues at a time of fiscal crisis. Thus, the stabilization of state finances was necessary for implementing structural reform.[17] Under Gaidar's direction, a team of market rationalizers hastily began work on a new tax regime for the transition economy.[18] The main features included: a valued-added tax (VAT), replacing the old turnover tax on enterprises; an unreformed profits tax on enterprises; new excise taxes on the business sector; and a personal income tax (PIT) on households.

The legislation also provided a bureaucratic-legal framework, empowering the state with the right to make revenue claims on society and transposed over society a set of categorical assignments denoting the legal status of taxpayers. While the legislation formalized the authority of various state actors to make claims on taxpayers as well as the obligations of taxpayers to abide by these claims, it did not provide a countervailing set of rights or protections of society against the revenue claims of the state. The reluctance to establish well-defined and restrictive formal limits on the right to make claims on society, particularly regarding economic resources, would become an enduring feature of the Russian postcommunist state.

In principle, the new tax regime fit an emerging market economy; in practice, it retained features of the command economy. Tax rates were high, but consistent with rates throughout Europe. The design of the new tax code was modeled after existing tax systems of advanced industrial economies. Such tax systems, however, had evolved over the course of a century and were structured to collect income from richer and wider revenue bases than existed in Russia. For example, personal income tax covered more than a quarter of total tax receipts as an average among the Organization for Economic Cooperation and Development (OECD) countries.[19] Yet Russia could not realistically come close to matching that figure, given the low levels of household income and the underdeveloped administrative capacity to monitor household transactions.

The state's new tax policy did not attempt to cultivate the nascent small business sector with temporary exemptions or reduced rates on the expectation of future revenue returns.[20] Instead, the Russian government focused its collection efforts on a select set of big revenue targets, particularly in the energy export sector. The introduction of radical economic reform spurred rising inflation and contracting production. Within a year, the Russian state was on the verge of fiscal collapse. Collecting revenue through the state's sprawling and fragmented administrative apparatus proved far more difficult than had been anticipated.

To forestall the disruption of revenue flow, the Gaider government utilized existing sources of income, especially commodity exports.[21] This approach required minimal cost, since the large Soviet-built firms in the export sectors were already penetrated by the tax administration. Tax reforms introduced at the outset of the transition placed the heaviest tax burden on these corporations. In 1989, the turnover tax and the profits tax accounted for 64 percent of total revenue; in 1993, after the first year of radical reform, the VAT and the still un-reformed profits tax accounted for more than 60 percent of total revenue.[22] This strategy was intended to facilitate the state's effort to locate and collect revenues given its limited administrative capabilities. But it also made the state revenue-dependent on the large corporations, which quickly acted to lessen the burden.

The government of market rationalizers that engineered Russia's economic breakthrough did not have the opportunity to revise the new tax regime. It is noteworthy that the authority of Gaidar to make economic policy came per-sonally from the president. Although Russia's path to regime breakdown was elite-driven, Gaidar's policy team of liberal economists had few connections to the industrial and regional elite. While they had ties to Russia's democratic movement, this movement never developed into a strong sociopolitical force, such as those in postcommunist Eastern Europe.[23] They were dependent on the disposition of the president for political support, which would become apparent when "extraordinary politics" ended. By the summer of 1992, the Russian transition was mired in elite conflict and institutional stalemate. The president needed to find political allies and looked to the new business and regional elites. Consequently, market rationalizers would no longer dominate the management of state finances as the interests of corporate collaborators and fiscal federalists were incorporated into the policy process.

Elite Bargaining and the "Swiss Cheese" Tax Regime

Russia's transition was consumed by a power struggle, in which the executive, the legislature, and the regions laid claim to the state's rule-making powers. This political conflict was finally resolved after a display of coercion from the president and the imposition of a new constitution. In general, the new con-stitutional order gave the president control over the government and provided opportunities for the executive side to circumvent the legislature in the poli-cymaking process. The legislature, however, was given a role in state finances and budget making. Meanwhile, the political challenge of regional elites was resolved through a series of ad hoc agreements over the division of power and resources. The institutional consequences were that the policymaking process came to feature multiple access points from which a large number of players in-fluenced policy outcomes. Extraordinary politics gave way to elite bargaining.

Tax policy was especially affected by elite bargaining. While the government was responsible for submitting budgets and drafting tax legislation, the legisla-ture was assigned the formal power to approve budgets and tax policies as well as the right to introduce its own initiatives regarding state finances. Regional governments, meanwhile, sought to consolidate their claim over local revenue sources. While the tax regime created by the market rationalizers remained in place throughout this period, it was enforced unevenly and amended repeatedly. Representatives of various industrial and regional groups succeeded in securing concessions on tax rates and other privileges. Corporate lobbying was conducted mostly on an individual firm or personalistic basis. Tax privileges were negotiated discretely with particular state agents, often without the consent of other state agencies involved in policymaking and collections.

Across the government, tax policy was made and remade in an idiosyncratic and personalistic manner. In 1992, Yeltsin named Viktor Chernomyrdin, the former head of the Soviet energy sector, as new prime minister. As the principal target of the state's extraction efforts, corporate elites pressed for special exemptions, rate reductions, and negotiated loopholes. Corporate collaborators were most active lobbying government officials under the industry-friendly Chernomyrdin. Among his first acts as prime minister, Chernomyrdin cut the VAT rate by 8 percent and allowed corporations to defer the payment of the profits tax.[24] As deputy prime minister, Anatoly Chubais, in 1994, intervened to force the tax administration to drop its claim to $7 million in disputed taxes from a multinational firm. While acting as first deputy prime minister, Vladimir Potanin, in 1996, granted special tax breaks to his own company, Norilsk Nikel, which saved $100 million for the metals export giant.[25] In 1996, an ad hoc government commission unilaterally cut the vodka excise by 5 percent, while the Ministry of Economy declared beer a nonalcoholic beverage, at the bequest of Russia's four largest brewers, in order to exempt beer from a tax hike on spirits.[26] In 1996, the Ministry of Finance amended the VAT rules so that they did not apply to a variety of banking operations, such as purchasing securities or transferring funds.[27]

The presidential administration, meanwhile, was the main access point for fiscal federalists seeking tax privileges. In early 1994, a presidential decree was issued effectively decentralizing tax policymaking. Regional and local administrations were allowed to introduce their own taxes without limits on the rates.[28] Also, at that time, the precedent was established for negotiating bilateral treaties with defiant regions. The federal government's agreement with Tatarstan allowed the rebellious republic to withhold an additional 25 percent of VAT revenues. Similarly, Sverdlovsk Oblast' was able to reduce its total tax burden to the center by almost 30 percent.[29] In the division of tax spoils, the regions seized a larger share of the VAT and profits taxes, which produced the most income and were the easiest to collect. In 1992, the territorial division of the VAT was 80 percent to the center and 20 percent to the regions, but in 1996 the ratio shifted to 75 percent to the center and 25 percent to the regions. In 1992, the profits tax was divided so that 41 percent went to the center and 59 percent remained in the regions, but in 1996 the ratio had become 34 percent to the center and 66 percent to the regions.[30]

The tax code was modified and manipulated through other institutional channels in the fragmented state. The Duma came to be known as the "black hole"
in the budget process, because of its readiness to grant special exemptions and
create "offshore" tax havens.[31] Even the state's revenue-extracting bureaucracies were accorded discretion over the application of rates and privileges. The
customs agency was notorious for granting privileges. A government commission estimated that over $2 billion of revenue was lost to the budget in 1996, via
customs-determined exemptions. By contrast, the tax administration earned a
reputation for applying higher tax rates than intended by policy makers. As
example, in early 1997, the Ministry of Finance authorized an exemption on
the 15 percent profits tax on treasury bills. Through a loophole in the legislation, the tax administration not only still tried to collect the tax, but raised it to
43 percent.[32]

One prominent outside specialist characterized the Russia case as a "Swiss
cheese" tax system, since it was full of holes.[33] As a result of multiple access
points to the policy process, the tax system grew increasingly convoluted and
complex through incremental and piecemeal revisions. By 1997, the tax code
consisted of nearly two hundred different taxes, augmented by twelve hundred
presidential decrees and government orders; three thousand legislative acts; and
four thousand regulatory acts and instructions from ministries and agencies.
In addition, regional governments added more than one hundred of their own
additional taxes to the system.[34] At a time when the state desperately needed
income, the numerous manipulations of tax policy had negative cumulative
effects on revenue extraction.

Fiscal-Administrative Incapacity in the Postcommunist State

In the command economy, state revenues flowed through a bureaucratically
coordinated and centralized system. The Soviet tax administration never developed into a professional and autonomous bureaucracy. Instead, tax administration was a subordinate department within the finance ministry and tax collection was just another form of interenterprise resource reallocation. In this
system, tax administrators were regionally based employees, who monitored
the finances of local enterprises. Revenue was not extracted automatically from
enterprises; instead tax administrators held discretionary powers to negotiate
tax claims with the managers. After the Soviet collapse, Russian state leaders
chose to build the new system of revenue extraction on top of the regionally
dispersed tax administrative offices.[35]

The market rationalizers sought to enhance the powers of the new tax administration and consolidate the fiscal-administrative system.[36] Instead, tax
collection and revenue flows were decentralized. A variety of state and private

agents were involved in the fiscal-administrative process. Revenue was collected by the tax administration, the customs agency, special off-budgetary funds, and the state property committee. The coercive arm of the tax administration was spun off into an independent tax police, which competed for tax revenue.[37] The overall system of revenue flow included the Central Bank and its regional branches, which received tax payments from accounts in the state-managed and commercial banks. In addition, various government ministries had their own discrete funds outside the regular budget process. To oversee and coordinate the flow of revenues in and out of the state budget, the finance ministry created a new treasury.[38]

The main bureaucratic instrument of revenue extraction was the tax administration. With the introduction of radical reform, the territorial-based revenue departments of the Ministry of Finance were reorganized into an improvised tax administration, which could not immediately begin to fulfill its expanded mandate. It was hindered by three organizational constraints. First, the far-flung territorial dispersion of the staff led to an inefficient allocation of resources. The tax administration covered all corners of the country, but it lacked sufficient manpower in places where economic activity was most heavily concentrated. The internal structure and practical routines varied from one region to the next, which made it difficult to coordinate activities and process information.[39] In 1995, the central office had 710 employees, directing a workforce of more than 160,000 employees.[40] Second, the field office staffs were dependent on regional political leaders for administrative assistance and financial support. This arrangement created a situation in which conflicting demands were placed on tax administrators. Regional leaders often protected large corporations from the coercive threats of tax authorities. Finally, the personnel of the tax administration lacked the technical expertise and resources to locate and claim revenue from the transition economy, especially the emerging cash-based private sector. As a result, the tax administration remained a decentralized, narrowly focused state agency.

The tax administration could not follow transactions and income flows in the transition economy. Even its ability to monitor the large corporations waned as the former socialist enterprises were privatized and restructured, and their financial accounts were transferred to commercial banks. The large corporations, especially in the oil and gas sector, created elaborate networks of banks and shell companies to avoid or evade taxes.[41] The tax administration lacked technical means and practical experience to monitor transactions of small and medium businesses in the emerging cash-based private sector. The narrowly focused capabilities of the tax administration were revealed during the first limited experiments with market socialism. By January 1990, roughly two hundred thousand quasi-private, profit-driven cooperatives, employing over four million workers, were officially registered and operating in the Soviet Union. Yet the state managed to collect in taxes only 1 percent of the reported income of the cooperatives.[42] Meanwhile, the tax administration could not adequately track the income of households. In 1994, in a labor force of seventy million, less than three million individuals filed the required income tax statements. By 1996, only 16 percent of taxpayers paid on time and in full; another 34 percent did not pay at all. The tax administration and its leadership came in for harsh public criticism.[43] The situation deteriorated to the point where the Yaroslavl tax administration went on strike to protest its own woeful economic situation.[44]

Meanwhile, the central state had difficulty keeping track of revenue flows. Fiscal federalists and corporate collaborators took advantage of the decentralized administrative structure. Development of a centralized treasury system progressed slowly. In 1993, a network of territorial branches was supposed to be established, but a year later treasury offices existed in only seventeen of the federation's eighty-nine regions.[45] Those regions that secured special revenue deals with the center avoided having the treasury involved in the handling of locally collected revenue. As an alternative to the treasury, the government gave authorization to selected commercial banks to collect and distribute special budgetary funds. This practice was followed in regions, where private bankers subverted the establishment of a centrally coordinated treasury system.[46]

The decentralization of revenue extraction led to confusion in the treasury over the actual volume of tax receipts. The tax administration and the tax police were separately filing income statements, claiming the same revenue sources. Moreover, the head of the tax administration complained that neither the treasury nor the Ministry of Finance knew how much revenue existed in the special off-budget accounts of the various power ministries.[47] On the eve of fiscal collapse, the decentralized structure of fiscal administrative capacity continued to undermine tax collection efforts in the postcommunist state.

The Russian state survived the fiscal crisis of the early postcommunist transition, but the new tax regime was fundamentally flawed. The cumulative negative financial effects of elite bargaining undermined the effort to strengthen the fiscal capacity of the state. In the second half of the 1990s, this weakness became glaringly apparent as the threat of fiscal crisis once again loomed.

FISCAL COLLAPSE OF THE POSTCOMMUNIST STATE

The Making of a Fiscal Crisis

The steady erosion of state finances and deepening budget deficits led to a growing recognition of the need to restructure the tax regime. In his second term, Yeltsin put together a new team of market rationalizers to work out a major tax policy reform and thorough overhaul of the fiscal-administrative system. But its efforts were thwarted by corporate and regional elites, whose economic interests were served by the existing tax regime, in alliance with fiscal populists, whose political interests were served by continuing hostilities toward the government. The result was the fiscal collapse of the postcommunist state.

Fiscal capacity of the new Russian state was built on shaky foundations. With a constant barrage of demands from industry, regions, and populists, the Chernomyrdin government could not maintain tight spending limits. Budget deficits were a chronic feature of the transition. With revenue in short supply, the fiscal-administrative system eventually unraveled. Wages and pensions went unpaid; basic public services could not be performed. In finding a solution, the government was constrained in working the usual instruments of state finance: currency reform was off limits, income receipts were in decline, and credit became too easily had.

The Russian ruble was overvalued, but the government feared the return of inflation that would accompany currency reform. By the mid-1990s, one of Yeltsin's few economic boasts was that the government had managed to control inflation. Suggestions for a gradual devaluation were rejected on political grounds. As a result, the artificially strong ruble unintentionally made domestic producers less competitive in consumer markets and effectively stalled the pace of economic recovery. To cover budgetary expenses, the government came to rely on credit. The Chernomyrdin government began to subsidize its budget deficits by issuing short-term credits at highly attractive rates to entice Russia's new financiers. A vicious cycle began in which the cost of paying off the promised interest on short-term debt issues consumed increasing amounts of the state's budgetary income. The government, meanwhile, fell deeper into debt. It opened the short-term debt market to foreign investors, lured in by prospects of easy profit. To sustain the short-term credit strategy, income needed to rise, but instead it was falling.

In the second half of the decade, economic conditions conspired to undermine tax receipts. The corporate sector upon which the government had become income-dependent was unable and unwilling to fulfill their tax obligations. Official figures indicated that corporate profits in 1996 fell to almost half of what they had been in 1995. The steep decline in corporate profits tore a gaping hole in the budget. According to the government's 1996 designated income targets, the central state underfulfilled its budgetary tax collection goal by nearly 20 percent, but the profits tax was underfulfilled by more than 33 percent. Whereas the profits tax accounted for almost 30 percent of total tax income to the central state in 1995, it plummeted to just 18 percent in 1996.[48]

Even more trying, world prices for energy exports plummeted to twenty-year lows. Prices for Urals crude fell from $22 per barrel at the end of 1996 to $10 per barrel in early 1998.

In addition to economic conditions, the decline in tax revenue was the result of the deliberate actions of corporate and regional elites, who were entwined in the state's elite bargaining revenue strategy. According to the Ministry of Finance, in 1995, special tax exemptions cost the budget roughly $6 billion in lost revenue; in 1996, the cost of such exemptions was estimated to have grown to $30 billion.[49] The amount of revenue lost through tax privileges was close to one-third of the total taxes collected for the consolidated budget, and more than two-thirds of the total taxes collected for the federal budget.[50] The uncertainty about tax rates and revenue claims had a negative effect on compliance.

The state's effort to enforce its tax claims was met with widespread avoidance schemes, delaying tactics, and outright evasion. In 1996, unpaid taxes topped $20 billion, or 5 percent of gross domestic product (GDP); seventy-three corporations accounted for over 45 percent of the tax debt to the central state budget. In 1996, only six of eighty-nine regions either met or surpassed their designated tax obligations to the central budget and only thirteen additional regions managed to send in more than 80 percent of their designated tax obligations. More than half of the regions failed to collect 70 percent of their designated tax obligations to the central state budget.[51] The donor regions, in particular, were lagging behind in tax collection. At the end of 1997, the donor regions topped the list of regions with the highest tax debt to the federal budget. Nearly one-third of all tax delinquent firms were located on the territories of these ten regions.

The state strategy of using short-term credit to finance budget deficits could only be sustained if subsequent revenue earnings were sufficient to cover the costs. Thus, the steady erosion of tax income from the mid-1990s made the state vulnerable to fiscal crisis. The sorry state of state finances prompted market rationalizers to call for radical tax policy reform and more aggressive tax collection, but the presence of corporate collaborators and fiscal federalists at strategic points in the policy process stymied their efforts, bringing the state closer to a fiscal collapse.

Failed Attempt to Reform the Tax Regime

Despite the woeful performance of the new tax regime, it was elite bargaining as usual until Yeltsin's reelection was secured. In the summer of 1996, the government finally turned its attention to the growing fiscal crisis. With tax income in sharp decline, market rationalizers pushed for tax policy reform and more vigorous collection efforts.

As early as 1993, then-finance minister Boris Fedorov created a commission to study tax reform. But the commission never completed its assignment. In 1994, Fedorov was discharged and the commission's acting head concluded that reform was unnecessary.[52] The issue returned the next year, when the Ministry of Finance formed a group to draft a reform plan. The group was headed by Sergei Shatalov, an economist from St. Petersburg, who had chaired the tax committee of the Supreme Soviet in the early nineties. Suggesting the seriousness of the venture, Shatalov was named deputy minister of finance. A draft reform was completed and circulated, but the issue did not generate political support.

The dismal tax collection results for the year 1996 finally brought together a loose coalition in favor of reform. They agreed that tax collections would not improve without first restoring simplicity and fairness to the tax code. Thus, the proposed tax reform included significant rate reductions and strictly uniform enforcement. The market rationalizers were the most vocal proponents of tax reform, arguing that tax policy must facilitate economic growth. They were joined in the Duma by the centrist Yabloko Party, led by the respected economist Grigory Yavlinsky, which also supported reform. The tax administration, whose agents were left to sort out the vagaries and contradictions of the existing tax code, joined the pro-reform coalition.[53] Perhaps the biggest boost came from an external force, the International Monetary Fund, which threatened to withhold financial assistance until the government produced a tax reform plan.

Tax policy was one area in which the president could not govern by decree. In his 1997 state of the union message, Yeltsin announced that tax reform was a priority and instructed the government to submit a new tax code to the Duma. Deputy Prime Minister and Finance Minister Anatoly Chubais was charged with the unenviable task of shepherding the project through the legislature. In spring 1997, Chubais sent a draft to the Duma. The reform package sought to simplify the tax code from two hundred to thirty taxes, to lower rates in order to create incentives for businesses to come out of the shadow economy, to shift the burden away from the largest corporations and broaden the tax base, to shift the tax regime away from production and to consumption, and to eliminate tax exemptions that were facilitating evasion.[54]

The Duma was slow to respond. Citing problems with the draft, Communist Party member and Duma speaker Gennady Seleznev at first refused to schedule a reading and suggested the government withdraw the proposal. But insistent pressure from the executive compelled the legislature to act. Just before summer recess, the Duma passed the reformed tax code, subject to amendment in the fall session. By the time deputies reconvened in September, corporate collaborators, fiscal federalists, and fiscal populists had submitted more than four thousand proposed amendments to the government's document. The draft code and pile of amendments were exiled to the Budget Committee for further study. The urgency for tax reform faded and the project was abandoned until next year.

In spring 1998, Yeltsin dismissed Prime Minister Chernomyrdin and replaced him with political novice Sergei Kiryenko. With tax policy firmly in the hands of market rationalizers, the new government took up the battle for tax reform.[55] The short-lived Kiryenko government displayed a heightened resolve to enact tax reform. The Duma once again tried to revise and delay the bill. This time Yeltsin threatened to dismiss the legislature. Reluctantly, the Duma passed a partial tax reform in late spring. It was too little, too late. In August 1998, the Russian government reneged on its outstanding debts and unilaterally devalued its currency. Kiryenko was forced to resign. The fiscal collapse of the state marked a watershed event in the Russian transition. The weaknesses of the postcommunist state were laid bare. At the highest levels, state and corporate elites began to reevaluate how the power resources of the state, coercion and concessions, might be redeployed to better effect.

Fiscal Collapse of the State: Coercion and Concessions Reassessed

The failures of the government to introduce tax reform and to increase tax collections were crucial aspects of the 1998 fiscal collapse. The fiscal crisis prompted both state actors and the new business elite to try to change the nature of their relationship, each to their own advantage. For the state, there was an effort to free itself from the entangling web of the elite bargaining revenue extraction strategy. In response to the pervasive disregard to its revenue claims, the central state sought to mobilize coercion against the noncompliant corporate elites as the means by which it would rebuild fiscal capacity. For the corporate elite, the financial crisis created an opportunity to fortify the boundary line between the state and their economic holdings. They offered a bargain to the state by which they would cooperate in fulfilling their tax obligations in exchange for the formalization of their claims over the economic concessions they had recently acquired. In the late 1990s, neither side prevailed in their attempts to redefine state–big business relations.

The government resisted action against the corporate elite until the issue of the president's reelection was resolved. In late 1996, the government at last demonstrated a newfound determination to take on the big tycoons, whose companies were the largest debtors to the state budget. Anatoly Chubais, who was brought back into the government to lead the effort, stated succinctly: "our bankers think that they are the bosses. Even after the election, they will keep trying to take advantage of us. We need to sock them in the teeth for once in our lives. We won't achieve anything unless we do this."[56] The president decreed the formation of a special commission, the Extraordinary Commission on Tax Collection, formally chaired by Chernomyrdin and its Operational Committee headed by Chubais.[57] It targeted the big corporate taxpayers in an effort to settle their outstanding debts to the state budget or force them into bankruptcy. Despite this display of resolve, the commission did not succeed in reversing the situation. In 1997, the number of firms with large tax debts grew from eleven hundred to over thirty-three hundred, while bankruptcy proceedings were initiated against only one firm.[58]

When Sergei Kiryenko was appointed prime minister, he summoned former finance minister Boris Fedorov to take over the tax administration. Tax collection efforts were temporarily energized under Fedorov, who sought to strengthen single-handedly the state's revenue extracting capacity. "The hands of the tax administration will not be empty for long," he vowed, "we'll arrest you, take your property and make you bankrupt. I will be like a tank."[59] Fedorov launched an aggressive campaign to collect outstanding debts to the state treasury. He created a "black list" of the worst tax delinquents, who, he vowed, would either pay up or end up in jail. He initiated a confrontation with energy giant Gazprom for reneging on a special tax agreement negotiated with the Extraordinary Commission. And, in the name of administrative recentralization, he proposed the consolidation of the state's three main revenue extracting organs—tax administration, tax police, and customs committee—into a single overarching bureaucracy, the Ministry of Incomes.[60]

These initial efforts to mobilize coercion were ineffective. Fedorov's tenure proved short-lived: he was sent packing when the Kiryenko government fell. In little more than a year, Yeltsin would surrender the presidency to his chosen heir, Vladimir Putin, who proved to be much more proficient at using coercion to reassert the interests of the central state.

Russia's corporate elite, meanwhile, bid to secure their claims on the economic concessions they had acquired during the Yeltsin administration. The tycoons tended to act individually, and they thrived in the system of elite bargaining through which they effectively reduced their tax burdens. But the 1998 fiscal crisis forced the tycoons to put aside personal rivalries temporarily to preserve their gains. The crash resounded with an angry chorus of demands for the state to strip the big tycoons of the holdings. In response, the corporate elite appealed to the new prime minister, Yevgeny Primakov, offering a compromise. In this deal, they would pay off their tax obligations in full and cooperate with the state in finding a way out of the financial wreck; in exchange the state would formally recognize their property claims.[61] The deal was rejected.

The corporate elite did not give up on a grand bargain, but continued to appeal to the state to make the economic concessions into private property. After leaving the government, Primakov was appointed the head of the Russian

Chamber of Commerce and Industry. When the Putin administration began to use coercion against the corporate elite, Primakov attempted to broker a deal between the tycoons and the state. He proposed a pact in which big business would stop avoiding taxes and pay higher fees to the state as long as the state would grant an amnesty on the redistribution of the wealth in the 1990s.[62] This state–business grand bargain, which would have more clearly delineated public prerogative from private property, failed. The Russian state did not relinquish its claim on economic resources and the corporate elite remained concessionaires, instead of proprietors.

RETURN OF THE STATE AND THE RUSSIAN TAX REVOLUTION

Redefining Political Constraints and Tax Policy Reform

The 1998 fiscal collapse revived president–parliamentary conflict and hastened the departure of Boris Yeltsin. His successor, Vladimir Putin, was determined to restore political stability and to strengthen the central state. Moreover, he sought to rebuild fiscal capacity through the reassertion of the interests of the central state against the corporate and regional elites. To accomplish this, Putin was much more willing to use the coercive resources of the state. This reinvigorated central state coupled with favorable economic conditions led to the "Russian Tax Revolution," in which a radical tax policy reform was enacted and tax collection efforts finally improved.

The repeated failure of the government to enact tax reform was the result of political constraints in the policymaking process. The presidential succession from Boris Yeltsin to Vladimir Putin created an opportunity to redefine these constraints. Putin's leadership style differed notably from his predecessor's. Putin was not inhibited by the political alliances that Yeltsin had built during his tumultuous reign. Instead, he displayed a willingness to use the coercive powers inherent in his office against intractable regional and corporate elites. The new president reshaped three features of the policy process: executive–legislature relations, center–regional relations, and state–business relations. With this, Putin limited the access points through which regional interests and fiscal populists could influence tax policy and transformed the bargaining process with corporate collaborators from one that was idiosyncratic to one more corporatist in style. In so doing, the central state regained the initiative over tax policy reform.

Putin entrusted tax reform to a team of market rationalizers, led by Aleksei Kudrin, the new finance minister. Like the new president, Kudrin was formally a member of the reformist city government in St. Petersburg, who made his way to the Moscow stage via the patronage of Anatoly Chubais. When Kudrin headed the St. Petersburg financial department during the mid-1990s, his solution to the chronic budget deficit was simple: "Do not raise taxes, lower taxes. Everything else is secondary."[63]

In 2000, the new team presided over a comprehensive set of reforms, known as the Russian "tax revolution."[64] The success of Unity, the progovernment political party, in the 1999 Duma election and the confirmation of Putin in the 2000 presidential election finally created the opportunity for executive–legislative cooperation over tax reform. This time, the government proved adept at building an alliance between market rationalizers and corporate collaborators in the Duma for this radical reform package. The reform package dramatically reduced tax rates, eliminated many tax privileges, and simplified the tax code. In so doing, the reforms lowered the costs of compliance for taxpayers and facilitated the collection efforts of the tax administration.

The main features of the reform package included the introduction of a 13 percent flat rate on personal income tax. The profit tax on corporations was reduced by one third from 35 percent to 24 percent, while many profit tax exemptions were eliminated. And, a single social security tax consolidated five different taxes. A single raw mineral resource tax with an unambiguous rate was created in place of three different taxes, which had previously been administered differently by central ministries and regional governments.[65] Reforming the VAT has been more complicated. It was finally lowered in 2003 from 20 percent to 18 percent, but the Ministry of Finance has been reluctant to lower it further because of the concern for income loss.

Under Putin, the influence of the fiscal federalists on tax policy was significantly limited. In alliance with the Duma, the president pushed through constitutional changes that removed regional governors from the upper house of parliament and acquired the right to fire governors who violated federal law. The central state then reclaimed a greater share of tax revenue from the regions. The center–regional division of VAT receipts, for example, was revised in favor of the center. By the end of 2001, the state center received 98 percent of its revenue take from the four most lucrative and easiest to collect taxes (VAT—42 percent, excise—22 percent, profits—18 percent, user fees on raw materials—16 percent).[66] In addition, the center imposed a lower marginal rate on the profits tax that regional governments were allowed to levy on corporations.[67] Finally, and most significantly, the special concessions that particular regions had negotiated under Yeltsin were withdrawn. Putin refused to extend the terms of the bilateral treaties, thereby ending the special revenue deals enjoyed by some regions.[68]

Finally, in Putin's first term, bargaining over tax policy between the state and corporate elite was remade into a more routinized and corporatist process.

Corporate interests were not removed from the policy process, but the manner of interest articulation was organized more collectively, rather than individually. In 2001, Kudrin began to chair a special commission that met with industry representatives to set tax rates.[69] In the same year, the Union of Industrialists and Entrepreneurs established a special committee on tax policy that continues to meet regularly with the government. Through this committee, the Union was made part of the process of tax policymaking by introducing its own reform proposals and responding to government initiatives.[70] In the profitable energy sector, oil and gas duties were regularly discussed and revised by government commissions on tax and tariff rates in consultation with industry representatives.[71] The government further introduced a reform in the budgetary process, by which state expenditures were directly linked to revenue bargaining with the large oil and gas corporations.[72]

The corporatist trend in state–big business bargaining patterns was motivated by a convergence of political and economic interests. From the perspective of the central state, there was a desire to consolidate and rationalize the process of interest representation in the policy process. Likewise, from the perspective of big business, there was a desire to reduce tax rates and to define more clearly the limits of the state in the economy. But the reworking of the bargaining process is still ongoing. Beginning in 2003, Putin showed that he was not adverse to using coercion to bolster the position of the central state vis-à-vis the corporate elite on tax policy issues.

The Russian tax revolution was carried out through an alliance of market rationalizers and corporate collaborators. But after the initial policy breakthrough, the alliance came apart over the issue of "super profits" in the energy sector. Division existed within the corporate elite, as manufacturers supported rate hikes for energy exporters in order to subsidize lower rates for themselves, thereby encouraging more widespread economic growth. Within the government, some ministers supported this tax stimulus plan, while others argued for a more cautious fiscal strategy of maintaining balanced budgets, paying down the debt, and building a reserve fund. As Putin's first term drew to a close, world market prices for oil and gas exports climbed higher and higher. The issue of the "super profits" aroused political passions and set off an intra-elite contest over Russia's most coveted economic resource.

Rebuilding Fiscal-Administrative Capacity in the Postcommunist State

Upon coming to office, President Putin vowed to strengthen the "vertical structure" of the state, that is, for the central executive to assure that its policies were implemented, its laws obeyed, and its taxes collected. In order to do the latter, the fragmented fiscal-administrative apparatus of the state had to be reconsolidated and revamped. This task was begun incrementally and rather reluctantly during the end of Yeltsin's tenure, but now the energy and resolve of the new president was directed toward rebuilding the fiscal-administrative capabilities of the central state. In its second decade, the postcommunist state was doing a much better job at gathering information, monitoring transactions, and enforcing its revenue claims than it had previously done.

The tax administration has overcome the organizational constraints that initially hindered its efforts to locate and extract revenue in the transition economy. To better coordinate fiscal activities, the once independent tax administration was subordinated to the Ministry of Finance. In addition, internal reorganizations reduced the number of federal offices in the regions, including tax inspectorates, customs agencies, and central bank branches, leading to a more concentrated and efficient deployment of labor and resources.[73] In response to tax arrears, the tax administration established a regular bargaining process for clearing up the debts of corporate taxpayers, while the Ministry of Finance announced the creation of a single department to deal with state debts, instead of four separate departments.[74] The overall improvement in performance is the result of a gradual process of personnel training and technical adaptation.

The most notable organizational innovation, however, was the creation of sector-based, interregional departments, which enabled the tax inspectorate to monitor more closely the economic activities of the largest taxpayers. These special departments have set up offices on the premises of the largest taxpayers, from which tax inspectors can monitor transactions on a daily basis. In 2001, the tax administration set up three special interregional departments: oil, natural gas, and alcohol and tobacco. Interregional Department No. 1 included Lukoil, Rosneft, and Slavneft as clients, while Interregional Department No. 2 included Gazprom. According to the head of the Federal Tax Service, after the formation of Interregional Department No. 2, tax receipts from Gazprom to the state budget increased by more than 13 percent.[75] In 2003, four additional interregional departments were established: electricity and energy, metallurgy, transportation, and telecommunications.

Besides the big taxpayers, the tax administration also improved its ability to gather information from small businesses and households. Tax audits have now become routine, rather than exceptional. In 2001, the tax administration carried out 440,000 audits on companies and another 311,000 on individuals, bringing in an additional R52 billion in revenue to central and local budgets, an increase of R4.5 billion from the previous year. In 2002, the tax administration assumed responsibility for registering businesses to keep better track of taxpayers in the small business sector. Meanwhile, individual taxpayers were assigned taxpayer identification numbers to establish income profiles for households. At first, local Orthodox priests stirred popular protest to this measure by warning the faithful to refuse any sacrilegious personal identification. The controversy was resolved only after a well-publicized high-level meeting between tax administration and church officials, who determined that accepting the number would mean the loss of income, but not salvation. Since the enactment of the flat tax, the state has notably improved its collection of personal income tax.[76]

Further, the fiscal-administrative capacity of the state was strengthened through developing the means to monitor the state revenue flows more closely. In early 1997, Chernomyrdin announced that only the treasury would be involved with the implementation of the federal budget. Taxpayer accounts and budgetary funds handled by commercial banks would have to be transferred to Central Bank branches or Sberbank. Firms would now have to pay taxes directly to these accounts.[77] In March 2001, the treasury finally established a branch office on the territory of Tatarstan, the last region to do so.[78] In practice, private commercial banks still are used to administer state revenues, particularly in the regions, although now the practice requires the approval of the treasury.[79] Also, under former police chief and prime minister Sergei Stepashin, the Audit Chamber has emerged as a more effective control instrument, investigating the misuse of state funds and nonpayment of taxes.[80]

The Russian tax revolution enhanced the extractive capacity of the post-communist state. The introduction of tax reform and recentralization of fiscal-administrative capacity coincided with a surge in tax receipts. While overall conditions have been favorable for economic growth under Putin, tax reform helped to facilitate the rise in revenues to the state budget. Since the enactment of these reforms, the total tax burden in Russia as a percentage of GDP dropped from nearly 35 percent to 31 percent. Yet in 2004, the state budget registered its fifth consecutive surplus.

Despite the successes, the reforms have not succeeded in one key area. The Russian state continues to depend heavily on income from a select group of big businesses. According to the tax administration, the twenty largest corporate taxpayers accounted for more than one third of all the revenue received in the consolidated budget.[81] In particular, the tax reforms have not yet significantly shifted the tax burden away from the fuel and energy sector for incomes.[82] What tax reform and fiscal-administrative improvements could not accomplish, the state opted for a dramatic display of coercion.

The Taxman Cometh: Coercion, Concessions, and the Yukos Affair

While the state may be dependent on the largest corporations for tax revenue, Russia's corporate elite remains dependent on state patronage for wealth and status. The infamous "oligarchs" were created by the state and never succeeded in securing their outright autonomy from the state. Indeed, the Putin presidency reinforced their dependency. The corporate elite was no longer tolerated in high government posts, while state agents were placed on the governing boards of their firms. Those businessmen who pushed too strongly to limit the reach of the state and protect their property claims found themselves embattled. Under Putin, the central state displayed a new willingness to employ coercion and to reclaim and redistribute the economic concessions that had been doled out by Yeltsin.[83] In this regard, the Yukos affair demonstrated unequivocally the state's preeminence over Russia's newly arrived corporate elite.

The Putin administration managed remarkably to achieve a budgetary surplus following the 1998 fiscal collapse. But this was the result more of soaring world energy prices and more favorable ruble exchange rates. The state remained revenue dependent on profits gleaned from oil and gas exports. While the government was at last able to pay pensions and balance its books, the increasingly high profits being reaped in the energy sector proved too attractive. Government-led efforts to claim a larger share of the energy wealth brought President Putin into conflict with the young oil tycoon, Mikhail Khodorkovsky, principal shareholder in the Yukos Oil Company.

Khodorkovsky enjoyed a phenomenal rise to riches during the Yeltsin years by adeptly manipulating his access to both political patronage and economic assets. By 2003, he was reported to be the wealthiest man in Russia. When the central state began to assert itself more vigorously into the affairs of big business, the confident Khodorkovsky acted to protect his prospering fiefdom. In this effort, he was the most visibly ambitious tycoon seeking to impose limits on the central state's ability to intervene in and make claims on the private sector.

When the government tried to raise the excise tax rates on oil exports in the 2002 Duma session, Khodorkovsky orchestrated an alliance of communist and liberal deputies to reject the proposal. It was a rare legislative defeat for the government that year.[84] Next, Khodorkovsky led a private initiative to expand the outdated Soviet-era pipeline infrastructure. But this venture threatened to undermine the existing state monopoly over oil transport, which provided the government with information about transactions and revenue from user fees. In addition, Khodorkovsky sought to check the powers of the central state through his financial support to opposition political parties and nongovernmental organizations. Finally, this former "robber baron" endeared his company to foreign capitalists by adopting international financial standards of corporate governance.[85] Presumably, the more that a Russian firm becomes embedded in a network of foreign capital, the less it can be easily manipulated as an economic concession of the state.

In February 2003, Putin gathered the corporate elite in Catherine's Hall in the Kremlin, where he spoke about efforts to improve the performance of the state administration. At the meeting, Khodorkovsky was outspoken in his criticisms of official corruption. Putin replied that Khodorkovsky had his own problems with paying taxes, explicitly linking the two issues.[86] Five months later, a close business associate of Khodorkovsky was arrested for improprieties related to the privatization of a fertilizer firm in the early 1990s. The Yukos affair had begun. In October, masked commandos seized Khodorkovsky from his private plane at a Siberian airport; eighteen months later, he was still in confinement and had yet to be brought to trial. The case against Yukos involved several core allegations: defrauding the state of privatization revenues, setting up an illegal offshore company to hide oil profits, evading corporate and personal income taxes, and stiffing the pension fund. The company was hit with bills for unpaid taxes and fines, covering the years 2000–2003, for more than $15 billion. Khodokorvsky's personal debt to the state for unreported income was nearly $2 billion. Much of the bill comes from questionable tax loopholes, but the tax administration does not recognize a distinction between tax avoidance and tax evasion.

The Yukos affair was a showcase of unchecked coercive powers. The formidable forces of the secret police, the justice ministry, the audit chamber, the tax police, and the tax administration were collectively mobilized to compile a succession of criminal cases against the company and its top directors. The legal system provided no protection against the assault. The courts followed the prosecutor's recommendations in close step. On the occasion when a Moscow magistrate made a decision in favor of Yukos, she was quickly removed from the case. Due process was ignored. The accused were not permitted adequate time to review the charges to prepare a defense. Yukos bank accounts were frozen and assets seized, the firm's business operations were paralyzed. Even the media was an instrument of the state offensive, airing a documentary that tied Khodorkovsky to Chechen terrorists and murdered journalists.

The Yukos affair also highlighted the way in which the postcommunist state views the most valued economic resources inherited from the old regime. At the time of Khodorkovksy's arrest, Boris Gryzlov, former police chief and later parliament speaker, made the point succinctly: "the country's natural resources do not belong to any corporation or particular person, but to all the people of Russia."[87] These economic resources, such as access to raw materials and control over the largest corporations, are not private property. They are economic concessions that the state maintains its claims on. As such, attempts by Yukos officials to reach a settlement and repayment schedule, as if it were a private firm, were rejected by the tax authorities. Instead, steps were taken to dismantle the company and redistribute its assets to more compliant members of the corporate elite.

The showdown between the Kremlin and Khodorkovsky was prompted over disputed revenue claims and noncompliance. In response, the tax collection system was mobilized as a coercive instrument by which the central state reasserted its dominance over the corporate elite. The once richest tycoon in Russia and the most profitable corporation were essentially crushed in less than a year's time. The ramifications of the case were felt all across the corporate elite. Further tax investigations revealed billions of dollars in back taxes owed by other oil tycoons, who expressed a willingness to settle. Tax rates in the energy sector were increased with the begrudging consent of industry leaders. Oil firms voluntarily stopped taking advantage of ambiguous offshore loopholes that enabled them to report profits at half the established corporate rate. The Russian state may still be lacking in fiscal-administrative capacity for routine monitoring and enforcement, but by concentrating its coercive resources at one highly visible target, it fundamentally transformed its relationship with the corporate elite.

CONCLUSIONS: COERCION, CONCESSIONS, AND STATE CAPACITY

As Putin entered his second term, in 2004, the fiscal capacity of the postcommunist Russian state was significantly stronger than it had been at any time during the transition. The state successfully extended its revenue claims to the richest companies, most notably in the additional taxes imposed on the energy sector. The corporatist bargaining structures that now connect big business to the state still provide a mechanism for business interests to have a voice in the tax policy process, but not the final say. Moreover, after the Yukos case, big business showed a greater willingness to comply with the state's revenue claims and to abandon many of its tax avoidance schemes. The case of tax collection reveals deeper insights about Russia's postcommunist state.

The failures to construct effective checks on coercive power and to formalize private property rights stand out as the crucial developments in the postcommunist state. This outcome was made possible as a result of the political conflicts of the early transition. The enactment of the 1993 constitution upheld the central state's claims on power resources and concentrated those claims in the executive branch. The institutional checks established in the constitution would prove to be ineffective in constraining the executive power was it was capable of realizing those claims. Notable in this regard would be the subordination of the coercive organs of the new state to the executive, essentially beyond legislative control. In addition, the failure of a grand bargain to be reached between political power and the new economic elite was an underappreciated nonevent in Russia's postcommunist transition. As a result, the line between public and private, state and society has never been clearly defined. The ill-gotten gains of the privatization campaigns would remain state concessions, not private property.

The state's campaign against Yukos was motivated more than anything else by Khodorkovsky's relentless efforts to define more clearly the line that separates public and private, state and society. Any question before as to the distribution of power resources between the state and the new economic elite was answered by this confrontation. The Yukos case provides a strong disincentive to engage in elite collective actions against the state. The early protests from other business leaders about the state's handling of Yukos and defenses of Khodorkovsky were quickly muted when it became apparent that the campaign had the blessing of the president. Once again, a Russian ruler is able to keep the elite internally divided. The Yukos case emphasized that Russia's postcommunist elite remains dependent on the state for its elite status.

If there are recurring themes or cycles in Russian history, then it is because of the way in which "the state" has for so long succeeded in maintaining its monopolistic claims over power resources. The constraints on the state are determined more so by the personality of and circumstances surrounding strong executives, rather than by organized elites, constitutional rules, or popular opinion. While Russia has experienced plenty of intra-elite conflict throughout history, no significant elite faction has ever managed to develop and secure its own claim on and access to power resources. Russia's elites are not autonomous, but dependent on the state for their elite status. As a result, the state has consistently managed to use coercion and concessions to keep elites divided against each other, incapable of collective action.

NOTES

1. Mary McAuley, *Soviet Politics, 1917–1991* (New York: Oxford University Press, 1992), 107.

2. The president's personal intervention in the redistribution of state assets through rigged auctions is acknowledged in Yeltsin's memoirs (Boris Yeltsin, *Midnight Diaries* [New York: PublicAffairs, 2000], 88–95).

3. A. V. Tolkushkin, *Istoriia nalogov v Rossii* (Moscow: Iurist, 2001), 264.

4. *Finansy v Rossii: staticheskii sbornik* (Moscow: Goskomstat, 1996), 13, 14.

5. D. G. Chernik, A. P. Pochinok, and V. P. Morozov, *Osnovy nalogovoi sistemy*, 2nd ed. (Moscow: Iuniti, 2000), 152.

6. Chernik et al., *Osnovy nalogovoi sistemy*, 156.

7. V. M. Rodionov, ed., *Finansy* (Moscow: Finansy i statistiki, 1992), 273.

8. Tolkushkin, *Istoriia nalogov*, 290.

9. Yegor Gaidar, *Dni porazhenii i pobed* (Moscow: Vagrius, 1996), 96, 97.

10. The term *fiscal trap* is developed by Janos Kornai, *Highways and Byways: Studies on Reform and Post-Communist Transition* (Cambridge, MA: MIT Press, 1995), chap. 5.

11. Vito Tanzi, "Inflation, Lags in Collection, and the Real Value of Tax Revenues," *IMF: Staff Papers*, vol. 24 (March 1977).

12. *Finansy v Rossi, 2001* (Moscow: Goskomstat, 2001), 99, table 3.7.

13. *Russian Economy: Trends and Outlooks, 2000* (Moscow: Institute for the Economy in Transition, 2001), 196, table 2.4.

14. Vladimir Tikhomirov, *The Political Economy of Post-Soviet Russia* (New York: St. Martin's, 2000), 66, table 2.3.

15. Notable representatives of the market rationalizers included: Yegor Gaidar, Grigory Yavlinsky, Boris Fedorov, and Alexei Kudrin. Particularly influential corporate collaborators included individual businessmen, such as Vladimir Potanin and Boris Berezovsky, who briefly occupied high-level government posts, as well as organized lobbies, such as the Union of Industrialists and Entrepreneurs. The tax association Nalogi Rossii, based in Yekaterinburg, was a prominent advocate of the interests of "donor regions" in tax reform debates. The "donor regions" included Moscow, St Petersburg, Sverdlovsk, Samara, Nizhny Novogorod, Tyumen, and Krasnoyarsk. The fiscal populists included the Communist Party and the Agrarian Party. Several individuals do not fit this scheme so easily, most notably, Anatoly Chubais, who at times acted as a market rationalizer and at other times as a corporate collaborator.

16. The term *extraordinary politics* was coined by Leszek Balcerowicz, the architect of economic reform in postcommunist Poland. Leszek Balcerowicz, "The Interplay between Economic and Political Transition," in *Lessons from the Economic Transition: Central and Eastern Europe in the 1990s*. ed. Salvatore Zecchini (Dordrecht, the Netherlands: Kluwar, OECD, 1997), 160.

17. Gaidar, *Dni porazhenii i pobed*, 99.

18. Tolkushkin, *Istoriia nalogov*, 297.

19. The overall OECD average for PIT as percentage of total tax revenue in 1997, for example, was reported to be 26.6 percent. The average was 24.8 percent for OECD Europe, where social taxes tended to be higher. PIT averages were higher for OECD countries where social taxes were lower, these included Canada—38 percent, the United States—39 percent, and Australia—42 percent.

20. This had been the strategy in postcommunist Poland, where market rationalizers created a tax policy that supported the development of small private business (Maciej Grabowski and Stephen Smith, "The Taxation of Entrepreneurial Income in a Transition Economy: Issues Raised by the Experience of Poland," in *Tax and Benefit Reform in Central and Eastern Europe*, ed. David Newbury [London: Centre for Economic Policy Research, 1995], 106–13).

21. Gaidar, *Dni porazhenii pobed*, 100.

22. Piroska Nagy, "The Fiscal Component of the First Russian Stabilization Effort, 1992–3," in *Fiscal Policy and Economic Reform*, Mario Blejer and Teresa Ter-Minassian (London: Routledge, 1997), 235.

23. For a good description of the unraveling of Russia's democratic movement, see Michael Urban, *Rebirth of Politics in Russia* (New York: Cambridge University Press).

24. Nagy, "Fiscal Component," 239.

25. As part of the "loans for shares" scheme, Potanin's Uneximbank secured 38 percent of Norilsk Nikel in 1995 for $170 million ($140 million short of the government's asking price) (*The Moscow Times*, September 1, 2003).

26. *The Saint Petersburg Times*, August 23–29, 1994; May 26–June 2, 1996; January 6–12, 1997; March 24–30, 1997.

27. *Nalogovyi vestnik*, no 1 (1997): 62.

28. Chernik, Pochinok, and Morozov, *Osnovy nalogovoi sistemy*, 202.

29. Lev Freinkman, Daniel Treisman, and Stepan Titov, "Subnational Budgeting in Russia" (World Bank Technical Paper, no. 452, 1999), 32. *Oblastnaia gazeta* (Yekaterinburg), January 24, 1996, February 8, 1996.

30. *Russian Economy: Trends and Outlooks, 2002* (Moscow: Institute for the Economy in Transition, 2003), 60, 61.

31. Boris Fedorov, *Pytaias' poniat' Rossii* (Saint Petersburg: Limbus, 2000), 112. *Rossiiskaia gazeta*, November 5, 2001. *Saint Petersburg Times*, November 9–14, 1994. *RFE/RL*, no. 27 (February 7, 1997).

32. *Kommersant'*, February 15, 1997; *Segodnia*, February 19, 1997. *Saint Petersburg Times*, January 27–February 2, 1997.

33. Vito Tanzi, "Creating Effective Tax Administrations: The Experience of Russia and Georgia," in *Reforming the State: Fiscal and Welfare Reform in Post-Socialist Countries*, ed. Janos Kornai et al. (New York: Cambridge University Press, 2001), 56.

34. Tolkushkin, *Istoriia nalogov*, 312, 313; *Saint Petersburg Times*, March 2–8, 1997.

35. D. G. Chernik et al., *Nalogi: Uchebnoe posobie* (Moscow: Finansy i statistiki, 1998), 91.

36. Fedorov, *10 bezumnykh let*, 194–96.

37. Gerald M. Easter, "The Russian Tax Police," *Post-Soviet Affairs*, vol. 18, no. 4 (October–September 2002): 332–62.

38. N. G. Ivanova and T. D. Makovnik, *Kaznacheiskaia sistema ispolneniia biudzhetov* (Saint Petersburg: Piter, 2001), 34.

39. *Vedomosti*, February 1, 2001.

40. Tolkushkin, *Istoriia nalogov*, 302.

41. Andrei Yakovlev, "'Black Cash' Tax Evasion in Russia: Forms, Incentives and Consequences at the Firm Level," *Europe-Asia Studies* 53, no. 1 (2001): 33–55. Viacheslav Soltaganov, *Nalogovaia politsiia: vchera, segodnia, zavtra* (Moscow: Dashkov, 2000), 31–39.

42. Anthony Jones and William Moskoff, *Ko-ops: The Rebirth of Entrepreneurship in the Soviet Union* (Bloomington: Indiana University Press, 1991), 16, 71.

43. *Segodnia*, February 5, 1997; *Finansovaia izvestiia*, February 6, 1997.

44. *Nezavisimaia gazeta*, January 14, 1997.

45. Ivanova and Makovnik, *Kaznacheiskaia sistema*, 35.

46. *Rossiiskaia gazeta*, August 7, 1998, *Delovoi kvartal*, February 5, 1998, *Saint Petersburg Times*, March 31–April 6, 1997.

47. *Delovoi liudi*, no. 113 (August 2000): 9.

48. *Nalogovyi vestnik*, no. 1 (1997).

49. *Kommersant'*, February 20–21, 1997.

50. *Finansy v Rossii: statisticheskii sbornik* (Moscow: Goskomstat, 2000), 24.

51. V. N. Koshkin, "O dopolnitel'nykh nalogakh i sborakh, vvodimykh organami vlasti sub'ektov RF," *Nalogovyi vestnik*, no. 28 (March 1997): 33–35. Tikhomirov, *Political Economy of Post-Soviet Russia*, 66.

52. Boris Fedorov, *10 bezumnykh let* (Moscow: Overseen secretor, 1999), 188, 189.

53. A lead article in the tax administration journal claimed that "tax policy had turned into a system of special assistance. It is better to have lower rates and fewer privileges, than higher rates and many privileges" (*Nalogovyi vestnik*, no. 3 [1997]).

54. *Nezavisimaia gazeta*, October 23, 1996; *Rossiiskaia gazeta*, July 17, 1997; *Saint Petersburg Times*, April 21–27, 1997.

55. Mikhail Zadornov, a member of the Yabloko Party and chair of the Dumas Committee for Budget, Taxes and Finances, replaced Chubais as finance minister, who was forced to resign under the cloud of financial scandal. Mikhail Motorin, the administrative head of the same Dumas committee, replaced Catalog, who resigned in frustration over the previous year's failure to enact reform. Boris Fedorov, meanwhile, was brought back into the government as the head of the tax administration.

56. Yeltsin, *Midnight Diaries*, 90.

57. Pave Kuznetsov and Aleksandr Fomin, "Osushchestvlenie vlastnykh pol-nomochii koordinatsionnymi organami: na primere operativnoi kommissii," *Effektivnost' osushchestvleniia gosudarstvennogo upravlennia v Rossii: period prezidentsva el'tsina* (Moscow: Institut prava i publichnoi politiki, 2002), 220–37.

58. Tanzi, "Creating Tax Administration," 62, 63.

59. *Komsomol'skaia Pravda*, August 1, 1998.

60. *Obshchaia gazeta*, no. 23, June 1998; Fedorov, *10 bezumnykh let*, 196.

61. Evgenii Primakov, *Vosem' mesiatsev plius* (Moscow: Mysl', 2002), 39.

62. *Komsomol'skaia pravda*, September 25, 2003.

63. *Saint Petersburg Times*, September 12–18, 1995 and July 8–14, 1996. Sergei Shatalov also returned to the ministry as a first deputy with responsibility for overseeing state finances. Motorin continued to work out the details of tax policy. The new head of the tax administration, Gennadi Bukaev, was on record in support of the market rationalizers' tax reform plan. *Rossiiskaia gazeta*, July 31, 2001.

64. For an overview of the process of tax reform, including the working groups, see T. F. Iutkin, *Nalogi i nalogoblozhenie* (Moscow: Infra-M, 2002), 529–41.

65. *Rossiiskaia gazeta*, October 17, 2001.

66. *Argumenty i fakty*, June 12, 2002.

67. *Russian Economy in 2001: Trends and Outlooks* (Moscow: Institute for Transition Economy, 2002), 129.

68. *Izvestiia*, October 11, 2001.

69. *RFE/RL: Newsline*, January 7, 2002.

70. *Kommersant'*, February 20, 2003. *Moscow Times*, November 29, 2001, February 27, 2002.

71. *RFE/RL: Newsline*, April 30, 2002. *Moscow Tribune*, May 17, 2002.

72. *Moscow Times*, March 8 and December 7, 2001.

73. *Vlast'*, no. 14 (April 2000).

74. *Rossiiskaia gazeta*, November 5, 2001.

75. Interview with G. Bukaev, *Interfax* (March 5, 2002).

76. As a percentage of GDP, PIT increased from 2.5 percent in 1999 to 3.3 percent in 2002. See *Russian Economy: Trends and Outlooks, 2002* (Moscow: Institute for the Economy in Transition, 2003), 60, table 7.

77. *RFE/RL*, no. 31 (February 13, 1997).

78. Ivanova and Makovnik, *Kaznacheiskaia sistema*, 35.

79. *Finansovaia gazeta*, no. 17 (April 2002).

80. *The Moscow Times*, November 1, 2001, November 6, 2001, April 16, 2002.

81. *Vedomosti*, February 1, 2001.

82. *Russian Economy in 2000: Trends and Outlooks* (Moscow: Institute for Transition Economy, 2001), 61. In 2003, when the VAT was finally reduced from 20 percent to 18 percent, the government compensated for lost revenue by raising excise taxes on oil and gas production and increasing the export tax on gas from 5 percent to 30 percent (*Moscow Times*, June 23, 2003).

83. Early in his tenure, Putin gathered Russia's newly rich business leaders and explained that their economic holdings would be safe as long as they did not obstruct his state-building agenda. Shortly thereafter, two of the most prominent businessmen, Boris Berezovsky and Boris Gusinsky, were forced to flee the country, rather than face criminal prosecution when they apparently provoked the new president.

84. It was widely presumed that the voting, particularly of the Communists, was a political tradeoff to secure Khodorkovsky's continued financial backing.

85. Since 1999, Yukos has increasingly employed foreign employees for its top executive positions. The company ceased relying on a group of French advisors and instead enlisted an American team. Khodorkovsky hired a U.S. citizen to serve as the company's chief financial officer. These seemingly internal governance issues had larger implications, however, for the Russian state.

86. *Kommersant'*, February 20, 2003.

87. *Moscow News*, October 30, 2003.

Chapter Three

The Transformation of State Statistics

Yoshiko M. Herrera

The Central Statistical Administration [TsSU] should not be "academic" or "independent"... but an organ of socialist construction.

—Vladimir Lenin, 1922

Unfortunately the virus of the TsSU-Goskomstat occupational disease—the embellishment of reality—is still alive.

—Viktor Belkin, 1992

It seems to me that the present Goskomstat in large measure preserves the frame of mind of the old USSR Central Statistical Administration [TsSU] and, having made some changes, has turned into a kind of mutant that has yet to restructure its work fully.

—Valentin Kudrov 1993

The statistics emanating from the new statistical agencies are in some respects more reliable than those published in the Soviet period. They suffer however, from serious gaps in coverage and distortions caused by biases in reporting.

—James Noren, 1994

By and large, we can conclude that the Goskomstat Russia has done relatively well since the declaration of Russia's independence, particularly

given the weight of the Soviet past, immensely complex tasks which faced
Russian statisticians, the chaotic state of the Russian economy, special conditions of the transition period, and the widespread corruption of public and
private organizations and institutions.

—Vladimir Treml, 2001

If one reviews assessments of Russia's state statistical committee over the last
twenty years, and in particular over the period of perestroika to the end of the
Yelstin era, there is a clear trajectory of substantive improvement over time. Indeed, the restructuring of the Russian state statistical committee (Goskomstat)[1]
in the 1990s is a remarkable story of major institutional transformation in a very
short period. What makes this transformation noteworthy is the traditionally
politicized and guarded status of information, and especially state statistics, in
the Soviet Union and Russia.

The control of information—about society and the state, as well as about
other societies and states—during Soviet times was a hallmark of communist
rule. As Lenin famously remarked, "Socialism is accounting!" Because the
state was to replace all markets as the means of distributing resources, the state
had to meticulously monitor the economy in order to determine every detail
about consumers, firms, and production; that is, it had to collect a massive
amount of information in order to determine what was to be produced, in
what quantity, and for whom. And, because it was a regime based on force
rather than popular will, the state had to keep close tabs on society, vigilantly
watching for signs of opposition and resistance. In this sense, Goskomstat and
its organizational predecessors functioned as "the eyes" of the Soviet state.[2]
However, in addition to the state collecting information about society and the
economy, information had to be hidden from society. Keeping people in the
dark about shortcomings and deficiencies of socialism, and hiding the truth
about successes in noncommunist systems was a means of controlling the
population by manipulating the basis on which beliefs could be founded and
choices could be made. As the early Soviet secret police, the Cheka, ominously
noted, "information is the alpha and omega of our work."[3]

Not surprisingly then, glasnost, which entailed increased access to alternative, non-state controlled sources of information and which encouraged discussion of what was really going on in the Soviet Union and abroad, dealt
an enormous blow to the system of control in the USSR. Whereas Gorbachev
thought glasnost would be an informational one-way street, providing more
information about society to the state in order to allow for improved central planning, in fact, glasnost worked in two ways, giving the state more
information while at the same time allowing society more information about
the state, and about society itself including, for example, more information

about historical events, the economy, the environment, and conditions in other countries.

In the post-Soviet period, that is, in the era where instead of socialism the country is supposed to be engaged in trying to build markets and democracy, information once again plays a crucial role. Markets are based on access to information about the quality of goods and services, just as elections are based on access to information about the quality of candidates. Neither market purchases nor elections can happen without information in the hands of consumers and voters, as well as state regulators. That is, the state needs information about society, while society too—in the form of consumers, firms, and voters— also needs information. Thus, the transformation of Goskomstat—the primary state information institution in Russia—is enormously important, along with the development of civil society informational institutions, such as the media, to the course of political and economic development in Russia. Information of course is not the only ingredient for success, but it is a necessary condition, and therefore the transformation of Goskomstat has important implications for our understanding of institutional development, and the process of postcommunist state formation.

Goskomstat, formerly known as the Central Statistical Administration (TsSU), had been the sole domestic source of demographic and economic information in the Soviet Union. In compiling all social and economic statistics in the USSR, TsSU/Goskomstat was responsible for monitoring and assessment of fulfillment of state five-year plans, as well as for conducting censuses. TsSU/Goskomstat's data were also used by other ministries for planning, as well as by scientific and educational institutes. During the Soviet period, non-state or societal sources of information were limited to what individuals could see with their own eyes or privately calculate, because discussion, let alone publication, of alternative information about the USSR was restricted.

Goskomstat has traditionally been thought of as a highly secretive organization renowned for publishing a very limited amount of largely incommensurable data that were of dubious quality. However, this image belies a more complicated reality. The tasks facing Goskomstat after the end of the USSR were colossal. The organization had to very quickly adapt to the changing demands of a new political, social, and economic system, and like all other Russian state institutions, the organization faced enormous resource constraints. Nevertheless, beginning in 1987 and continuing through most of the 1990s, the Yeltsin era, there was a sea change at Goskomstat, organizationally as well as methodologically. Most of the departments of Goskomstat were renamed and given new responsibilities, and the goals as well as methods used to collect and process data were significantly changed in comparison to those that existed in Soviet times.

In the post-Soviet period, Goskomstat necessarily lost most of its functions related to state-socialist goals (such as monitoring plan fulfillment because there were simply no more plans), and gained new responsibilities related to collecting information necessary for building a market economy (whether or not markets were actually built). These new market-oriented responsibilities included the transition to the UN's 1993 System of National Accounts (SNA). The SNA affected all economic data and resulted in the production of gross domestic product (GDP) estimates for the first time in Russia. Concomitant with this move to the SNA, Goskomstat also began collecting and publishing data on previously ignored areas such as services, environmental issues, regional data, the shadow economy, and capital flight. Although many of these data series remain inadequate and incomplete, their mere existence is an improvement over the past. Because Goskomstat is a state institution with a specific mandate to produce information, the organization's publications provide a ready metric for assessments of progress in institutional reform. In this realm, the publications of Goskomstat of the late 1990s bear little resemblance to those of 1985.

It would be a mistake to conclude that Goskomstat has overcome all of its problems, or that there is no Soviet-era legacy within the institution. It would also be premature to assume that the successes achieved in the 1990s will be permanent. Indeed, as state interests consolidate under President Putin, some of the conditions that allowed for the development of professionalism at Goskomstat may be at risk. Nevertheless, if one compares the progress of Goskomstat to other informational institutions, such as the media, it is clear that for Goskomstat the Yeltsin era was a relatively successful one. And during the Putin era, while the creeping restrictions on independent media and organized political opposition gather steam, Goskomstat has, thus far, not become merely an agent of the executive. Goskomstat is still a long way from an efficient, reliable, democratic, state institution, but it is not the same old Soviet state bureaucracy.

What is interesting then, is to ask what has actually changed in Goskomstat as an institution, and how were these changes possible. What is new, and what is left of the Soviet legacy? Similarly, how was all this possible? In this chapter I examine the organizational and methodological changes at Goskomstat during the 1990s, as well as the causes of those changes. The first section is an analysis of organizational changes since perestroika and continuing challenges. The second section is an examination of the main methodological changes at Goskomstat including the expansion of access to data, the reduction of secrecy and obscurantism regarding methods, and the change from Marxist-Soviet to international categories of analysis. I also discuss the issue of manipulation of data. In the third section I consider the causes of the institutional transformation at Goskomstat in terms of structural changes, norms, actors, and resources.

ORGANIZATIONAL CHANGES

The Central Statistical Administration (Tsentral'noe statisticheskoe upravlenie SSSR—TsSU) was initially formed on the basis of a respectable legacy of prerevolutionary Russian statistics. TsSU USSR existed from 1918 until 1930, when its personnel and work were transferred to the department of Economic Accounting (Sektor narodnokhoziaistvennovo ucheta) in the State Planning Commission (Gosplan). In 1931 this section became the Central Administration of Economic Accounting of the Gosplan of the USSR (Tsentral'noe upravlenie narodnokhoziaistvennovo ucheta—TsUNKhU, Gosplana SSSR). The changes in 1930–1931 were very significant because they were the culmination of Lenin and Stalin's attempts to destroy the institutional and methodological independence of the state statistical institutions.[4] By subordinating TsSU to Gosplan, Stalin made it clear that statistics would work for socialism and the state rather than toward abstract scientific or objective goals. Some improvement in organizational autonomy came in 1948, however, when the state's main statistical organization was removed from Gosplan and given independent status under the Council of Ministers of the USSR, and renamed TsSU.

The first sign of significant institutional change for TsSU came in the midst of perestroika in 1987. On July 17, 1987, the Central Committee of the Communist Party passed resolution no. 822, "On measures for fundamental improvement of statistical work in the country."[5] The resolution grew out of debates at the seventeenth congress and party plenums in December 1986 and June 1987, and it specified thirty points aimed at reforming the state statistical administration in order to promote social and economic development.[6] Also in July, the organization was promoted to the level of "State Committee" status, and TsSU was renamed Goskomstat USSR (Gosudarstvennyi komitet SSSR po statistike). Later, the Council of Ministers passed another resolution on October 9, 1987, "Acceleration of the restructuring of the work and organizational structures of state organs," which underscored the plans in the party resolution and outlined designs for organizational restructuring within Goskomstat.[7]

In addition to perestroika-style organizational restructuring, glasnost also came to Goskomstat beginning in 1987, including attempts to improve methodology and access to state statistics. In accordance with resolution 822, an information-publication center (Informatsionno-izdatel'skii tsentr) was created. This center was one of the first open points of access for foreigners as well as ordinary citizens to Goskomstat data.[8] In addition, Goskomstat was subject to scathing public criticism, for example, from the economist Grigorii Khanin.[9] Goskomstat's relations with foreign organizations visibly changed at this time as well. For example, in 1987 the U.S. Bureau of the Census and Goskomstat began a program of cooperation that included exchanges of

official delegations, methodological information, and publications.[10] This was
an extraordinary step for an organization that had previously not allowed a
single Western foreigner into its building. The American demographer Murray
Feshbach was the first to enter Goskomstat's building, and he was followed
in February 1988 by Vladimir Treml, an American economist who delivered
a lecture to Goskomstat officials on the problems with Soviet statistics from
the point of view of a Western analyst.[11] This type of foreign interaction
grew in terms of frequency and scope throughout the late 1980s. In May
1989 Goskomstat began a telecommunication link with the UN Economic
Commission for Europe.[12] And by 1990, international institutions, including
the International Monetary Fund (IMF), World Bank (WB), Organization for
Economic Cooperation and Development (OECD), and European Bank for
Reconstruction and Development (EBRD) were also making inroads into the
methodological debates in Goskomstat.[13]

As was the case for so many Soviet state institutions, perestroika brought
its share of chaos as well as positive change. Goskomstat was forced to rapidly
consider a plethora of changes in a difficult context of dynamic economic
and social conditions, while state funding of the institution was very limited
due to general shortages and economic difficulties throughout the country.
Owing to the hurried pace of change and the lack of both trained personnel and material resources, one analyst called the 1985–1987 period one of
"fundamental breakdown in the Soviet statistical system."[14] In a sense that
was correct, but the end of the *Soviet* statistical system turned out to be a pro-
gressive step in terms of the quality of statistical information about the Soviet
Union.

The last years of perestroika witnessed further organizational restructuring,
including the replacement of Goskomstat's chairman.[15] And the end of the
USSR, for Goskomstat as well as for nearly all other state institutions, meant
yet another round of organizational shake-ups. With the end of the Soviet Union
in 1991, Goskomstat USSR was broken up into republican units, but the central
apparatus became Goskomstat of the Russian Federation.[16] In October 1992,
the Supreme Soviet of the Russian Federation formally approved a program
for transitioning to a market-oriented international statistical and accounting
system, called "The State Program for the Transition of the Russian Federation to the Internationally Accepted System of Accounts and Statistics in
Accordance with the Demands of Market Economic Development."[17] Also in
1992, a new organization, the Statistical Committee of the Commonwealth
of Independent States (Statisticheskii Komitet Sodruzhestva Nezavisimykh
Gosudarstv—Statkom CIS) was established, with former Goskomstat chairman M. A. Korolev as its chairman.[18] Statkom CIS was created mainly to
work on the development of a System of National Accounts (SNA) and the

implementation of international methodology for all CIS countries.[19] Statkom CIS was (and still is) located in the same building as Goskomstat Russia and its material resources and human capital were essentially taken from Goskomstat Russia (which took most of its resources from Goskomstat USSR).[20]

All of these organizational changes inevitably resulted in short-term disruptions of previous work.[21] Although at the time some feared that the breakup of Goskomstat USSR into constituent units and Statkom CIS would drain Goskomstat Russia of skilled workers and resources, in fact the changing political and economic environment, as well as the new methodological demands, were the real hurdles.[22] Noren wrote, "the truth is that most of the old apparatus is still in place but is ill-equipped to handle the problems inherent in dealing with reporting units no longer operating under central planning while at the same time trying to introduce new methodologies more in line with international practice."[23] It is fair to say that at the time of the end of the USSR there was no organized group of outside interests capable of, or devoted to, controlling the methodological and organizational course of Goskomstat.

The period from 1991 to 1993 in Russia was one of general institutional instability, much of it caused by the lack of a constitution and the power struggle between the executive, President Boris Yeltsin, and the legislature, the Supreme Soviet. In the end, as is well known, the executive was triumphant and authority in many state institutions throughout the federation was shifted from the legislative to the executive branch. Goskomstat too was affected by this particular institutional context. Goskomstat had been under the control of the Supreme Soviet of the Russian Federation since 1991. But in the fall of 1993, as in many federal institutions, authority shifted to the president, and in particular the Council of Ministers. There was another leadership change at this time as well: Iurii Iurkov became chairman, and Vladimir Sokolin became deputy chair. Both had been midlevel managers in Goskomstat USSR.[24] In addition to the question of authority from above, Goskomstat in the early 1990s also had to begin to seriously address horizontal relations with other state organizations, in particular, the issue of cooperation with the Ministry of Finance and the Central Bank on questions of macroeconomic and financial data.

It is important to note that at the time of the greatest methodological openness in the organization's history (due to increased contacts with foreign organizations), society and the economic system of Russia were in flux, and the executive and legislative branches of government were weak. This gave the leadership of Goskomstat unprecedented latitude for reorganization and institutional change. While the executive and legislature were too busy battling each other to pay attention to Goskomstat, the structural changes in the economy and society also provided an apparently reasonable basis for reworking the goals and methods of the organization.

Amidst this organizational instability, Goskomstat set itself a range of ambitious goals, including further movement toward international standardization and greater interaction with international organizations. As of 1993 Goskomstat had already joined as a member of the UN Statistical Commission and the Confederation of European Statistics.[25] And at the same time Goskomstat was also already submitting data regularly to the IMF, EBRD, and other international organizations. This is not to suggest that all data provided by Goskomstat to international organizations were unproblematic, unbiased, or complete. During a time when Russia was negotiating loans from the IMF, WB, and EBRD there were obvious incentives to provide information that met the perceived demands of these international organizations. However, in general the pressure on Goskomstat per se, as opposed to the Ministry of Finance or Central Bank, was to conform to the categories and practices of international organizations rather than to meet specific data targets.

One can conclude that despite some continuing problems with resources as well as methodology, Goskomstat by 1994 was a very different organization than it had been in 1991. For example, Koen reported on the change in his interactions with Goskomstat over the 1990s.[26] In 1991, he visited Goskomstat and met with both the Russian and USSR statistical committees. However, in the course of the visit he was only allowed to talk to high-level managers, and at all times during discussions, in the room with him was a deputy director who was an open critic of G. Khanin (the well-known perestroika era critic of TsSU). Koen also reported that almost all of the information he got was what was accessible already in publications, and he noted that even publicly available information, such as what was published in newspapers, was told to him reluctantly as if it were secret.[27] But by 1994, Koen reported that his meetings "could hardly have been more different."[28] He writes,

> Although access had by no means become straightforward, it was possible to talk with competent specialists, to informally request data, and to exchange critical views on the credibility of the numbers. Indeed, during those years, spectacular improvements took place, helped by a changing of the guard at the top, and reflected *inter alia* in an explosion of the volume of information released by the statistical authorities. The opening up was favoured by the growing number of contacts between Russian and foreign statisticians, by the many technical assistance programmes undertaken under the aegis of several international organizations, by the rising demand for data, and naturally by the new tolerance, or indifference, *vis-à-vis* novel or dissenting ideas.[29]

Koen's reference to "indifference" is important because it signals one of the reasons why such radical change was possible. It is not so much that there was a directive from above to support dissent, but that there were, in contrast with the pre-perestroika period, no specific directives against international cooperation.

The post-1993 period was one of relative organizational stability. There were no major structural changes and the overall goals of the organization, including movement toward international methods, continued. This is not to suggest, however, that the post-1993 era was an easy period for the organization. Goskomstat faced very serious resource constraints throughout the decade. The most public example of this was the postponing of the scheduled 1999 census until 2002, which was explicitly due to a lack of resources.

In addition, during the course of the 1990s the organization's staff was cut by nearly half, and while Goskomstat employees did not face wage arrears problems, many employees and regional managers reported that their official salaries were the only resources they received.[30] That is, no funds whatsoever for equipment, supplies, renovation—all this in a period when the organization was supposed to be moving toward international standards requiring major technological improvements and retraining of staff. It appears that the personnel changes, including staff reductions and acquiring appropriately skilled workers, were accomplished not by mass layoffs or sudden large-scale hiring of new workers, but by a combination of attrition of older employees and closing of irrelevant departments (such as those related to plan monitoring), some retraining of younger employees, and gradual hiring of skilled younger employees beginning mostly in the later 1990s.[31]

The one significant exception to organizational stability in the 1990s was the unusual change in top leadership in 1998. In June 1998, the chairman of Goskomstat, Iurii Iurkov; the first vice chairman, Valerii Dalin; and the head of the data processing center, Boris Saakian, along with more than twenty other top officials, were arrested and charged with "systematic distortion of statistical data" for the purposes of helping certain large enterprises avoid taxes. It was reported that Iurkov pleaded guilty. Later, there were more specific charges, namely that Goskomstat officials understated production in exchange for bribes and that they sold confidential information about firms to competitor firms.[32] The details of this case and its conclusion remained murky, until over five years later, when the case was finally decided in court in February 2004. In the end, Iurkov, Saakian, and another department head, Viacheslav Baranovskii, were found guilty of forming "a criminal group that in 1995–98 sold information both to private firms and government departments, including the Labor Ministry and the former the Federal Agency of Governmental Communications and Information (FAPSI)."[33] Following Iurkov's arrest and his immediate dismissal in 1998, Vladimir Sokolin, who had been a deputy chairman of Goskomstat Russia and a former methodologist at USSR Goskomstat, became chairman. The other elite positions were also filled from within the ranks of the Goskomstat bureaucracy rather than from outside.

The Iurkov et al. affair and its effect on Goskomstat's institutional transformation remains puzzling. On the one hand, if the arrests were in fact prosecution of corruption, then they may have been a positive step. But on the other hand, some people have speculated that Iurkov was close to then prime minister Victor Chernomyrdin and that his arrest was linked to Chernomyrdin's fall from grace. Because selective enforcement of laws, including politically motivated arrests, was so common in Russia especially in the late 1990s and during the Putin era, and because the details of the case are not available to the public, it is hard to know exactly why Iurkov et al. were arrested and what effect their arrests have had on the organization. In my interview with him, when asked about this case the current chairman, Vladimir Sokolin, said that the main result of the arrests was a decline in prestige and trust of the organization by the public, but that internally the organization had not really been affected.[34]

In terms of an overall organizational trajectory, it seems that Goskomstat itself has been streamlined or downsized, but the complexity of its relations with foreign as well as other Russian organizations has increased substantially over time. Rather than just being open to sharing its data with other organizations, Goskomstat in the 1990s increasingly had to coordinate core aspects of its work with other organizations. Domestically, the disaggregation of informational sources in the post-Soviet period has necessitated Goskomstat's cooperation with other organizations in order get access to basic data that it does not collect itself. At the central level, these organizations included principally the Ministry of Finance and the Central Bank, and the presidential administration. At the regional level, Goskomstat offices work of course with firms and individuals, as well as with the tax authorities and regional executive administrations.

But work with other state agencies as well as with private firms has not been entirely smooth. There have been conflicts over which agency is to collect which data, for example, with the Ministry of Finance and Central Bank or the Ministry of Foreign Trade and the Customs Office. And there has also been corruption of this process as demonstrated in the charges made during the Iurkov affair, including the illegal selling of information to both firms and other state agencies. In addition, as many citizens and organizations in Russia will attest, getting basic information from Goskomstat almost always involves paying some kind of fee, and these fees may or may not be legal or officially sanctioned.

Another aspect of Goskomstat's relationship with other organizations, which was apparent especially with international organizations in the 1990s, was that Goskomstat collected and processed data in cooperation with the demands of outside entities, rather than just presenting data as finished products to international organizations. These included a range of international and foreign organizations, such as the UN, WB, IMF, EBRD and state statistical agencies of the United States, Germany, France, Italy, and the Netherlands.[35] The necessity of deep cooperation with these outside organizations suggests that in the post-Soviet period, the autonomy of state institutions or the ability of any one organization within the state to develop as an autarkic system is less and less possible.[36]

Goskomstat has never been fully autonomous from other state structures, nor has it been accountable to the public. Although interference is less than it was in Soviet times, today other powerful state institutions still occasionally exercise some control over Goskomstat. For example, the Committee on the Census of the Presidential Administration, in consultation with Goskomstat, decided most questions related to the conduct of the census and to the publication of results. But the problem is not just that Goskomstat is subject to pressure from above, but rather that intrastate relations, that is relations between Goskomstat and other state agencies, remain unstable and subject to delays as well as corruption. One reason for this intrastate instability is the weak legal framework for statistics in Russia. A comprehensive law on statistics that governs the use and sharing of data between state organizations and citizens was only passed in 2004 and its implementation is ongoing.[37]

The conduct of the 2002 census illustrates this Soviet legacy of problematic intrastate relations and practices aimed at serving the will of the government. During the preparation and conduct of the census other state agencies (e.g., local executive administrations, police, passport offices, and housing authorities) and private organizations (e.g., media) often provided free services, such as administrative support, security of offices and personnel, advertising and publication of state information, transportation, and information about the population. The norm of interaction among these state and private organizations, however, was informal in the sense of not being specified in writing or law, and at the discretion of local executives rather than for payment specified in contracts. On the one hand this appears to be a legacy of Soviet-style mobilization of all resources to fulfill central directives (e.g., the census).[38] But on the other hand, this is a concrete example of the use of "administrative resources," a contemporary phenomenon that has been well noted in election campaigns.

While some analysts attribute the willingness of local authorities to go along with executive demands—be it for getting out the vote for a particular party, or in this case, achieving a certain level of participation in the census—as a function of force or the resources of the executive, I believe that the explanation lies in a mixture of carrots and sticks as well as ideational context. As in any bureaucracy or firm, recalcitrant lower-level managers can be punished or rewarded for their performance (or lack thereof) in meeting organizational targets in a variety of ways; this was also the case with Goskomstat. However, based on observation of practices as well as interviews with local Goskomstat officials, I also found that that the idea of doing whatever necessary to meet normatively positive goals was widespread among local officials. That is, regardless of potential gain or threat of punishment, many local officials agreed that the census was a decent and good project, and therefore it was obvious to them that any means necessary to achieve the highest level of participation should be used.

While it was a common Soviet practice to use state agencies for whatever purpose suited the party leadership, this ad hoc requisition of services and information from other state organizations opens the door to politicization of data. In the post-Soviet era, the state does not own, and is not supposed to control local administrations and media. And, other state organizations such as local police or transport authorities are not supposed to be working at the discretion of local executives, no matter how virtuous the goal (carrying out the census with limited resources). This final aspect of organizational development, the institutionalization of rules for intrastate relationships and organizational boundaries, is one of the most important future tasks facing Goskomstat and other Russian state institutions.

METHODOLOGICAL CHANGES

In concert with the organizational changes of the 1990s, Goskomstat experienced radical methodological changes. Because methodology structures the categories of analysis as well as the process by which data are constructed, Goskomstat's methodology provides the foundational framework for all of the organization's statistical output. This output, in the form of publications, is the primary product of Goskomstat—indeed the raison d'être of the whole organization—and the publications provide a metric upon which to evaluate progress in institutional reform. By considering the changes in Goskomstat's methodology in light of established international and scholarly norms, we are able to evaluate the primary activity of the organization, and hence evaluate the *quality* of institutional reform.

Of course, established international and scholarly norms are themselves socially constructed in particular contexts. Those economic and demographic indicators that we might take for granted today as a reasonable and useful, were not always considered so. We have no choice but to measure objective reality via a series of agreed upon conventions, and those conventions change over time and in response to particular demands. For example, indicators such as gross domestic product (GDP) and infant mortality do not grow on trees; rather, they are the product of decades of debate and consideration of how to make quantifiable and comparable very complicated concepts, in this case the overall level of a nation's productivity or one aspect of the health of a nation (infant deaths in comparison to live births).

Statistical indicators are never politically neutral, and always have consequences for the way in which societies and governments characterize and monitor problems and conceptualize and compare solutions. Indeed the fact that Soviet statistics were so different in terms of content and categories, that is, methodology, from Western statistics is evidence of the political content of statistical methodology. But it is not that Soviet methods had political content, and Western ones do not. Rather, in both systems statistical methodology is (and was) a function of particular power relations and interests, as well as the demands of the object of analysis. Were statistics themselves actually objective and free of political content, we would not expect differences in methods, as opposed to data, across types of political regimes. But it is precisely because there is no naturally occurring objective way to quantify the complexity of reality in a manner that allows for comparisons across societies that we have to rely on debate and deliberation over methods and information processing, in the form of international and scholarly methodological norms, in order to evaluate the quality of a country's statistics. That is, in the absence of objective standards, we have to rely on a shared sense of what is reasonable, recognizing of course that that sense may change over time and in different contexts.

Thus it is with recognition of the situatedness of international and scholarly methodological standards that we can analyze Goskomstat's methodology during the 1990s in order to establish what the problems of Soviet statistics were, what needed to be changed, and how much has changed. The issue of methodological change can be broken into four areas of analysis, which are suggestive of types of problems that have traditionally confronted Soviet statistics: limitations on access to data; secrecy and obscurantism regarding methods; Marxist or Soviet-specific categories of analysis; and finally, manipulation, errors, and other distortion of data. Below I discuss each of these problems, and progress during the 1990s.

Data Limitations

One of the traditional problems with Goskomstat and its Soviet predecessors was the ignorance (both deliberate and unintentional) of whole classes of activity. These limitations took two primary forms: accidental or purposeful non-collection of data and suppression or limitations on access to collected data. In the former, some areas were specifically ignored, such as services and military activity, but others, such as the informal economy or unemployment were not captured due both to methodological issues and to political or ideological debates over the existence of such activity. Underreporting and ignorance of specific areas became widely known under glasnost, but the changing economic environment of the 1990s, including the emergence of private enterprises, the growth of the shadow economy, and the new demands for banking and financial statistics, more sharply emphasized the need for Goskomstat to adapt its categories to fit current conditions.

The second facet of the data limitation problem concerned the suppression of collected data. In general, information about the economy that was publicly released was always relatively minimal in the Soviet Union. The government released a fraction of what was available in Western countries, and they did this by limiting the scope of the data as well as by simply limiting the number of copies of works published, and then also limiting access to those publications.[39] But even amongst the economic data it did release, the exclusion of data related to the military industrial complex, which obviously accounted for a large part of the economy, rendered what was released to be incomplete at best. In addition, data limitations extended to noneconomic areas. It was long suspected that detailed publication of the 1979 Soviet census was held up for more than ten years, not because of any technical or methodological flaw in the census, but rather for political reasons.[40] And when the 1979 census data were finally released, only 368 pages, in contrast to over three thousand for the 1970 and 1959 censuses, were published.[41] A final issue in the limitations on data was that only official TsSU/Goskomstat data were available for public discussion and publication, and, as Treml writes, "one could freely cite and use in other ways the available TsSU statistics but not to change, interpret, or criticize them."[42] Thus it was not just that Goskomstat publications were incomplete or lacking, but that supplemental or alternative statistics were strictly forbidden. That is, until glasnost.

One of the ways in which access to Goskomstat USSR data was forced open during glasnost and perestroika was the decentralization of publications by regional- and republican-level statistical offices. The Baltic states in particular took an active role in publishing republican-level data that were not being published by the central Goskomstat. In addition, regional scholars such as G. Khanin from Novosibirsk were able to publish their own calculations and alternative statistics in journals and newspapers.

Goskomstat responded first in the area of social and demographic data with new publications and new data series, and additional and improved economic data came later.[43] Already by the late 1980s there had been a significant increase in the number of publications as well as volumes of data within publications, and it became possible for ordinary citizens to subscribe to certain statistical publications.[44] Moreover, official discussion, if not solution, of the problem of previously ignored areas such as the military and the shadow economy, as well as "moral" statistics like crime, arrests, alcoholism, divorce, and abortion, got underway in the 1990s. In some areas there has been substantial progress. For example, during the Soviet era almost no regional (sub-republican level) data were published, but by the end of the 1990s Goskomstat was publishing almost all of its data at least disaggregated to the regional level. However, the problems of data limitations, stemming from both noncollection of data and restrictions on access to what has been collected, have still not been solved— or have been only superficially addressed—in a number of areas including, for example, public health statistics on HIV rates, the shadow economy, and other types of activities or processes that are both hard to measure as well as embarrassing to report.

Methodological Secrecy and Obscurantism

In addition to limiting access to data (by not collecting or publishing it), another major methodological problem in Soviet statistics was the secrecy and lack of explanation of the content of indicators or categories, as well as the lack of explanation of changes to, or problems with, published data. As someone who spent most of her career deciphering Soviet statistics, Gertrude Schroeder wrote, "the information dearth was compounded by the government's penchant for concealing the economy's problems and exaggerating its performance and by the obscurantist framework of Marxist jargon used for compiling statistics and analysis."[45]

Gregory Grossman's concept of "descriptive distortions" is another way to put this obscurantism problem; that is, stating that an indicator means one thing when it really means something else.[46] For example, Treml noted that the number "doctors" might include dentists; or "grain weight" might include dirt, water, and other matter not initially separated during the harvest; or "meat" might include lard and other inedible animal parts.[47] A higher profile example of obscurantism concerns the category of "defense expenditures," which turned out to mean only pay and current material expenses, but not research, construction, or weapons purchases, which together are estimated to have represented 70 percent of the actual defense budget.[48]

The reason that "descriptive distortions" were so prevalent was twofold. First, Soviet statistics used similar terms but different content for a number of indicators (e.g., national income included only material production, not services; or infant mortality was measured differently from international standards). But a second important reason for the existence of descriptive distortions was that Goskomstat so rarely published methodological descriptions of its indicators. These reasons for the existence of obscurantism are important to its reduction.

By moving to international standards, including international categories of analysis, the space for nonstandard content has been increasingly squeezed out (but not eliminated entirely). Second, once Goskomstat committed to making clear what was in the indicators by publishing methodological notes, in the right conditions, transparency could become a self-enforcing outcome. If analysts have access to accurate descriptions of the content of indicators, it becomes increasingly hard to fool audiences with labels that do not correspond to what they are supposed to correspond to.

On the economic front, since 1996 Goskomstat has published five volumes of methodological notes as well as extensive methodological commentary in the pages of *Voprosy statistiki* (*VS*).[49] In addition, the 1993 SNA methodology used in Russia was published jointly with the World Bank in 1995.[50] If these types of steps are not reversed, and if analysts continue to investigate Russian statistics, then the level of descriptive distortions should continue to decrease over time. But this trajectory depends both on continued publication of methodological notes and continued vigilance on the part of outside analysts.

The discussion of methodology in *VS* in the run-up to the 2002 census provides an illustration of measured and relative progress in terms of reducing methodological secrecy and introducing a greater level of transparency in the workings of Goskomstat. The articles in *VS* include discussions of past and future censuses, census pretrials, conferences with scholars or others outside Goskomstat, regional participation, methodological questions, and discussion of the content and categories of the census.[51] There was definitely more information about Goskomstat's internal processes available to the public than had existed in the past, and there was clearly engagement with the international and domestic scholarly communities on a range of methodological and organizational issues.

However the reliability of the 2002 census data has been compromised by the nontransparent use of, and lack of citation of, non-census data sources. In a largely secret, last-minute decision, census forms were filled in by census officials for individuals who were not enumerated voluntarily, on the basis of data from the housing authorities, employment records, and the passport office. Only three items were filled in: the number of people living in an apartment, their ages, and their sex. But these forms, which were filled in on the basis of older data rather than current enumeration, were not distinguished from other census forms, and therefore the 2002 census data, at least for the number of people, age, and sex, will contain data from other, possibly outdated, sources combined and presented as 2002 census data, without proper citation or identification of differences in data sources.[52] This presentation of 2002 data is reminiscent of Soviet descriptive distortions insofar as the data do not exactly correspond to what they are purported to represent.

Beyond methodological secrecy, another aspect of obscurantism in Soviet statistics was, and continues to be, the silence regarding changes or problems with published statistics. Its causes are likely incompetence as well as reluctance to acknowledge errors. For example, in January 1992 Goskomstat published a net 2.2 percent decline in industrial production for 1991, but in 1993 they published a net 8 percent decline for 1991, without any commentary on the discrepancy between the 1992 and 1993 publications.[53] In addition, Goskomstat published figures for budget deficits, similarly without any commentary or explanation on where they came from.[54] In interviews conducted with economists and other consumers of Goskomstat data in Russia during 2003–2004, the lack of *specific* methodological notes (i.e., explanation of particular changes and discrepancies) was one of the most frequently cited problems still characterizing Goskomstat data. In general one must conclude that Goskomstat still has some work to do in coming to terms with past problems of obscurantism. There has never been an official apology or systematic accounting of past errors during the Soviet period.[55] Even in Goskomstat's 1996 auto-history, there is hardly a hint of any problems during the past 194 years of Russian and Soviet statistics.

Marxist-Soviet Categories of Analysis

A third area of problems in Soviet statistical methodology concerned the use of Marxist or Soviet categories of analysis that had no Western equivalents and which when combined with the other methodological problems (limitations on data, secrecy about methods, and errors and manipulation) made information about the Soviet Union extremely difficult to compare with that from other countries.

This difference in categories mainly affected economic statistics, and it was not accidental. Rather, it was a function of organizational norms regarding the relationship of economies and statistical systems: many Soviet statisticians believed that capitalist and communist economies demanded different types of statistical systems. This organizational norm at Goskomstat developed in response to the increasing gap, since the 1950s, between the work of international and Soviet statisticians. In the postwar era, as the SNA became more and more widely accepted and used by countries around the world, Soviet statisticians found themselves at odds with international practice. This created a problem in reconciling how their work fit with international practice, because they had long been committed to the science of statistics and did not want to be ostracized internationally. To get around this conflict, Soviet statisticians defended and rationalized their commitment to an alternative statistical system (the Soviet system of Net Material Product [NMP] as opposed to the SNA), on the basis of structural differences in the economy. The logic behind this differentiation was that the SNA was appropriate for capitalist, market-based economies, and that a different statistical system, the NMP, was appropriate for communist economies.[56] There was some support for this structure-based differentiation in that the SNA does demand market prices, which the USSR did not have. But rather than moving to market prices, as international statisticians would have preferred, for a variety of reasons the Soviets promoted their system as an alternative, given the structure of the economy. In this sense, the Goskomstat norm of two alternative statistical systems was conditional on the type of economy.

Regardless of the justifications for different types of economic indicators and statistical systems, the differences between Marxist-Soviet categories of analysis and Western categories served to divide the content and categories of Soviet economic statistics from international practice. Thus the shift to Western categories represented a major step toward making data about the Russian economy more accessible to international audiences, and the establishment of the SNA was the emblematic step in that process.

The first phase of SNA implementation was 1992–1996.[57] In 1997 Goskomstat embarked on a second stage that entailed full and systematic internationalization of all Goskomstat statistical information. Despite certain problems, in general Goskomstat's implementation of the System of National Accounts in such a short period in the 1990s stands as a remarkable achievement. On a variety of UN assessments of SNA implementation that were carried out in the late 1990s, Russia scored above the average of other countries in the world, and even further above other countries at similar levels of income.[58] In addition, Goskomstat moved away from Marxist-Soviet categories in a range of other areas.[59] And, this trajectory of international standardization at Goskomstat is discernable from its own publications. A survey of Goskomstat yearbooks or of *Voprosy statistiki* (and its predecessor *Vestnik statistiki*) from the mid-1980s to 2004 demonstrates clearly a fundamental change from the discourse of Marxism-Leninism to one of international statistical methodological norms. This change is also evident at the highest levels: for example, if one compares the language of the 1987 Central Committee resolution to the 1992 program for statistical reform or the 1993 program on the shift to a System of National Accounts. These changes have made Goskomstat publications more and more similar in form, as well as content, to their Western counterparts.

Manipulation and Other Errors

A final issue in the discussion of methodological change at Goskomstat concerns the issue of manipulation of data and other methodological errors. While many analysts are convinced that Goskomstat actively falsified data,[60] and there was the Iurkov et al. accusation in 1998 of systematic distortion (see above), many scholars have argued against the idea that Goskomstat officials routinely and deliberately falsified data; instead they focus on the complexities of the system and some of the methodological issues described above. For example, in trying to explain Goskomstat's "numerous and puzzling inconsistencies," Vladimir Treml concluded, "as a general case, I believe that these puzzles are the product of archaic and often conflicting methodologies and conventions, faulty and biased price and output indexes and formulae, and poorly designed classifications and not of outright *ad hoc* manipulation and deliberate falsification of data."[61] To the extent that Treml is correct, outright falsification of published data was not an area for institutional change at Goskomstat in the 1990s, because even in the Soviet period it had been a limited phenomenon.

However, while the question of active falsification was not a priority for Goskomstat in the 1990s (except in the Iurkov incident), the issue of increasing unintentional errors does demand attention. Soviet data given in physical units were always the most reliable; data in value terms were suspect due to faulty price indices; and the indices in general were the poorest types of Soviet statistics (e.g., indices of prices, production, sales, income, etc.) due to problematic (biased) formulas and methods.[62] These problems were compounded by the inflationary context of the early 1990s and its effect on the price indices used to convert current value terms from volume or real production terms. While Goskomstat moved away from Soviet-type price indices, their new deflators nevertheless were (and are) extremely sensitive to small changes in the rate of inflation.[63] In addition, the rapid methodological changes at Goskomstat may themselves have contributed to erroneous appearances of changes over time. As Goskomstat updated and revised its methodology throughout the 1990s, it frequently created apparent changes over time, which it has only occasionally addressed in methodological notes.

A final issue related to methodological errors at Goskomstat in the 1990s concerns the goals and incentives involved in reporting information. Whereas there were well-known incentives for overestimation of production to fulfill plan targets during the Soviet period, in the current period, the opposite incentives are in place because taxation makes underreporting desirable.[64] Moreover, the change in incentives would not only affect yearly estimates, but would also affect "changes" over time. For example, the incentive shift alone, that is, from overreporting to underreporting, may be responsible for suggesting declines in production that were more severe than actually were the case.

But it is not just in economic matters where incentives affect the type and quality of data collected. In any area, for example, drug use or HIV infection, where data are linked to some type of sanctions (be they material, nonmaterial, formal or informal), one can expect underreporting. Also, where the use and privacy of data are unclear, as in census data, individuals will have incentives not to report for fear of fines, harassment, or other punishment. Finally, where data reporting is costly and the benefits are minimal, such as in filing criminal reports or registering for unemployment, one can also expect underreporting. These incentives suggest that to improve the quality of data about the economy and society in Russia, reliance on changes in Goskomstat methodology and practices may be insufficient. Rather, changes in society and the political system that are aimed at generally increasing trust in government agencies and reducing the costs and punishment as well as increasing the benefits associated with reporting will be needed. Thus, in the areas of unintentional errors and incentive-driven biases, there continues to be room for substantial improvement.

In summary, if we evaluate Goskomstat on the basis of its publications over the course of the 1990s, and if we use situated international methodological standards as a metric, there is substantial evidence that Goskomstat has made significant progress in addressing its traditional problems including reducing limitations on access to data, reducing secrecy and obscurantism regarding methods, and shifting its categories of analysis away from Soviet or Marxist categories toward internationally standardized indicators. However, these problems have not been entirely eliminated. Moreover, changes made during the 1990s are not necessarily permanent, and especially in the Putin era, much remains to be done in terms of strengthening both institutional autonomy and transparency and addressing incentives for reporting.

CAUSES OF CHANGE AT GOSKOMSTAT

In order to understand the sources of the transformation of Goskomstat in the 1990s, as well as the potential for continuation of those reforms, in this section I discuss the structural changes, norms, actors, and resources that contributed to institutional change at Goskomstat. To begin with, it is impossible to imagine the specific institutional development of Goskomstat in the 1990s without perestroika and glasnost. All post-Soviet Russian institutions were in some way affected by the end of the Soviet Union and the necessary restructuring that followed. However, glasnost was a crucial period for serious reevaluation and reconsideration of the ideological bases of the Soviet Union, and perestroika provided the seeds for radical institutional reorganization. The general demand under glasnost for more openness and discussion of politics, economics, and society extended to public discussion of TsSU's statistics.

The trajectory of criticism of Goskomstat took a familiar path. As in other state institutions, critiques began during glasnost and perestroika with revisionist historical articles criticizing statistics during the Soviet period.[65] Then there were calls for a return to true Leninist principles and criticism of current practices was framed as a deviation from socialism.[66] But these critiques, which were initially framed as a means of revitalizing Soviet power, evolved into critiques of the system itself. Moreover, TsSU and Goskomstat were forced to respond to criticisms, as it was no longer possible after 1987 to either suppress or ignore them. And, in addition to demands from society for change at Goskomstat, during perestroika there was also top-down pressure to "reform" and support restructuring.[67]

The dissent and criticism of Soviet and Russian statistics that started under glasnost and perestroika did not end with the end of the Soviet Union. Instead, external criticism—that is, analysis and review emanating from outside Goskomstat—continued to provide checks on the process of institutional reform in Goskomstat throughout the 1990s. Initially, alternative data and alternative models for the construction of state statistics, which were presented by foreign or non-state actors under glasnost, and which were available in scholarly journals or books as well as newspapers, functioned as a substitute or supplement to official statistics. However, rather than simply existing as alternative data, as was the case during Soviet times, in the post-Soviet period, these alternative statistics, and the methodologies used to construct the data, themselves became models for official Russian state statistical work. In other words, rather than just functioning as a part of civil society or a check on the state, alternative sources of information and methods were important to the transformation of Goskomstat's own methodology.

The international context and in particular the end of the Cold War and the related decline in the ideological power of the Soviet system played a role in the reorientation of Goskomstat personnel toward international standards and methods. Whereas the autarkic Soviet system had provided some justification for methods that were consistent with Marxist ideology and specific to the needs of central planning—for example, excluding services from national income estimates, and using state-defined prices to derive values—the end of that system and the move to market prices in Russia, consolidated the view amongst statisticians in Russia that the methods of Goskomstat would have to change.

The commitment by Goskomstat employees to the Soviet statistical system, the NMP rather than the SNA, was premised upon structural economic differences. Once Russia began to move toward a market economy by eliminating state plans, allowing for private firms, and freeing market prices, the structural economic distinction, which had been used for decades to rationalize a different statistical system, also disappeared. With the structural changes in the economy, Goskomstat employees, who were primarily Soviet statisticians, embraced the move to the SNA. However, it was the conditionality of organizational norms upon the economy, rather than the material incentives created by the structural change in the economy, that accounts for the changing interest in reform by long-time Goskomstat employees.

The idea of international commensurability, that is, the notion that Russia was now part of a global, market-oriented world and that its statistics would therefore have to be comparable, was evident in every level of the organization. Former Goskomstat chairman Pavel Guzhvin ended his 1993 article with a very familiar sentiment: "we hope to raise statistics to a level that will satisfy the demands of the market economy and will make it possible to compare indicators of the Russian national economy's development with analogous indicators of other countries."[68] In addition, in interviews with lower-level regional Goskomstat personnel, in response to the question of why there had been so much change in methodology at Goskomstat, respondents almost universally noted that the new conditions of the market economy demanded change and it was important for Russian statistics to be compliant with international practice.

A very interesting aspect of the transformation of Russian statistics is that the primary actors involved—that is, the statisticians in the organization, including the leadership and the rank-and-file employees—were largely Soviet-era bureaucrats. In other words, the organization was not taken over by outside reformers; instead there was tremendous internal demand for radical institutional change. As noted above, the structural change in the economy was an important catalyst for the conditional norms about the appropriateness of the move to the SNA, but those norms were based upon a commitment to some level of professionalism during the Soviet period. Were it not for the aspiration to be accepted as part of the community of international statisticians during the Soviet period, there would have been no need for any rationalization of the Soviet system via conditional norms or any other mechanism. Thus, professionalism, stunted though it was during the Soviet period, turned out to be enormously important to reform once the organization achieved a significant degree of institutional autonomy in the Yeltsin period.

The specific outside actors involved in Goskomstat's transformation included of course Mikhail Gorbachev and Yeltsin's government, especially Prime Minister Yegor Gaidar, who was a strong supporter of the move to the SNA and reform of state statistics in Russia. Even after Gaidar, however, subsequent Russian governments generally supported institutional and methodological reform at Goskomstat. But outside dissidents, such as the economist Grigorii Khanin, also called attention to the need for change at TsSU/Goskomstat. Khanin's articles in *Novyi Mir* and *Kommunist* represented a watershed in the debate over Soviet statistics.[69]

International organizations including the UN Statistical Commission, IMF, and World Bank in particular were also absolutely critical to the reorganization of Goskomstat's methodology, although they largely followed rather than precipitated internal demand for reform. Ironically, for all their efforts in deciphering Soviet statistics, established Sovietologically oriented organizations such as the U.S. Central Intelligence Agency (CIA) played little role, if any, in the transformation of Goskomstat in the 1990s (that is, beyond the data and analysis they had provided previous to the end of the Soviet Union). CIA work on Soviet statistics stopped completely in 1991, and in any case their methods were no longer relevant. Whereas CIA analysts poured over published material from afar with almost no direct contact with Goskomstat, analysts from other international organizations worked from inside Goskomstat with the direct cooperation of Goskomstat's top leadership.[70]

In addition to specific actors and organizations, however, the constellation of elite political actors or the general context of the state was also an important factor. In the 1990s, as is well known, the Russian state was very weak. Neither political opposition, nor the government were very well organized or consolidated. Unlike in the pre-Gorbachev era or in the Putin era, the demands of the government leadership during the 1990s were not unified. The dissident republics like the Baltics took the initiative during the perestroika era to publish their own data, sometimes in the local languages. As with challenges from individual and international organizations, the alternatives and criticisms presented by republican statistical committees in the late 1980s compelled the central Goskomstat to take action.[71] And yet there was no agreement from the Gorbachev government on what action to take. Similarly, the divided and weak-state Yelstin era afforded a level of autonomy to Goskomstat in which professional norms and international standards went relatively unchallenged. In the absence of strong governmental directives, international organizations, foreign governments, and private firms, as well as other state organizations, all influenced the organizational and methodological changes at Goskomstat during the 1990s. In contrast, President Putin has made strengthening of the state a priority. While this may entail greater institutionalization of some 1990s changes, it also signals an end to relative competition of political and economic interests and demands that characterized the 1990s and perhaps also the relative autonomy of Goskomstat from the demands of the executive and government.

Once change had been initiated, certain decisions within Goskomstat became self-reinforcing mechanisms for further change. For example, once the decision to publish methodological notes had been made, and the content and categories of analysis at Goskomstat had become more transparent, it became harder and harder to hide information through "descriptive distortions" or other mechanisms involving methodological secrecy. In other words, transparency in methods led to increasingly less space for concealing undesirable facts, greater overall transparency in data, and greater ability for outside analysts to check the accuracy of Goskomstat's publications.

In many ways, the transformation of Goskomstat is not a resource-driven story, but resource constraints played an interesting role nonetheless. The organizational and methodological changes of the 1990s required extensive resources, but like most other state institutions, Goskomstat was greatly constrained in this area. The development of massive surveys to collect data on the population and the economy, which were both technically complicated and expensive, as well as the development of computer science and information technology to process the data created a formidable burden that Goskomstat was not always able to meet (e.g., the postponement of the census for three years).

Moreover, in addition to the generally difficult financial position of all state institutions in the 1990s, Goskomstat suffered in other ways, most notably human capital constraints. Relative to other state institutions that required technical and statistical skills, such as the Ministry of Finance or the Central Bank, Goskomstat offered much lower prestige as well as pay, and therefore had greater difficulty in attracting and keeping skilled workers. International institutions that worked with Goskomstat were another source of "brain drain" for Goskomstat's most talented staff. An indicator of the level of prestige and employee compensation at Goskomstat is apparent in the gender breakdown. Goskomstat is overwhelmingly—between approximately 90 and 95 percent— staffed by women, except of course in the highest management positions, which are overwhelmingly held by men.[72]

So, given these resource constraints, how did Goskomstat manage to carry out such sweeping reforms? The professionalism amongst the employees mentioned above was very important. Another part of the answer is that Goskomstat was the recipient of aid from some international organizations, notably the World Bank. But without the internal support for reform within the organization, these funds would not likely have been as effective as they were. Most of the international aid went to the central Goskomstat office in Moscow or to pay for technical assistance from Western consultants. This expertise, however, did filter down through the organization via nationwide conferences dedicated to retraining as well as through educational materials that were distributed to regional offices.

But in addition, some of Goskomstat's resource constraints turned out to be blessings in disguise. First, financial constraints restricted the number of employees at Goskomstat, where Goskomstat was forced to reduce its workforce by approximately one-half during the 1990s. This hard employment constraint provided incentives for elimination of redundant and less skilled workers, and retention of the best workers. Second, while the large number of female work-ers was a signal of low prestige for the organization, reflecting sexist attitudes and restricted opportunities for women in Russia, it is also the case that Russia has an enormously skilled female workforce, and that skilled female workers tend to be reliable and willing to work for low pay. Thus, I would argue that the existence of so many female workers may have actually boosted productivity and may have been one of the ways that Goskomstat was able to proceed with reforms in a low-compensation environment.[73]

Another way in which low prestige may have actually supported reform at Goskomstat is that the organization was not a high-profile site of contestation for political elites. There was far more attention by political elites to the inner workings and production of data at the Central Bank and Ministry of Finance than to Goskomstat. While this prestige differential is partly a function of the division of labor and the fact that Central Bank and Ministry of Finance work with macroeconomic data of high importance to the government, it is also the case that some of the most politicized data, specifically on government budgets and tax receipts, came from the Central Bank and Ministry of Finance rather than from Goskomstat (although all three organizations did share information). Thus, Goskomstat's low prestige, regardless of its source, may have had the effect of affording the institution more autonomy from political interests and therefore greater space for professionalism to grow.

A third resource constraint that turned out to have positive implications for institutional reform was the implementation of "self-financing" in the late 1980s. The primary means for Goskomstat to raise revenues was through the sale of its publications. Although Goskomstat received most of its funding from the federal budget, since the mid-1990s both the central and regional offices began selling services privately, especially specialized data sets. All Goskomstat offices claim that all the funds from these operations go back into the federal budget, but regional offices claim that they can draw on the funds they have sent in to be used for equipment or other needs of the regional office.

While analysts did (and continue to) raise concerns about the opportunities for corruption via the sale of publications, not to mention the unfairness in the fact that Russian citizens are required to pay for data that have been col-lected and processed already at citizen expense, the sale of publications forced Goskomstat to produce products worth selling. According to one analyst, "in a way, openness was also forced upon Goskomstat by hardened budget con-straints, as selling statistical publications became a way to raise revenue."[74] Of course Goskomstat is a monopoly collector of data in many areas (especially disaggregated, lower-level statistics), so competition is limited. Nevertheless, revenue prospects have increased the incentives for Goskomstat to meet the needs of businesses and consumers in its publications.

In general, the role of resources in the transformation of Goskomstat was complicated. On the one hand, the infusion, small though it was, of international aid and expertise was critical, and more resources for equipment and training would likely have furthered reform efforts. On the other hand, in the context of professionalism and a commitment to move toward international practices, other hard resource constraints may have also served to promote reform within the institution. But overall, the role of resources in Goskomstat's transformation is deeply connected to its impact on the development of human capital at Goskomstat, which happened in concert with other changes in the institution. The human capital that was necessary for reform at Goskomstat in the 1990s, moreover, was dependent on resources committed during the Soviet period, especially education. Despite changes in the specifics of training programs, it remains to be seen whether the current educational system in Russia, hampered by massive resource constraints, will continue to produce high-quality statisticians.

CONCLUSION

Goskomstat made remarkable progress in organizational and methodological reform during the 1990s. The goals of the institution have shifted away from serving state socialism, and there was substantial improvement in the volume and scope of data released. The organization also reduced the level of methodological secrecy and moved vigorously toward implementation of international standards and categories of analysis. A very important indicator of Goskomstat's continued methodological and organizational progress in the post-Yeltsin era will be whether new data that are collected are made fully available and in what form. Outright falsification is unlikely, but the institutional legacy of secrecy and limitations on access to data suggests that monitoring the quality of state information will remain a complicated task.

The primary area of concern for the future is the establishment of rule-based intrastate organizational relationships. Data and statistical institutions can be used by the state not only for welfare-enhancing policies, but for increased policing, surveillance, and other nondemocratic purposes as well. Economic and demographic information is a crucial link between state and society; it allows society to make decisions and allows the state to shape issues and solutions. It is clear that the Soviet state used information and statistics to shape a particular type of society. If professionalism and institutional reform are to proceed at Goskomstat, then processes of data collection and presentation must be transparent, and data must be treated confidentially and used for their intended purposes only, and Goskomstat as well as other state agencies must shore up their institutional boundaries so that they do not become agents of the executive.

In reviewing the specific process of institutional reform at Goskomstat, we can draw some lessons about the process of postcommunist institutional development and state formation more generally. First, the larger institutional context, both domestic and international, matters for institutional reform. The end of the USSR and structural changes in the economy of Russia precipitated changes in understandings about the appropriateness of particular statistical systems at Goskomstat. In addition, the institutional struggles within the USSR and later within the Russian Federation affected Goskomstat though the top-down reform-oriented programs that successive Russian governments supported at Goskomstat, but also by distracting the executive and other interested elites enough to allow Goskomstat a level of autonomy where professionalism could flourish. Second, in this case, Soviet-era organizational norms and professionalism were important to the acceptance and implementation of later institutional reform. The swiftness and scope of change at Goskomstat would have been impossible to achieve without the widespread and deep appreciation of the need for Russian statistics to meet international standards.

Third, the role of resources in institutional change is not linear. At a basic level, resources for equipment, retraining, and salaries were crucial. And it is to Goskomstat's credit that the institution managed to avoid wage arrears and make small improvements in equipment and training, given its very limited budget. More resources may have made these tasks easier. However, the resource constraints also forced Goskomstat to make difficult but necessary reductions in personnel and they forced Goskomstat to adapt its services to the needs of businesses, organizations, and consumers. And, the primary resource that Goskomstat relies on is its human capital. This is something developed over time and largely on the basis of other more diffuse state resources, primarily education. Thus, increases to Goskomstat's budget in the 1990s would not in itself have created a more productive, skilled, and reliable workforce. Why Goskomstat's staff has worked as hard as it has and for such minimal compensation is not a question than can be answered by the staff's monthly paychecks. Resources matter, but they do not provide the full explanation.

Finally, Goskomstat's transformation sheds some light on the issue of institutional corruption. In Goskomstat's case, the incidence of deliberate falsification of data was very limited, but the level of misrepresentation of the social and economic conditions in the Soviet Union was very high. The complexity of the way in which data were limited and manipulated suggests that in examining institutional corruption, we should focus not just on crude bribery, lying, and cheating, but rather on the more subtle ways in which the tasks and output of an organization become distorted. In particular, Goskomstat's experience suggests that the issue of corruption hinges on institutional autonomy, which can protect it from other political actors, such as the executive (or a dominant party), and transparency, which allows outside actors to check the quality of the work of the institution. Russian statisticians, like all state employees everywhere, are subject to informal pressure from other organizations, which can lead to exploitation of loopholes or wiggle room in order to enhance or improve the appearance of the state. But transparency, in this case methodological transparency, can serve to reduce the incidence of selective and obscurantist tactics. Similarly, the strengthening of institutional autonomy and development of rule-based, rather than outcome-based, relationships with other state organizations can reduce pressure on state employees to use any means, legal or illegal, to achieve executive goals. While Goskomstat provides a specific case of this, the principle of attention to institutional autonomy and transparency can be applied more generally to combating corruption in institutional reform.

NOTES

Research for the chapter was made possible by the generous support of NCEEER, IREX, the Project on Russian Governance, the Davis Center for Russian and Eurasian Studies, and the Weatherhead Center for International Affairs at Harvard University. Interviews were conducted with Sergey Sokolovskii. George Georgiev, Darya Nachinkina, and Kuanysh Batyrbekov provided excellent research assistance. I thank Timothy Colton, Stephen Holmes, and Vladimir Treml for comments on an earlier version.

1. Goskomstat is an acronym derived from the full name of the organization, Gosudarstvennyi komitet po statistike, or State Committee for Statistics. In 2004 the Committee was renamed the Federal Service for State Statistics (Federal'naia sluzhba gosudarstvennoi statistiki). Throughout this chapter I use the acronym *Goskomstat*, because that was the term in use during the 1990s, the period under review here.

2. On the concept of making society "legible," see James Scott, *Seeing Like a State* (New Haven, CT: Yale University Press, 1999).

3. Cheka circulars, 1920–1921, as cited by Peter Holquist, "'Information Is the Alpha and Omega of Our Work': Bolshevik Surveillance in Its Pan-European Context," *Journal of Modern History* 69, no. 3 (September 1997): 415.

4. See E. Seneta, "A Sketch of the History of Survey Sampling in Russia," *Journal of the Royal Statistical Society. Series A (General)* 148, no. 2 (1985): 118–25; and Samuel Kotz and Eugene Seneta. "Lenin as a Statistician: A Non-Soviet View," *Journal of the Royal Statistical Society, Series A (Statistics in Society)* 153, no. 1 (1990): 73–94.

5. "O merakh po korennomu uluchsheniyu dela statistiki v strane," *Sobranie postanovlenii pravitel'stva Soyuza Sovetskikh Sotsialisticheskikh Respublik* 34 (1987): 706–16.

6. For additional discussion of this Central Committee resolution see Tim Heleniak and Albert Motivans, "A Note on *Glasnost'* and the Soviet Statistical System," *Soviet Studies* 43, no. 3 (1991): 474, 476–77.

7. "Uskorit' perestroiku deiatel'nosti i organizatsionnoi struktury statisticheskikh organov," *Vestnik statistiki*, no. 12 (December 1987): 3–6. For additional discussion of this see Heleniak and Motivans, "A Note on *Glasnost'* and the Soviet Statistical System," 477.

8. To date, the center retains the same name and is the current site of the Goskomstat store where publications are on sale; it remains the only part of the Goskomstat building open to the public without a special permit (*propusk*).

9. Among Khanin's publications, the two most prominent were Vasilii Seliunin and Grigorii Khanin, "Lukavaia Tsifra," *Novyi Mir*, no. 2 (February 1987): 181–201; and G. Khanin, "Ekonomicheskii rost: al'ternativnaia otsenka," *Kommunist*, no. 17 (November 1988): 83–90. Khanin is a complicated figure; while his work is well known, there are few economists today who agree with him. Nearly everyone, however, agrees that his articles in the late 1980s were influential.

10. Heleniak and Motivans, "A Note on *Glasnost'* and the Soviet Statistical System," 473–90.

11. Vladimir Treml, "*Perestroyka* and Soviet Statistics," *Soviet Economy* 4, no. 1 (January–February 1988): 65–94, provides a detailed analysis of changes at Goskomstat from 1985 to 1988, and an overview of problems with Soviet statistics.

12. Heleniak and Motivans, "A Note on *Glasnost'* and the Soviet Statistical System," 479.

13. Victor Belkin, "O dostovernosti informatsii," *Svobodnaia mysl'* no. 10 (1992): 102.

14. Jan Vanous, "The Dark Side of 'Glasnost': Unbelievable National Income Statistics in the Gorbachev Era," *PlanEcon Report* 3, no. 6 (February 13, 1987): 1.

15. On July 12, 1989, Mikhail Korolev was replaced as chairman of Goskomstat by Vadim Nikitovich Kirichenko ("Pervaia Sessiia Verkhovnogo Soveta SSSR," *Pravda*, July 13, 1989, 1).

16. Goskomstat, *Rossiiskaia Gosudarstvennaia Stastistika, 1802–1996* (Moscow: Izdat-Tsentr, 1996).

17. "Postanovlenie Verkhovnogo Soveta Rossiiskoi Federatsii: O Gosudarstvennoi Programme perekhoda Rossiiskoi Federatsii na priniatuiu v mezhdunarodnoi praktike sistemu ucheta i statistiki v sootvetstvii s trebovaniiami pazvitiia rynochnoi ekonomiki," *Rossiiskaia gazeta*, November 6, 1992, 4. This document was also published in English as "The National Program of the Transition of the Russian Federation to the Internationally Accepted System of Record-keeping and Statistics According to the Demands of Market Economic Development" (International Statistical Institute Occasional Paper, 2nd ser., 1993), 8–33. For details on the contents of the program see Pavel F. Guzhvin, "Rossiiskaia statistika segodnia i zavtra," *Voprosy ekonomiki*,

no. 5 (May 1993): 7–8; James Noren, "Statistical Reporting in the States of the Former USSR," *Post-Soviet Geography and Economics* 35, no. 1 (1994): 32–35; and *Vestnik statistiki* issues during the fall of 1992 and winter 1993.

18. Noren, "Statistical Reporting," 13–37.

19. For discussion of Statkom CIS's early activities, see Noren, "Statistical Reporting," 31–32. The original documents are published in "Informatsionnii biulleten'," *Statkomiteta SNG* 1, no. 1 (1992): 13–20 and "Informatsionnii biulleten'," *Statkomiteta SNG* 1, no. 4 (1993): 5.

20. In the breakup of Goskomstat USSR into independent republican state statistical committees and formation of Statkom CIS there were several shifts of skilled personnel among these different organizations. Vladimir Treml observed that during the Soviet period, the central, Moscow-based Goskomstat USSR, in comparison to the republican level committees, had most of the best-trained statisticians in terms of methodological and theoretical work. On the one hand, due to the shared geographic location, after the USSR broke up, Goskomstat Russia was the primary recipient of the most skilled employees of Goskomstat USSR. However, on the other hand, some of the most qualified Moscow-based statisticians were lured to newly independent republican committees with higher salaries and benefits. In addition, while Statkom CIS initially attracted methodologically sophisticated employees, as time went by, it also became a place for senior officials who were removed from Goskomstat Russia, such as, for example, M. Korolev, Iu. Ivanov, N. Belov, and V. Shevchenko (Vladimir Treml, e-mail correspondence with author, May 10, 2004).

21. Valentin M. Kudrov, "Nadezhny li raschety tempov rosta ekonomiki SSSR i Rossii?" *Voprosy ekonomiki*, no. 10, 1993: 129; and James Noren, "The FSU Economies: The First Year of Transition," *Post-Soviet Geography* 34, no. 7 (September 1993): 420.

22. See I. Demchenko, "Nel'zia upravliat' stranoi, ne imeia nadezhnoi informatsii," *Izvestiia*, August 26, 1992, 1–2, on fears of resource losses. For counter arguments see Noren, "Statistical Reporting," 23 and P. Guzhvin, "Doverie k statistike," *Vestnik statistiki*, no. 9 (September 1992): 9–10.

23. Noren, "Statistical Reporting," 23.

24. Vladimir Treml, "Ten Years of Change in Russian State Statistics," unpublished manuscript (2001): 4.

25. Guzhvin, "Rossiiskaia statistika segodnia i zavtra," 12.

26. Vincent Koen, "Russian Macroeconomic Data: Existence, Access, Interpretation," *Communist Economies & Economic Transformation* 8, no. 3 (September 1996): 321.

27. Koen, "Russian Macroeconomic Data," 321. This practice has not gone away entirely. In 2001 I tried to purchase old statistical yearbooks from Goskomstat's store, but was told I could not because the books contained "secret material." However, these books had previously been on sale, were on the open shelves of the store, and were available in public libraries.

28. Koen, "Russian Macroeconomic Data," 321.

29. Koen, "Russian Macroeconomic Data," 321; see Treml, "Ten Years of Change," 21, for a similar assessment.

30. Regarding figures for the entire organization, Goskomstat Russia claimed in 1996 to have over fifty thousand employees (Goskomstat, *Rossiiskaia Gosudarstvennaia Stastistika, 1802–1996* [Moscow: Izdat-Tsentr, 1996]). In a 1997 report Goskomstat was said to have 31,484 employees (Goskomstat, *Osnovnye indikatory kadrovogo potentsiala organov gosudarstvennoi vlasti v Rossii*. Moscow: Goskomstat, 1997: 44). On their website (www.gks.ru/) in 2001, they claimed to have thirty thousand employees (April 18, 2001), and at the end of 2005 they report 20,000 employees (December 10, 2005). These figures correspond with regional interviews in 2003, where nearly all offices claimed their staff was approximately half the size it had been in 1991.

31. Goskomstat regional managers, interviews by author, fall 2003.

32. Michael Gordon, "Statisticians Accused of Aiding Tax Evasion," *New York Times*, June 10, 1998, A3. Also, see Treml, "Ten Years of Change," 6, on the Iurkov arrest details.

33. *Radio Free Europe/Radio Liberty* 8, no. 21 (February 3, 2004). Iurkov and Saakian were given four and a-half years and four years, respectively, in a strict-regime labor camp; Baranovskii was given a four-year suspended sentence. The five other defendants were given amnesty. Interestingly, Iurkov et al. don't seem to have been convicted of the "systematic distortion" charge, which is comforting given that Goskomstat has never issued a correction for the supposedly distorted data (or even a statement of what exact data were supposed to have been distorted).

34. Vladimir Sokolin, interview by author, Moscow, June 28, 2004.

35. V. A. Vlasov, "V perepisnoi komisii Goskomstata Rossii," *Voprosy statistiki*, no. 4 (April 2001): 60; "O sostoianii informatsionno-statisticheskoi bazy po sotsial'no-demograficheskim kharakteristikam naseleniia," *Voprosy statistiki*, no. 10 (October 2001): 69–70; Treml, "Ten Years of Change," 21.

36. Some of the international cooperation during the 1990s seems to have been driven by the rewards of technical and material assistance, but resources cannot explain the enthusiasm with which lower-level actors within Goskomstat, who did not have much contact with international organizations, embraced reform.

37. See Pravitel'stvo Rossiiskoi Federatsii, "Polozhenie o Federal'noi sluzhbe gosudarstvennoi statistiki, no. 399, 30 July 2004" at www.gks.ru/ (last accessed January 8, 2006).

38. For example, university and institute students were forced to work for the census or face expulsion; this type of corvée labor is similar to the practice of students being forced to pick potatoes in the old Soviet days.

39. Gertrude Schroeder, "Reflections on Economic Sovietology," *Post-Soviet Affairs* 11, no. 3 (1995): 200. For discussion of lists of available publications see Heleniak and Motivans, "*Glasnost'* and the Soviet Statistical System."

40. Lee Schwartz, "USSR Nationality Redistribution by Republic, 1979–1989: From Published Results of the 1989 All-Union Census," *Soviet Geography* 32, no. 4

(April 1991): 209–48; Chauncy D. Harris, "Research Note on the Release of More Detailed Data from Three Soviet Censuses," *Post-Soviet Geography* 35, no. 1 (January 1994): 59–62.

41. W. Ward Kingkade, "Content Organization, and Methodology in Recent Soviet Population Censuses," *Population and Development Review* 15, no. 1 (March 1989): 122.

42. Treml, "Ten Years of Change," 10.

43. Heleniak and Motivans, "*Glasnost'* and the Soviet Statistical System," 474.

44. See Heleniak and Motivans, "*Glasnost'* and the Soviet Statistical System," 480–88, for an extensive discussion of the content of new publications and changes to existing ones up to 1991. On the availability of various statistics in detail for the pre-1991, 1991, and 1992 periods in the CIS see Noren, "Statistical Reporting."

45. Schroeder, "Reflections on Economic Sovietology," 200–201.

46. Gregory Grossman, *Soviet Statistics of Physical Output of Industrial Commodities* (Princeton, NJ: Princeton University Press, 1960), cited in Treml, "Ten Years of Change," 9.

47. Treml, "Ten Years of Change," 10.

48. Treml, "Ten Years of Change," 10.

49. See Goskomstat Rossii, *Metodologicheskie polozheniia po statistike*, 4 vols. (Moscow: Goskomstat Rossii, 1996–2003) and Rosstat, *Metodologicheskie polozheniia po statistike, vypusk 5* (Moscow: Rosstat, 2005).

50. Goskomstat and World Bank, *Russian Federation: Report on National Accounts* (Moscow: Goskomstat Rossii; Washington, DC: World Bank, October 1995).

51. Yoshiko Herrera, "The 2002 Russian Census in Comparative Perspective: Institutional Reform at Goskomstat," *Post-Soviet Affairs* 20, no. 4 (2004).

52. For example, the over-count in Chechnya is largely a function of this use of outdated sources, which were presented as 2002 census data. See Herrera, "2002 Russian Census."

53. I. Pogosov, "Ekonomicheskie reformy I informatsiia," *Voprosy ekonomiki*, no. 5 (May 1993): 20; and also Kudrov, "Nadezhny li raschety tempov rosta," 128.

54. For example, in a very detailed analysis of SNA data for the 1989–1995, period Tabata reported that there remained a scarcity of data on SNA. And he also noted the continued existence of the old problem of frequent changes (published later without comment) to previously published figures (Shinichiro Tabata, "Changes in the Structure and Distribution of Russian GDP in the 1990s," *Post-Soviet Geography and Economics* 37, no. 3 [1996]: 130).

55. However, *Voprosy statistiki* does contain scattered articles on specific problems, for example, the manipulation of the 1937 census. See A. Volkov, "Kak stalo krivym zerkalo obshchestva (k 60-letniiu perepisi 1937 goda)," *Voprosy statistiki*, no. 3 (March 1997): 14–21.

56. For additional discussion of the Soviet concept of net material product see Abram Bergson, "The USSR before the Fall: How Poor and Why," *The Journal of Economic Perspectives* 5, no. 4 (Autumn 1991): 29–44; and Kudrov, "Nadezhny li raschety tempov rosta."

57. For discussion of efforts to develop the SNA in Russia, see "Aktual'noe interv'iu," *Vestnik statistiki*, no. 2 (1993): 26–28; Noren, "Statistical Reporting"; Tabata, "Changes in the Structure and Distribution of Russian GDP"; and Leonid I. Nesterov, "National Wealth Estimation in the USSR and the Russian Federation," *Europe-Asia Studies* 49, no. 8 (December 1997): 1471–84. The earliest attempts were not without problems. Noren called these perestroika era attempts at GDP "half-hearted" and "feeble at best" (Noren, "Statistical Reporting," 14). For a discussion of the state program, see "Postanovlenie Verkhovnogo Soveta Rossiiskoi Federatsii."

58. United Nations Economic and Social Council, Statistical Commission, "30th session, Milestone assessment of the implementation of the System of National Accounts, 1993 by member States, Report of the Secretary-General." E/CN.3/1999/3 (March 1–5, 1999). See also subsequent reports in 2000 and 2001, as well as quality assessments by the IMF.

59. Guzhvin, "Rossiiskaia statistika segodnia i zavtra."

60. On falsification claims see for example, Belkin, "O dostovernosti informatsii," 97; Kudrov, "Nadezhny li raschety tempov rosta," 130; Vanous, "The Dark Side of 'Glasnost,'" 13.

61. Vladimir G. Treml, "Dr. Vanous's 'Dark Side of Glasnost' Revisited," *Comparative Economic Studies* 31, no. 4 (Winter 1989): 96.

62. Noren, "The FSU Economies," 421.

63. The inflationary context emphasizes the sensitivity and assumed context of Western methods, for example in the concept of GNP. It is very hard to understand how yearly value indicators could be useful in a context where "value" is changing daily. In highly inflationary times, physical volume indicators might provide much more real information about the economy than the price-sensitive value indicators.

64. B. P. Orlov, "Illusions and Reality of Economic Information," *Problems of Economics* 32, no. 1 (May 1989): 15–32; Noren, "Statistical Reporting," 23–25.

65. See various articles in *Vestnik statistiki* in the late 1980s. Also, a new journal, *Istoriia statistiki (History of Statistics)*, was established in the late 1980s.

66. See for example, Orlov, "Illusions and Reality." This reversion to Lenin is ironic given Lenin's views on TsSU and the independence of statistics.

67. For more discussion of this point, see Heleniak and Motivans, "*Glasnost'* and the Soviet Statistical System," 474.

68. Guzhvin, "Rossiiskaia statistika segodnia," 13.

69. See Khanin and Seliunin, "Lukavaia Tsifra"; and Khanin, "Ekonomicheskii rost."

70. For example, in working on the transition to SNA, Misha Belkindas of the World Bank met regularly or talked on the phone weekly with the chairman of Goskomstat.

71. For further discussion of this point see Heleniak and Motivans, "*Glasnost'* and the Soviet Statistical System," 479–80.

72. These figures are the author's own estimates. It should also be noted that gender breakdown as a signal of prestige and compensation is not limited to Russia. It is generally true that occupational categories that are primarily staffed by women have

lower pay and prestige. Of course this is not a signal of the lower qualifications of women or the true value of the work; rather, it is a reflection of societal attitudes that devalue, or value at lower rates, work done by women.

73. Of course more systematic and comparative studies would have to be done to confirm this point. It is also the case that the difficulty in finding skilled workers is not trivial. As other opportunities expand, for both men and women, Goskomstat faces increasing challenges given its low wages—currently about 100–150 dollars a month for college graduates.

74. Koen, "Russian Macroeconomic Data," 321. See also Heleniak and Motivans, "*Glasnost'* and the Soviet Statistical System," 474, for a similar point.

Chapter Four

Resistance to the Central State on the Periphery

Kathryn Stoner-Weiss

This chapter addresses the issue of state capacity by examining the impediments to central state authority in the Russian periphery throughout the 1990s. Policymaking authority devolved quickly from center to periphery in the decade immediately following the collapse of the Soviet Union such that Russia went from a country tightly governed by the institutional constraints of the Communist Party of the Soviet Union and the planned economy to a situation in which the center lost an effective governing presence in many Russian provinces. Even just prior to the collapse of the Soviet Union in 1991, regional governments had begun to openly defy the central state and usurp central authority. This phenomenon accelerated throughout the 1990s as regional political actors declared their laws sovereign on provincial territory, usurped federal taxation privileges, imposed illegal internal tariffs, established citizen requirements distinct from those of the Russian Federation, and even issued their own currencies. Unbridled provincial ambition at times threatened the cohesion of Russia as a single political and economic expanse. In a seemingly desperate attempt to address this problem once and for all, Vladimir Putin moved to eradicate elections for the eighty-nine heads of executives in Russia's regions (governors in oblasts and presidents in republics). From February 2005 onward, regional heads of executives were appointed on the "recommendation" of the presidential administration.

In this chapter, I view the Russian state's inability to extract compliance from lower levels of government through the 1990s as a symptom of a broader problem caused by a rift within Russian state and society relations more generally. That is, I argue that a key reason that the Russian central state was not able to ensure reliable regional government compliance to its policies and laws through the 1990s in particular is because regional government actors often were effectively captured by or actively colluded with key regional economic interests against the central state.

This chapter consists of five main parts. In part I, I outline the structure of Russian federalism and why the center–periphery dimension of Russian governance became so problematic in the course of Russia's transition away from communism. In part II, I examine the persistence and patterns of regional noncompliance with federal law and the constitution from 1994 through 1999. In part III, I lay out the argument that the main impediment to central state authority in the provinces was the collusive relationship that often existed between many regional political and economic elites wanting to protect what they had gained (or prevent further losses) in Russia's rough and unruly first transitional decade. In part IV, I provide an evaluation of the degree to which Putin's "centralizing" reforms have had the desired effect of overcoming this impediment and actually strengthening central state authority. While there is reason to think changes to central state structures in the periphery since 2000 have been successful in some ways, there is also a good deal of evidence— not the least of which is Putin's move to further limit electoral democracy in Russia's regions by 2004—that indicates we might want to question the depth and durability of these successes. Finally, in light of the questions I raise regarding the success of Putin's attempts to reassert the central state in the periphery, part V offers alternative institutional solutions that might better accomplish this task.

I. WHY RUSSIAN FEDERALISM MATTERS

Boris Yeltsin's political jockeying with then Soviet president Mikhail Gorbachev in 1990 and 1991 for Russia's supremacy over the unraveling USSR clearly hastened the devolution of power from center to periphery. His now infamous exhortation to regional leaders within Russia to "take as much autonomy as you can swallow" paralleled his own struggles against Union supremacy and Gorbachev's desperate attempts in 1991 to hold the Soviet Union together.[1] Yeltsin likely did not anticipate, however, just how much autonomy Russia's regional governments would grab through the 1990s. Nor did he anticipate the effect their efforts would have on the Russian central state's ability to govern.

By 1991 the Russian Federation was comprised of twenty-one republics, forty-nine oblasts and six *krais*; the two special status cities of Moscow and

St. Petersburg, both of which had oblast status; ten autonomous *okrugs*; and one autonomous oblast. The Chechen republic, of course, declared itself independent (and waged two wars of independence with the contemporary Russian Federation from 1994 to 1996 and 1999 to time of writing). The Chechen leadership does not consider the republic to be a part of the Russian Federation today, but it is still counted as such since its formal relationship with Russia is yet to be decided conclusively.

In part, the early confrontation in Russian center–periphery relations stemmed from the institutional vacuum left in the wake of the collapse of the Soviet Union. Boris Yeltsin proved himself particularly adept at tearing apart the institutional bulwarks of the Soviet state, but the task of building new institutions that might have enabled him to actually govern his country proved far more difficult. Initial resistance to the new central state was both a reaction to Soviet hypercentralization and a result of the clash of views between central authorities and regional political leaders regarding the appropriate distribution of power between levels of government. The center favored a national federal system—a type of "federalism from above"—where the central government would clearly take the lead in determining the distribution of power between itself and the federation's constituent units, whereas regional leaders advocated (and continue to advocate) a more contractually based federal system, where regions would sign individual or collective agreements with the central state that would govern their membership in the federation. The "war of laws" where regions passed laws that directly contradicted federal law, and chronic noncompliance to existing federal law of the 1990s between the federal center and almost all of Russia's eighty-nine provinces, should be viewed in the context of these conflicting perspectives on the shape of the Russian state.

Some scholars have argued that the Russian center was able in fact to maintain some degree of control over regions through strategic dispensation of budgetary transfers. Daniel Treisman made the case that regions and republics who "most adroitly manipulated the weapons of early sovereignty declarations ... managed to extract substantially more [from Moscow] than those that were more docile."[2] By effectively buying off the most aggressive and noncompliant regions, Treisman maintained, Moscow was able to stem a secessionist tide in the early 1990s. That is, despite sovereignty declarations by a number of republics of the Federation, only Chechnya actually attempted to secede, while others gained budgetary concessions from Moscow in return for their remaining in the Federation.

The picture of the central state that this argument provides is a coherent unit able to act adroitly and resolutely, if in a limited way. But faced with the array of examples (in the following section of this chapter) of regional governments defying the central government through the late 1990s, it is difficult to accept this conceptualization of center–regional relations as completely accurate. While Treisman may be correct that the center's strategic distribution of budgetary funds helped to curb regional secessionism in the early 1990s—perhaps the most extreme form of noncompliance to the central state—this practice does not appear to have been successful in stemming the tide of smaller, regular infractions against federal law and central policy as the transition continued. Indeed, regions that the center allegedly bought off in this way tended to be among the biggest noncompliers with federal laws and the constitution. This kind of "legal separatism" and noncompliance was clearly pervasive.[3] It is this de facto regional autonomy that has proven particularly damaging to central authority and the policy effectiveness of the central government in practice in the provinces. So, at best, even if control over fiscal flows was an important instrument in curbing regional secessionism, it proved an imprecise and clumsy instrument in curbing less dramatic, but equally damaging, regional grabs for power from the center. Indeed, in apparent recognition of the failure of this and other central attempts to limit regional recalcitrance, Putin himself used the unreliability of regional political actors in the Beslan school tragedy in the fall of 2004 (where Chechen rebels seized a school in southern Russia, eventually resulting in the deaths of 330 children and their parents in the course of a botched rescue attempt) as a pretext for eliminating elections for regional heads of executives in the region.

Certainly, under the Yeltsin administration, there were instances of forced regional compliance to the constitution and federal law in certain key instances in some regions,[4] but these tended to be interventions on big issues of symbolic importance to the federal government. In the long run, this kind of direct intervention proved infeasible in the range of areas that were simply beyond the president's personal control and in situations of limited information.

Similarly ineffective was the center's attempted practice of strategically distributing patronage to key regional elites perhaps to impede their collective action against the center by dealing bilaterally with regions rather than as a group.[5] Moreover, these attempts at taming regional interests were expensive and grew increasingly unreliable as the center ran out of money and privileges to distribute in the first decade following the collapse of the Soviet Union.

II. PATTERNS OF REGIONAL NONCOMPLIANCE TO FEDERAL LAW AND THE CONSTITUTION

A more complete picture of the challenges the Russian central state faced in governing the periphery requires a methodology that can discern more systematically the temporal, spatial, and policy patterns of Russia's war of policy authority through the 1990s. Previous analyses of the issue, however, largely were limited to either sporadic reports from the Russian Ministry of Justice or anecdotal accounts of regional defiance of central state edicts. As a result, I compiled a modest database from a variety of electronic news sources. My research assistants searched Russian national newspapers for articles containing reported instances of regional noncompliance to federal law and the constitution from January 1994 (the month immediately following the adoption of the constitution in December 1993) through December 1999 and the end of the Yeltsin era.[6] Although in many ways it would be ideal to have a data set culled from data collected from the Russian Ministry of Justice, I abandoned hope of ever gaining access to it after being unceremoniously rebuffed in several attempts to do so. Nonetheless, the data set I managed to compile from the database of articles provides a good sense of the scope of the phenomenon. Although the number of violations in our data set appears to be far smaller than the sporadic reports issued in the press by the Russian Ministry of Justice, there is good reason to think that this sample is representative of what is possibly a larger population of violations. That is, there may be biases in the ways in which newspapers reported these violations, but there is little reason to think that they are systematic or that they would render this data unrepresentative. Indeed, it is possible that the data we gathered are more representative of the total population of violations than reports by the Ministry of Justice in that newspaper coverage may be more objective. With these data, therefore, I am able to explore the general patterns of noncompliance across time, policy area, and region.

Variations across Time

Clearly regions became bolder in their dealings with the central state through the 1990s.[7] Although reported instances of noncompliance appeared to peak toward the end of the decade, there was a slow but steady increase in reported noncompliance through the six years for which we have data. It is important to note the other political and economic events with which the central state was dealing that might have influenced regional government behavior in becoming more or less compliant at particular points in time. First, noncompliant activity on the part of regional governments appears to have peaked when the national economy was in crisis. As the economy recovered somewhat, noncompliance slackened. This was the case in the year or so run-up to the financial crisis in August 1998, and by 1999, when the economy began to show signs of recovery (the first year of positive gross domestic product [GDP] growth), noncompliance tapered to precrisis levels.

Second, it is notable also that noncompliant activity was consistently high from the third quarter of 1996 through the third quarter of 1999, following the first Chechen conflict and immediately prior to the second. During the three-year period of relative calm in Chechen–Russian Federation relations, regional governments stepped up their political/legal defiance of central authority, perhaps less fearful of (violent) retribution given the disastrous performance of the Russian military in Chechnya.

Moreover, following the spike in noncompliance in 1998 after the financial crisis, noncompliance remained high as regional governments sought to protect their localities from the fallout of the devaluation of the ruble in particular. This illegal behavior was relatively short-lived, however, and noncompliance declined steadily and then rather precipitously as the second Chechen conflict began in the fall of 1999. This big dip in noncompliant behavior may have been a result both of the start of Russia's (still mild) economic rebound, and Putin's resumption of the Chechen conflict following several incidents of domestic terrorism. This second Chechen conflict was (at least initially) far more popular among the Russian electorate than the first conflict and it may be that regional governments made a strategic calculation, as they appear to have done during the first conflict between 1994 and 1996, that this was not a good time to aggressively pursue more legal and political challenges to central state authority.

Variations across Policy Areas

Figure 4.1 shows the general patterns of violations by policy area. The data relatively naturally fell into the nine policy areas that appear in the figure. That is, we did not attempt to force fit it into some preconceived policy areas. Rather, these were the nine into which the data could be easily sorted.

The fact that four (general economic, taxation, trade, and misdirection of federal funds) of the nine policy areas concerned financial-economic issue areas indicates that the preponderance of reported regional noncompliance concerned money flows into and out of regions. Combined, the three main economic categories, labeled in figure 4.1 as general economic, trade, and misdirection of federal funds to regional purposes, comprised three of the top five violation categories—respectively 171, 81, and 78 violations for a total of 330 violations (of 846 in the dataset) or 39 percent of the total violations. If we add taxation (58 violations) to this total, then violations directly related to the struggle over economic policymaking authority between center and periphery in Russia comprised 46 percent (almost half) of total violations included here. Further, although the category entitled regional structure encompasses the greatest number of violations—196—a majority of the violations that we included in this category were also clearly closely intertwined with regional economic policy. Violations concerning regional political structure and authority encompassed statements within laws or constitutions of regional

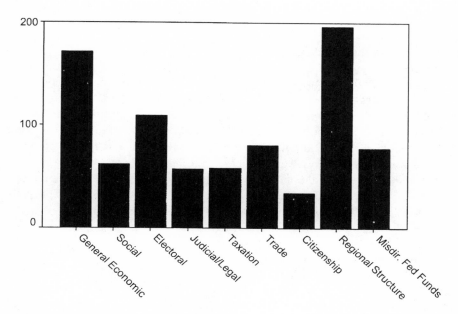

Violation Type

Figure 4.1.   Patterns of Noncompliance by Policy Area, 1994–1999.

Key to Violation Type

General Economic = Includes violations of antimonopoly regulations; pursuit of independent banking policies; pursuit of independent land, property, or real estate laws; imposition of price controls; privatization violations.

Social = Includes civil/human rights abuses, violations of social welfare provisions, crackdown on regional media, violation of federal ban on death penalty, violations of language rights.

Electoral = Electoral Requirements for candidates and voters, local parliamentary immunity from prosecution, non-Russian language requirements for candidates, residency requirements for candidates, etc.

Judicial/Legal = Includes illegal judicial appointments, interference in the adjudication of law, usurpation of federal judicial or law enforcement authority, introduction of separate legal system (Sharia law in Chechnya).

Taxation = Includes introducing regional taxes in areas where federal government has exclusive tax authority; other violations of federal tax law.

Trade = Includes pursuing international trade deals without the express consent of the federal government; maintaining trade restrictions on goods entering or exiting the region.

Citizenship = Includes residency registration requirements, regional laws indicating that regional citizenship is primary and citizenship in the Russian Federation is secondary for regional residents.

Regional Structure = Includes statements within laws or constitutions of regions indicating that the regional document supercedes federal law and the constitution; infringing on the rights of cities by appointing mayors; creating institutions that would administer regional policies in an area that is exclusively federal jurisdiction.

Misdir. Fed Funds = **Misdirection of federal funds** to regional projects including using federally transferred funds for a purpose other than that directed by the federal government; violations of federal budgetary policies.

governments that proclaimed the supremacy of regional over federal law, or that created regional institutions for administering policy in an area that was to be exclusively federal jurisdiction; generally these intersected with economic policy areas in that the violations made changes to regional administrative structures with strong economic ramifications. These included, for example, declaring regional ownership of federal property located in a particular region, or announcing jurisdiction over a federal economic agency in the region.

Regional governments were far less interested in challenging federal authority in areas of social policy, where we uncovered only sixty-two reported violations. This was likely because policy responsibility for expensive social programs was undesirable for cash-strapped regional governments and so challenges to federal authority in this policy area were fewer. Indeed, the abuses of social welfare provisions included in this category are not so much instances of regional authorities grabbing policy authority as much as simply shirking responsibility for unfunded federally mandated programs and thereby violating federal laws.

When we compare the rate of noncompliance in all economic policy areas (classified as general economic, tax, trade, and misdirection of federal funds in figure 4.1) to all social policy areas (social, judicial/legal, and citizenship in figure 4.1 above), we find that economic policy was the focus of noncompliance activity in the regions over time.

Variations across Type of Region

When we examine patterns of noncompliance by region, there is further support for the argument that regional economic interests were often at stake in resistance to central authority. As a group, the most frequent noncompliers

Table 4.1. Top Ten Regional Noncompliers by Region Type (Republic or Oblast/*Krai*)

Rank	Oblasts	Republics	Number of Violations
1		Chechnya	123
2		Kalmykia	65
3		Bashkortostan	50
4		Tatarstan	37
5		Mari-El	32
6		Karachia-Cherkessia	25
7		Sakha	24
8		Komi	21
9 (tie)		Udmurtia	20
9 (tie)	Kemerovo		20
10	Primoriia		19

were the twenty-one ethnically non-Russian republics of the Russian Federation, as opposed to the ethnically Russian oblasts. Only two oblasts were among the top ten noncompliers, for example.

In terms of the total number of violations, the twenty-one republics (comprising 24 percent of the total number of Russia's eighty-nine subnational units) accounted for a disproportionately high number (513 or 60.1 percent) of all violations in the data set. Further, table 4.2 breaks down the number of violations of each type of region by the nine policy areas described in figure 4.1.

In particular, looking at the proportion of policy type that each type of region claimed, the twenty-one republics accounted for 34.5 percent of what we classified as economic violations, 82.3 percent of social, 82.6 percent of electoral, 86 percent of judicial/legal, 37.9 percent of taxation, 48.1 percent of trade, 64.7 percent of citizenship, 77.8 percent of regional structure, and 37.2 percent of misdirection of federal funds.

If we exclude the Chechen Republic from the data as an outlier given that its leadership viewed the republic as a separate country with its own legal system and economy, table 4.3 indicates that the remaining twenty republics still outpaced the fifty-five oblasts and *krais* and the two special status cities of Moscow and St. Petersburg (included under the category oblasts) in total number of violations of federal law and the constitution (390 versus 322) or 19.5 violations per republic and 6.4 per oblast.

The ten autonomous *okrugs* and one autonomous oblast of the Russian Federation (categorized as "autonomies" here) clearly did not play a leading role in the noncompliance battles of the 1990s (with only eleven violations in total among them or one per geographical unit). This was most likely a result of the fact that their interests were subsumed in the noncompliant actions of the oblasts of which they were geographically located. Further, for several of the autonomies—in particular, Yamalo-Nenets and Khanti-Mansii, located in Tiumen' oblast—their political struggles tended to be concerned with negotiating more policy autonomy with the oblast leadership, in some ways paralleling the battles of the other regions of Russia with the central state during this period.

The high number of republican violations in the social policy areas as well as electoral violations and those concerning citizenship and the establishment of their own judicial and legal systems in particular indicate that for republics *as a group*, noncompliance was not just about economics. Many republican violations included the attempts of regional elites to establish their respective republic as a more or less juridical equal with the Russian Federation, ostensibly in pursuit of greater ethnic self-determination. Indeed, aside from social policy (violations of human rights being a leading area with thirty-five violations) most of Chechnya's 123 violations were in the areas of judicial/legal structure as a partial result of the republican leadership declaring Sharia law in

Table 4.2. Violations of Federal Law or the Constitution by Region Type and Policy Area, 1994–1999

	Oblasts			Republics			Autonomies			Total	
Policy Type	N Events	% of Total Events	% of Policy Type	N Events	% of Total Events	% of Policy Type	N Events	% of Total Events	% of Policy Type	N Events	% of Policy Type
Economic	111	34.5	64.9	59	11.5	34.5	1	9.1	0.6	171	100.0
Social	10	3.1	16.1	51	9.9	82.3	1	9.1	1.6	62	100.0
Electoral	19	5.9	17.4	90	17.5	82.6	0	0.0	0.0	109	100.0
Judicial/Legal	8	2.5	14.0	49	9.6	86.0	0	0.0	0.0	57	100.0
Taxation	36	11.2	62.1	22	4.3	37.9	0	0.0	0.0	58	100.0
Trade	42	13.0	51.9	39	7.6	48.1	0	0.0	0.0	81	100.0
Citizenship	12	3.7	35.3	22	4.3	64.7	0	0.0	0.0	34	100.0
Regional Structure	20	6.2	10.2	152	29.6	77.6	4	36.4	2.0	196	100.0
Misdirection of Federal Funds	44	13.7	56.4	29	5.7	37.2	5	45.5	6.4	78	100.0
Total	322	100.0	38.1	513	100.0	60.6	11	100.0	1.3	846	100.0

Table 4.3. Violations of Federal Law or the Constitution by Region Type and Policy Area, 1994–1999 (excluding Chechnya)

Policy Type	Oblasts			Republics			Autonomies			Total	
	N Events	% of Total Events	% of Policy Type	N Events	% of Total Events	% of Policy Type	N Events	% of Total Events	% of Policy Type	N Events	% of Policy Type
Economic	111	34.5	66.9	54	13.8	32.5	1	9.1	0.6	166	100.0
Social	10	3.1	37.0	16	4.1	59.3	1	9.1	3.7	27	100.0
Electoral	19	5.9	17.8	88	22.6	82.2	0	0.0	0.0	107	100.0
Judicial/Legal	8	2.5	34.8	15	3.8	65.2	0	0.0	0.0	23	100.0
Taxation	36	11.2	62.1	22	5.6	37.9	0	0.0	0.0	58	100.0
Trade	42	13.0	53.8	36	9.2	46.2	0	0.0	0.0	78	100.0
Citizenship	12	3.7	40.0	18	4.6	60.0	0	0.0	0.0	30	100.0
Regional Structure	20	6.2	12.8	112	28.7	71.8	4	36.4	2.6	156	100.0
Misdirection of Federal Funds	44	13.7	56.4	29	7.4	37.2	5	45.5	6.4	78	100.0
Total	322	100.0	44.5	390	100.0	53.9	11	100.0	1.5	723	100.0

the mid-1990s (generating thirty-four violations) and regional governmental structure (generating forty violations) such that the republic's leadership repeatedly declared independence from the Russian Federation and unilaterally elevated its status to that of nation-state.

In most other republics, although not nearly as extreme as Chechnya, the pattern was the same in that violations tended to reflect the desire to elevate the republic's status to a near juridical equal of the Russian Federation. Pursuant to this, violations that involved changes to the structure of republican governments (declarations of the supremacy of republican law over federal law if the two conflicted, for example) were disproportionately high relative to oblasts (112 violations for republics and 40 for oblasts) as were violations of federal electoral law to the advantage of republican electoral laws. Often electoral violations included ethnic and language requirements for candidates for republican office—that is, for example, establishing republican laws requiring that candidates had to speak the language of the titular nationality in violation of federal electoral law specifically proscribing such requirements for electoral office.

Nonetheless, economic authority over their regions clearly remained a primary, although not the only, concern for republican and oblast political actors alike. Indeed, with Chechnya removed from the dataset in table 4.3, the economic policy category becomes the area in which there was the greatest number of violations (166). The mean rate of noncompliance in this policy area for the twenty republics is 2.7, and for oblasts it is 2.2, making it the area in which noncompliance was third highest for republics (behind regional structure with a mean of 5.6 violations per republic and electoral violations with a mean of 4.4 violations) and highest for oblasts. It should also be noted, of course, that pursuit of more cultural self-determination and economic authority are not at all independent projects—more of one could certainly lead to more of the other. In the statistical analysis that follows, clearly republican status made a big difference among regions in determining which were most likely to defy central authority, but among republics and non-republics alike, economic variables mattered more than the percentage of the population that was ethnically Russian in identifying the most recalcitrant regions.

Variations in Regional Economies and Noncompliance Patterns

A natural question to explore is: What drives the tendency of republics to be more noncompliant than oblasts in particular? Further, within region types, why are some republics and some oblasts far more noncompliant than others? The comparative politics literature provides a rich trove of hypotheses that we can submit to statistical tests. It may be, for example, that the non-Russian republics were more resistant to the central state's incursion into their affairs or more determined to set policy independent of central state dictates in the interest of ethnic self-determination. This theory would predict that republics with a lower concentration of ethnic Russians and/or a higher concentration of non-Russian ethnicities were more likely to be noncompliant with central state law. Relatedly, it may be that poorer republics were determined to gain increased control over their regional economies, perhaps to sustain their ethnic project.[8]

Alternately, however, challenges to central state authority may have come from republics that had the most to lose if the central state became overly involved in their affairs. This hypothesis, then, would predict that it was republics that have more industry, or more enterprises with strong market presence that were more likely to resist the central state through noncompliance in an effort to avoid central state oversight.

Previous work by Daniel Treisman regarding the roots of Russia's apparent "ethnic revival" in the early 1990s following republican declarations of sovereignty indicated that ethnic regions with high industrial output and that were major raw materials producers or had high industrial exports showed greater separatist activism.[9] It seems reasonable therefore to explore similar variables in explaining differences between the degree of republican noncompliance to the central state during the same period and beyond.

Similarly, with respect to oblasts where the population was predominantly ethnically Russian, there were significant variations in rates of noncompliance. As with the republics, variations among oblasts could as easily be explained by relative regional economic structure or power. That is, oblast leaders tended to be most noncompliant in economic policy areas in order to protect what property and privilege they managed to amass during the first decade of the transition from plan to market. Thus, we might see higher rates of noncompliance among regions that had significant industrial sectors, for example.

I am able to test these hypotheses through regression analysis, reported in tables 4.4 and 4.5 below.[10] These results indicate that noncompliance through the 1990s was highly correlated with a region's status as a republic, but that in republics and oblasts alike, noncompliance was driven by the industrialized structure of a region's economy, and the presence of economically powerful enterprises located in the region. In republics, it was also driven by wealth (a republic's status as a net donor to the federal budget as opposed to being a net recipient), although natural resource endowments also appeared to matter in model 3a in table 4.5. This indicates that while non-Russian ethnicity matters somewhat in explaining a republic's noncompliance pattern, clearly economic variables mattered more.

Models 1 and 2 in table 4.4 indicate that a region's status as a republic makes a big difference in determining the degree to which it is likely to be

Table 4.4.   Explanants of Noncompliant Behavior

Variable Frequency of Noncompliant Events	Model 1 (Oblasts, Republics, Autonomies)	Model 2 (Republics & Oblasts Only)	Model 3 (Republics Only)	Model 4 (Oblasts Only)
Republic	15.4***	12.8***	—	—
	(3.1)	(3.10)		
Donor status	1.24	3.4	9.57*	−.967
	(2.97)	(3.43)	(4.86)	(3.04)
% population Russian	−0.008	−0.0494	−0.183*	.0527
	(0.047)	(0.0636)	(.088)	(.0493)
Leading enterprises	.385**	0.141*	1.45*	.1999*
	(0.213)	(0.173)	(1.35)	(.170)
Industrial production	0.0010**	.000125**	.000125**	.000119**
	(0.000046)	(.0000428)	(.000034)	(.0000561)
Constant	2.29	6.56	22.6	−1.92
	(0.213)	(5.62)	(8.4)	(4.33)
R squared	0.44	0.43	0.29	0.24
N	88	77	20	57

Notes: Chechnya is excluded from these models. I report robust standard errors to control for heteroscedasticity in the data.
*** = significant at .01 or better
** = significant at .05
* = significant at .1

Table 4.5.   Republican Natural Resource Endowments (Oil, Gas, Diamonds, etc.) and Noncompliant Activity

Variable Frequency of Noncompliant Events	Model 3a (Republics Only with N = 14)
Donor status	−1.20
	(6.70)
% population Russian	−0.115**
	(.051)
Leading enterprises	3.52*
	(.818)
Volume of Industrial Production	.0001804***
	(.0000139)
Raw materials exports as a percentage of total	1.11*
	(.53)
Russian Federation exports	12.8
Constant	(3.8)
R squared	.84
N	14

Notes: I report robust standard errors to control for heteroscedasticity in the data.
*** = significant at .01 or better
** = significant at .05
* = significant at .1

noncompliant to federal law and the constitution, as indicated by the highly significant and large coefficients for the republican dummy variable in both models. But if we look as to why this might be, we see that non-Russian ethnicity (in models 1 and 2) did not appear to play a significant role. Although the coefficients for percentage of a region's population that was ethnically Russian are negative (indicating that the lower the ethnic Russian population, the more likely is noncompliant behavior), neither is significant at .1 or better. Thus, in these models, whether a region was predominantly ethnically Russian or non-Russian does not matter in determining whether or not it defied central state authority. The noncompliant phenomenon then, does not appear to have ethnic self-determination at its root when we do not distinguish between region type.

The only indication of ethnicity mattering in determining a region's behavior comes in model 3, which examines variation in noncompliant behavior among republics only. Here, we see a small negative coefficient (but significant at .1) for percentage of the population that was ethnically Russian. Among republics only then, there is some evidence that non-Russian ethnicity mattered somewhat in explaining noncompliant behavior.

Significantly, however, variables designed to measure the effect of regional economies on noncompliant behavior are more compelling in explaining the patterns of regional behavior. Although, as a measure of wealth, a region's status as a net donor to the federal budget did not have a significant effect on its propensity for noncompliant behavior in models 1, 2, and 4, the sign is positive.[11] Among republics alone, however, in model 3, a region's status as a net donor to the federal budget had a large effect on a region's noncompliant activity (a donor republic did not comply 9.57 times more than a non-donor republic) and is significant at the .01 level.

Interestingly, this variable falls out as significant, however, when we add a variable measuring resource wealth (regional percentage of Russian Federation raw materials exports) in a refined version of this model (3a). Republics that constituted a larger percentage of national resource wealth had 1.11 more noncompliant events than those that did not (significant at the .1 level). Donor status likely falls out of this model as significant because donor republics were generally those that had a high percentage of natural resource exports. This model, however, should only be considered suggestive of the importance of natural resource endowments among republics since the number of republics for which data were available was only fourteen (as opposed to twenty in the original model 3). Thus although a region's relative wealth as measured by donor status appears to be less important in model 3a than in model 3, the fact that natural resource wealth made a difference in explaining why some republics were more noncompliant than others is strongly suggestive of an economic (and perhaps natural resource) basis to republican resistance to the central state.

Finally, in all five models, the coefficient measuring the effect of the volume of industrial production by region (in millions of rubles, 1998) on frequency of noncompliance, for example, is positive and consistently significant at .05. This follows Treisman's findings concerning industrial republics and their assertive behavior toward the central state early in the 1990s, but the results here indicate that the relationship appears to hold at the oblast (ethnically Russian) level as well.[12] Further, and perhaps most significantly for the argument concerning the strength of economic interest groups on regional politics, the coefficient of the measure that we employ to test the economic importance of particular enterprises to a region's economy (the number of leading enterprises having over 35 percent of market share of a particular commodity) is both positive and statistically significant in all five models. The coefficient for this variable is particularly large in models 3 and 3a (1.45 and 3.52 respectively) that look only at republics. Again, this is highly suggestive of the argument that it was regional economic structure among the republics that helps to explain the behavior of political elites toward the central state. These variables also prove significant for oblasts.

Generalizations about Noncompliance Patterns

There are three main generalizations coming out of the noncompliance patterns, all of which point to the importance of regional economies in explaining their behavior toward the central state.

First, regarding temporal variations, events at the center apparently affected the noncompliant activity of regional governments. In particular, although events in Chechnya might have played a role in explaining the temporal pattern of regional noncompliance to the federal law and the constitution, noncompliant activity clearly increased when the national economy worsened in the 1990s and tapered off when the economy was more stable.

Second, the link between the condition of the Russian economy and noncompliance is particularly important when viewed in conjunction with the patterns of noncompliance across policy area and type of region. The data showed that almost half of all recorded violations were related to regional finances or economics, and that republics as a group were more noncompliant than oblasts in particular.

Third, regression results presented in table 4.4 confirmed that republican status is a key indicator of noncompliant behavior, but beyond this, it appears that economic variables are also crucial in explaining republican behavior. A republic's status as a net donor to the federal budget, its industrialized structure, and the presence of large, economically powerful enterprises made it more noncompliant with central laws and the constitution. Among oblasts, the non-Russian ethnic factor did not seem to matter in determining regional behavior, but like republics, economic measures (with the exception of donor status, which was not significant), including volume of industrial production and the presence of economically powerful enterprises within the region, mattered more.

These findings then provide some initial support that the root of noncompliant behavior is rooted in the interaction between regional politics, economic structure, and the coalitions that they generated.

III: THE SOURCE OF REGIONAL RESISTANCE TO THE CENTRAL STATE: THE BUSINESS–GOVERNOR NEXUS

In large part, the resistance to central regulation of the economy in particular is related to the simultaneity of Russia's political and economic reforms. During the first ten years of Russia's transition, a combination of new and old interests found themselves empowered in sometimes unanticipated ways. Newly elected regional political leaders and powerful economic groups entered the central state's political arena as they tried to limit its incursion into their economic affairs. That is, an apparently unanticipated political consequence of the economic transition was the rise of narrow, social forces that were not incorporated into emergent national political frameworks.

On the one hand, the rapid privatization of industry of the early 1990s created a new class of private owners and destroyed the formerly powerful Soviet ministries charged with controlling the planned economy. This, on the face of it, was positive if the goal was to provide the foundation of a market economy—private ownership. But at the same time, the speed and scope of the privatization process, and the compromises made to achieve privatization (including allowing managers to become owners), created a pocket of super rich private interests capable of capturing parts of the state for personal gain. The economic transition therefore created a segment of society with a vested interest in keeping the state weak in exactly those areas that a competitive market requires that the state be effective. These interests remained untamed and directly challenged the degree to which the state could regulate markets and implement policy beyond the Kremlin. Throughout the 1990s, there was often strong resistance to central state policies and regulation at the local level, and few institutional solutions to overcome this resistance. The impetus to contradict and failure to comply with central policies came not from elected public officials alone, but from the small circles of business interests by whom they were captured, to whom they often became accountable, and with whom their futures became closely intertwined.

These early beneficiaries from the transition had little interest in promoting central state regulation of their activities. In order to protect their early financial and property gains, effectively they carved up and captured parts of the state— particularly at the regional level—for personal financial advantage. As a result, regional governments in Russia tended to pass legislation that contradicted the federal constitution predominantly in ways that affected economic conditions in their regions, thereby undermining the central state's ability to even minimally regulate their activities. Even violations that seemingly had little direct economic basis had clear economic effects. For example, the underlying cause of a region establishing a citizenship requirement for voters, or language requirements for elected officials in contradiction to the federal constitution, was to limit and control who was entitled to select regional leaders, who those regional leaders would be, what policies they would pursue, and what interests they would promote. Regional violations of federal housing and privatization policies were designed to ensure that regional interests controlled valuable regional real estate assets. Restructuring of judiciaries was another strategy to control mechanisms by which ownership disputes might be resolved, ensuring once again that regional interests were protected and advantaged. The imposition of illegal tariffs and taxes on goods entering many regions was a more overt strategy to protect regional business from competition by ensuring that local goods and services were privileged over those from outside the region. Restrictions on freedom of movement through the residence permit system that persisted in many regions was a strategy for limiting labor mobility in local production facilities, maintaining the prevailing economic balance of power and preventing further reform. Finally, declarations of regional ownership of natural resources were other overt mechanisms by which regional governments, under the influence of regional economic interests, aimed to ensure they benefited the most from what lay under their soil.

To provide more detail regarding how exactly regional economic interests became entangled in regional government, it will be useful to both review evidence from other studies of the transition experience in the 1990s as well as to recall some of the compromises made during the early phases of privatization in Russia. Recent work done by the World Bank supports the argument and evidence here that both regional governments and enterprise insiders had vested interests in maintaining the status quo and therefore working to keep the central state from upsetting this regional balance of forces.[13]

The interdependence and collusion between regional enterprises and governments stems back to the Soviet era, but was further extended through the 1992 privatization program that institutionalized the de facto ownership that many managers had established over their factories in the late 1980s. All three variants of the 1992 mass privatization program under Yeltsin (and under which fifteen thousand firms were privatized) enabled insiders—both managers and workers—to purchase up to 51 percent of shares outright. The fact that privatization vouchers were also tradable under the program allowed insiders to buy additional vouchers. This ended up being about 65 percent on average.[14] Thus, the early compromises built into the 1992 privatization program enabled insiders to maintain effective control over their enterprises. This, in turn, initiated a property rights regime that has proven both difficult to change and a drag on investment and productivity.

The 1992 privatization program made this huge concession to managers of large Soviet-era enterprises in order to effectively buy and ensure their participation in the privatization program.[15] This compromise was also a way to provide some assurance to newly elected regional governments that regional outsiders would not immediately be empowered to substantially interfere with the regional economy for which they were now accountable through elections. Nonetheless, the hope was that gradually, outsiders would invest in these firms and that ownership and management would become separated. Almost a decade later, however, there is general agreement that managers and employees continued to hold 50 to 60 percent of shares in privatized enterprises.[16]

Managers' de facto control often exceeded their actual direct ownership of shares of their companies since many employee shares did not come with voting rights. Managers also routinely employed tactics (like threatening layoffs or firings, withholding wages, etc.) to prevent employees from selling their shares to outsiders. Moreover, "despite other positive signs in the Russian economy, the enterprise sector remained in a low investment, low productivity trap."[17] Wage, supply, and tax arrears persisted, and inter-enterprise barter payments reached half of all industrial sales by mid-1999.[18] Insiders received particularized benefits while the general state of productivity and investment declined. Although the original argument for rapid privatization was to prevent asset stripping by industrial managers in state-owned enterprises, in fact they persistently grabbed and resold assets since their firms were privatized. World Bank analysis indicates that

> instead of increasing a firm's value through reinvestment, enterprise manager-owners have typically extracted income streams from these firms at the expense of minority shareholders. The managers have diverted cash flows to offshore accounts and shell corporations, concentrated losses among subsidiaries held by outsiders . . . and delay[ed] payments of dividends.[19]

Other studies by the World Bank characterize the dynamic between enterprises and the state in some postcommunist countries—including Russia—as indicative of a "capture economy."[20] This denotes both the influence a firm may have on the formation of laws as well as administrative corruption, which may entail not only conflict of interest of government officials, but also private payments by firms to public officials to "distort the prescribed implementation of official rules and policies."[21]

Analyses employing the 1999 Business Environment and Enterprise Performance Survey (or BEEPS) of over three thousand firms in twenty countries in Eastern Europe and the former Soviet Union indicate that both older and newer firms engaged in attempts to influence and often capture the state. This behavior on the part of firms was to ensure the perpetuation of the property regime described above that favors them (by limiting competition and entry into their markets, receiving a favorable tax regime, thereby preserving their rent-seeking opportunities and otherwise protecting them from central state regulation and oversight), but that provided negative externalities to the economy as a whole.

It would be a mistake, however, to assume that regional governments were merely victims of state capture rather than frequently willing participants in an interdependent or more collusive relationship. For their part, regional governments sought to maintain involvement in and sometimes control over the operations of regional enterprises particularly important to the regional economy—even if the latter were formally privatized. This was often to prevent large-scale changes within enterprises that might threaten the local workforce with unemployment and "to preserve the rent-seeking opportunities for vested interests."[22] Moreover, a system of interdependence grew up between regional business and government that favored the economic status quo:

> In certain regions . . . the nexus of interdependence between government officials and enterprise management typically grant[ed] management quasi-governmental powers, including influence over executing and law-enforcing apparatus in a given locality.[23]

Evidence of the influence of regional business circles, versus other social forces, on regional politics and politicians comes also from responses of public officials to survey questions regarding their career paths. A relatively small contingent of respondents in a 1999 survey of 824 officials in 72 of Russia's 89 regions (11.9 percent) reported that at the same time they worked for the regional government, they also worked outside of the regional government and legislative structures. Of those, 46.9 percent reported that their private-sector position was in an enterprise within the region, and that they held some sort of leadership position in the enterprise.[24] In the absence of strong conflict of interest laws, this provides some evidence of the penetration of regional government by powerful business interests. This also demonstrates that while there was obviously some direct incursion into regional government by regional economic interests, these groups obtained a remarkable degree of influence without actually having to assume administrative positions themselves.

The penetration of regional economic interests went far beyond these tentative forays into the bureaucracy itself to more determined and far-reaching penetration of legislatures and executives of many regions. From detailed analysis of regional electoral data, we know that regional legislatures were frequently filled with deputies elected to represent powerful local economic interests throughout the 1990s. In 1997, the Central Electoral Commission reported that

In practically all legislative organs of the subjects of the Federation it is possible to meet leaders of strong enterprises and commercial structures of the region. In the Republic of Sakha (Yakutia) it is the leaders of diamond and gold enterprises, in the Republics of Komi and Tatarstan and Tiumen and Sakhalin oblasts it is oil companies. In Cheliabinsk oblast it is metallurgical factories, and in Murmansk oblast, it is the Kol'skii Nuclear Power Station.

As the Central Electoral Commission itself noted, this results in the "strengthening of the influence of economic lobbyists on the economic policies of subjects of the Russian Federation. Aside from this is the threat of confrontation of the regional elite with the federal center in constructing the interests of the regions."[25]

There is reason to believe, moreover, that the underlying cause of the central state's growing inability to govern in the Russian periphery throughout the 1990s was a result of the collusive activity of regional business interests and policy makers.[26] This has important implications for the past and future policy instruments and institutional mechanisms that the central state might use to enhance its capacity to govern the economy in the Russian periphery.

IV. PUTIN'S SOVIET SOLUTIONS TO RUSSIA'S POST-SOVIET PROBLEMS

Almost immediately after his May 2000 inauguration, President Putin moved swiftly to address regional resistance to central authority. Vowing to reestablish and reassert the strength of the Russian state, and the "vertical" chain of authority from center to periphery in particular, Putin launched a multifront war on regional resistance to Moscow.

First, his attack included the establishment of seven federal districts within his presidential administration, each encompassing approximately twelve subunits of the Russian Federation. This did not involve a redrawing of formal borders between provinces, but was an administrative change in that each of the seven districts would be headed by an appointed representative charged with coordinating the tasks of the federal bureaucracy in particular, as well as attempting to check the overt flouting of central authority on the part of elected regional governors and republican presidents. This was a controversial move in that the reform attempted to place appointed presidential representatives higher in the political-administrative hierarchy than elected governors and presidents of regions.

Second, in an effort to remove overly active governors from excessive regional involvement in national politics, Putin proposed, and the Duma accepted, a plan to reorganize the Federation Council, Russia's upper house of parliament, such that regional political leaders (governors, presidents, and heads of regional legislatures) would no longer automatically gain seats. Instead, each region would be represented in the upper house by two appointed representatives—one put forward by the governor or president of the region and the other by a vote of regional parliament.

Third, to address the noncompliance problem, Putin quickly passed through the Duma a set of laws that would allow for the legal removal of governors and regional legislatures once it was proven in the courts that these officials were knowingly passing legislation in violation of the constitution and federal law. He also issued demands that regions reverse existing contradictory legislation. Finally, in an apparent effort to reduce the asymmetries between regions in their dealings with Moscow, Putin and his administration quietly moved to dissolve all but eight of the bilateral treaties the Yeltsin administration had signed with forty-two regions of Russia between 1994 and 1999.[27]

Despite the somewhat heavy-handed nature of Putin's solutions to the breakdown of central state authority in the periphery, it is not entirely clear that these moves actually did a great deal to challenge the heart of regional resistance. As noted in the introduction to this chapter, the most compelling evidence of the apparent inefficacy of these reform attempts under the first Putin administration was Putin's decision to eradicate completely the election of regional executives. While it does seem true that Putin's early efforts to curb regional challenges to central state authority may at best have temporarily tamed regional political leaders, without further institutional reform, it is entirely possible, perhaps likely, that should the Russian economy sour, we will see the reemergence of overt regional resistance to the central state yet again—regardless of whether or not regional political elites are elected or appointed. Under Yeltsin, after all, regional executives were centrally appointed for the most part and Yeltsin opted for elected regional heads by 1995 since he had become concerned about their loyalty to him and his reform efforts. Putin also appears to have forgotten that under the Soviet system regional leaders were also appointed and it was these officials who led the exodus of republics from the Soviet state. Appointment by the center, therefore, is clearly no guarantee of loyalty. Although Putin correctly identified the danger of regional resistance to central authority in rebuilding the Russian state as an effective policymaking and implementing device, he offered the wrong solutions. That is, while he rid Russia of some of the symptoms of what ails the central state in the periphery, he still has not cured the disease.

Putin's remedies thus far can be characterized as Soviet solutions to post-Soviet problems. As a result their depth, durability, and ultimate efficacy (given that the Soviet system ultimately failed on many fronts) are questionable. In creating the federal districts, for example, he simply increased the size of the central state, but did not increase its effectiveness. As with the two previous iterations of this office under Yeltsin, Putin's new representatives of the federal executive had poorly defined responsibilities. It was unclear, for example, to what degree they were supposed to oversee the actions of regional governments in general or merely federal bureaucrats in the regions.[28] Their staffs were small relative to the size of a typical regional administration, and the presidential representatives were given no responsibility for spending federal funds, or for attending to the implementation of federal laws. Finally, the wide variation in how presidential representatives have carried out their roles is a testament to how poorly their roles were defined and what they understood their functions to be.[29] It was unclear, for example, to what degree they were supposed to oversee the actions of regional governments in general or merely federal bureaucrats in the regions.[30] Further, both heads of regional administrations and federal bureaucrats, like the heads of the regional branches of federal funds, quickly became resentful of what they perceived as ineffective interference in their activities.[31]

By 2002, the overall effectiveness of the federal envoys as a remedy to weak central state capacity in the provinces was in serious question. In a study of the results of the reform in the southern federal district, Natalia Zubarevich reported that the governor general there had done little to stop gubernatorial patronage of local companies. She concluded, "the presidential envoy's battle with corruption is selective, of little impact . . . and achieves its purposes only when the envoy's interests coincide with the interests of another level of government [either city or oblast level]."[32] Referring to the activities of the president's envoy in his region, the governor of Leningrad oblast asserted that by the summer of 2002, "results are not visible" and that "We need to create the appropriate conditions for business, not set up gosplans [referring to the huge former Soviet economic planning agency]."[33]

Just as some regions were more assertive than others vis-à-vis their authority with the federal government through the 1990s, according to a 2002 report compiled by a group of Western analysts of Putin's federal representatives "weak governors tend to heed and meet with federal representatives, while powerful ones keep their distance."[34] In sum, Putin's creation of these seven federal districts headed by representatives accountable directly to him did little to interrupt previous patterns of center–periphery relations in Russia.

Moreover, the creation of the federal districts headed by new presidential representatives merely created yet another layer of the Russian state—a strategy that has already proven ineffective in enhancing governing capacity in post-Soviet Russia.[35] The Russian state apparatus actually grew steadily through the 1990s relative to its size in the first few years following the collapse of the Soviet Union. The Russian State Committee on Statistics reported in 1999 that despite central state efforts to cut the size of the Russian bureaucracy, it actually increased in terms of the number of officials employed in federal agencies and regional administrations. Where in 1994, for example, there were a reported 1,004,000 officials employed at all layers of the state, that number had increased each year to reach 1,133,000 by the end of 1999. Not surprisingly therefore state spending on this apparatus also increased steadily since 1994 (the first year for which figures were available) from 1.73 percent of all state spending in 1994 to 2.4 percent in 1998. More than two years after the ascent of Vladimir Putin in 2000 to the top of the Russian state hierarchy, a Russian bureaucrat was born every eighteen minutes.[36] Indeed, the number of bureaucrats has increased in the last ten years as Russia's total population has declined, such that about 10 percent of Russia's population worked in the civil service.[37] Remarkably, there are about three hundred more Russians employed in the civil service than in the Russian army.[38]

Putin has not used his other two main sticks on errant governors or regional legislatures. He did not remove a regional leader nor disband a legislature over legislation not conforming to the constitution or federal law. Indeed, although this authority was thought to be a none too subtle way in which to rid Russia of its more recalcitrant and possibly corrupt regional leaders, this proved not to be the case in practice. A crucial test of this authority was the example of Yevgenny Nazdratenko of Primorskii Krai in the Russian Far East. Although Nazdratenko was seemingly corrupt and long a thorn in the side of the Yeltsin administration, rather than removing him from power and trying him in the courts for corruption under the pretense of his new authority to remove governors, Putin instead chose to secure Nazdratenko's resignation in exchange for a plumb position at the Federal Ministry of Fisheries. Indeed, most observers assumed that Putin would be able to use his new authority to remove those leaders of regions that lead the noncompliance war of the 1990s. But it is likely that the presumed popular (and perhaps international) backlash that might result from actually removing an elected representative from office rendered this weapon against the regions largely unusable.

In July 2003 this authority was rendered even more useless by a ruling from the Constitutional Court of Russia in a case brought to it by the governments of Tatarstan and Bashkortostan, two of the leading noncompliant regions. The court ruled that federal prosecutors based at the regional level did not have the legal authority to file cases against regional governments that they believed passed legislation that violated the constitution of the Russian Federation. According to the ruling, only the Constitutional Court itself had this authority. Given the mammoth task of monitoring the legislative output of eighty-nine regional governments and legislatures, by removing the ability to file suits against offending regional governments from the offices of federal prosecutors based in each region, the ruling rendered a serious blow to the authority of the central state to ensure uniformity in Russian laws.[39] Some analysts predicted that this ruling ushered in a quiet counterrevolution in regional legislation against Putin's centralizing initiatives.[40]

Far from being able to summarily rid himself of the leaders of regional resistance in Russia, which the evidence here has indicated tended to be the wealthiest regions (net donors to the federal budget), Putin has suffered several legal and political defeats that have left the regional leadership structures of the 1990s largely intact. In July 2002, the Constitutional Court ruled that all terms served by regional governors prior to the passage of the October 1999 federal law on the organization of regional government did not count toward the two-term limit established by the 1999 law. This meant that many regional leaders would be able to run for third and fourth consecutive terms: in 2002 there were fifty-three governors of eighty-nine regions that could potentially rule their provinces for another four to eight years such that in total their rules could last for as long as twelve to twenty years.[41] Further, despite strong presidential administration involvement in regional elections between October 2000 and January 2002, the incumbency rate for regional governors and presidents was a startling 65.4 percent.[42] There was reportedly high participation by business elites in regional elections—either trying to run candidates of their own or backing incumbent candidates in exchange for preferential tax and budgetary treatment.[43] Despite the purported spread of "Unity" (now "Unified Russia") among regional politicians, the "gubernatorial regimes" of the 1990s remained in power—with Unity's backing or without it.

It is also unclear as to the concrete effect on Russian federal relations of the dissolution of many of the bilateral treaties that helped to confuse the already complicated system of federalism. Notably, however, the eight treaties that have been left in place are the ones that the federal government signed with the more notorious and persistent noncompliant regions, donors in particular (most notably, Tatarstan). Signing these agreements did little to stem the tide of noncompliance, and as a result they did little to clear up the muddy waters of jurisdictional transparency or equity. Beyond this though, the treaties were so widely variable that some regions like Tatarstan and Sverdlovsk negotiated considerable economic and tax privileges for themselves, while others amounted to little more than expressions of friendship and solidarity between the regional signatory and the federal government. It is unclear then, what effect, if any, dissolving these documents would actually have on Russian federal relations and the practical authority of the central state in particular.

Forced resolution of noncompliance may be Putin's biggest success, but the longevity of this is questionable if we look at past patterns from the 1990s. We know, for example, that noncompliance declined when the economy began to improve in 1999 and was higher when the economy was relatively worse (the third quarter of 1998 and the financial crisis). For the last three years, the Russian economy has been steadily growing and reports of noncompliance have decreased markedly. But if past is predictor, and economic growth slows, regional resistance in the form of non-compliance to federal law and the constitution may well increase again.[44]

As Stephen Holmes has argued, despite what Putin and his team may want us all to believe, his Russia may not be that different in important respects from the Russia of Boris Yeltsin.[45] That is, the fundamental structural problems are still there. This is particularly true of regional–central relations. So far, Putin's state "strengthening" reforms do not go to the heart of the collusive relationship between certain sectors of regional business and political elites. It may be that there is in fact too much strong resistance to breaking down these relationships and this may also explain why it is, despite dizzying popularity ratings, seemingly strong support from the Duma the likes of which Yeltsin never experienced, and a growing economy, Putin did not undertake the serious microeconomic reform that would put Russia on a more stable economic footing in the event of a decline in world oil prices in particular. It may be that he intended to undertake this kind of reform of the economy, but that he simply did not possess the political authority in practice to do so.

V. ALTERNATIVE INSTITUTIONAL SOLUTIONS TO STRENGTHEN RUSSIA'S DEBILITATED STATE

State building is a process, not an event. Despite its various deficiencies, the post-Soviet Russian state has nonetheless come a remarkably long way in a very short period of time. In many respects it is not at all surprising then that the state in Russia is not yet a well-oiled machine. That said, given that the durability and efficacy of Putin's attempts to strengthen the central state in the periphery can be questioned, with the benefit of hindsight from the 1990s as well as comparative experience in institution building, what further institutional changes should be made to better ensure the transparent and reliable authority of the Russian central state in the periphery? That is, rather than further eroding Russia's standing as an electoral democracy—which is the net effect of eliminating elected executives in the eighty-nine regions of Russia—what could Putin have done to bolster the central state's governing presence in the provinces?

The evidence in this chapter is that the root of regional resistance to central authority throughout the 1990s was the collusive relationship that frequently existed between economic and political elites in wealthy (donor) regions in particular. Further reform must therefore target these relationships. Despite numerous attempts, Putin has not (yet?) built political institutions that are capable of breaking the stranglehold of regional economic notables on local politics. His most desperate attempt aimed at the very heart of Russia's status as an "electoral democracy." Ironically, however, Putin might instead have leveraged one of the main advantages of democracy—accountability. If more elections were held at the regional level for more offices, public officials would be liberated from career dependence on either central or regional officials, and increase their sense of public responsibility and accountability. If national political parties provided candidates claiming their name with financing to run their campaigns, and maintained some sort of programmatic discipline over their members, then perhaps chains of reciprocity between national and local elected officials and chains of accountability would be broadened and strengthened. In particular, political institutions could have been constructed to heighten the electoral dependency of elected regional political actors on a national political party organization and the electorate rather than a narrow set of local economic notables. Building up the presence of national political parties at the local level would better link regional actors to national actors. If President Putin himself formally joined a political party and ran with a party label, this might help signal the importance of parties to the political process. The 2002 law introducing the mixed proportional representation and single mandate system in regional dumas should help to encourage party development at the regional level, but is not a panacea. Just as there is compelling evidence that there is strong resistance to the central state on the part of regional elites, there is similarly strong resistance to building political parties in the periphery that widen the sphere of accountability of regional political actors.[46] Building political parties capable of creating reciprocal links between national and regional political leaders is obviously a long-term project, but it would not only make Russia's political landscape more transparent and more broadly accessible, it would also have the effect of providing policy coherence across the Russian expanse.

In sum, however, in the absence of this sort of political institutionalization and broadening of political and economic relationships beyond the sort
of clientelistic politics that has long ruled Russia, there is no reason to assume that the authoritarian state Putin is apparently building will actually have
any more authority in the regions than the incomplete democratic state that
preceded it.

CONCLUSION

The Russian case highlights the tension between the necessities of decreasing the role of the state in postcommunist economies while at the same time
ensuring that the new states that replace them are capable of regulating the
economy sufficiently to produce well-functioning markets and providing basic protections and services to citizens. Even the minimal state pictured by
Russia's early neoliberal reformers should not have become a weak state. On
the contrary, for the successful transition from plan to market, the state had to
be capable of providing sufficient legal protections for the equal protection of
property rights and the separation of private from public interest.

Paradoxically, however, almost fifteen years after the initiation of its dual
economic and political transition, the post-Soviet state is neither minimalist
nor capable of providing many of the conditions that a fully functioning market
economy demands or democratic society requires. The empirical evidence and
arguments here indicate the dilemma of dual transitions: economic change
and the simultaneous reorganization and reconstitution of state institutions are
not always complimentary processes. On the contrary, economic interests that
emerge out of the shift from public to private property rights regimes may work
to weaken or stall the establishment of a state capable of regulating their new
economic activities. Thus the process of economic transition itself sometimes
works to undermine further political and macroeconomic change.

We see evidence of this in the patterns of regional noncompliance to federal
law and the constitution such that the Russian central state proved increasingly
incapable over the last decade to effectively and reliably transmit its authority
across territory. Its authority in this regard was challenged not by regional
government actors alone, but by regional economic actors made politically
powerful through the early processes of economic change—particularly the
reform of property rights. These groups benefited from a central state that was
incapable of regulating their activities and circumscribing their power through
regulation. As a result, they worked to penetrate, co-opt, and control branches
of federal bureaucracies based in the regions, regional bureaucracies, and most
importantly, regional politicians.

This dynamic presents a serious challenge to the future of Russia's political and economic reform effort. For regardless of the quality of its fiscal or social policies, the budgetary and political threats issued by the president, or even whether regional governors are elected or appointed by the president himself, if the central state remains stymied in its efforts to extend its authority to govern across territory, then positive changes will continue to come slowly if at all to the lives of average Russians.

NOTES

Prepared for Program on Russian Governance headed by Timothy Colton and Stephen Holmes and funded by the Carnegie Corporation. Revised as of April 7, 2006.

1. See Jeffrey Kahn, "The Parade of Sovereignties: Establishing the Vocabulary of the New Russian Federalism," *Post-Soviet Affairs* 16, no. 1 (January–March 2000): 58–89.

2. Daniel Treisman, "The Politics of Intergovernmental Transfers in Post-Soviet Russia," *British Journal of Political Science* 26 (1996): 327.

3. The term *legal separatism* comes from former first deputy prime minister Anatoly Chubais. See "Center Continues to Rail against 'Legal Separatism,'" *Institute for East West Studies, Russian Regional Report* 1, no. 10 (November 6, 1996).

4. For example, Yeltsin issued a decree to compel Udmurtiia's parliament to follow a constitutional court ruling and end its practice of appointing mayors in the republic. See "Newly Elected Governors Grapple with Moscow, Regional Problems," *Institute for East West Studies, Russian Regional Report* 3, no. 2 (January 15, 1998).

5. Steven L. Solnick, "The Political Economy of Russian Federalism: A Framework for Analysis," *Problems of Post-Communism* (November–December 1996): 13–25.

6. This data set was compiled using the LexisNexis electronic database as well as Radio Free Europe/Radio Liberty Electronic Archives and the Eastview Publications electronic archives purchased by Firestone Library at Princeton University. The search of Russian national newspapers (that is, with news coverage and circulation across the country, rather than any particular region) generated approximately five hundred articles cataloguing regional noncompliance to the constitution. With the assistance of two of my graduate students, Eric McGlinchey and Marc Berenson, I devised a list of policy areas by which to classify noncompliance into nine categories (economic, social, electoral requirements, judiciary/legal, taxation, trade, citizenship, regional government structure, misdirection of federal funds). Next, my team coded the articles gathered from the database so that each infraction was assigned a policy area. Many of the articles yielded more than one infraction per region, so the final number of observations was 846.

These data provide a thumbnail sketch of the extent of the center's noncompliance problem in the regions. I do not know if the various newspapers would emphasize one region more than another in their reporting, or if some acts of compliance were simply easier to observe and were therefore overreported. In thinking about this problem, however, I have no sense of the ways in which biases would run nor what weighting scheme would make sense in attempting to correct for this problem in the data. I am confident this data is the best available, however.

7. We have some confidence that the temporal patterns we observe are not merely a result of fluctuations in the quality of newspaper coverage of the phenomenon through the 1990s in that Ministry of Justice reports issued regularly from about 1996 onward also indicate a steady increase in reported infractions. Thus, the patterns the ministry reported seem to be parallel to what our data show.

8. See for example, Donald Horowitz, *Ethnic Groups in Conflict* (Berkeley: University of California Press, 1985).

9. Daniel S. Treisman, "Russia's 'Ethnic Revival': The Separatist Activism of Regional Leaders in a Postcommunist Order," *World Politics* 49, no. 2 (January 1997): 239.

10. I employ ordinary least squares regression analysis here for ease of interpretation.

11. In other versions of the model I included regional per capita gross domestic product for 1998 and it was never statistically significant in any of the five models, suggesting that wealth alone is not what drives the behavior of the regions toward the center as much as economic structure.

12. Note that in another version of model 3, I added a variable to measure the interactive effect of a region's status as a republic and volume of industrial production that produced a coefficient of .00001777, statistically significant at the .07 level.

13. In particular, see Raj M. Desai and Itzhak Goldberg, "The Vicious Circles of Control: Regional Governments and Insiders in Privatized Russian Enterprises," Policy Research Working Paper 2287 (Washington, DC: The World Bank, Europe and Central Asia Region Private and Financial Sectors Development Unit, February 2000); Joel S. Hellman, Geraint Jones, and Daniel Kaufmann, "Seize the State, Seize the Day: State Capture, Corruption and Influence in Transition," Policy Research Working Paper 2444 (Washington, DC: The World Bank, World Bank Institute Governance, Regulation and Finance Division and Europe and Central Asia Region, Public Sector Group, and European Bank of Reconstruction and Development Office of the Chief Economist, September 2000); Joel S. Hellman, Geraint Jones, Daniel Kaufmann, and Mark Schankerman, "Measuring Governance, Corruption and State Capture: How Firms and Bureaucrats Shape the Business Environment in Transition Economies," (Washington, DC: The World Bank, World Bank Institute Governance, Regulation and Finance Division and European Bank for Reconstruction and Development Chief Economist's Office, April 2000).

14. Desai and Goldberg, "Vicious Circles," 4.

15. Andrei Shleifer and Daniel Treisman, *Without a Map: Political Tactics and Economic Reform in Russia* (Cambridge, MA: MIT Press, 2000), 27–34. Note that I am not making any normative argument or judgment regarding the wisdom of these concessions. I am merely pointing out their political effect on regional government relationships with enterprises.

16. Desai and Goldberg, "Vicious Circles," 5.

17. Desai and Goldberg, "Vicious Circles," 7.

18. Desai and Goldberg, "Vicious Circles," 7. Their source for this economic data is Russian Economic Barometer and Russian Economic Trends. World Bank, "Dismantling Russia's Nonpayments System: Creating Conditions for Growth," 1999.

19. Desai and Goldberg, "Vicious Circles," 9.

20. Hellman, Jones, and Kaufmann, "Seize the State." The BEEPS data indicates that Russia is a comparatively "high capture" economy.

21. Hellman, Jones, and Kaufmann, "Seize the State," 2.

22. Desai and Goldberg, "Vicious Circles," 10.

23. Desai and Goldberg, "Vicious Circles," 10.

24. This is a survey of public officials completed in the autumn of 1999 in seventy-two of Russia's eighty-nine regions. It is easier to list which of Russia's eighty-nine regions were not included in the interviewing process than those that were. Because of the danger involved in going to the North Caucasus in the fall of 1999, neither Chechnya nor Ingushetia were included in the sample. In addition, it proved impossible to complete interviews in the city of Moscow, Moscow oblast, or Leningrad oblast. Since we were primarily interested in the relationship between republics and oblasts and *krais* and the center, none of the ten autonomous *okrugs* nor the one autonomous oblast were included. The survey was conducted in cooperation with Aleksandr Gasparishvili and Sergei Tumanov of the Opinion Research Center, Moscow State University. We employed the network of interviewers Gasparishvili and Tumanov constructed in the provinces during the 1990s. Teams of interviewers conducted person to person interviews of a list of respondents that we provided. On average, interviews lasted forty minutes.

I am also grateful to Beth Mitchneck of the Department of Geography and Regional Development at the University of Arizona for her assistance in devising the survey instrument and in generously providing copies of her questionnaire, part of which is replicated here, and which she used in a similar survey of public officials at the city and oblast levels in Russia in 1997. For more on Mitchneck's survey and results see her "The Regional Governance Context in Russia: A General Framework," *Urban Geography* 2001, and her "Regional Governance Regimes in Russia: The Case of Yaroslavl' and Udmurtia," in Jeffrey W. Hahn, ed., *Regional Russia in Transition: Studies from Yaroslavl* (Washington, DC: Woodrow Wilson Center Press, 2001).

25. Central Electoral Commission of the Russian Federation, *Vybopry v zakonodatel'nie organi gosudarstvennoi vlasti sub'ektov Rossiiskoi Federatsii, 1995–1997* (Moscow: Tsentral'naia Izbiratel'naia Kommissiia, 1998), 637.

26. See chapter 5 of Kathryn Stoner-Weiss, *Resisting the State: Reform and Retrenchment in Post-Soviet Russia* (Cambridge University Press, 2006) where the media noncompliance data and survey data of elected and appointed regional officials are merged to demonstrate statistically the relationship between noncompliant behavior and the degree to which regional business groups influence regional political leaders.

27. Nikolay Petrov, Carnegie Endowment for International Peace, Moscow office confirmed this as the most up to date number at time of writing in a personal communication with the author, February 23, 2005.

28. See Soobshenie Press-Sluzhbii Prezidenta Rossiiskoi Federatsii, 2000-05-13-002 Ukaz "O polnomochnom presdstavitele Prezidenta Rossiiskoi Federatsii v federal'nom okruge" (Decree on the authority of the representative of the president of the Russian Federation, May 13, 2000). See also the interview with Sergei Samoilov, head of the Presidential Administration of the Russian Federation in the *Russian Regional Report* (New York: EastWest Institute), August 4, 2000.

29. See also Peter Rutland, "The Role of the Presidential Representative (polnomochyii predstavitel' prezidenta): Reflections on the North-West Federal Okrug, Prepared for the EastWest Institute Conference on Putin's Relationship with the Regions, September 21–22, 2001." See also *Russian Regional Report* 6, no. 36 (October 17, 2001).

30. See Soobshenie Press-Sluzhbii Prezidenta Rossiiskoi Federatsii, 2000-05-13-002. See also Samoilov, August 4, 2000.

31. Robert Orttung, "Leningrad Governor Critical of Federal Reforms," *Russian Regional Report*, August 2, 2002, and Robert Orttung, "Putin's Governors General," *EastWest Institute's Russian Regional Report* 7, no. 20 (June 17, 2002).

32. Natalia Zubarevich, "Kazantsev Has Little Impact in the Southern Federal District," *EastWest Institute's Russian Regional Report* 7, no. 29 (November 25, 2002).

33. As quoted in Orttung, "Leningrad Governor Critical of Federal Reforms."

34. Orttung, "Putin's Governors General."

35. These numbers are reported in Vitaly Golovachev, "Russian Bureaucrats Reproducing Like Rabbits," *Trud*, June 14, 2000. Data on state spending comes from the federal law on the budget for each of the corresponding years. These laws are published in *Sobrianie aktov gosudarstvennogo zakonodatelstva Rossisskogo Federatsii* (Moscow: Government of the Russian Federation, 1994, 1995, 1996, 1997, and 1998).

36. Vladimir Kovalyev, "A Bureaucracy That Cuts Just One Way," *St. Petersburg Times*, May 21, 2002, Johnson's Russia List, #6260 May 22, 2002.

37. Mikhail Dmitriev, first deputy minister Russian Ministry of Economic Development and Trade, "Public Administration Reform in Russia," Carnegie Endowment for International Peace, May 1, 2002 (available at www.ceip.org/files/events/events.asp? Event ID=482) and Kovalyev, "A Bureaucracy That Cuts Just One Way."

38. Kovalyev, "A Bureaucracy That Cuts Just One Way."

39. "Constitutional Court Rules in Favor of Curbing Prosecutors' Rights in Battles with Regions . . ." RFE/RL Newsline, vol. 7, part 1, July 22, 2003.

40. See "Constitutional Court Decision Opens Way for Quiet Revolution," *Radio Free Europe, Radio Liberty Newsline*, vol. 7, no. 137, part 1, July 22, 2003.

41. Vladimir Ryzhkov, "A New Era of Stagnation," *Moscow Times*, July 25, 2002 in Johnson's Russia List, #6371, July 26, 2002.

42. Rostislav Turoskii, "Itogi i uroki gubernatorskikh vyborov," in *Politika v regionakh: gubernatorii I gruppy vlianiia*, ed. Boris I. Makarenko (Moscow: Center for Political Technology, 2002), 11.

43. Turovskii, "Gubernatory i oligarkhi: istoriya otnoshenii," 76–107.

44. Indeed, reports have surfaced in the summer of 2002 of the resurgence of 1990s phenomena like barter and increased wage arrears to doctors and teachers in seventeen regions of Russia, despite federal insistence that these practices end.

45. Stephen Holmes, "Simulations of Power in Putin's Russia," Carnegie Endowment for International Peace, Russian and Eurasian Affairs Program, June 2001. Available at www.ceip.org/files/publications.

46. See Kathryn Stoner-Weiss, "The Limited Reach of Russia's Party System: Underinstitutionalization in Dual Transitions," *Politics and Society* 29, no. 3 (September 2001): 385–414.

Chapter Five

State Capacity and Pension Provision

Linda J. Cook

Countries in Eastern Europe and the former Soviet Union face the typical problems of middle-income countries with publicly managed pay-as-you-go /pension/ systems. . . . But the problems are magnified in the transitional economies because they have the aging demographic profiles, widespread coverage, system maturity, and aspirations of high income countries but the resources, tax systems, and government capacities of middle- and low-income countries.[1]

This chapter deals with the capacity of the Russian state to provide for the welfare of its population, focusing on the case of pension provision. While Russia's failures in the social sphere during the 1990s are many, this case is particularly salient because pensions constitute by far the largest welfare state program, accounting for about 6 percent of gross domestic product (GDP) in the 1990s. More than a quarter of Russia's population was eligible for pension payments, and these payments constituted a critical source of cash income for many poorer households as well as one of the few mechanisms of effective income redistribution by the state.[2] Moreover, the pension system fared better than many other social programs. It did not anywhere collapse completely, is credited with keeping the incomes of most pensioners above the poverty level until the 1998 financial crisis, and was the subject of much attention from reformist policy makers. Yet in the Yeltsin period the new Russian state failed to effectively administer or restructure the pension system it had inherited. Payment arrears mounted unevenly across the Federation, tax evasion and enterprises' debt to the Pension Fund became chronic problems, and reform efforts faltered because of policy deadlock or poor design.

In attempting to explain these failures this chapter will focus on the institutions of the Russian state: the executive, the Pension Fund, government ministries, and intragovernmental policy processes, as well as executive–legislative relations. It might be assumed that the problems of Russia's social provision were largely the result of structural economic conditions rather than of the state or its capacities—that the Russian economic collapse and prolonged recession led to an unavoidable social crisis. Economic pressures were indeed intense, and will be discussed at various points. But, as has been shown by studies of both the Great Depression in the West and the postsocialist transitions in Eastern Europe, states may respond more or less effectively to the welfare consequences of economic crises, including with policies that restructure social provision and expand relative spending; as the introduction to the current volume notes, crises in the social sphere may be "capability-elevating."[3] We will focus on why the Russian state of the Yeltsin era failed to respond effectively.

During the Putin period the Russian state has demonstrated improved capabilities to deliver pension security. It effectively addressed the immediate crisis, clearing arrears, raising pensions, paying them reliably across the Federation, and stabilizing the Pension Fund budget. A major, long-term program for restructuring the pension system was approved by the government and passed through the legislature, and is being implemented. Though many problems remain, improvement of the state's effectiveness in this area is indisputable. This chapter will identify the major factors that explain the growth in state capacity, and explore its limitations.

The first part sets out the conceptual framework. The second part presents the pension system as it operated at the outset of the Yeltsin period, placing that system in international context. The next two sections apply the framework in comparative case studies of pension provision and reform during the Yeltsin and Putin periods. The conclusion proposes an explanation for the comparative performance of the state across the two periods.

STATE CAPACITIES AND SUPPLY OF PUBLIC GOODS

The introduction to this book has defined state capacity as encompassing "the relative ability of constituted authorities to recognize societal problems, fashion cogent responses to them, and effectively deliver corrective action, both in reaction to urgent crises and through planning ahead and steering social change."[4] The literature distinguishes different dimensions of state capacity. We will be concerned primarily with distributive capacity, defined as the capability to supply public goods and services and to regulate transfers of income and wealth. The state's ability to deliver programs of social welfare depends first and foremost on whether it can redistribute income and allocate spending to social services. States may transfer resources between generations, among income groups, and over the life cycles of individuals. Formal pension systems, which cover some 40 percent of the world's labor force, provide a major source of income and security for older age groups.[5] Pensions are a valued public good that contributes to the legitimacy of the state and encourages tax compliance. Especially in societies where traditional modes of caring for the elderly have broken down and there is little accumulation of personal wealth, as in the Russian case, pensioners depend for their welfare on the state's distributive capacities.

In order to fund the pension system, in particular to collect wage-based social security taxes, the state has to rely also on its infrastructural power to extract revenue. It must monitor transactions in the labor market, generate reliable information about wages and incomes, and enforce compliance on powerful economic actors. In the transitional economy of the 1990s, Russia's inherited institutions proved inadequate to these tasks.[6] There emerged several distinct forms of evasion, with different implications for the state's power. At one end of the state–society relationship workers and wages escaped into the informal economy, evading the state's reach. At the other end powerful economic actors used their access to political elites in order to negotiate tax avoidance. Much of the remaining formal sector relied on strategies of minimal or formal compliance, taking advantage of the state's limited information to understate wages. The federal nature of the Russian state, the noncompliance of regional units with the federal tax regime, also complicated the picture. Cumulatively, the central state's weakened capacity to monitor financial transactions and tax individuals and economic and federal units seriously eroded its ability to finance the inherited pension system.

The state's ability to provide public goods and services, especially in a period of radical socioeconomic transition, also depends critically on state elites' potential to fashion cogent responses to problems; to innovate and adapt; to formulate feasible, coherent, and effective policies. Two factors are key here: first, the cohesion of the elites, the extent to which they share a common set of policy goals, priorities, and interests, strengthens capacities, while the presence of veto points in the system may weaken them.[7] Secondly, capacities will be stronger to the extent that policy makers can use background knowledge about their own societies, appreciate the complexity of the problems they face, have adequate expertise, and draw on a dialogue with academic experts and civil society.

Russian political elites of the Yeltsin era were far from cohesive in their social policy goals, and the design of the institutional system lent itself to polarization and fragmentation of power. For much of the Yeltsin period the left-dominated legislature functioned as a veto actor against efforts to reform pension entitlements, while the pension system's key institution, the Pension Fund, defended its corporate interests against both regulation and reform. The government itself divided at key points between ministerial appointees who favored radical systemic change and more conservative interests. The president's power to choose ministers with little consultation exacerbated divisions both within the government and with the legislature. Presidential unilateralism—the use of executive decree powers to make arbitrary and ad hoc changes in pension distribution—added to policy incoherence.

At the same time, the transitional nature of the system, the great instability in institutions, economics, and politics, made it difficult for policy makers and experts to gain a thorough understanding of the policy environment. Much accumulated background knowledge became obsolete. Old mechanisms for pension provision collapsed, and new ones were created hurriedly. The circumstances frustrated policy makers' efforts to analyze or model the pension system's performance, or to design effective innovations. High inflation undermined the predictability of operations of the pension funds, while large shifts in the structure of the labor force and macroeconomic instability complicated efforts at projection and planning, especially planning ahead and steering change.

Finally, we consider the state's capacities for implementation, the adequacy of the administrative, informational, technical, and regulatory mechanisms that newly adopted policies require. An important factor affecting implementation capacities in Russia and other postcommunist states was the degree of international intervention in social policy reform agendas. As in other policy areas, Russia has been "subject to incessant pressure to conform to the expectations of . . . supranational bodies as to institutional design."[8] Global and international influences on states' institution building are of course not new, but in the past, existing institutional capacities constrained policy choice. According to Skocpol's work on the 1930s depression, for example, state authorities "take into account . . . capacities of the state structures in which they are located. If a given state structure provides no existing, or readily foreseeable, 'policy instruments' for implementing a given line of action, government officials are not likely to pursue it."[9] By contrast Russian state authorities did pursue policies in the pension sphere for which they lacked the necessary instruments. Encouraged and pressured by international financial institutions (IFIs), they followed international models of insurance- and market-based pension provision. Such models required administrative and regulatory capacities and information flows that were absent or deficient in Russia. These policies lacked feasibility, and institutional deficits often distorted or blocked their implementation.

The reform agenda also evoked normative conflicts over the scope of the state's role in old-age security, and social welfare more broadly. The dominant neoliberal reform model called for the state to withdraw from direct provision of most social welfare benefits. These functions were to be transferred to individuals and markets, with the state's role restricted largely to targeted aid for the poor. In the pension sphere, reform proposals called for movement from the existing solidaristic state-run system toward one based on individual accounts invested in markets. While such changes required an increase in the state's regulatory functions, they would at the same time diminish its social responsibilities and redistributive capabilities. Normative conflicts over the scope and speed of this transition, within the government and in the broader policy community, complicated efforts at reform.

ACCOUNTABILITY AND RESPONSIVENESS

This chapter is also concerned with the accountability and responsiveness of state elites to their society. In democratic states both rule of law and periodic elections constrain state actors. In the pension sphere, where real levels of payouts have to be renegotiated frequently because of economic pressures on pension systems (i.e., inflation, falling tax collection), analysts have stressed the importance of short-term electoral constraints.[10] Under the prevailing system of semidemocracy in the 1990s, the Russian state was able to impose substantial losses on pensioners. I will argue, however, that the electoral process did provide a constricted accountability that limited the kinds of losses. In the Yeltsin period the Duma functioned as an effective veto actor against efforts to dismantle the statutory base of the pension system, though the president was able to determine much about the scale and patterns of pension financing.[11]

Moreover, limited accountability does not necessarily imply strength. Pension provision reached beyond the recipient population to tie the broader labor force into a system of social security that facilitated the state's monitoring of incomes, and contributed to its distributive capacities. When the state failed to deliver on pension obligations it undercut the credibility of its welfare and distributive roles. Poor credibility in turn encouraged defection into the informal sector and state avoidance. In other words, society disconnected from and weakened the state.

THE PRE-TRANSITION RUSSIAN PENSION SYSTEM

The new Russian state inherited from the Soviet Union a mature pension system that carried extensive financial obligations to the population.[12] The system

Table 5.1. Pension Expenditure, % GDP, Selected Countries, 1996

Russia	5.7
Czech Republic	8.4
Ukraine	8.6
Hungary	9.7
Latvia	10.8
Poland	13.9
Spain (1993)	11.2
Germany (1993)	14.3

Source: Irina Denisova, Maria Gorban, and Ksenia Yudaeva, "Social Policy in Russia: Pension Fund and Social Security," *Russian Economic Trends* 1999. 1: 12; IMF.

had a broad normative basis in federal law, with the key 1956 Pension Law extending coverage to all civilian state employees upon retirement, those disabled by work-related accidents or illnesses, and deceased workers' surviving dependents. Given virtually full employment in the Soviet economy and high labor force participation rates for women as well as men, coverage was quite broad, nearly universal for those retiring at the end of the Soviet period.[13] Pensions were financed from the state budget and administered by social organizations and trade unions. There was no specified contributory mechanism; retiring workers became eligible for a defined benefit based on their wages and years of service. Overall, Russian pension spending was low in comparison with levels in Europe and other transitional economies (see table 5.1).[14] (It should be kept in mind, though, that housing, transport, utilities, and other basic goods often remained subsidized in Russia, somewhat limiting the value of the comparison.) This was a system of entitlements or social benefits rather than insurance, with the state determining and carrying the full obligation for payment.

Eligibility requirements in the Soviet pension system were quite liberal by international standards. Men could collect at sixty and women at fifty-five. Moreover, the Soviet government had used enhanced pension benefits as incentives for various types of labor force and other behavior. These became incorporated into the system as "privileges" and exceptions: those who worked in difficult or dangerous occupations, or in severe climatic conditions, could retire early, as could several categories of white-collar workers under specified conditions. The broad system of early retirement effectively lowered the pension age still further, while some 10 percent of pensioners received privileges.[15] Those eligible to collect could continue working without penalty, and Russia had some seven million "working pensioners." In 1992 more than thirty-five million people, almost one-fourth of the population, received pensions, as against 15–19 percent in Organization for Economic Cooperation and Development (OECD) countries.[16] Both the liberal rules for general eligibility and the various privileged exceptions formed a legacy of entitlements that was embedded in Soviet legislation and in the expectations of the population. The efforts of the Russian state to retrench and reform this system became a major test of its capabilities.

When Russia emerged as an independent state in 1991–1992 the legislature (Supreme Soviet) reorganized the institutional and financing bases of the pension system. An independent, extrabudgetary Pension Fund (PF) was established, and made responsible for collecting taxes from employers' wage bills to fund pension payments. In order to meet the accumulated obligations of the system, the tax was set at the comparatively high level of 29 percent. Combined with other social insurance taxes it produced a total payroll tax of 38 percent, a very high rate by international standards. (The World Bank views a payroll tax over 25 percent as unacceptably high and likely to generate evasion.)[17] The pension system established in Russia at this point was a single-pillar, defined-benefit pay-as-you-go (PAYG) system, based largely on an intergenerational transfer of income. Current benefits were financed from current contributions. Enterprises paid a lump sum for their employees with no accounts for individual workers, making the connection between payments into the fund and pensions received remote. The sudden move from state funding to PAYG, with virtually no reserve fund, constituted a radical change.

Even at the time of its creation in 1991, before the economic chaos of the 1990s, the Russian pension system presented serious problems of viability and sustainability. PAYG systems are common in advanced industrial societies with strong taxing and state-administrative capabilities. In comparison to these systems the Russian was quite demanding. It required a very high payroll tax and administered benefits for an exceptionally large proportion of its population. Moreover, many types of pensions (privileged, early retirement, etc.) that are normally funded separately were folded into the PAYG system. And while eligibility was broad, pension levels were comparatively low, leaving little scope for reductions without serious damage to pensioners' welfare. Established PAYG systems were under pressure everywhere by the 1980s because of the worsening ratios between contributors and beneficiaries caused by the aging of populations. Russia's system also faced these demographically driven problems of medium-term viability, and in the mid-1990s it was confronting simultaneously both immediate and systemic crises.

THE YELTSIN PERIOD

The Crisis of Russia's Pension System

From the early 1990s Russia's pension system moved into an escalating crisis that was characterized by rapidly declining real pension payments, arrears, and rising poverty among pensioners. The economic collapse of the early 1990s had dramatic negative effects on the pension system. It brought a decline of more than 40 percent in the level of real wages, the main revenue base for pensions. Very high inflation in these years—averaging over 1500 percent in 1992 and almost 900 percent in 1993—undercut the real value of pensions and wiped out pensioners' savings.[18] At the same time the collapse significantly increased demands on the pension system: labor force cuts pushed older workers out of jobs onto pensions, the numbers claiming invalid pensions increased significantly, unemployment reduced the size of the labor force, and the growth of the informal sector further reduced payments into the fund.[19] As a result the ratio between those paying into the system and those receiving pensions—the payor/recipient ratio—officially shifted from 2.1 in 1991 to an unsustainable 1.7 in 1996. Extensive tax evasion worsened the situation significantly. Experts' estimates that took account of evasion and wage arrears put the actual ratio at 1.4.[20] In the face of similar pressures Poland and Hungary, for example, substantially increased their spending on pensions, then moved rapidly toward building a consensus on systemic reform. Russia succeeded in doing neither.

Problems of the Pension Fund

At the core of the system and its problems was the Pension Fund, an independent off-budget fund that was responsible for collecting contributions and, with social security offices, distributing them throughout the Federation.[21] The fund relied on a wholly inadequate inspection service to enforce tax compliance.[22] According to its own data, the "dynamics for efficiency of insurance contributions collection" fell steadily from 1992 to 1996, and again in 1998, while overdue arrears in enterprises' payments grew (see tables 5.2 and 5.3). In the

Table 5.2.   Dynamics of Efficiency (%) of Pension Insurance Contributions Collection, Russian Federation, 1992–2000

1992	1993	1994	1995	1996	1997	1998	1999	2000
100.1	90.7	86.3	82.5	76.0	84.4	78.6	95.4	95.1

Source: The Pension Fund of the Russian Federation: The Main Data on the Financial-Economic Activities for 1990–2000 (Moscow: Contemporary Economy and Law, 2000).

Table 5.3. Overdue Arrears of Contributors to the Pension Fund, 1993–2001 (Trillions of Rubles for 1993–1997; Billion New Rubles from 1998)

1993	1994	1995	1996	1997	1998	1999	2000	2001*
1.1	7.0	22.7	55.5	87.7	129.3	142.7	145.9	150

Source: The Pension Fund of the Russian Federation, 2000.
*For 2001, *Foreign Broadcast Information Service: Central Eurasian Daily Report*, April 24, 2001, citing *Rossiiskaia Gazeta*, April 24, 2001; figure is approximate.

early 1990s the fund managed to remain solvent because of high inflation, but once inflation was controlled in 1995, deficits mounted. The government reported that in 1997 fewer than 25 percent of corporate entities were paying into the fund punctually.[23] In that year enterprises cumulatively owed over R87 trillion, nearly 50 percent of the total inflow.[24] It became routine for enterprises to underreport their wage bills to the Pension Fund, contributing only enough to make their employees eligible for minimum benefits, a pattern of "minimal compliance" that is also common in weak Latin American states. The Pension Fund never succeeded in penetrating the finances of new private businesses that typically pay high wages.

Part of the Pension Fund's problem was the influence of the largest debtors within the state and their ability to bargain with high-level executive officials for exemptions and offsets, or to simply ignore pressures for payment. Among the largest debtors were the natural monopolies Gazprom, United Energy Systems, the railroads, and oil companies. When the government was struggling to pay off pension arrears in early 1997, the Pension Fund designated thirty companies, out of some 120 with debts of more than R50 billion, to appear before the Temporary Extraordinary Commission for Tax and Budget Discipline.[25] The commission threatened a range of sanctions against debtors, including threats to sell off parts of their companies, to limit their oil exports through the state-owned Transneft, and to force them to issue bonds, all to little avail.[26] The larger story of the struggles with these large tax debtors has been well told elsewhere.[27] Essentially these economic actors had sufficient power vis-à-vis the state to resist its efforts at enforcing the taxes that were required to fund inherited welfare obligations.

The Pension Fund also had serious problems of accountability and legal regulation. Established rather hastily in 1991, the fund was by far the largest standing pool of money in the social security system, and its governance structure shielded it from external oversight over money flows. The administration of the Pension Fund was dominated by the executive, with no representation of contributors, and pensioners' organizations represented at the government's discretion.[28] Originally subordinated to the Supreme Soviet, the fund was transferred to the government by Chernomyrdin during the October 1993 crisis, and Vasilii Barchuk was appointed head by a presidential *ukaz*. Especially from this point it functioned as a highly nontransparent institution. The fund was largely unaccountable for its use of funds, and was regularly subject to charges that it lent money to the budget, took credits from commercial banks at high interest rates, and badly mismanaged pension funds. The central Fund's control over employees in its regional offices was weak.[29] Pension Fund officials segregated regions on the basis of their success at collecting contributions and bargained with powerful governors over the division of taxes, undermining the uniformity of the pension system.[30]

Pressure for improvements in the Pension Fund's oversight and management came from a range of governmental and nongovernmental actors. Both Finance and Social Welfare Ministries supported a proposal that pension funds be transferred only through Sberbank structures, ending "diversions" to the commercial sector.[31] Anatoly Chubais, chair of the Extraordinary Commission for Improving Tax Discipline, proposed transferring collection of pension contributions to the state tax service, an idea that drew some broader support and was eventually implemented under Putin.[32] The World Bank made auditing of the Pension Fund a key condition of its major social sector loan (discussed below). None of these proposals was implemented. The Russian government forfeited the third tranche of the World Bank loan, scheduled for release in the precrisis spring of 1998, in part because it failed to carry out the Pension Fund audit. Under both Barchuk and his successor Zurabov the Pension Fund exemplified the "winner take all" phenomenon in the social sphere: its leaders gained largely unaccountable control over a large pool of funds in the first round of reform, then stood as a major obstacle to either legal regulation or further reform of the pension system.[33]

More mundane problems of administrative capacity also plagued the pension system, and affected citizens' ability to claim their pension rights. Survey evidence shows that social security offices, which calculated and distributed pensions, had low levels of information technology and often failed to receive, or to understand, normative documents instructing them on calculations of pension levels.[34] Because work records and wages were hard to verify in the chaotic new economy, officials often had difficulty processing eligibility claims of retiring workers. As a consequence some workers had difficulty making legitimate claims, while others inflated their pensions by falsifying wage levels, a practice that was reportedly common. Local offices had insufficient technical and administrative capacity to keep up with the frequent recalculations of pensions, contributing to delays and arrears.

State Capacities and Efforts to Resolve the Pension Crisis

The Russian government faced three short-term possibilities for dealing with the shortfall in Pension Fund collections: it could increase spending by supplementing the fund's revenues with transfers from the federal budget; restrict eligibility; or cut real pension benefits.

The government did transfer money from the budget to the Pension Fund, but only sporadically and against a background of chronic debts for social and other budget-funded pensions. Between 1995 and 1997 the federal budget itself ran a deficit to the fund that grew from R1.6 trillion to R15 trillion, making the budget sector one of the fund's largest debtors.[35] In the first half of 1997, when the arrears crisis was at its peak, the Ministry of Finance paid off these debts (in rubles devalued by inflation, which had continued at lower rates of over 300 percent in 1994 and almost 200 percent before stabilizing in 1995), and transferred several trillion rubles to clear arrears and raise pensions, relying in part on a large World Bank social sector loan.[36] Arrears mounted again almost immediately, peaking during the 1998 financial crisis. The Primakov government, appointed in September, managed to pay off arrears and compensate pensioners for part of the year's inflation with money from the federal budget and a R10 billion Sberbank credit.[37] In other words, the government did not pursue a policy of considered and consistent aid to the Pension Fund, but an erratic and crisis-driven one. The best measure of the outcome, the percent of GDP spent on pensions, remained relatively flat through the 1990s as GDP fell and real spending declined (see table 5.4). According to an estimate by the OECD, the real value of average and minimum pensions declined to about 60 percent and 40 percent of their respective 1991 levels by 1998.[38]

Restricting Eligibility: The Duma as a Veto Actor

Beginning in the mid-1990s the government did propose numerous changes in the rules of pension entitlement. They targeted the liberal eligibility criteria and special benefits, bonuses, and privileges inherited from the Soviet period, proposing, for example, to raise the retirement age; restrict rights to early

Table 5.4. Russian Pension Expenditure as a % of GDP, 1994–2001

1994	1995	1996	1997	1998	1999	2000	2001
6.0	5.2	5.6	6.4	5.7	5.2	5.2	5.5

Sources: Sotsial'noe polozhenie I uroven' zhizhi naseleniia Rossii: Statisticheskii Sbornik, 1997:194; 2003:194 (Moscow: Goskomstat, 1997, 2003).

retirement; cut benefits to working pensioners; and eliminate various types of privileged pensions. Reformist Russian government officials and ministers periodically floated one or another of these proposals, then backed down in the face of protest from the public, press, and Duma. For example, in early 1997 Pension Fund head Barchuk caused a national outcry when he announced that the government had discussed proposals to abolish or reduce payments to working pensions (some seven million of the total) in order to raise minimum pensions, and Yeltsin quickly issued a reassurance that no such cuts would be introduced. None of these measures was enacted during the period under review, though they continued to be viewed as essential to the fiscal balance of the pension system. They were not abandoned but delayed, written into reform programs to be phased in gradually in the future, or moved to separate pension tiers that would be financed by employers, strategies commonly used in democratic polities in order to blunt opposition to pension cuts.[39]

The key factor in the short-term failure of these policies was the opposition of the Duma, which stood as a veto actor against such immediate and highly visible cuts in pensioners' entitlements. The Duma would have had to approve any changes in the statutory base of the pension system. The Left parties, which depended heavily on older voters for political support, generally opposed in principle any diminution in the legal rights of pensioners. After the 1995 election, when the crisis of the pension system became severe, the Communist-led Left controlled nearly enough votes to reject legislation, and it became futile for the government even to propose such reforms. In February 1997, for example, the Duma passed a ruling, backed by 281 deputies, dismissing as "inadmissible" attempts to solve the pension problem by extending the retirement age or stripping working pensioners of their entitlements.[40] The lower house also blocked the government's repeated attempts to cut taxes on employers. Overall, government and Duma sparred over pension policy throughout this period, with the Duma blocking government initiatives while Yeltsin vetoed at least fifteen pieces of pension-related legislation between 1994 and 1998.[41] The Duma functioned as a constricted kind of accountability mechanism that constrained the government, producing a stalemate on structural reforms of the pension system, as in many other policy areas.

Cutting Real Benefits: Arrears and Presidential Unilateralism

Given limited budget transfers and political blocks to eligibility restrictions, the pension shortfall was dealt with mainly by cuts in real pension payments. This was accomplished in two ways: by changes and manipulation in pension benefit formulas, and by the large-scale accumulation of pension arrears, which became a major political issue in 1996–1997.

In any pension system, pensioners' real incomes tend to be eroded by inflation, and their relative incomes by generalized wage increases. The main hedge against erosion is indexation of pensions, either to prices or to wages, and the schedules and formulas for indexation form much of the stuff of routine pension politics in established systems. Given extremely high inflation in Russia, especially in 1992 and 1993, indexation became critical to the real value of pensions. Russian legislation provided that pensions were to be indexed periodically by the legislature, but in 1992 the system of pension distribution became one of the subjects of executive–legislative struggle. According to Andrea Chandler, who has analyzed pension policy in this period, "The legislature's arguments were normative and legal, arguing for the importance of a systematic legal framework in order to guarantee that the individual had an inalienable right to a decent standard of living. The executive's argument was . . . instead to introduce short-term *ad hoc* cash supplements to pensioners."[42] The differences were critical to the distribution of pension funds. Indexation increased all pensions by the same percent (or coefficient), at regular intervals, maintaining differentiation and some correspondence to past wages. Compensation meant an increase of all pensions by the same absolute sum, or enhanced for minimum pensions by a lump-sum supplement. It produces a compression of pension levels. Beginning in 1992, Yeltsin began to supplement and replace indexation with presidentially decreed pension "compensation" payments.

Compensation was an *ad hoc* procedure, allowing Yeltsin to determine the timing and payment formula, and its political uses were blatant. The president periodically vetoed some (though not all) modest indexation measures passed by the Duma, deriding them as fiscally irresponsible, and in this he was generally supported by the Finance and Labor Ministries, the Pension Fund, and the Federation Council.[43] Then he decreed compensation payments. In the lead-up to the 1996 presidential election Yeltsin issued two decrees raising compensation payments, to R75,000 in January and to R150,000 in April, nearly doubling the minimum pension.[44] Numerous other changes were also made in the formulas for calculating benefits. The overall effect was compression of pensions along with overall downward pressure on their real level, as inflation far outpaced the combined effects of indexation and compensation. By 1998 pensions for the majority in Russia were a virtually flat benefit barely above the poverty level.[45] Some compression of pensions may have been a reasonable policy goal given the financial constraints on the system, but it was pursued in a highly politicized and arbitrary manner that undermined the coherence and predictability of the pension system along with any sense of earned entitlement. In the view of one critical former Duma deputy, because of Yeltsin's control and intrusions, the pension system qua system was destroyed.[46]

The most socially and politically significant failure of the pension system in the 1990s was the accumulation of arrears in payments to pensioners. Already present in 1994, payment arrears grew from 3 percent of entitlements in that year to 9 percent in 1995 and 34 percent in 1996.[47] The minister of Social Protection reported that pensions were delayed up to a month in sixty-three of Russia's eighty-nine regions during 1995, and in 1996 the RLMS (Russian Longitudinal Monitoring Survey) showed that one-third of those eligible had not received pensions in the previous month, and in some regions arrears exceeded 60 percent, meaning that pensioners received only about one-third of expected payments.[48] Arrears were cleared in mid-1997, but mounted again in the fall, sparking some protests in the spring of 1998, though these ended with the arrival of payments. Moreover, substantial variation in arrears across regions, their accumulation in poorer regions, and their concentration in rural areas, delayed payments disproportionately to the poorest. The trends toward regionalization and informalization of the pension system peaked with the 1998 financial crisis, as more regions refused to remit taxes and distributed benefits to pensioners in-kind and by various *ad hoc* means.[49]

The overall effects of these trends were declining real pension levels and rising poverty among pensioners. Minimum pensions at or near the subsistence level might be taken as a measure of the bare adequacy of a pension system. According to official data the minimum in Russia, received by nearly four million pensioners, fell below that level during the 1990s, and after the 1998 financial crisis average pensions also fell below (see table 5.5). Arrears especially constituted a massive failure of the social security system on which millions of Russians depended, a betrayal of public trust.

Pensioners responded in several ways. Those with special access lobbied for exemptions and new entitlements. The influential Union of Veterans gained passage of a law that significantly expanded the social privileges of war and labor veterans, compensating somewhat for their loss of pension income.[50] Civil servants negotiated separate pensions at a high rate of wage replacement, guaranteed by the federal budget. Some pensioners pursued their rights in court, and in at least one particularly egregious case of benefit manipulation they mounted

Table 5.5.   Average and Minimum Old Age Pensions (with Compensation Payments) as % of Pensioners' Subsistence Minimum, Russian Federation, 1993–2001

	1993	1994	1995	1996	1997	1998	1999	6/2000	6/2001*
Min.	79.1	42.8	47.9	82.2	80.0	46.3	53.8	49.1	—
Avg.	136.1	100.8	110.3	126.2	131.5	85.3	81.9	82.9	85

Source: The Pension Fund of the Russian Federation, 2000.
*OECD, Russian Federation: Economic Survey: 2002/5 (February) (Paris: OECD, 2002): 48, estimated.

a broad, successful campaign to challenge the government.[51] But pensioners did not create organizations on any scale dedicated to the broad representation of their interests. Trade unions, which might have played some role here, had little influence on the policy process.[52] The Communists represented pensioners according to their own lights, with an unrealistic restorationist agenda that produce mainly policy deadlock.

Flawed Efforts at Systemic Reform

By the mid-1990s Russian policy makers and pension experts broadly recognized the need not just to address the Pension Fund deficit, but to reform the system. In crafting reform proposals they turned to models of insurance- and market-based pension provision used in the West, while international organizations, primarily the World Bank, advised and aided their efforts. But Russia lacked, or had in only rudimentary form, the administrative and regulatory infrastructures that undergird these systems, and the resulting "institutional deficits" created blocks to successful implementation. Pension experts also found it very difficult to make the necessary projections, for example, about the tax base, numbers of contributors and recipients, partly because the Pension Fund withheld information but mostly because of the economy's instability. Despite these problems the executive remained fairly united around reform proposals in the mid-1990s.

The first major reform proposal, the 1995 "Concept," was prepared by the Ministry of Labor and Social Development and pension specialists and approved by the government.[53] Its main goal was to move the pension system to an insurance basis, tying pensions directly to individuals' contributions and registering contributions in individual accounts. The "Concept" also provided for supplementary, voluntary, privately held, and invested non-state pensions. Overall this was a modest reform, reflecting the belief of Russian pension specialists and policy makers that the "group" nature of the existing pension fund and the poor correlation between earnings/contributions and payments were the main disincentives to workers' participation.[54]

The 1995 Concept constituted a general framework for pension reform that would govern the elaboration of laws and policy documents in the mid-1990s. Even, perhaps especially, at this conceptual level we can see some of the limits of the system's capacities for innovation, of elites' ability to take account of the policy environment. The 1995 Concept failed to address many aspects of that environment. It focused narrowly on insurance mechanisms to solve contribution problems. It largely ignored many other reasons for unwillingness to contribute, such as high levels of distrust in the Pension Fund and government, the unreliability of pension payments, and uncertainty about the future rules of the pension system and the economy generally.[55] There was a disconnect between the guarantees in the document and the rampant payment arrears, arbitrariness, and institutional corruption in the policy environment. A potentially effective reform would have had to address simultaneously problems of tax collection, Pension Fund finances, and public trust in the system. All of these problems were worsening as the reform was elaborated.

The Concept also required institutional and market infrastructure that was absent. Implementing legislation mandated the registering of individual contributions of current workers to the Pension Fund, while the Russian Federation had in place very limited administrative capacity to begin keeping such accounts.[56] According to pension expert Grigorii Degtiarev the legislation left much about the mechanism of personalized registration unclear or imprecise and, "The procedure of individual registration is labor-intensive and expensive, /requiring/ the Pension Fund and its territorial organs to process a huge mass of information."[57] The World Bank provided technical aid for creation of individual accounts, but the necessary technology had been introduced in fewer than one-third of Russia's regions by late 1998.[58] The Pension Fund claimed that the system was fully in place by 2000, a claim that is belied by a well-known incident in which the labor minister challenged fund officials to produce the record of his personal pension contribution account, and they could not.

Legislation based on the Concept also provided for private employer-sponsored professional pension schemes and voluntary individual pension schemes. It assumed that Russia's unstable industrial sector and poorly regulated and volatile financial markets could play a role—though at this point a supplementary one only—in providing pension security. The problems with this assumption are well-specified by a group of Russian pension specialists: "Russian financial markets are almost totally undeveloped, the banking system is very weak, law enforcement is poor, corporate governance is very bad, and protection of shareholders' and creditors' rights is inadequate. If we add macroeconomic instability and high inflation to these failings, then we will have to conclude that saving for retirement on a private basis in Russia is very difficult if not impossible."[59] In fact non-state pension funds fared poorly in Russia's chaotic financial markets. They were subject to corruption. In the 1998 financial crisis all lost money and several collapsed, showing the credibility of doubts about whether the Russian state could construct an adequate regulatory regime for market-based pension provision.[60]

The Conflict over Radical Reform

In 1997, seeking to revitalize pension and other social sector reforms, Yeltsin appointed a group of radical outsiders to oversee or bypass the ministries, ultimately provoking major intragovernmental conflicts. Mikhail Dmitriev, the man appointed as deputy minister of Labor and Social Development and placed in charge of pension reform, was a policy maverick known for his promotion of a radical "Chilean" variant, the rapid transfer of most pension provision in Russia to market-based, or funded, schemes.[61] In funded schemes employees save for their own retirement, usually through investment of pension earnings, and pensions depend on the accumulation in individuals' accounts; the state's role and responsibility are minimized. Dmitriev developed his proposals while a fellow at the Moscow Carnegie Institute, and his appointment and ideas polarized the pension reform debate. The appointment of a key minister whose views were strongly at odds not only with the Duma majority but with much of the government and policy experts, again illustrates the potential of the presidentialist system to introduce changes with little consultation and disrupt the policy process.

World Bank officials also became more involved in the policy process at this point, monitoring an $800 million social protection adjustment loan (SPAL), with progress on pension reform a key conditionality, and providing policy and technical assistance. The Bank did not prescribe the terms of the reform, but it strongly recommended the introduction of funding as well as transition from the existing "defined benefit" system to a notional "defined contribution" system in which benefits would be left unspecified.[62] In the Bank's "optimal structure," the second or main tier would eventually be fully funded, a major departure from the existing system as well as the 1995 Concept.[63] Though less radical than Dmitriev's proposal, the Bank's recommendations pushed in the same direction, encouraging the state to solve the problems of its pension system by transferring at least part of provision to private markets.

The proposal for rapid transition to funding divided the government, with the Labor Ministry internally divided and the Pension Fund and a broad range of independent experts opposing it, while the Ministry of Economics and the Inspectorate for Non-State Pension Funds stood in favor. Much of the criticism was normative. There was substantial opposition to abandoning the redistributive and solidaristic elements of the existing system, to radically weakening the state's role in pension provision.[64] Many also criticized the proposal on feasibility grounds, with Labor Ministry officials arguing that Russian financial markets were not prepared to preserve pension accounts. The process also exacerbated divisions: Dmitriev's commission bypassed both moderates within the Labor Ministry and the Pension Fund, antagonizing their leaders even as his proposals threatened their vested interests in running the existing system. The highly visible involvement of the World Bank, and the pressure for rapid transition to at least partial funding of the pension system, as well as changes in other areas of social policy, also produced resentments.[65] Dmitriev was removed from the pension reform, a compromise draft was produced, and it was approved by the government in May 1988. However, divisions in the government over the 1998 draft remained significant,[66] and the August financial crisis soon brought a halt to reform efforts.

Having lost months in internal policy conflict, the Yeltsin government ended its tenure with poverty among pensioners at record levels and a still-disputed reform program. More rapid agreement within the government would not have made much difference in moving reform forward if the Duma had opposed it. It is worth noting, however, that while the Duma rejected most measures imposing immediate and visible costs on pensioners, it sometimes approved organizational reforms that did not have such consequences, and Yeltsin might conceivably have tried to cultivate a more constructive relationship with legislators. In any event, in 1998, under pressure from the International Monetary Fund (IMF) to balance the Pension Fund budget, the government proposed to shift funds from health and other social insurance funds, then decreed a special temporary tax on nonwage income that had no legal standing.[67] The Primakov government, appointed in September 1998, paid off arrears and compensated pensioners for part of the year's inflation with budget funds and a Sberbank loan, as noted above. The government continued falling back on *ad hoc* measures to fund a faltering pension system.

By contrast with Russia, East European states demonstrated considerably stronger capabilities to carry out pension reform. Poland and Hungary, for example, inherited similarly unviable pension systems. These states also first tried, and failed, to restrict pension eligibility. They then increased expenditures to sustain the system in place while moving on to comprehensive reform proposal, debated the extent of funding, and by 1996 settled on mixed systems. The World Bank played an advisory role in both reforms.[68] There was much less *ad hoc* and parcelized policymaking, and intragovernmental divisions over systemic reform, pitting pro-funding finance ministries against pro-PAYG Labor Ministries, were better contained and effectively mediated.

Accountability and Responsiveness

How accountable was the Russian state, how responsive to pensioners? I have argued that the state was subject to a limited accountability through the electoral mechanism that kept in place pensioners' formal rights and some claim on resources. The executive could not summarily change the statutory base of the pension system (as was done, for example, in Pinochet's Chile and Nazarbaev's Kazakhstan) because of the legislature's opposition. Moreover, the Communists kept the pension issue on the political agenda, and Yeltsin's need to compete with Zyuganov for the presidency pressured him to raise pensions and pay off arrears. As Anders Aslund has argued, pension spending, more or less sustained as a percent of GDP during the 1990s, fared better than some other types of social expenditures, and pensioners suffered lower poverty rates than other vulnerable groups, particularly children.[69] Still, real pension spending was cut drastically, in arbitrary ways, and it left most pensioners barely above the subsistence level. The structure was kept in place but significantly de-funded. Large costs were imposed on pensioners.

THE PUTIN PERIOD: TOWARD A MORE CAPABLE STATE

One of the central goals of this chapter is to determine whether there has been an evolution in the Russian polity from the incoherence of the Yeltsin period toward greater coherence, rationalization, and effectiveness in policymaking and implementation. In the pension sphere there has been such an evolution. Since 1999 arrears have been cleared; pensions have been reliably paid throughout the Federation; and the government has drafted, passed through the legislature, and begun to implement a major reform of the pension system. Why has the Putin administration been more effective than its predecessor? Much did not change between the two periods: reform ideas and agendas remained quite similar, in pension policy and in the social sphere more broadly. Many of the key policy elites remained in place,[70] and staffing of the state administration did not improve markedly. Moreover, all of the social sphere's problems were exacerbated by the 1998 financial collapse. Russia's steady and significant economic growth since then is certainly part of the story, but the state can be effective in providing public goods only if it is able to tax this growing resource base and allocate funds to social provision. It must also design and agree on workable policies that take account of available resources and conditions. The Putin administration has succeeded in both.

Improved State Capacities in Pension Governance

First, the Putin administration began with a blueprint for reform in the social policy sphere, formulated in the Gref program.[71] Most of the principles and proposals in the program's social policy section were not new; they had been developed during the Yeltsin period, by some of the same experts and policy elites. But the program reflected a deeper understanding of the complexities and requirements of these policies; in the words of a man who was involved in social policy formulation across both administrations: "The Gref program involved . . . for the first time in government really deep analysis. . . . In many cases in the 1990s nobody could implement plans because they were technically impossible; with the Gref program there was much deeper analysis of substantive possibilities."[72] The Putin-era government from the beginning proposed more coherent and elaborated pension reform policies than its predecessor. This is surely in part a consequence of learning from the flawed efforts of the Yeltsin period.

Secondly, the new government took a comprehensive approach to the political and economic problems of the pension system, most of which the Yeltsin administration failed either to confront or to resolve. Issues of unreliable payments, distrust of the Pension Fund, high taxes and weak collection, and the structure of the pension system itself were all addressed. The government treated these as a set of linked problems that had to be resolved if participation in a system of state-mandated pension provision was to be restored. In other words, it took much fuller account of the policy environment and background information.

The Pension Fund cleared arrears in 1999, and has since paid pensions regularly throughout the Federation. It has delivered phased payment increases that have compensated for inflation and gradually raised real pension levels. By 2002 average pensions stood slightly above the pensioners' subsistence minimum. While the government continued to rely on a combination of indexation and compensation payments, the system was made less arbitrary. It should be stressed that these increases have been modest: payments to pensioners have remained quite low in real terms, while welfare state effort in this area—the percent of GDP spent on pensions—has not risen above the levels of the 1990s (see table 5.4). Still, real spending increased significantly with economic growth, and pensions again became a reliable source of cash income provided by state institutions to older Russians and their households.

Predictable pension payments are premised on more effective tax collection, and here problems of the excessively high payroll tax level, evasion, and minimal compliance were addressed. Legislation was passed that unified and slightly lowered the social security tax, and restructured it to regress against wages. Employers who report high average wage bills pay steeply reduced social tax rates (from 35 percent on incomes to R100,000 down to 5 percent on those above R600,000), giving them incentives to report the full wages of their higher-paid employees. The new tax system, introduced in January 2001, is designed both to improve collection and to generate for the state information about actual wage levels and upper-bracket incomes that was obscured in the transition economy. It is essentially a state-capacity building measure. The new social security tax, combined with the 13 percent flat income tax, gives Russia a markedly regressive tax structure.

New rules, designed to address incentive problems for pensioners, also eased restrictions on the size of pensions relative to average wages. Such new

Table 5.6. Tax Receipts of the Pension Fund, 1991–2000 (Trillions of Rubles for 1993–1997; Billion New Rubles from 1998)

1993	1994	1995	1996	1997	1998	1999	2000	2001
10.2	36.1	73.7	115.1	151.1	149.1	250.4	379.3	494.9

Sources: *Obzor ekonomicheskoi politiki v Rossii za 1999 g.* (Moscow: TEIS, 2000), 301; *Sotsial'noe polozhe-nie i uroven' zhizhi naseleniia Rossii: Statisticheskii Sbornik.* 2001 (Moscow: Goskomstat, 2001), 157; *Rossiiskii statisticheskii ezhegodnik* (Moscow: Goskomstat, 2002), 198; figures exclude payments from federal budget.

incentives have been combined with broader measures to improve tax compliance, discussed by Gerald Easter (chapter 2, this volume), including efforts to rein in the oligarchs and limit abusive tax concessions. Pension Fund receipts have improved significantly under the new social security tax structure (see table 5.6), with the fund running surpluses. There are claims that the amount of legal earnings has increased, but it remains to be seen whether pervasive patterns of minimal compliance have changed; in March 2001 Pension Fund head Zurabov reported that 60 percent of employers were paying minimal contributions that would make employees eligible for "subsistence-level pensions at best."[73]

The Kasyanov government also confronted the massive reputational and credibility problems of the Pension Fund. Most importantly, it transferred the collection of social security taxes from the fund to the tax service, so that there is external oversight and accounting of contribution inflows, as well as potentially more effective collection. There were extended discussions of collapsing the social security funds into the budget, and proposals to simply eliminate the fund. Pension Fund head Zurabov effectively used both the financial weight and informational monopoly of the fund to preserve its independence, but he was placed under pressure to improve performance and accountability. The movement toward funded pension accounts, at least some of which would be managed independently, also subjected the fund to potential competition, forcing the management to defend its credibility as the main guarantor of pension security. The fund responded, both with more efficient payment of pensions and with an innovative effort to create a version of Medicare for Russian pensioners. Problems of credibility and transparency, however, have remained serious. A 2003 ROMIR (Russian Public Opinion and Market Research) Monitoring poll showed that more than three-quarters of the public distrusted the fund. At least one pension expert who worked closely with the government on technical calculations for the reform program regarded pension finances as a "black box."[74]

The executive under Putin was also more consultative with the broader expert community in its policy formulation process. According to one government advisor, "Four people created the Gref program, but they worked for several months and discussed it with many people. They sent letters to many research institutes asking for materials—executive summaries—of what researchers proposed for the national economy and for social programs. Most institutes got these letters."[75] This was a serious effort to get in distilled form the accumulated knowledge, at least from the Moscow institutes, of the transition years. In the preliminary meetings as well there were broad consultations with people of varied perspectives. The document itself, with the final policy recommendations, was, however, as the quote suggests, written by a very narrow group from or closely connected to the executive, who continued to dominate policy initiative in the social sphere. This was a more inclusive and consultative, but still narrowly dominated, policy process.

One especially good example of the improved capacity to formulate policy relates to management of funded pension accounts. During the Yeltsin period there was a serious proposal by a newly appointed deputy minister to move immediately to a Chilean-style, almost fully funded system, with little prior discussion. During the Putin period there was a two-year-long debate over the extent of funding, the risks, the available mechanisms and agencies for managing funded accounts, and the kinds of regulations and guarantees that could or should be provided by the state, a discussion broadly informed by international experience.[76] Leaving aside the wisdom of this policy direction, the discussion was far more substantive, and produced more feasible and potentially effective policies.

Constructing a Compromise on Systemic Pension Reform

The Putin executive was, like its predecessor, divided over movement toward a funded (accumulative) pension system, but it managed to construct a compromise through the use of internal conciliation mechanisms. The major protagonists, Mikhail Dmitriev, this time more appropriately placed in the Ministry of Economic Development and Trade, and Pension Fund head Zurabov, were divided on both ideological and instrumental grounds. Dmitriev and the Economic Development Ministry favored a larger funded component to minimize the pension system's pressures on the federal budget, and to maximize investment of pension funds in order to deepen capital markets and promote economic growth. Zurabov favored retention of a larger insurance element and the Pension Fund as predominant manager of funds, and was supported by the much weaker Labor Ministry. In a policy process approximating those used in Eastern Europe, a conciliation council, the National Council on Pension Reform, was convened under the prime minister to resolve the standoff (dubbed the "Pension War") and move the reform along. Ministry and fund lobbied the legislature on behalf of competing reform drafts. The World Bank was discouraged from taking a direct part, easing tensions over external intervention (though the Bank's earlier interventions had broadly set the reform agenda).[77]

The compromise broadly resembled that discussed in 1998, combining distributive and accumulative elements, showing again that the Yeltsin period had laid the groundwork. The system had three tiers: a basic, guaranteed pension that was redistributive; individual insurance accounts; and investment accounts for all but those nearing retirement. It was by comparative international standards a modest reform, with only 2–3 percent of contributions initially going to the funded component, a smaller part than most countries redirect. Still, the amount of money involved was quite significant, with anticipated accumulation of R35 billion in 2002 and R80 billion by 2004, increasing gradually to an estimated 35 percent of GDP by 2040.[78] Initially, the Pension Fund would administer all three components. The outcome was clearly a compromise: the Economic Development Ministry got pension investment accounts; the Pension Fund got them limited in size at least initially. In sum, at least in this case Putin-era elites were not more cohesive in their policy preferences, but the process was more effective at promoting compromise.

Finally, in the Putin period the Duma ceased to function as a veto actor. As Gerald Easter points out, the 1999 Duma election ended the Left's dominance and "made it possible to transform the legislative branch from a constant opponent to an ally of the executive branch in the implementation of social reforms."[79] Whereas Yeltsin had treated the Duma as a hostile force, Putin assiduously cultivated allies there, bringing together rival parties under the executive's tutelage and constructing a dominant pro-presidential block that was committed to the government's agenda. Passage of the pension reform through the Duma was nevertheless a long and contested process, with the last and most contentious bill, on investment of the accumulative part of the pension, delayed for months.

Implementing Reforms

There remain major questions about Russia's capacities to implement the new pension system, both about the technical capabilities of the Pension Fund to process and generate the necessary information, and about the adequacy of markets, financial, and regulatory structures. Only months after the investment law was passed, the World Bank issued a report on the reform's design and implementation that featured a litany of doubts about the Russian financial system's ability to handle private investment of pension funds. According to the report:

the private investment of pension funds requires financial safeguards not currently present.... The weakness of financial and capital markets poses serious risks for the shift to the private sector.... A well-functioning government securities market is not in place to circumvent financial market weakness.... Regulatory structures are weak and pose risks for reform.... There is a need for a core set of solvent banks and asset custodians...to improve the quality of asset managers and the market's absorptive capacities...for an accurate, integrated, national database for tracking credits and accounts.... The scope of available instruments for investment of pension funds needs to be expanded quickly, and requires major reforms of financial markets.[80]

It reflects the doubts, long-voiced by many, about the wisdom of relying on new, still poorly regulated markets for social provision, about the risks of investing trillions of pensioners' rubles in Russian markets. It advises the Russian government, for the time being, to deal with these problems by increasing the amount of pension funds invested abroad.

Accountability and Responsiveness

The Russian state under Putin is more responsible to its population, but not more accountable. It is worth noting that improved payment of pensions has not been linked to greater political influence of recipient groups. On the contrary, the traditionally pensioner-supported Left has been weakened and, as a legislative force, marginalized. The dominant parties in the Duma are "parties of power" created by central political elites, with very shallow roots in the electorate, few and vague programmatic commitments, and virtually no constraining ties to broader societal constituencies. These parties, and the President, will still need votes in future elections, so electoral considerations provide one motive for restoring pension payments. One senses, though, that the larger motives have to do with strengthening the state, improving tax compliance, and gaining the confidence of the population in the state-run pension system so that it will invest pension savings in the long term.

Society has also been weakly represented in the system's reform. The institutions that usually represent current and future pensioners in democratic policy processes—trade unions, Labor Ministry, pensioners' organizations—all of which typically defend solidaristic and redistributive principles—are comparatively weak in Russia and have played a peripheral role in the reform.[81] The Pension Fund has defended solidaristic principles, but the reform debate most resembled a struggle between the fund and the Ministry of Economic Development and Trade, each with its own primary agendas, in which the interests of pensioners were at best secondary. It was a process in which "state agencies vigorously lobb/ied/ each other, crowding out /most/ non-governmental voices and constituencies."[82] There was broader representation of social organizations on the National Pension Council, but the council was created too late in the process to have much influence on policy formulation.[83] The public played little part, and it is not clear that many would have supported these reforms. Available evidence from public opinion polls indicates that, while many people recognize the need for pension system reform, most distrust the financial institutions that will now play a role in pension security as well as the government's intentions.[84] With a more cooperative Duma, the government is in fact subject to fewer constraints in reforming the social sphere, in weakening both the inherited obligations of the state and the entitlements of society, than it was in the Yeltsin period.

CONCLUSION: EXPLAINING IMPROVED STATE CAPABILITIES

Why has the Russian state under Putin been more effective than its predecessor in providing pension security? How has it built stronger distributive capacities? We will first review the failures of pension provision and reform in the Yeltsin period, then their comparative success under Putin.

I have argued that the Russian state in the Yeltsin period could not respond effectively to the crisis of its pension system for several key reasons: It lacked the capacity to tax and allocate enough of the financial resources available in the system to fund adequate pension provision. State elites were divided over the directions reform should take, and the legislature in any case rejected most proposals. The key institutions of the pension system were unregulated or corrupt. Presidential unilateralism contributed to the system's disorganization and opacity. The resulting failures, particularly low and compressed pension payments and arrears, progressively undermined the pension system.

Russian society was not inert in the face of state failures; instead as Bela Greskovits has argued for the transitional economies more broadly, many responded to hardship by escape.[85] The large costs imposed on pensioners ramified through the system as younger and higher-income workers and their employers defected from state-mediated social security mechanisms, further diminishing the state's distributive capacities, its ability to tax and allocate resources and provide public goods. As Peter Evans argues, states may be largely autonomous of societal accountability, but "a state that is only autonomous would lack both sources of intelligence and the ability to rely on decentralized private implementation."[86] Rather, the connections between states and societies can be mutually empowering. It is significant here that Putin, in his campaign to strengthen the Russian state, has stressed efforts to restore the credibility of social security programs and has used their tax structures to craft incentives for the legalization of incomes.

Some scholars have argued that the state's failure to pay pensions was a result not of weakness but of indifference to the needs of a passive society, or a strategic choice that allowed powerful economic actors to evade taxes at the expense of pensioners.[87] While this view has a certain plausibility, the evidence seems stronger that the state could not collect taxes. Easter and others argue that state institutions lacked the ability to monitor transactions, and a detailed study by Shleifer and Treisman shows that state agencies repeatedly tried and failed to pressure large tax debtors.[88] There was deep concern within state agencies, not so much about the well-being of pensioners as about the defection from the social security system, and constant discussion about reforms and incentives that would bring back especially middle and higher-income strata. This concern was central to every discussion of pension reform from 1995 through the Putin period, and it was increasingly linked with the potential for accumulated pension savings to fund economic development. In the end, it seems that the inability of the Pension Fund and other federal agencies to collect, administer, and allocate funds was the major cause of arrears and low payments. Even if they faced little effective protest on the streets or at the ballot box, state officials were deeply concerned about the corrosive effects of pension system failures for the state.

The Putin administration succeeded in reconstructing both the political and fiscal dimensions of the state's distributive capacities. It improved capabilities to collect social security wage taxes by simplifying the tax structure, reassigning collection responsibilities, giving employers strong financial incentives to report high incomes, and reliably providing a public good (i.e., pension payments) in exchange for tax payments. As other chapters in this volume show, it has also limited tax concessions to powerful economic actors, and demanded uniformity in social security administration from regions. It improved monitoring of the Pension Fund, and increased political and competitive pressures on the fund's leadership. It has built some of the institutional and regulatory infrastructure for a reformed pension system, though major questions about its ability to implement the new system remain.

The state's policymaking capabilities have also improved. Here the stabilization of both political and macroeconomic environments has contributed greatly. The transitional nature of the policy environment under Yeltsin, which we have seen in the pension sphere—the collapse of old institutions for pension provision, the hurried creation and poor design of new ones, economic instability and governmental arbitrariness, the effort to implement internationally promoted market reform models while simultaneously creating the instruments for these models—made planning and projection especially difficult. The resulting policies were often piecemeal and infeasible, and did little to respond to pensioners' problems. By contrast, Western states during the Great Depression relied on and expanded capacities in place to address the problems of severe economic downturns; while the East European states' economies had stabilized before they set out to transform social sector institutions in new directions adopted from market models.

The state has also improved its policymaking capabilities by developing a more regularized, substantive, and consultative policy process, and by utilizing institutional mechanisms for conflict resolution to achieve compromise and move forward on long-term reforms. Here the institutional power of the presidency has been key. Yeltsin used those powers, of decree, appointment, and intrusion, in ways that made policy in the pension sphere *ad hoc* and arbitrary, shielded the Pension Fund and its finances from scrutiny, and exacerbated policy divisions. Abuse of executive power damaged policy coherence, and contributed to further weakening the state's distributive capacities. The power of the presidency was used in ways that militated against compromise or the building of consensus, either with the legislature or within the government. The current President has, by contrast, committed the power of his office to stabilization and state strengthening, to consultation, and coherence, demonstrating that the same institutions can be put to very different uses.

This Russian state is stronger and more effective, but it is both less accountable to its society and explicitly committed to reducing the public sector. It behaves more responsibly in the social sphere, but its program is one of retracting the state from inherited obligations, shrinking its role and responsibilities for social provision, and its capacities for redistribution. The goal is to shift most social provision to individuals and markets, to move to the model of a "subsidiary state" that provides mainly for the poor.[89] The role of the state is being shifted toward creation and regulation of social security markets. The elite discourse about pension reform is only secondarily concerned with the security of pensioners or the state's welfare function; it is centrally concerned with the creation of, and control over, investment mechanisms that will make pension savings available to Russian capital markets. In the words of one critical Russian pension expert, the aim of the reform is "not so much for raising pensions as for developing the economy."[90] Russia is becoming a more strongly regulatory, weakly distributive, state.

NOTES

I would like to thank Timothy Colton, Stephen Holmes, Elena Vinogradova, and members of the Russian Governance Project for comments on earlier drafts of this chapter.

1. *Averting the Old Age Crisis*: *Policies to Protect the Old and Promote Growth* (New York: Oxford University Press, 1994 [for the World Bank]), 284.

2. See OECD, *The Social Crisis in the Russian Federation* (Paris: OECD, 2001), 21–22.

3. On responses to the depression see Margaret Weir and Theda Skocpol, "State Structures and the Possibilities for 'Keynesian' Responses to the Great Depression in Sweden, Britain, and the United States," in *Bringing the State Back In*, ed. Peter Evans, Dietrich Rueschemeyer, and Theda Skocpol (New York: Cambridge University Press, 1985), 107–68; on Eastern Europe, see *Balancing Protection and Opportunity: A Strategy for Social Protection in Transition Economies* (Washington, DC: World Bank, 2002); Mitchell A. Orenstein, *Out of the Red: Building Capitalism and Democracy in Postcommunist Europe* (Ann Arbor: University or Michigan Press, 2001).

4. Timothy Colton, "Introduction" (this volume), 8.

5. *Averting the Old Age Crisis*, 39.

6. For a more extended discussion of tax collection see Gerald Easter, "Building Fiscal Capacity" chapter 2 (this volume).

7. Here I am drawing on R. Kent Weaver and Bert A. Rockman, eds., *Do Institutions Matter? Government Capabilities in the United States and Abroad* (Washington, DC: Brookings, 1993).

8. Colton, "Introduction," 8; this point draws on the arguments in Anna Grzymala-Busse and Pauline Luong, "Reconceptualizing the State: Lessons from Post-Communism," *Politics and Society* 30, no. 4 (December 2002): 536.

9. Weir and Skocpol, "State Structures and the Possibilities for 'Keynesian' Responses to the Great Depression in Sweden, Britain, and the United States," 118.

10. See, for example, Paul Pierson, *Dismantling the Welfare State: Reagan, Thatcher, and the Politics of Retrenchment* (New York: Cambridge University Press, 1994).

11. This last point owes much to a paper by Ilean Cashu and Mitchell Orenstein, "The New Politics of Pension Reform in Russia" (Xerox, no date).

12. The chapter is concerned mainly with retirement or labor pensions, including early retirement and various types of privileged pensions. A separate, much smaller category of "social pensions" for those who were not in the labor force, that is, orphans, disabled, etc., remained funded directly from the state budget and provided very low, administratively set payments.

13. The best account remains that in Alistair McAuley, *Economic Welfare in the Soviet Union: Poverty, Living Standards, and Inequality* (Madison: University of Wisconsin Press, 1979), 269–76.

14. By a more inclusive measure, Russian pensions in 1992 were 2.5 percent of GDP below the international average for eighty countries, controlling for population

over age sixty; *Russian Federation toward Medium-Term Viability* (Washington, DC: World Bank, 1996), 68.

15. Tatyana Maleva, ed., *Sovremennye Problemy Pensionnoi Sfery: Kommentarii Ekonomistov I Demografov* (Moscow: Carnegie Center for International Peace, 1997).

16. OECD, *Social Crisis in the Russian Federation*, 118. In a sample of OECD countries pensioners accounted for about 15–19 percent of the population. All have standard pension ages of sixty-five or over; the main factor distinguishing Russia is the low retirement age.

17. See *Averting the Old Age Crisis*, 263.

18. Ben Slay, "The Russian Economy: How Far from Sustainable Growth," *Russia's Uncertain Economic Future* (Washington, DC: JEC, December 2001), 28.

19. Maleva, *Sovremennye Problemy* 1997, 17; the number of employed declined by more than five million between 1991 and 1996 while the number of pensioners grew by more than three million.

20. *Rossiiskaya Gazeta*, August 23, 1995.

21. The Pension Fund was a centralized organization, with a federal office, 88 regional offices, and 2,342 local offices; all contributions were to go to transitional accounts of regional offices, then be distributed to regional, then local social welfare departments. The actual calculation and distribution of pensions was originally assigned to social welfare offices under the Labor Ministry, though these functions were gradually consolidated in the Pension Fund.

22. Hjalte Sederlof, program team leader, Social and Human Development Programs, Europe and Central Asia Region, World Bank; interview by author, Providence, RI, April 29, 1999.

23. See *Rossiisskaia Gazeta*, January 30, 1997.

24. Valentina Bochkareva, senior researcher, Institute for Social and Economic Problems of the Population, Russian Academy of Sciences; interview by author, Moscow, February 1999.

25. *Rossiskie Vesti*, January 30, 1997.

26. *Radio Free Europe/Radio Liberty*, April 8, April 10, 1997.

27. See Andrei Shleifer and Daniel Treisman, *Without a Map: Political Tactics and Economic Reform in Russia* (Cambridge: MIT Press, 2000), 143–56.

28. Grigorii Pavlovich Degtiarev, "Pensionniia reforma v Rossii: 1991–1999 gody," (paper prepared for the Russian Governance Project, 2001), 13–19.

29. On this point see Kathryn Stoner-Weiss, "Resistance to the Central State on the Periphery," chap. 4 (this volume).

30. Elena Romanova, "Pension Arrears in Russia: The Story behind the Figures," *Russian Economic Trends* 8, no. 4 (1999): 15–23.

31. Interview with Social Welfare Minister Bezleplina, *Rossiskiie Vesti*, 23 April 1998, 1–2.

32. *Rossisskaia Gazeta*, May 30, 1997, 2. This proposal was also supported by a representative of one of the more sophisticated pensioners' organizations; Vladimir Petrov, assistant to the president, Russian Pensioners' Party; interview by Elena Vinogradova, Moscow, June 1999.

33. Joel S. Hellman, "Winners Take All: The Politics of Partial Reform in Postcommunist Transitions," *World Politics* 50, no. 2 (January 1998): 203–34.

34. Elena Vinogradova, "Public Administration in Social Services: The Need and Capacities for Reform," in *Social Capital and Cohesion in Post-Soviet Russia*, ed. Judyth Twigg and Kate Schecter (Armonk, NY: M.E. Sharpe, 2003), 50–72. These surveys did not, however, include Pension Fund offices.

35. Romanova, "Pension Arrears."

36. Maleva, *Sovremennye Problemy*.

37. *Russian Economic Development* (Moscow: Institute of Macroeconomic Research and Forecasts, Higher School of Economics, 1999), 11.

38. OECD, *Social Crisis*, 119.

39. For example, the 1998 Pension Reform Program called for the standard eligibility age to be increased by five years over a ten-year period, beginning in 2002; while early retirement ages for those working in difficult conditions would be phased out beginning in 1999. For strategies of pension reform in democratic systems that rely on delaying and phasing in cuts, see Pierson, *Dismantling the Welfare State*.

40. *Foreign Broadcast Information Service: Daily Report, Central Eurasia*, February 21, 1997.

41. Andrea Chandler, "Presidential Veto Power in Post-Communist Russia, 1994–1998," *Canadian Journal of Political Science* 34, no. 3 (September 2001): 487–516.

42. Andrea Chandler, "The Origins of Post-Communist Russia's Pension Crisis, 1990–1993" (paper presented at the thirty-one National Convention of the American Association for the Advancement of Slavic Studies, St. Louis, MO, November 1999), 16–17.

43. See, for example, *Rossiiskie Vesti*, February 14, 1997.

44. See *Rossisskaia Gazeta*, April 17, 1996; the April edict No. 5550, "On Urgent Measures to Improve Pension Provision for RF Citizens." On Yeltsin's calculated attention to the pension arrears problem as well as other social issues, in the months before the election, see *Epokha El'tsina: Ocherki Politicheskoi Istorii* (Moscow: Vagrius, 2001): 552–64.

45. OECD, *Social Crisis*, 119. The ratio between the minimum and average pension fell to 1.72 in 1998 and 1.37 in early 2000.

46. Anatolii Golov, director, Institute of Social Policy, interview with author, Moscow, June 24, 2002.

47. Romanova, "Pension Arrears in Russia," 15–16.

48. See *Rossisskaia Gazeta*, May 8, 1996; Irina Denisova, Maria Gorban, and Ksenia Yudaeva, "Social Policy in Russia: Pension Fund and Social Security," *Russian Economic Trends* 8, no. 1 (1999): 13; Romanova, "Pension Arrears."

49. Marina Baskakova, senior researcher, Moscow Center for Gender Studies, Russian Academy of Sciences, interview by author, Moscow, February 4, 1999.

50. See the law, "O Veteranakh," *Sobrianie Zakonodatel'stva*, no. 3, January 16, 1995, 168; many of the law's guarantees, however, went out as unfunded mandates and were not fulfilled. On the pervasive phenomena of privileges, social and other, see *Epokha El'tsina*, 428–29.

51. See Ilean Cashu and Mitchell Orenstein, "The Pensioners' Court Campaign: Making Law Matter in Russia," *East European Constitutional Review* 10, no. 4 (Fall 2001): 1–7.

52. On the situation with unions, and the largely sham experiments with tripartism in the early 1990s, see Walter D. Connor, *Tattered Banners: Labor, Conflict, and Corporatism in Postcommunist Russia* (Boulder, CO: Westview, 1996); Linda J. Cook, *Labor and Liberalization: Trade Unions in the New Russia* (New York: Twentieth Century Fund, 1997).

53. For a discussion of the 1995 Concept, see V. I. Mudrakov, "Programma Pensionnoi Reformy v Rossiiskoi Federatisii vstupila v sily," *Rossiisskaia Gazeta*, August 23, 1995.

54. Valentina Bochkareva, senior researcher, Institute for Social and Economic Problems of the Population, Russian Academy of Sciences; interview by Elena Vinogradova, Moscow, June 25, 1998; Oleg A. Shenkarev, deputy, member of Committee on Labor and Social Policy, Russian Federation State Duma; interview by author, Moscow, February 3, 1999.

55. For related arguments see Denisova et al., "Social Policy in Russia," 16–18.

56. See the 1996 Law on Individual (Personalized) Registration in the System of State Pension Insurance in *Sobrianie Zakonodatel'stva*, 14, April 1, 1996, 140.

57. Degtiarev, "Pensionnaia Reforma v Rossii," 31–32.

58. World Bank Public Information Document (PID), "Russian Federation—Pension Reform Implementation Project," prepared October 15, 1998. According to the PID, at this point, "The PF has already designed /introduction of individual accounts/ in 26 of 89 subjects of the Federation."

59. Denisova et al., "Social Policy in Russia," 15. There comments were actually directed to the 1998 reform, which relied more heavily on market investment.

60. Tamara Pushkina and Maria Turovskaia, "Negosudarstvennym pensionnym fomdam trebuetcia gosudarstvennaia podderzhka, *Chelovek I Trud* 4 (1999): 36–37; Marina Baskakova, senior researcher, Moscow Center for Gender Studies, Russian Academy of Sciences, interview by author, Moscow, February 4, 1999; Alexie S. Avtonomov, director of Legal Department, Foundation for the Development of Parliamentarism in Russia; interview by author, Moscow, February 1, 1999.

61. The Chilean pension system provides the model for neoliberal reformers; it is, however, strictly regulated, and its exceptional claims to success have been questioned. On regulation of the Chilean pension system see *Averting the Old Age Crisis*, chap. 6.

62. On NDC systems see Louise Fox, "Pension Reform in Post-Communist Transition Economies," in *Transforming Post-Communist Political Economies*, ed. Joan Nelson, Charles Tilly, and Lee Walker (Washington, DC: National Academy Press, 1997) 370–84.

63. World Bank, "Report and Recommendation of the President of the International Bank for Reconstruction and Development to the Executive Directors on a Proposed Social Protections Adjustment Loan in the Amount of US$800 million to the Russian Federation," June 5, 1997, 44.

64. Degtiarev, "Pensionnaia Reforma v Rossii," 36–38; Baskakova, interview by author, Moscow, February 4, 1999.

65. Vladimir Gimpelson, director, Center for Labour Market Studies, Higher School of Economics; interview with author, Moscow, June 26, 2002.

66. See, for example, "Zadachi I osnovnye polozheniia khoda pensionnoi reformy v Rossiiskoi Federatsii," *Pensiia*, 7, 22 (1998): 14–16.

67. See *Rossiiskaia Gazeta*, July 25, 1998 (Decree 800).

68. Katharina Muller, *The Political Economy of Pension Reform in Central-Eastern Europe* (Northampton, MA: Elward Elgar, 1999).

69. See Anders Aslund, "Social Problems and Policy in Postcommunist Russia," in *Sustaining the Transition: The Social Safety Net in Postcommunist Russia*, ed. Ethan Kapstein and Michael Mandelbaum (New York: Council on Foreign Relations, 1997).

70. Examples of holdovers are Yevgeniy Gontmakher, chief of the Social Development Department of the Government Apparatus; Mikhail Dmitriev, vice-minister of Economic Development and Trade with responsibility for the social sector; and Deputy Prime Minister for the Social Sphere Matvieyenko.

71. "Prioritetnye Zadachi Pravitelstva Rossiiskoi Federatsii na 2000–2001 gody po Realizatsii Osnovnykh Napravlenii Sotsial'no-Ekonomicheskoi Politiki Pravitelstva Rossiiskoi Federatsii na Dolgosrochnyiu Perspectivy," Tsentr Strategicheskikh Razrabotok, 2000 g. (Gref Plan), accessed at: www.kommersant.ru/documents/high-priority-task.htm; "Proekt Strategiia Rossiiskoi Federatsii do 2010 goda," Fond 'Tsentr Strategicheskikh Razrabotok, 2000 g, accessed at: www.kommersant.ru/documents/Strat1.htm.

72. Author's interview with government advisor, Moscow, June 6, 2001.

73. See *Rossisskaia Gazeta*, March 20, 2001.

74. ROMIR poll cited in "Zurabov Risks Pensions," Gazeta.ru. Aug. 23, 2003, at www.gazeta.ru; author's interview with pension expert, Moscow, June 2002.

75. Svetlana Misikhina, expert, Municipal Economic and Social Reform, TACIS, interview with author, Moscow, June 7, 2000.

76. Anatoli Kolesnikov, deputy chair of the Board of the Pension Fund of Russia, interview with author, Moscow, June 2001.

77. An essentially similar version of this process was reported by a range of interviewees and reflected in the press.

78. World Bank, *Pension Reform in Russia: Design and Implementation* (Human Development Sector Unit: Europe and Central Asia Region, November 2002, at www.worldbank.org; esp. p. 24.

79. Easter, "Building Fiscal Capacity," chap. 2 (this volume).

80. *Pension Reform in Russia*; quoted material is from various pages of the report. The report is ironic, in light of the Bank's major role in pushing this reform forward since the mid-1990s.

81. Informed observers generally agreed on the peripheral role played by these institutions.

82. Tim Colton, "Governance Project Proposal" (Xerox, 2000); voices from the private financial sector were heard, but remain difficult to document.

83. Trade unions, veterans', and employers' organizations were represented, though the council was dominated by government and Duma members; "Sostav natsional'nogo soveta pri Prezidente Rossiiskoi Federatsii pri pensionnoi reforme" (mimeo, 2001).

84. See "Russian Surveys on Pension Reform Support Examined," *FBIS Daily Report: Eurasia*, July 18, 2001, citing *Vremya MN*, July 18, 2001.

85. Bela Greskovits, *The Political Economy of Protest and Patience: East European and Latin American Transformations Compared* (Budapest: Central European University Press, 1998). Greskovits's main point is that the dominance of the escape strategy explains political stability in transitional systems.

86. Peter Evans, *Embedded Autonomy: State and Industrial Transformation* (Princeton, NJ: Princeton University Press, 1995), 12.

87. See, for example, Michael McFaul, "The Political Economy of Pension Reform in Russia," in *Left Parties and Social Policy in Postcommunist Europe*, ed. Linda Cook, Mitchell Orenstein, and Marilyn Rueschemeyer (Boulder, CO: Westview, 1999).

88. Schleifer and Treisman, *Without a Map*.

89. For the concept of the "subsidiary state," see "Proekt Strategiia razvitiia Rossiiskogo Federatsii do 2010 g." (Moscow: Tsentr Strategicheskikh Razrabotok, 2000) downloaded at: www.kommersant.ru/documents/Strat1.htm.

90. Author's interview with pension expert, Moscow, June 6, 2002.

Chapter Six

Governing the Banking Sector

Timothy Frye

For many observers the banking sector offers a paradigmatic case of business state relations in Russia in the 1990s. Formed by seizing assets from collapsing state and party organizations, private banks grew from bit players in Russian politics in the early 1990s, to become a crucial source of state finance in the middle of the decade. During the glory days, the cliché of Russia's "high flying" banks became a staple of news reports. Yet the shaky institutional foundations on which Russian banks were built soon proved their downfall. Having bet heavily against a devaluation of the ruble, new private banks suffered an ignominious crash in August 1998 that impoverished many ordinary citizens and revealed the fault lines of the Russian transition. Since the crash, Russia's banks have begun to rebound, but governance on the sector remains weak, particularly in comparison to other countries in the region.

Despite agreement on the frailty of banking institutions in Russia, there is heated debate about the source of this weakness. The dominant views root poor governance in private economic interests that captured the state or in a rapid economic liberalization that impoverished the state.[1] Evidence from Russia and the region, however, casts doubt on important elements of these arguments. The former raises as many questions as it answers, while the latter has little empirical support.

This chapter traces how budget deficits, political struggles between neo-communist and anticommunist elites, and state ownership of banks shaped the incentives of bankers and state officials to strengthen (or more often weaken) regulatory institutions in Russia. It finds that budget deficits generated largely by subsidies to other sectors of the economy encouraged private banks to lend to the state rather than to private firms. As a result, banks expressed little demand for institutions to protect their property rights or to promote lending to the private sector. A focus on how banks translated budget deficits generated by other, more powerful interest groups in the early 1990s into leverage over policy later in the decade offers a twist on traditional capture theory. Relatively weak social groups can come to have vast influence over policy by feeding off the rents created by other groups.

In addition, intense political struggles between powerful neocommunist and anticommunist elites not only blocked the passage of legislation to strengthen regulatory institutions; they also heightened policy uncertainty by increasing the possibility of sharp swings in policy. Policy uncertainty encouraged banks and regulators to adopt short-term strategies at odds with the long-term requirements of building capable state institutions. This intense political polarization between neocommunists and anticommunist elites sheds light on why, in contrast to many theories of regulation, private banks continued to weaken state institutions even after they grew wealthy and politically influential.

Finally, state ownership undermined governance by allowing state banks to use their privileged access to the state to inhibit competition, while it also exacerbated conflicts of interest between regulators and the regulated. This insight reinforces the importance of drawing sharp boundaries between public and private entities in transition environments. The ongoing influence of state ownership also provides a partial answer to the puzzle of why governance over the banking sector has improved only marginally in recent years, despite a steep drop in the political power of private banks after the financial crash of August 1998.

THE QUALITY OF GOVERNANCE

Well-governed banking sectors have high levels of transparency, clearly defined property rights between borrowers and savers, and a level playing field for all. The organization best able to govern banks is the state due to its economies of scope and scale and monopoly on coercion.[2] To promote good governance, states protect property rights inherent in contracts between banks and their clients, and also ensure that banks abide by a set of prudential norms that reduce systemic risks. This is no easy task as indicated by the frequency of banking crises in middle-income countries, the savings and loan debacle in the United States, and the repeated bailouts of banks in Japan in the 1990s.

Creating good governance over financial markets in the postcommunist world has been more difficult than expected, especially in Russia.[3]

As in all command economies, the Soviet Union operated with a monobank system consisting of a state bank (Gosbank SSSR) that operated both as a central bank and a commercial bank, but primarily performed accounting functions for the state plan. In 1988 the government created a handful of *spetz* banks, such as Agroprombank and Promstroibank to fund specific state programs in agriculture and industry, respectively. Through the 1988 Law on Cooperatives, the government allowed the creation of "zero banks" that were formed ostensibly from private capital, but reportedly were often financed by elements of the Communist Party. In addition, it permitted firms to open "pocket banks" that acted as accounting (or money laundering) agents for their founding companies. Pocket banks lent almost exclusively to their founding companies and had few ties to other firms. By 1992, the number of licensed banks in Russia exceeded thirteen hundred, including hundreds of small pocket banks, hundreds of weakly capitalized zero banks, hundreds of banks closely attached to state bodies, and a few large state banks.[4]

Primary responsibility for governing these banks fell to the Central Bank of Russia (CBR). Yet this task was complicated as the CBR was intertwined with commercial banks. Many former branch banks of the Soviet-era Central Bank transformed themselves into private commercial banks. In addition, the largest banks, Sberbank, Agroprombank, and Promstroibank, remained in state hands.

Since 1990, the Central Bank has been a prominent player in Russian politics. In addition to being the majority owner of the country's dominant bank, Sberbank, the Central Bank has offices in all of Russia's eighty-nine regions, controls the money supply, and manages currency markets. In the early 1990s, the head of the CBR, Viktor Gerashchenko, was a vocal and colorful opponent of President Yeltsin's stabilization policies who enjoyed strong support in parliament. The CBR also has a large and well-paid workforce. According to the Audit Chamber of the Russian Federation, the CBR has eighty-six thousand employees, thirty times more than the Bank of England, and three times more than the Federal Reserve of the United States. The wage bill of the CBR in 1998 was $1.2 billion, or roughly $14,000 per year per employee. In 1997, then head of the CBR Sergei Dubinin earned an official salary of $240,000, almost twice as much as then head of the U.S. Federal Reserve Bank Alan Greenspan.[5]

Despite the size and wealth of the CBR, by most yardsticks—expert ratings of the quality of governance, the frequency of banking crises, compliance with international regulatory standards, the extent of lending to the private sector, the existence of nonperforming banks, and the extent of preferential treatment— the banking sector in Russia is governed poorly, even in comparison to others in the region. Each year the European Bank for Reconstruction and Development

(EBRD) rates the quality of banking institutions on a scale where (1) equals "little progress beyond the establishment of a two-tiered system; (2) equals significant liberalization and interest rates and credit allocation; and limited use of direct credits; (3) equals substantial progress in establishment of bank insolvency; full interest rate liberalization and significant lending to private enterprises; (4) equals significant movement of banking laws and regulations to BIS (Bank of International Settlements) standards; well-functioning banking competition and effective prudential supervision and 4+ equals standard and performance norms of advanced industrial economies; full convergence of banking laws and regulations with BIS standards." The average score for the twenty-five economies in transition from 1990–2002 was 2.1, while for Russia it was 1.7. In 2000, the average score for all countries was 2.5, while for Russia it was 1.7. Between 2000 and 2003, only four countries in the region had weaker banking institutions than did Russia according to this EBRD ranking.

The financial crash of August 1998 provides the most striking example of weak governance on the banking sector. The CBR failed to monitor the vast exposure of Russian banks to swings in the exchange rate. Private Russian banks often backed their loans to buy state treasury bonds known as (GKOs) with ruble-based forward contracts with other Russian banks. Some of these contracts were fictitious and were used to reassure foreign investors that Russian banks could afford the massive dollar-denominated loans that they had taken on to buy GKOs. Given the size of the loans relative to the banking sector, it is hard to believe that the CBR was unaware of this problem.[6] The vast unsecured borrowing of foreign currency by Russian banks with the tacit approval of the CBR ensured that even small changes in the exchange rate would bring the liabilities of the banks to the fore. The crash of August 1998, was in many respects, a banking crisis. One observer noted: "The default/devaluation by the government was precipitated by the imminent collapse of several leading banks. The August default/devaluation should thus be viewed as a desperate remedial measure, rather a cause of the sector's insolvency."[7] Another noted: "In our view, the banking sector was already insolvent prior to the crisis, and contributed directly and indirectly to it."[8] This governance failure robbed a small and nascent middle-class of its meager savings and impoverished many who had placed their nest eggs in Russian banks. Moreover, it was a particularly clear example of the failure of the Russian state.

POTENTIAL EXPLANATIONS

Observers have offered several general arguments for the weakness of state institutions in Russia that can also be applied to the banking sector.[9] The most frequently cited reason for the stunted development of governance on the banking sector is that oligarch-dominated banks exerted pressure on the state to keep regulations weak and opaque. Indeed, there is good evidence that large banks linked to powerful economic interests favored weak governance and got their wish.[10] This state capture explanation, however, also raises several questions. Why would a handful of large banks seek to weaken rather than strengthen the regulatory regime? One economic theory of regulation emphasizes that wealthy and well-organized economic interests support stronger state institutions to protect their property rights.[11] Historical studies from Europe find that property holders often strengthened the state to protect their interests.[12] Based on this argument, some expected that privatization in Russia would clarify property rights and generate demand from property holders for better governance and a more capable state.[13] More cynically, the oligarch banks may have strengthened the state if only to weaken their rivals. Yet, this did not happen.

The oligarch capture explanation raises another point. If the oligarchic banks were the main impediment to better governance, one might have expected rapid progress on banking reform following the crash of oligarch banks in 1998. While the oligarch banks have not disappeared, they have lost much influence to the energy and raw materials lobbies. Nonetheless, governance on the banking sector remains poor.[14] Similarly, in the early 1990s private banks in Russia were bit players, but governance was weak. Finally, it is not clear to what extent the oligarch banks created bad governance or bad governance created the oligarch banks. There is much to be said for the state capture explanation, but it also leaves many questions unanswered.

Others argue that neoliberal reforms have gutted the state, leaving it too poor to govern well.[15] That economic reforms impoverished the Russian state is far from clear. Per capita gross domestic product (GDP) in Russia is roughly one-fifth the Organization for Economic Cooperation and Development (OECD) average, but state spending as a percentage of GDP was roughly similar in both in the 1990s (42 percent versus 48 percent). State spending in middle-income countries outside of the postcommunist world is typically about a quarter of the GDP.[16] In other words, Russia spent like an OECD country on the earnings of a middle-income country. In addition, the most liberal economies in the postcommunist world tend to have the strongest banking institutions. Countries with higher than average scores on the EBRD's four-point Price Liberalization Index in the 1990s had stronger banking institutions according to the EBRD Index of Banking Institutions (2.4 versus 1.1, t = 14.5).[17] If anything, liberal reforms foster better governance in the postcommunist world.

Another explanation emphasizes that the institutional legacy of the Soviet Union left institutions poorly adapted to a market economy.[18] This is true, but countries with similar legacies, like Russia, Ukraine, and Belarus have very different banking sectors. Moreover, this explanation fails to explain why some aspects of banking quickly became rather sophisticated, while others did not. Russian banks traded forward contracts, bought foreign stocks, and played currency markets, even as they took weeks or months to transfer funds.[19]

While many factors have fostered weak governance in the banking sector, this chapter focuses on several that seem especially salient. First, macroeconomic instability is a critical component for creating sound banking sectors. Budget deficits—whether financed through inflation or state treasury bonds—divert the interests of banks from their normal function as intermediaries between savers and borrowers. Because banks in Russia reaped vast gains from various forms of financing the state budget deficit, they expressed little interest in promoting good governance in activities typically associated with banks.[20] Economists have long argued that macroeconomic instability and high budget deficits crowd out lending to the private sector, but they also crowd out demand for good governance.

Perhaps more importantly in the Russian case, budget deficits produced tremendous benefits to banks that turned them from marginal to influential players in politics. This point is important because many have criticized governments in the region for focusing on macroeconomic reforms and neglecting institutional development.[21]

Second, state ownership undermined governance on the banking sector.[22] The two largest banks in Russia, Sberbank and Vneshtorgbank, are majority state-owned, and have dominated almost all segments of the market since 1990.[23] State ownership generated conflicts of interest that blocked regulatory changes that would erode the commanding position of state banks. Politicians also benefited from Sberbank's politically motivated lending and purchases of state treasuries bonds. As state ownership increased after 1998, this explanation helps account for the ongoing difficulties in improving state institutions on the banking sector after August 1998.

Third, political conflict between neocommunist and anticommunist elites led to weak state institutions in at least two ways.[24] First, because neocommunist and anticommunist camps had very different preferences over policy, and it was far from certain which camp would hold power in the future, businesspeople and bureaucrats alike expected drastic swings in policy. Rather than devoting their efforts to the long-term task of building institutions, businesspeople and bureaucrats adopted more short-term strategies, like corruption and asset-stripping.[25] In addition, because political power was roughly balanced between neocommunist and anticommunists, it was very difficult to pass legislation to improve governance. By contrast, in countries where either anticommunist or neocommunist factions dominated, it was easier to pass reform packages, other things being equal, because bargaining took place among factions whose policy preferences were similar.[26]

BRIEF CROSS-COUNTRY ANALYSIS

To begin, I analyze the quality of governance on the banking sector in twenty-five postcommunist countries from 1990 to 2002. If these three arguments hold across countries, it is likely that they hold within Russia as well. I briefly examine how the three factors highlighted above are related to the quality of banking institutions as measured by the EBRD's Index of Banking Institutions. As noted previously, this measure ranges from 1 to 4.3, depending on assessments made by country specialists at the EBRD.[27] To assess relations between budget deficits and the quality of banking institutions, I divide the sample of twenty-five countries into years in which countries have higher than average and lower than average budget deficits and compare the quality of banking institutions in these two groups. Doing so reveals that countries experiencing higher than average budget deficits in a given year had significantly weaker banking institutions (EBRD 2001). As reported in table 6.1 countries with a larger than average budget deficit have a mean banking institution score of 2.0, while countries with a lower than average budget deficit have a mean score of

Table 6.1. The Argument in Comparative Perspective

	EBRD Bank Score	T-Statistic (p-value)
Budget Balance		
< average	2.0	4.0
> average	2.4	(.0000)
		n = (270)
Political Polarization		
> average	1.8	5.2
< average	2.4	(.0000)
		n = (236)
State Ownership		
> average	2.2	4.0
< average	2.6	(.0001)
		n = (219)

Source: EBRD Transition Report, various years.
Notes: This table reports a comparison of means of bank reform scores for countries with higher than average and lower than average budget balances, rates of political polarization and state ownership in the banking sector. Data are from twenty-five postcommunist countries from the years 1990–2002. No data from Serbia or Mongolia. n = number of observations. Variables described in text.

2.4 (t = 4.0, significant at .0000). Thus, balanced budgets are associated with stronger bank institutions.

I take a similar tack to examine the association between state ownership of banks and the quality of banking institutions. The EBRD provides data on the percentage of assets controlled by state and private banks for each country for most years in the 1990s. In a typical year, the average country has 37 percent of its banking sector assets in state hands. Countries with higher than average portions of the banking sector in state hands have significantly lower quality banking institutions (2.2 versus 2.6, t = 4.0, significant at .0001). This result underscores that state ownership can weaken state institutions.

Political polarization may also attenuate regulation. I measure polarization by the percentage of seats in parliament held by the largest neocommunist (anti-communist) party when an anticommunist (neocommunist) politician controls the executive branch.[28] This measure excludes the reformed communist successor parties of Poland, Hungary, Lithuania, and Slovenia.[29] In many years in the sample, Russia, Bulgaria, Kyrgyzstan, Albania, and Romania have relatively high polarization scores. Countries whose dominant political factions reside within either the neocommunist or anticommunist camp, such as Estonia, Latvia, the Czech Republic, Turkmenistan, and Kazakhstan, tend to have low polarization scores. Countries with higher than average polarization scores have lower-quality banking institutions (1.8 versus 2.4, t = 5.2, significant at .0000).

This brief comparative analysis is hardly definitive, but it provides a benchmark for comparing banking institutions across postcommunist countries. It also identifies three factors that appear to be associated with the quality of banking institutions in the region.[30] The next section traces in more detail how macroeconomic conditions, state ownership, and political polarization shaped the quality of banking institutions in Russia in two periods.[31] From 1990 to 1999, these factors contributed to a poorly governed banking sector and a banking crisis in August 1998. However, when the federal budget turned a surplus and polarization declined after 1999, state officials and private bankers began to address governance problems in earnest for the first time since 1990. Nonetheless, the role of state-owned banks increased after the crash and has limited progress in improving the quality of state institutions on the banking sector.

THE STATE AND THE BANKING SECTOR, 1990–1999

Throughout the 1990s, capital accumulation in the banking sector lay in budgetary instability, rather than in lending to the private sector. As such, banks devoted their energies to extracting resources from the state rather than to creating institutions to govern the market. The means by which banks extracted these rents varied over time, but none generated incentives for banks to invest their efforts in creating more capable state institutions that would encourage lending to the private sector.

Facing great pent-up demand for goods, a large budget deficit, and powerful interest groups seeking subsidies, the first postcommunist government in Russia launched a stabilization program in January 1992. Initial efforts produced few results for society at large as inflation reached over 2000 percent in 1992 and 1200 percent in 1993. This burst of inflation, however, provided vast revenues to the banking sector. By some estimates, the transfer of wealth to banks through hyperinflation reached 6–9 percent of GDP.[32] Banks earned rents by disbursing (or not) government credits granted to specific sectors or firms.[33] Currency speculation also generated great wealth as banks held dollars against the declining value of rubles held by the population.[34] The weakened budget position of the government led to sharp declines in the ruble in the early 1990s. As a main store of hard currency, private banks saw tremendous appreciation in assets held in dollars, marks, and pounds at very little cost.

Banks turned to a new source of revenue in 1994 as the government began financing its deficit via state treasury bonds, or, GKOs. These ruble-denominated bonds had maturities of three, six, and nine months and were seen as a safe source of lending given the government's guarantee of repayment. Having prospered from inflation, the banking community successfully lobbied to exclude foreigners from the market, which greatly increased profits to local banks. In addition, the CBR sold GKOs only to a select group of banks, which concentrated wealth in a few hands. The rates of return on GKOs fluctuated wildly from 20 to 250 percent depending on the market's faith in the ability of the Russian government to make good on the bonds, but the transfer of wealth to the banking sector via state treasure bonds was vast. By some estimates from 1994 to 1998, GKOs provided about $15 billion for the Russian government, but the nominal value of the GKOs issued was about $70 billion, which left $50 billion to the holders of GKOs, mostly private commercial banks and the CBR through Sberbank.[35] Again, the inability of the government to finance its budget led to a vast transfer of wealth from taxpayers to a handful of banks.

In the early 1990s the banking sector prospered beyond its ability to influence state policy. Long-time Yeltsin economic advisor Aleksander Livshitz noted that the banking community played little role in policymaking prior to the mid-1990s.[36] Garegin Tosunian, president of the Association of Russian Banks noted: "the government didn't begin to listen to us until the mid-1990s."[37] The sources of inflation lay not so much in the power of the banking lobby. Rather, banks grew wealthy from inflation sparked by a sympathetic head of the CBR who opened wide the monetary spigot and a government unable to rein in the demands of sectoral lobbies and regional governments.[38] The inflation of the early 1990s generated a formidable banking lobby in the mid-1990s, but in the first years of the transformation, the banking lobby took a back seat to better-organized interests.

Having grown wealthy off distortions in the state budget generated largely by lending to other sectors of the economy, a small group of banks began to extract rents directly from the state by servicing government accounts. By the mid-1990s, many government agencies and regional bodies transferred their accounts to private banks. For example, Oneximbank and Menatep Bank held the lucrative account of servicing the funds of the customs agency and finance ministry respectively, while Most-Bank and Technobank grew wealthy managing the accounts of the Moscow city government. The State Audit Chamber estimated that the banking community earned more than 1.3 billion dollars from this practice in 1995 and 1996.[39]

Some private banks that earned rents from budget deficits in the early 1990s grew wealthier still off the "Loans for Shares" program. A handful of select banks approached the government with the prospect of alleviating the budget deficit by loaning money to the state using valuable state-owned assets as a pledge.[40] To raise revenue quickly and reward supporters in a year prior to elections, the Yeltsin team allowed select banks to run auctions for a controlling packet of shares in some of the largest companies in Russia in 1995. As specific banks also received the right to conduct the auctions, the outcome of the auctions was never in doubt. These banks or their related companies won the auctions with a price just slightly over the minimum established by the state. Oneximbank won the rights to Norilsk Nickel and Sidanko, while Menatep won the bidding for shares in the oil giant, Yukos. The government did not buy back the shares after the agreed upon three-year holding period and the banks eventually took ownership of these valuable assets.[41]

In the 1990s, banks earned great revenue from the inflation tax, state treasury bonds, authorized banking, and in some cases, "loans for shares" auctions. They earned little revenue from the types of borrowing and lending practiced by their nominal counterparts in more mature market economies. One prescient bank analyst noted that these were not banks at all, but "quasi-banks" because they earned little revenue from borrowing and lending.[42] The vast transfer of wealth from taxpayers to banks via hyperinflation and budget deficits "demonstrated to these new banks that real wealth was found in currency speculation, not prudent enterprise lending."[43] Thus, these banks had weak incentives to demand stronger state institutions to support borrowing from and lending to the private sector.

Polarization and the Supply of Regulation

Intense political polarization marked the 1990s in Russia as an anticommunist president tried to push a liberal economic reform program through a parliament largely controlled by groups opposed to these policies. Throughout the decade, the executive branch needed votes from the Communist Party of the Russian Federation and/or the Agrarian Party to pass major legislation.[44] As a result passing laws designed to improve state capacity was very difficult. On laws governing the Central Bank, the privatization of state-owned banks, and bank bankruptcies, the executive and the parliament found little common ground. One example is deposit insurance for banks. All recognized that deposit insurance promised to bring private funds from "under the mattress" into banks, but neither the neocommunist nor liberal factions generated sufficient support from the government and parliament to pass a bill that would guarantee bank deposits despite more than a decade of efforts. Before recounting the twists and turns of the history of attempts to pass a deposit insurance bill in the 1990s, one observer noted: "the draft legislation on deposit insurance may compete for the award for the most unlucky."[45]

The CBR was skeptical of deposit insurance unless private banks paid the lion's share of the costs in large part because Sberbank has an implicit guarantee that the state will bail it out in the event of a crisis—an advantage that it was loathe to cede. Sberbank has great political support among Duma deputies from rural regions—the strongholds of the Communist Party and its allies—because in most small and medium-sized towns Sberbank is the only local option for banking services.[46] Private banks, which also have a strong lobby in the legislature, have been wary of deposit insurance for fear that they would bear the bulk of the costs of the program, but have been willing to support legislation if the price is right.

Liberal deputies called for debate on a government guarantee for retail deposits in the early 1990s, but made little progress.[47] Spurred by the failure of pyramid schemes in 1994, the Duma tried to introduce deposit insurance, but was blocked by the private bankers' lobby and opposition within the government.[48] Following the financial crash of August 1998 and a rise of popular sentiment against banks, both houses of parliament passed legislation backing deposit insurance, but President Yeltsin vetoed the legislation, presumably to keep costs down on struggling private banks that were a base of his support.[49] The rough balance of political power between neo-communists and anticommunists in Russia helped block the adoption of important banking legislation for much of the 1990s.[50]

In addition, high levels of political polarization reduced the incentives of market participants to improve governance. Given the possibility that their economic gains would be at risk should President Yeltsin lose office, Russian bankers focused on short-term rent-seeking rather than supporting good governance. Banks' sensitivity to the political environment was apparent on markets for Russian privatization vouchers and for state treasury bonds—two markets on which banks were significant players. A surprisingly strong showing by the Communist Party in parliamentary elections in December 1993 and subsequent resignations of liberal ministers in favor of more statist replacements in January 1994 caused a sharp decline in the price of the voucher.[51] Similarly, in the run-up to the presidential elections in 1996, the price of state treasury bonds (GKOs) was tightly linked to the popularity of President Yeltsin relative to his neocommunist challenger, Gennadii Zyuganov.[52] Elections in less polarized settings, as in Poland and the Czech Republic, produced barely a ripple in financial markets, indicating market participants' longer-term view in these less polarized settings.[53]

One anecdote highlights how political polarization shortened time horizons. A prominent Russian banker recounted that in early February 1996 at the Davos meetings of the World Economic Forum George Soros told him: "'Boys, your time is over. You've had a few good years but now your time is up.' His (Soros') argument was that the Communists were definitely going to win. We Russian businessmen, he said, should be careful that we managed to get to our jets in time and not lose our lives."[54] This is hardly an environment conducive to building governance institutions for the long term.

State Ownership and Governance

State ownership of banking assets also promoted an uneven playing field and much politically motivated lending in the 1990s. Despite the creation of many private banks in the early 1990s, state banks dominated the market. The CBR was a majority owner in the country's largest bank, Sberbank, held 99 percent of the shares of the second largest bank, and owned five commercial banks in Europe that previously belonged to the Soviet Union. The inherent conflicts of interest in holding these shares reinforced the lack of a level playing field. For example, Sberbank was the only bank in Russia with an explicit government-backed guarantee on retail deposits, and this guarantee gave it a significant advantage over its competitors.

State ownership also generated a conflict of interest on the market for GKOs. Most observers focused on private banks, but the CBR was technically the largest player and the regulator of the market for state securities. In 1997 and 1998, the CBR and Sberbank held roughly two-thirds of GKOs, an arrangement that allowed the cash-strapped federal government to spend beyond its means and provide largesse to key constituents. The government had a strong interest in keeping the CBR and Sberbank in the GKO market.

This ownership arrangement also provided benefits to the CBR. According to the law "On the Central Bank," the CBR keeps half of its profits and turns over the other half to the federal government. As the government had few tools to compel the CBR to provide full information, many accused the CBR of underreporting its profits.[55] This ownership scheme added to the opacity of banking sector. The CBR used a variety of means to hide profits, including relying on agents in foreign banks owned by the CBR to buy GKOs. In addition, the CBR held funds in an obscure bank (FIMACO) on the island of Jersey that it did not report to the International Monetary Fund or the Russian government.[56] According to the Audit Chamber of the Russian Federation, more than $50 billion passed through FIMACO, making it a scandal of rare proportions, even for postcommunist Russia.

Recognizing the benefits of state ownership, the CBR blocked attempts to privatize its holdings. In 1995 the Duma passed legislation to reduce CBR stock in state-owned banks, but fierce lobbying from the CBR compelled the Duma to overturn its decision.[57] Moreover, following the crash of August 1998, the CBR pushed for a slow schedule of reducing its ownership in Sberbank, Vneshtorgbank, and the five foreign banks that were majority owned by the CBR. William Tompson notes: "the apparent lack of enthusiasm at CBR for either the privatization of Sberbank or the speedy introduction of deposit insurance further points to a desire to preserve the savings bank's unique position and to ensure that it remains under central bank control for the foreseeable future."[58]

The so-called spetz-banks that were formed as spin-offs from the former specialized banks of the command economy exhibited poor performance and little enthusiasm for good governance.[59] One study found that the "descendants of the 'former' *spetsbanki* appear to have higher labor costs, poorer loan quality, higher loan rates and marginally lower capital than other banks."[60] This poor performance is consistent with the argument made here as these "spetz-banks" and their descendants had extensive state ownership and retained close ties to state officials. In the 1990s state ownership of banks contributed to the opacity of the market and reinforced the lack of a level playing field.

In other countries in the region banking crises have spurred attempts to reform the sector, but the Russian Central Bank did little to address the roots of the 1998 financial crisis.[61] The CBR withdrew fewer licenses in the year after the crash than the year prior to the crash.[62] Moreover, "the percentage of bank licenses recalled during the year after the crisis, was higher among banks that did not have GKOs in their portfolios on the eve of the crisis than among those that did."[63] This indicates that the CBR and the government were loathe to address governance problems at the largest and most powerful banks.

The CBR and the government spent much of 1999 warding off plans put forward by the IMF and the World Bank to reform the banking sector. Then head of the CBR Gerashchenko proudly announced that he had not read the government's plan on bank reform. When asked about the possibility of having the CBR undergo quarterly audits as required by the G7 countries, Gerashchenko retorted: "To make us perform a striptease every quarter is a little bit stupid."[64] The CBR's plan to modernize the banking sector opposed efforts to reduce state ownership in the banking sector, was skeptical of sharply raising minimal capital requirements, and advocated a ten-year timetable for reform.

One aspect of the government's plans was the creation of ARKO, an agency designed to restructure collapsed banks. The CBR vehemently opposed the creation of ARKO and succeeded in keeping the organization poor and weak. Less than thirty problematic banks fell under its initial purview.[65] While the government and international financial institutions bargained over reform plans, Russian banks transferred assets to bridge banks with varying degrees of success. Oneximbank became Rosbank. Menatep became Menatep-St. Petersburg. Bank Rossisskii-Kredit emerged as Impex Bank. Those banks that had substantial industrial assets and/or patrons within the state suffered less than others. Foreign lenders and Russian depositors were big losers as both groups accepted pennies on the dollar for their losses. The massive asset-stripping that followed the crash, with the tacit support from the CBR and the government, did little to inspire confidence.

In sum, the demand for and supply of capable state institutions on the banking sector during the 1990s was low. Budget deficits and state ownership generated weak incentives for banks to support stronger regulation, while politicians in a polarized setting had little incentive to improve governance. Weak state institutions helped spur the financial crash of August 1998 and the poor performance of the sector more generally.

THE BANKING SECTOR 2000–2004

In addition to wiping out depositors' savings, the financial crash of August 1998 changed the landscape of Russian banking. Large private commercial banks saw their political and economic influence diminish relative to other interests. Some large commercial banks, such as MOST-Bank, SBS-Agro, and Inkombank were closed.[66] Others created bridge banks that were smaller and less aggressive than their predecessors. Two banks that increased their presence were Alfa-Bank, which sold most of its GKO holdings market prior to August 1998 and had a powerful industrial group that included the Tyumen Oil Company, and MDM-Bank, which benefited from ties to the metals giant, MDM-Group.[67]

In recent years foreign banks have become prominent players in Russia. Thirty-two banks have 100 percent foreign ownership. U.S.-based Citibank and Austria's Raifessenbank are among Russia's fifteen largest banks, and foreigners own five of the fifty largest banks in Russia.[68]

Some large private banks continue to operate primarily as treasury agents for a single firm or a small group of firms. Banks with founders in the metals and energy sector have displayed considerable growth over the last four years. Examples include GazpromBank, SurgetNeftegazBank, and Metcombank, a pocket bank for the metals giant, Severstal.

Medium-sized banks generally exited the crisis in good stead having largely avoided losses on the GKO market. Some of these banks have been at the forefront of the recent increase in private sector lending. Market observers often point to Bank Russkii-Standart, Probiznessbank, and Moscow Credit Bank as having found niches in the market for borrowing and lending. In addition, two foreign owned banks, KMB and Delta-Capital, have become leaders in lending to small businesses and the mortgage market. Nonetheless, many small and medium-sized banks continue to operate as pocket banks for enterprises or regional governments.

State-owned banks emerged after the crisis in a strong position as private banks offered weak competition. Sberbank and Vneshtorgbank benefited from vast infusions of capital from the federal government in 2000 and 2001. These two banks alone account for roughly 35 percent of all assets held in the banking sector, and state-owned banks combined account for 40 percent of all assets. In addition, Sberbank retains roughly two-thirds of all retail deposits making it by far the largest bank in Russia.

The economic and political environment in which these banks operate, however, has changed in important respects. Budget surpluses have limited opportunities for earning easy money by financing the government. In addition, parliamentary and presidential elections in 1999 and 2000 reduced political polarization.

Budget Balance and Governance

According to the explanation cited above, the outlook for raising the quality of governance on the banking sector should have improved after the crash of August 1998. The ruble devaluation, rising oil prices, and some restructuring within industry have markedly improved Russia's finances. The consolidated budget averaged a deficit of 8 percent of GDP from 1991 to 1999, but averaged a 2 percent surplus from 2000 to 2004. The stable economy ended the banks' most profitable practice—lending to the government. As such, the structural position of banks within the Russian political system is weaker than prior to August 1998. If in the mid-1990s, Russian banks had leverage over policy because they were central financiers of the state budget deficit, the budget surpluses of recent years have greatly eroded the political power of Russian banks.[69]

As banks have been less able to earn easy money from the state's fiscal imbalances, they are now repositioning themselves to lend to the private sector or leave the business. Bank lending to nonfinancial firms increased from eleven billion U.S. dollars in 1999 to seventy-seven billion in 2004.[70] Loan assets on average grew during the period 2000–2002 from 34 to 47 percent of all assets.[71] This figure is low in comparison to other countries in the region, but does indicate a sharp increase in loan activity in a relatively short period of time. Indeed, the CBR and others have worried that the rapid increase in loans may leave some banks vulnerable in case of a sharp economic correction.[72] Total retail deposits from individuals have also increased from eighteen billion dollars in 2000 to fifty billion in 2004.[73] The latter figure is twice the peak in the period prior to the crash. An increase in retail deposits in private banks has cut somewhat into Sberbank's market share, which has fallen from 77 percent of all retail deposits in 2000 to 64 percent in 2004 (OECD 2004).

One banker noted: "Those that are interested in banking are repositioning themselves to be banks, while those that do not want to do banking are getting out of the business."[74] Fifteen of the top one hundred banks are undergoing some form of ownership restructuring.[75] Several analysts agreed that banks that operate in financial-industrial groups now must justify their high cost of operations to their founders, given the opportunity for the latter to get loans from foreign banks or Sberbank at lower rates.[76] Gazprom reduced its holdings in the sector by selling its 37 percent stake in the National Reserve Bank in an effort to focus on its core business.[77] Moreover, large Russian corporations can turn to foreign banks, bonds, or state-owned banks for loans, an option that further reduces the attractiveness of holding a costly pocket bank.

Medium-sized banks that earn most of their revenue from borrowing and lending are also increasing their capital through mergers or acquisitions.[78] By doing so, they hope to reduce their risks of lending to fairly opaque firms and to compete with larger banks on specific markets. Small banks have begun to recognize their disadvantage and have sought buyouts from larger banks with some success.

This shift in strategy has sharpened incentives for creating stronger regulatory institutions that may promote borrowing and lending to the private sector. For example, in June 2001, the two largest private commercial banks in Russia announced a banking reform plan, in cooperation with the Russian Union of Industrialists and Entrepreneurs (the RSPP).[79] Alexander Mamut, then chairman of the Board of MDM-Bank, and Petr Aven, the head of Alfa-Bank, presented a largely self-serving plan that called for sharply increasing minimum capital requirements, privatizing state-owned banks, making a rapid transition to international accounting standards, and creating a three-tiered banking system, with small banks restricted to only minimal operations. The Mamut plan called for banks to have one billion rubles ($33 million) in capital before they receive their license and to increase their capital to three billion rubles ($100 million) within their first two years. As 80 percent of Russian banks at the time had less than $5 million in capital, this plan would have left only a handful of banks, including, not surprisingly, MDM-Bank and Alfa-Bank, in the market.

That the Russian government in concert with the CBR and an alliance of smaller banks blocked the Mamut plan indicates the degree to which the government was less dependent on large banks than in 1998. Self-serving elements aside, however, the Mamut plan marked the first time that the banking community had offered a plan to use the power of the state to bring a degree of order to the banking sector. In addition, the Mamut plan was backed by the RSPP, the largest industrial union in Russia, which indicated recognition from some in industry that an improved banking sector could serve as a source of investment capital. Recent statements by the head of Alfa-Group, Petr Aven, echo this sentiment for stronger regulation: "Banking supervision has to be strengthened, as tough as possible. . . . The Central Bank has to be tougher. . . . Hopefully 50 percent of Russian banks will die."[80]

These shifts in lending practices, merger and acquisition activity, and proposals to reform the banking system indicate an increased interest in governance as financial institutions position themselves to engage in the types of borrowing and lending commonly associated with banks. Indeed, the EBRD raised Russia's score on its index of the quality of banking institutions from 1.7 to 2.0 in 2002. While demand for good governance on the banking sector is still fairly low, it is increasing.[81]

Declining Political Polarization and Governance

In addition, political polarization fell after parliamentary and presidential elections in 1999 and 2000 gave the Putin team a rough working majority in the Duma. As argued previously, the decline in political polarization should strengthen incentives to create more capable institutions. The Ministry of Economics and Trade, the Ministry of Finance, and the executive branch have shown greater enthusiasm for cleaning up the banking sector. The executive branch took a more aggressive stance toward the CBR. In the summer of 2000, the government sought to make the CBR subordinate to the government, but could not get this plan approved by the Duma.[82] The government then pushed for a National Banking Council consisting of representatives from the Duma, the CBR, and the government to oversee the financial activities of the CBR. With members from the Federation Council, the Duma, and the Executive Branch, the council now oversees the spending of the Central Bank on its employees and operations.[83]

President Putin also stepped up criticism of the CBR noting: "it has not done its best to develop the banking system."[84] Facing pressure from a popular executive intent on whittling the powers of the CBR, Gerashchenko resigned in March 2002.[85] This move indicated that the Putin team was willing to risk some political capital on bank reform and removed an individual who was widely seen as a major obstacle to reform.[86]

The government pushed for banking reform on the legislative front as well. In 2000, it lobbied the Duma to pass the so-called "IMF package" that included amendments to the law "On Banks and Banking" that more clearly defined relations between banks and related companies; the law "On Insolvency of Credit Organizations," which made it easier to declare a financial institution bankrupt; and the law "On the Central Bank" that would increase the transparency of the budget and decision making at the CBR. Revealing his commitment to the IMF package, Finance Minister Aleksei Kudrin attended committee meetings every day for two weeks to push the legislation through the Duma.[87]

In the summer of 2001, the government pressed the legislature to pass a law "On Money Laundering" that would remove Russia from a list of countries whose financial transactions were seen as suspect by the international community. After intense bargaining, the Duma passed legislation that satisfied the Financial Action Task Force (FATF), which then removed Russia from its blacklist in October 2002.

The executive branch and the new team at the CBR have adopted a more aggressive regulatory strategy. Prior to Gerashchenko's resignation, the government adopted a five-year reform program. The Joint Strategy on Banking Reform published on September 27, 2001, promised to adopt international accounting standards for all banks by January 2004; to review the role of state ownership of banks, but also indicated that "a cardinal reformation" of ownership with regards to Sberbank was "not one of the tasks of banking reform"; and to support the creation of a system of deposit insurance, but offered only a vague paragraph on the topic.[88] The document was more limited than some observers expected.[89] Other observers, however, were pleased that the CBR and government had managed to put forward a plan that offered even these changes.[90]

The reforms put forth after the resignation of Gerashchenko in June 2002 were more ambitious.[91] The new CBR first deputy minister Andrei Kozlov reaffirmed a commitment to introduce international accounting standards for all banks by January 2004 and to strengthen efforts to clarify banks' notoriously murky ownership structures. The CBR also issued regulations designed to make it more difficult for banks to artificially inflate their capital and to disguise the identities of their true owners.[92] By 2002, the rating agency Standard & Poor's reported that of the fifteen largest banks, nine identified owners with at least a 30 percent ownership stake.[93]

Most importantly, after eleven years of discussion, the government finally adopted a Law on Deposit Insurance in December 2003. The OECD called the legislation "perhaps the most important banking reform adopted in recent years."[94] The plan insures individual (not corporate) deposits up to 100,000 rubles ($3,750) with a government guarantee and is mainly aimed at protecting small retail depositors.[95] Banks wishing to accept deposits from the public have to take part in the program or leave the market. They must submit to relicensing by the CBR and adopt international accounting standards. The relicensing program is perhaps the most important aspect of the law as it requires the CBR to conduct a thorough review of all banks accepting retail deposits. By the end of 2004, more than eleven hundred banks had applied for the program and four hundred firms had received new licenses.[96] Observers had mixed views on the quality of the reviews.[97] Richard Hainsworth, a long-time observer of banks in Russia noted: "The criteria that banks have to fill are very strict. Some of the big banks sweated blood, right until the end."[98] Others were more skeptical. Elena Trofimova of the rating agency Standard & Poor's observed that the initial results "present a disappointing picture; and even very weak banks have been admitted."[99] By pushing deposit insurance, the Central Bank also sought to increase transparency on the notoriously opaque banking sector. By the summer of 2003, about one hundred banks in total, including almost all the top fifteen banks, prepared their financial statements using international accounting standards.[100]

The treatment of Sberbank in the bill on deposit insurance provoked special interest. Sberbank is the only bank with a government guarantee on retail deposits and was reluctant to cede this advantage. While the bill was designed to level the playing between state and private banks, the legislation afforded several privileges to Sberbank. It maintains a separate fund for deposit insurance and it will only merge with the general deposit insurance fund in 2007 or until its market share of retail deposits falls below 50 percent.

The Russian government's stance in recent years toward foreign banks has been more mixed. In the 1990s, foreign banks could only own 12 percent of the total assets of the Russian banking system, but in November 2002 the CBR removed formal limits on the size of foreign ownership in the banking sector.[101] This move could have important impact on governance as many credit foreign ownership as promoting stronger financial institutions in Eastern Europe.[102] However, the CBR opposes allowing foreign banks to open branches in Russia, and only permits them to operate Russia-specific subsidiaries. Recently, the Ministry of Trade and Economic Development supported placing a 25 percent quota on foreign capital in the banking system.[103] It is too soon to tell if this is a bargaining chip for WTO organizations or deeply held policy position.

While it is too early to determine the success of the implementation of these plans, the passage of a law on deposit insurance and a higher profile for the regulatory bodies within the CBR contrasts with previous policy. Many of these efforts remain paper victories, but they are necessary first steps to a better-governed sector and indicate a change in policy from the Yeltsin years.

In addition to these formal changes in CBR policy, lobbyists at the Russian Union of Industrialists and Entrepreneurs, the Association of Russian Banks, and the Association of Russian Regional Banks note that they have found it easier to find a common language with the Putin administration and the new team at the CBR.[104] Some lobbyists noted that their ideas found a more welcome reception at the Ministry of Economics and Trade than elsewhere within the government. Representatives of the Ministry of Economics and Trade noted that this was a conscious strategy.[105] In designing their reform program, they had tried to reach out to the banking community—particularly those medium-sized banks that earned revenue through borrowing and lending—to gain political support and to help identify regulatory problems.

One institutional innovation that speaks to greater input from market participants is the creation of a state council (Gossovet) to develop a strategy for banking reform.[106] This council consists of about forty representatives of state bodies, such as the Ministry of Finance, the Central Bank, the Antimonopoly Committee, prominent bankers from Moscow and the regions, and experts on the banking sector in Russia. The initiative to create this body came from the government.[107] The first draft of the State Council became the subject of a lively discussion over the direction of bank reform, the current state of the banking system, and the role of the banking sector in promoting investment.[108]

Of course, a decline in political polarization is not a cure-all. While the Putin administration has displayed greater interest in improving governance, bank reform is not at the top of the agenda. In his address to the Federation Council on April 18, 2002, bank reform did not appear until the last third of the speech.[109] In addition, continued high oil prices may have dulled the government's sense of urgency in conducting institutional reforms. The overwhelming victory of President Putin's party in elections in December 2003 raises further concerns that the opposition will place few constraints on the executive, leaving the latter free to undermine governance should it choose to do so. Nonetheless, the longer-term view afforded by a less polarized political setting has, on balance, increased efforts to improve governance on the banking sector.

State Ownership and Governance

While lower budget deficits and political polarization promised to improve governance, the continuing large role of state-owned banks points to the limits of institutional reform. Indeed, state-owned banks dramatically increased their activity after August 1998, and may now be an even greater obstacle to increasing state capacity on the banking sector than prior to the crash. The government has pushed Sberbank and Vneshtorgbank to lend far more aggressively to large corporate entities. In 1997, Sberbank held only 14 percent of loans outstanding, but this figure reached 32 percent in 2001 and 30 percent in 2004. In contrast, no private bank controls more than 5 percent of lending.[110] State-owned banks lend at lower rates than private banks, in part because the government stands behind their loans. Recalling the ability of state-owned banks to lend at low rates, the president of the Association of Russian Regional banks noted: "Sberbank dumps its goods on the market" (Sberbank zanimaetsya dempingom).[111] This dominance reduces competition on the market and reinforces the disadvantage of private ownership of banks.[112]

Sberbank has engaged in dubious corporate governance practices in the postcrash era. In the summer of 2001, Sberbank board members voted to make five million shares available to majority owners, a move which raised $180 million for the bank, but also diluted the shares of minority owners by more than a third and deepened skepticism toward Sberbank's commitment to good governance.[113] Indeed, in the summer of 2003, Sberbank took the unprecedented step of suing one of its board members who claimed that the bank regularly provided below-market rate loans to its company managers, padded its two hundred thousand-strong workforce, and made money-losing loans at below market rates to politically influential companies.[114] For good measure, Sberbank also sued newspapers that printed his comments.[115]

The CBR and some within the government have been skeptical of reforms for the banking sector promoted by the IMF, particularly plans to reduce the ownership stakes of the CBR. The CBR is not the only beneficiary of state ownership in the banking sector. Politically motivated lending is a valuable tool for any government that seeks to reward supporters without running the gauntlet of budget approval from the Duma—a fact well understood by the current government. In December 2001, Vneshtorgbank placed $700 million at the disposal of Gazprom to help pay its taxes. Not only was the loan at below-market rates, the transfer was not announced to the market, which led to a mini-run on the ruble as traders reacted to a sharp and unexplained decline in CBR reserves.[116] Sberbank has made large loans to companies in which the state is the largest shareholder, such as RAO-EES, Svyaz'Invest, and Rosneft. Sberbank's loan portfolio is highly concentrated on loans to these clients, much more so than would be advisable for a bank that could not count on a government bailout if a client cannot repay a loan. As these firms are primarily state-owned, many doubt the ability of Sberbank to collect should these firms falter. In 1998 one observer noted: "it is no exaggeration to describe Sberbank as the country's number one 'pocket bank'—the pocket bank of the federal government."[117] This insight rings even more true today.

The government in the Putin era has shown increased interest in state ownership in the banking sector. It created two new state-owned banks designed to fund industry and agriculture. More importantly, it stalled efforts to divest the CBR of its 99 percent stake in Vneshtorgbank—the country's second largest bank. Initially, the government planned to sell a 20 percent stake of Vneshtorgbank to a strategic investor, and negotiations with the EBRD were under way. However, in June 2002, the government announced plans to merge Vneshtorgbank with Vnesheconombank, a largely moribund government agency created to trade Soviet-era debt. Such a move promised to delay attempts to sell a stake in the newly created entity. The head of the new entity quickly announced his intention to be a major creditor of strategic industries in Russia. While Prime Minister Mikhail Kasyanov threw cold water on the idea, the merger indicates that state ownership in the Russian banking sector is not diminishing. The prime minister also noted that the privatization of Vneshtorgbank was only likely in five to seven years.[118]

That the government named Vnesheconombank to oversee the state pension fund, despite the fact that it has no license for commercial banking and mainly acts to oversee the government's debt, is further evidence of the increasing role of state banks. One long-time observer of Russian banks noted: "I see no logic here." Another said: "This looks like another move in the Russian elite's game of 'who controls the nation's cash flows.'"[119] The government's resuscitation of the Soviet-era Vnesheconombank provides more evidence of the Putin administration's desire to increase the presence of the state on the banking sector.

As the government searches for new sources of investment capital outside of the energy sector, state-owned banks may play a larger role in the economy than prior to the crash of August 1998. Evidence from other postcommunist countries and Russia's first decade suggest that this does not bode well for governance on the sector.

In sum, the past four years have seen the first shoots of efforts to improve the regulatory environment for banks in Russia. Macroeconomic stabilization has ended the easy rents that banks could extract from the state. In turn, banks have increased borrowing from and lending to the private sector. Though much work remains to translate this interest into higher levels of demand for improved governance, recent budget surpluses have at least created a group of banks that would benefit from better governance. In addition, lower levels of political polarization have increased the supply of efforts to reform the banking sector, as indicated by recent government efforts in support of bank reform. By contrast, continued and expanding state ownership in the banking sector is a clear impediment to improving the governance of banks in Russia. As in the energy sector, the Putin administration appears intent on keeping the state as a prominent owner in the banking sector for the near future.

CONCLUSION

Creating strong banking institutions is a tall order. Yet even by the relatively low standards of the postcommunist world, state institutions in the Russian banking sector stand out for their weakness. This chapter found that two common arguments about the quality of banking institutions in Russia were lacking. Rapid economic liberalization was not associated with weak institutions in the banking sector, and while there was stronger evidence in support of the state capture argument, it raised as many questions as it answered.

This chapter examined how budget deficits, political polarization, and state ownership of banks shaped the quality of banking institutions. Obviously other factors are important as well, but concentrating on these three produces insights that help us understand the development of the Russian state. A focus on how banks benefited indirectly from macroeconomic instability adds some nuance to the state capture argument. In the early 1990s, new private banks were unlikely suspects to gain leverage over the state. The agricultural lobby, regional governments, and the natural resource sectors were far more influential players in Russian politics. Indeed, these groups were especially adept at obtaining subsidies from the state in the early 1990s. As the Russian budget deficit ballooned, however, Russian banks became the main financiers of the state deficit. By serving as a critical source of capital for the state, private banks in Russia became well placed to influence policy. The rise of Russian banks suggests that political influence early in the transition need not be translated into greater power later in the transition in a linear fashion. It also suggests the importance of examining state capture from a dynamic rather than a static perspective. Strategically located groups—even weak ones—can grow politically influential off rents generated largely by other, more powerful groups.

Paying attention to the distributional consequences of macroeconomic instability is also important because many have criticized governments in the region for paying too much attention to macroeconomic stabilization and neglecting institutional development. However, a macroeconomic policy that rewards banks for lending to the private sector rather than to the state is essential to raising demand for better governance.

A focus on political polarization between anticommunists and neocommunists provides some insights into why private banks, having grown wealthy in the early and mid-1990s, did not try to strengthen state institutions. Many expected that Russia's nouveaux riches bankers would be willing to invest their efforts in creating a more capable state, if only to protect their property rights. However, private bankers in Russia in the 1990s showed little enthusiasm about regulatory reform, even after they had amassed considerable wealth.

One factor that contributed to bankers' lack of support for long-term institutional reform was the extent of political polarization in Russia between neocommunists and anticommunists.[120] Facing the possibility of a sharp change in the direction of policy should President Yeltsin fall from office, bankers were reluctant to invest their efforts in the arduous and long-term task of building institutions. In contrast, in other settings where shifts in policy were less likely, banks exhibited considerable demand for improving the quality of institutions. For example, in Poland or Slovenia turnovers in government produced little change in policy in part because all major parties were largely committed to building a market-oriented economy.[121]

Political clashes between a large neocommunist delegation in parliament and a stridently anticommunist president also made it difficult to pass legislation in Russia. The need to gain support from the Communist Party and an anticommunist executive made passing regulatory reform in the banking sector particularly difficult in the 1990s. In far less polarized political systems like Estonia or Hungary, governments could cobble together legislation while relying on votes from like-minded parties. In Kazakhstan, and other neocommunist dominated political systems, the commitment of the elite to a state-dominated economy also made bargaining between branches of government a relatively minor problem.[122] Of course, countries experiencing little political polarization that are dominated by parties intent on maintaining state control may have weak banking institutions for other reasons. However, in Russia, opportunities for compromise between an anticommunist president and a neocommunist-led parliament in the 1990s were few and far between. An emphasis on political polarization recognizes that the political environment in which successive Russian governments made policy was far less conducive to building strong state institutions than in other settings where either neocommunists or anticommunists dominated the political scene, other things being equal. It also encourages analysts to trace how political configurations shape the incentives of state officials to strengthen or weaken state institutions.

Finally, while many have criticized privatization, or more often the manner in which it was conducted, for weakening state institutions, this chapter found that state ownership of banks is far from a solution. Indeed, state ownership of banks carries great risk to building strong regulatory institutions. In the Russian case, state-owned banks blocked regulatory reforms that would level the playing field, such as creating deposit insurance, for more than a decade. Extensive state ownership also intensified conflicts of interests within the Central Bank, an organization that operates as both a regulator and a player in the banking sector. A focus on the role of state-owned banks can help us understand why progress in banking reform has been so slow even after the financial crash of August 1998 trimmed the wings of Russia's most prominent new private banks.

Taken together these findings call into question the prevailing wisdom about the roots of weak banking institutions in Russia. Moreover, they identify the fault lines in Russian politics that shaped state institutions over the last fifteen years and will likely continue to do so for years to come.

NOTES

I would like to thank an anonymous reviewer, Gail Buyske, Timothy Colton, Stephen Holmes, Kim Iskyan, Kira Sanbonmatsu, and other members of "The State after Communism project" for helpful comments; Quintin Beazer and Sarah Wilson for research assistance; and the Carnegie Foundation and the Center for Law and Public Policy in Moscow for financial and logistical support.

1. Joel Hellman, "Winners Take All: The Pitfalls of Partial Reform," *World Politics* 50, no. 2 (Winter 1998) 203–34; Joel Hellman, Geraint Jones, Daniel Kaufman, "'Seize the State, Seize the Day'" (World Bank Policy Research Working Paper No. 2444, 2000); Joseph Stiglitz, "Whither Reform: Ten Years of the Transition," *Annual Bank Conference on Development Economics* (Washington, DC: World Bank, 2000); Juliet Johnson, *A Fistful of Rubles: The Rise and Fall of the Russian Banking System* (Ithaca, NY: Cornell University Press, 2000), 18–25.

2. Joseph Stiglitz, *The Economic Role of the State* (New York: Basil Blackwell, 1990).

3. Erik Berglof and Patrick Bolton, "The Great Divide and Beyond: Financial Architecture in Transition," *The Journal of Economic Perspectives* 16, no. 1 (Winter 2002): 77–100.

4. As banks were highly profitable in the early 1990s, allowing a powerful regional official or enterprise to open a bank was a means of gaining some political support. In addition, the granting of licenses offered a rich environment for corruption of CBR officials. From Alexander Khandruyev, former first deputy of the Central Bank of Russia, interview by author, September 19, 2001.

5. Catherine Belton and Igor Semenko, "The Commercial Empire of the Central Bank," *Moscow Times Business Extra*, October 19, 1999.

6. Margot Jacobs, "Russian Banks: Sailing Ahead or Sinking Fast?" (Moscow: United Financial Group Research Report, 1998).

7. David Kuenzi, "Banking on the Ruble: How Reckless Banking Contributed to Russia's Financial Collapse" (Moscow: Creditanstalt Research Report, 1998), 1.

8. Enrico Perotti, "Lessons from the Russian Meltdown: The Economics of Soft Legal Constraints" (Working Paper No. 379, Amsterdam: University of Amsterdam and CEPR, 2001), 1.

9. In some cases these arguments are based primarily on evidence from the banking sector. See Johnson, *Fistful of Rubles*, 2000; Stiglitz, "Whither Reform."

10. Christia Freeland, *The Sale of the Century: Russia's Wild Ride from Communism to Capitalism* (New York: Crown, 2000), 116–67; David E. Hoffman, *The Oligarchs: Wealth and Power in the New Russia* (New York: PublicAffairs, 2002), 297–325; Johnson, *Fistful of Rubles*.

11. George Stigler, "The Economic Theory of Regulation," *Bell Journal of Economics and Management Science* 3 (1971): 3–21.

12. Douglass North and Barry Weingast, "The Evolution of Institutions Governing Public Choice in 17th Century England," *Journal of Economic History* 49 (1989): 803–32; Charles Tilly, *Coercion, Capital and European States* (New York: Basil Blackwell, 1990).

13. Andrei Shleifer and Robert Vishny, *Privatizing Russia* (Cambridge, MA: MIT Press, 1995).

14. Of the so-called "seven bankers lobby" that existed prior to 1998, only Petr Aven and Vladimir Potanin have remained active in lobbying the government, and this is likely due to their holdings in oil, gas, and metals, rather than their ownership of banks. Moreover, of the "third generation" oligarchs that made much of their wealth following the crash of 1998, such as Aleksander Mordashov, Roman Abramovich, Vladimir Yevtushenkov, Oleg Deripaska, and Andrei Melnichenko, only the latter has significant interests in banking.

15. Most forcefully, see Stiglitz, "Whither Reform." Also Peter Stavrakis, "State Building in Post-Soviet Russia: The Chicago Boys and the Decline of Administrative Capacity" (Occasional Paper No. 254, Washington, DC: Kennan Institute for Advanced Studies, October 2003).

16. Geoffrey Garrett and David Nickerson, "Globalization, Democratization and Government Spending in Middle-Income Countries," New Haven, 2001.

17. *EBRD Transition Report 2000* (London: EBRD, 2000). This relationship holds using cross-sectional and panel data and more sophisticated statistical techniques.

18. Johnson, *Fistful of Rubles*.

19. Some argue that poor governance in Russia is generally rooted in the low salaries paid to state officials. If so, then the banking sector would be the best governed in Russia. The Audit Chamber of the Russian Federation reported that the average salary in the CBR was $14,000 (Belton and Semenko, 1999).

20. Banks that engage in borrowing and lending tend to oppose inflation as it reduces the value of their outstanding loans. However, where banks earn revenue primarily from funding the government, they may benefit from inflation.

21. See Stiglitz, "Whither Reform."

22. Rafael Laporta, Florencio Lopez-de-Silanes, and Andrei Shleifer, "Government Ownership of Banks," *Journal of Finance* (February 2002): 265–301.

23. Sberbank is the former state-owned retail savings bank that has deep roots in the Soviet and pre-Soviet period. Vneshtorgbank is a former specialized bank that operated in the Soviet period that was responsible for foreign trade. Both became joint-stock companies in 1990. See www.sbrf.ru and www.vtb.ru for details.

24. Jakub Svensson, "Investment, Property Rights and Political Instability: Theory and Evidence," *European Economic Review* 42 (1999): 1317–41. Here neocommunist elites refer to party leaders or executives who campaigned with backing of the largest communist successor party, held high office in the party or state apparatus prior to 1989, and advocate a large state sector in the economy. The ex-communist parties of Hungary, Lithuania, Poland, and Slovenia do not fit the criteria to be neocommunist parties at any point in the transformation.

25. Timothy Frye, "The Perils of Polarization: Economic Performance in the Post-communist World," *World Politics* 54 (April 2002): 308–37.

26. Alberto Alesina and Allen Drazen, "Why Are Stabilizations Delayed?" *American Economic Review* 81 (Fall 1991): 1170–89.

27. The measure actually includes plus and minus scores for each value (e.g., 2+, 3−, which are scored 2.3 and 2.7 respectively). Before publication these measures are circulated to experts at the World Bank and the IMF and are then defended before a board of specialists at the EBRD. This is a quality measure, particularly given the alternative of relying on dodgy financial statistics.

28. The executive is a president in a presidential system or the prime minister in a parliamentary system. See fn. 24 for a definition of *neocommunist elite*.

29. John Ishiyama, "The Sickle or the Rose? Previous Regime Type and the Evolution of Ex-Communist Parties," *Comparative Political Studies* 30 (June 1997): 299–330.

30. These results also hold in a cross-sectional analysis and in a time-series cross-section analysis using data from 1990–2002. See author for results.

31. See Joel Hellman, *Breaking the Bank: Bureaucrats and the Creation of Markets in a Transition Economy*, PhD dissertation, Columbia University, 1993; Gail Buyske, *The Development of Financial Systems in Post-Socialist Economies*," PhD dissertation, Columbia University, 1997; William Tompson, "Russia's Ministry of Cash: Sberbank in Transition," *Communist Economies and Economic Transformation* 10, no. 2 (1999): 133–57; William Tompson, "Financial Backwardness in Contemporary Perspective: Prospects for the Development of Financial Intermediation in Russia," *Europe-Asia Studies* 52, no. 4 (2000): 605–25; and Johnson, *Fistful of Rubles*.

32. William Easterly and Paulo Viera de Cunha, *Financing the Storm: Macroeconomic Crises in Russia, 1992–1993* (Washington, DC: World Bank, 1993).

33. See Mikhail Dmitriev, Mikhail Matovnikov, Leonid Mikhailov, Lyudmila Sicheva, and Eugene Timofeev, "The Banking Sector," in *Russia's Post-Communist Economy*, ed. Brigitte Granville and Peter Oppenheimer (Oxford: Oxford University Press, 2001), 213–39; especially 224–26 on incentives to collude with firms to gain low (or no) interest loans from the central government.

34. Easterly and de Cunha, *Financing the Storm*; Mikhail Dmitriev, ed. *Rossiiskie banki na kanune finansovoi stabilizatsii* (St. Petersburg: Norma, 1996); Dmitriev et al., "The Banking Sector," 220–21.

35. *Russian Economic Trends*, March 5, 1998.

36. Aleksandr Livshitz, former minister of finance, interview by author, Moscow, June 17, 2002.

37. Garegin Tosunian, president, Association of Russian Banks, interview by author, Moscow, June 19, 2002.

38. Aslund estimates that subsidies to the tune of about 8 percent of GDP went to agriculture in 1992, while massive tax breaks went to the oil and gas sector throughout the 1990s (Anders Aslund, *How Russia Became a Market Economy* [Washington, DC: Brookings, 1995], 164, 301). On lobbying by regional governments, see Daniel Treisman, *After the Deluge: Regional Crises and Political Consolidation in Russia* (Ann Arbor: Michigan University Press, 1999); on lobbying by economic sectors, including banks, see Vladimir Mau, *The Political History of Economic Reform in Russia, 1985–1994* (Moscow: CRCE, 1995).

39. Johnson, *Fistful of Rubles*, 122–23.

40. Freeland, *Sale of the Century*, 168–89; Hoffman, *Oligarchs*, 296–324.

41. Ira Leiberman and Rogi Veimetra, "The Rush for State Shares in the 'Klondyke' of Wild East Capitalism: Loans for Shares Transactions in Russia," *George Washington Law School Review of International Law and Economics* 29 (1996): 737–68.

42. Kim Iskyan, "The Russian Banking Sector: A Crisis of Stagnation" (Moscow: Renaissance Capital Research Report, 2001).

43. Tompson, 1999, 242.

44. Vladimir Mau, "Ekonomicheskaia politika: Rossii: v nachale novoi fazi," *Voprosy Ekonomiki* (January 2001).

45. Igor' Moiseev, "Sberbanku dali dva goda fori," *Vedemosti*, November 15, 2002.

46. Martin Shakuum, chair of banking subcommittee in the Duma, interview by author, September 18, 2001.

47. Joachim Bald and Jim Neilsen, "Developing Efficient Financial Institutions in Russia," *Communist Economies and Economic Transformation* 10, no. 1 (1998): 81–92.

48. Johnson captures the logic well: "The CBR wanted the commercial banks to design and fund it, while the bankers felt that the CBR should do so. Both wanted the security, but neither wanted to pay for it" (Johnson, *Fistful of Rubles*, 114).

49. Martin Shakuum, chairman, Duma Subcommittee on Financial Legislation, interview with the author, September 18, 2001.

50. The value of deposit insurance for transition and developing economies is debatable. One study finds that on average introducing deposit insurance in countries that

already have relatively capable state institutions leads to fewer banking crises. However, introducing deposit insurance into countries with weak institutions leads to more crises than in countries without deposit insurance (Asli Demirguc-Kunt and Edward Kane, "When Does Deposit Insurance Work?" *Journal of Economic Perspectives* 16, no. 2 [2002]: 175–96). Since Russia would likely end up in the "weak institutions" category, this suggests that for deposit insurance to work well, other institutions, such as courts and bureaucracies, should also be improved.

51. Timothy Frye, "Russian Privatization and the Limits of Credible Commitment," in *The Political Economy of Property Rights*, ed. David Weimer (New York: Cambridge; 1997), 84–108.

52. Roderick Kiewiet and Mikhail Myagkov, "The Emergence of the Private Sector: A Financial Market Perspective," *Post-Soviet Affairs* 14, no. 1 (1997): 23–47.

53. Frye, "Perils of Polarization."

54. Freeland, *Sale of the Century*, 192.

55. Victoria Lavrentieva, "Duma to CB: Show Us the Money," *Moscow Times*, December 21, 2001, 1.

56. Belton and Semenko, "Commercial Empire"; Johnson, *Fistful of Rubles*, 64–65.

57. Johnson, *Fistful of Rubles*, 114.

58. Tompson, 1999, 138.

59. The five USSR spetz-banks were Agroprombank, Promstroibank, Sberbank, Vneshekonombank, and Zhilsotsbank, and were responsible for the agriculture, industry, household, foreign trade, and housing sectors, respectively.

60. Koen Schoors, "The Fate of Russia's Former State Banks: Chronicle of a Restructuring Postponed and a Crisis Foretold," *Europe-Asia Studies* 55, no. 1 (2003): 75–100.

61. Helena Tang, Edda Zoli, and Irina Klytchnikova, *Banking Crises in Transition Economies* (Washington, DC: World Bank, 2001). That the CBR and government faced legal obstacles in closing insolvent banks is a flimsy excuse. Had they demonstrated an interest in improving governance, they would have pushed for stronger legislation on insolvency in the banking sector. Indeed, the CBR lobbied to exclude banks from the Law on Bankruptcy.

62. Perotti, "Lessons."

63. L. Sicheva, L. Mikhailov, L. Timofeev, E. Marushkina, and S. Surkov, *Krizis 1998 goda i vostanovlenie bankovskoi sistemi* (Moscow: Moscow Carnegie Center, 2000), 303.

64. Andrei Ivanov, "Russian Banking Reform: To Be or Not to Be?" Troika-Dialog Research Report (Moscow: Troika-Dialog, 2000), 1.

65. Indeed some have argued that ARKO's opaque decision-making structure and distribution of assets to some politically well-connected banks has, if anything, increased concerns about the stability of the sector. That ARKO lent money to Alfa-Bank, one of the most prosperous in Russia, to expand its regional operations raised particular concerns (see Dmitriev et al., "The Banking Sector," 235).

66. In a sign of the times, Inkombank, formerly one of the most prominent banks in Russia, was forced to sell to the state its collection of works by Kazimir Malevich, including his "The Black Square" in 2002.

67. It probably does not hurt Alfa-Bank's position to have one of its former top managers, Vladislav Surkov, as deputy head of the presidential administration or that Alfa-Bank had been the authorized bank of the St. Petersburg government while President Putin served there in the 1990s.

68. "Foreign Banks Race to Invest in Consumer Lending," *Russian Business Consulting News Service*, January 14, 2003.

69. Andrei Klepach, bank analyst, Center for Development, interview by author, June 17, 2002.

70. OECD, Economic Survey of the Russian Federation, Paris, 2004.

71. *Bulletin of Banking Statistics*, #4, 2002.

72. Elena Berezanskaya and Boris Safronov, "U bankov 'portyatsya' krediti," *Vedemosti*, September 17, 2002; Vlastya Demyanenko, "Russian Central Bank Worried about Too Fast Credit Growth," *Reuters*, September 30, 2002.

73. Boris Safronov, "Vremya roznichnikh bankov: Samii bistrii rost obespechivaiyut chastniie vkladi," *Vedemosti*, November 25, 2002.

74. Alex Kotcherguine, vice president, MDM-Bank, interview by author, June 20, 2002.

75. Mikhail Matovnikov, bank analyst, Interfax news agency, interview by author, June 13, 2002. See also Mikhail Matovnikov, "Banki: vremya menyat' strategiyu," *Kommersant'*, 18 June 2002.

76. Author interview with Natalya Orlova, bank analyst at Alfa-Bank, June 17, 2002.

77. *Moscow Times*, July 9, 2002.

78. Elena Berezanskaya and Svetlana Petrova, "Mamut dobilsya svoevo," *Vedemosti*, September 17, 2001, 1(B).

79. See "O deiyatelnosti rabochei gruppii byuro pravlenie RSPP po voprosam reformirovaniya bankovskoi sistemi," (Moscow: Russian Union of Industrialists and Entrepreneurs, 11 July 2001).

80. Petr Aven, "Aven: Let 50% of Banks Die Quickly," *Moscow Times*, August 8, 2003.

81. Indeed, the collapse of the fifty-second largest bank in Russia, IBK, in March 2002 after receiving a good bill of health from the CBR indicates the continuing opacity of banks in Russia (Mikhail Matovnikov, "Predvestniki krizisa," *Russkii Fokus*, 17, 2002, 1–3).

82. Igor' Moiseev, "Prezident khochet' sdelat' TsB 'gosuchrezhdenniyam,'" *Vedemosti*, September 29, 2000.

83. Aleksandr Shokhin, former head of the Duma committee on banking, recently applauded greater transparency in the use of funds within the Russian Central Bank (Vasilii Kudinov, Elena Berezanksaya, and Anastasia Onegina, "TsB poluchil rekordnuyu pribiil: Zabrav depoziti iz Vneshtorgbanka," *Vedemosti*, May 13, 2003).

84. Radio Free Europe/Radio Liberty Research Report, December 28, 2000.

85. Julia Tolkacheva, "New Russian Central Bank Seen as Welcome Reformer," *Reuters*, Moscow, March 19, 2002.

86. There is also evidence that the CBR is beginning to enforce restrictions on limits of lending to individual firms. If this rule is consistently applied, it would be fatal for most pocket banks (Evgenii Epshtein, "Gazprom zanyal 500m," *Vedemosti*, April 15, 2002).

87. Irina Kotelevskaya, head of department for relations with government bodies for the Russian Union of Industrialists and Entrepreneurs, RSPP, interview by author, June 20, 2002.

88. See "Sovmestnaia strategiia Banka Rossii i Pravitelstva Rossiiskoi Federatsii o razvitii bankovskoi sistemi," *Kommersant-Daily*, September 17, 2001, 4.

89. Svetlana Petrova, "Gerashchenko pobedil, no pobezhdenii svoevo dobilsya," *Vedemosti*, September 17, 2001.

90. Personal communication with Gail Buyske, bank consultant.

91. "Voprosy modernizatsii bankovskoi sistemi Rossii," eleventh International Banking Congress, June 6, 2002.

92. "Tsentrobank proverit bankovskiie krediti," in *Finansoviie Izvestiya*, accessed at www.finiz.ru/business/article.11360 on May 12, 2003.

93. Kiril Koriukin, "For Banks, Going Public Is a Very Private Affair," *Moscow Times, Special Report*, June 17, 2003. Christopher Kenneth, "Russian Banks Unprepared for New IAS Accounting," *Russia Journal*, June 4, 2003.

94. *OECD Economic Survey of the Russian Federation 2004: Banking Reform*, 1.

95. The limited funding of bank deposits may reduce moral hazard problems that plague deposit insurance in countries with weak institutions.

96. Greg Walters, "Key Changes Set Banking Reform in Motion," *Moscow Times*, February 9, 2005.

97. It is also potentially important that these reforms were put forward by the regulatory arm of the CBR. Kozlov has assumed a much higher profile than his predecessors and talks with the head of the CBR several times a day according to Sergei Ignatyev.

98. Greg Walters, "Key Changes," February 9, 2005; see also Ben Aris, "All Change," *The Banker*, April 2004.

99. Sveta Skibinsky, "State Muscle Could Be Key to Success for Real Reform in Russian Banking," *St. Petersburg Times*, December 7, 2004.

100. Christopher Kenneth, "Russian Banks Unprepared for New IAS Accounting," *Russia Journal*, June 4, 2003.

101. Oleg Anisimov, "State-Owned Banks May Face Foreign Challengers," *Russia Journal*, August 12, 2003. There is much debate about whether foreign banks will have the right to open branches in Russia outright or to rely on Russia-specific subsidiaries.

102. Berglof and Bolton, "The Great Divide and Beyond."

103. Russia against Foreign Bank Branching, February 11, 2004.

104. Irina Kotelevskaya, author interview, June 20, 2002; Aleksander Murichev, president of the Association of Regional Russian Banks, "Rossiya," interview by author, June 14, 2002; Garegin Tosunian, author interview, June 19, 2002.

105. Boris Shentsis, deputy head, Ministry of Economy and Trade who is responsible for financial sector reform, interview by author, June 19, 2002.

106. Elena Myazina, "Gossovet vzyalsya za banki," *Izvestiya*, June 15, 2002.

107. One member of the Gossovet recalled that at the first meeting he noted: "Why are we all here?" (Aleksander Khandruyev, former CBR deputy minister, interview by author, June 19, 2002).

108. Irina Granik, "Bankiri ni odobrili kontseptsiyu bankovskoi reformi," *Kommersant'*, June 15, 2002.

109. Poslanie Prezidenta Rossiiskoi Federatsii V. V. Putin Federalnomu Sobraniyu RF, April 18, 2002.

110. Gail Buyske, "Russia Case Study: World Bank Consolidation Project," draft, Moscow, October 2002.

111. Aleksander Murichev, interview with author, June 14, 2002.

112. Torrey Clarke, "Retail Banks Struggle under Sberbank Shadow," *Moscow Times*, June 26, 2001, 11.

113. Igor Semenko, "Sberbank Approves New Share Emission," *Moscow Times*, June 28, 2001, 5.

114. Vasilii Kudinov and Tatyana Lysova, "'Sberbank Zasudil Kleinera," *Vedemosti*, June 20, 2003.

115. Sberbank has a ratio of assets to employees of about \$132,000. The corresponding figure for Citibank is \$3.9m (Igor Semenko, "Sberbank on the Prowl for Negative News," *Moscow Times*, June 27, 2003).

116. *Vedemosti*, December 25, 2001.

117. Tompson, 1999, 134.

118. Interfax, June 19, 2002.

119. Victoria Lavrentieva, "Choice of Pension Agent Said Damaging," *Moscow Times*, January 27, 2003.

120. One alternative is that the new rich did not seek to strengthen the state domestically as long as they could park their money abroad in countries where their property would be protected. See Konstantin Sonin, "Why the Rich May Favor Poor Protection of Property Rights," ms. (Moscow: New Economics School, 2002); also Karla Hoff and Joseph Stiglitz, "After the Big Bang: Obstacles to the Emergence of the Rule of Law in Russia" (paper presented at Annual Meeting of the American Political Science Association, Washington, DC, September 2002).

121. See John Bonin, ed., *Banking in Transition Economies: Developing Market Oriented Banking Sectors in Eastern Europe* (Cheltenham: Elgar 1998).

122. Nonpolarized neocommunist-led governments, like Kazakhstan and Uzbekistan, have EBRD Bank Reform Scores that are statistically indistinguishable from that of Russia (1.6 versus 1.7) during the period under study.

Chapter Seven

Evaluating Exchange Rate Management

Daniel Treisman

In the ten years between December 1991 and December 2001, the Russian ruble lost 99.4 percent of its value against the dollar. In the two months of August and September 1998 alone, the currency depreciated by more than 60 percent. If one of the basic responsibilities of government is to provide stable money, this looks like a colossal failure.

It has seemed so to many observers. President Yeltsin himself referred to the August 1998 crisis as a "terrible financial disaster."[1] According to one liberal economist, ordinary Russians viewed it as "the gravest cataclysm to hit their country since the end of the Soviet era."[2] In his opinion, August 1998 had discredited the words *democracy* and *reform* in popular discourse and set the country back politically by ten years. A group of U.S. congressmen claimed in 2000 that the August events had "led to Russia's total economic collapse."[3]

A country's exchange rate, as Charles Kindleberger observed, is more than just a number: "It is an emblem of its importance to the world, a sort of international status symbol."[4] The stability of a country's currency is often taken as a summary indicator of the competence and probity of its economic decision makers. To many Western observers, as Timothy Colton and Stephen Holmes note in the introduction to this volume, the Russian government in the 1990s appeared "weak" and "dysfunctional," reminiscent of the predatory regimes of postcolonial Africa. The ruble's collapse and subsequent gyrations seemed to epitomize this weakness.

How unusual was Russia's record of currency instability in the 1990s? To what can it be attributed? And what—if anything—does it reveal about perceived failures of Russian governance? In this chapter, I try to answer these questions, examining the economic data on Russia's exchange rate performance and the arguments that have been proposed to explain it. Previous accounts have located responsibility for the ruble's instability at three different levels. Some blame the errors or ignorance of individual policy makers. Others attribute currency volatility to conflicts within the state and the poor articulation of governing institutions. Still others place the main cause not within the state but outside it. They blame powerful interest groups—usually the "oligarchs," believed by many to have "captured" Russian government in the mid-1990s—for pressuring the authorities to enact exchange rate policies that were not in the public interest.

My analysis suggests several conclusions that diverge from the conventional wisdom. First, I show that the decline and volatility in Russia's currency in the 1990s—although extreme when compared to currency changes in settled, highly developed countries—were not at all unusual for an emerging market economy. Many countries around Russia's level of economic development had similar problems, and some had currencies that were less stable than Russia's. One should probably not, therefore, seek explanations for the ruble's volatility in factors unique to Russia.

Second, although individual errors, institutional incoherence, and interest-group lobbying helped shape the context in which exchange rate policy was made, they appear to have played a smaller role in determining the outcomes than is usually thought. The macroeconomic challenges that Russia faced during this period were so severe and its resources to address them so limited that even had the country's Central Bank been perfectly insulated from politics and run by a student of Milton Friedman, Russia would probably have experienced similar turbulence. Russia's first postcommunist government inherited extreme price distortions, a state budget ballooning out of control, a major "overhang" of rubles, no government bond market, and almost no currency or gold reserves. Throughout the decade, international oil prices and investor sentiment swung sharply. In such conditions, major fluctuations of both the nominal and real exchange rates were simply unavoidable.

Third, I will argue that, in any case, economic ignorance, institutional incoherence, and oligarch capture generally do a poor job of explaining the pattern of policy choices and exchange rate performance in Russia. If these factors caused the nominal depreciation of 1992–1994, it is hard to account for the authorities' great success in stabilizing the nominal rate in 1995–1996. This occurred at a time when the most economically literate officials were being edged out by Soviet-era professionals; when conflicts between government and parliament and among state agencies remained intense; and when the oligarchs were approaching the peak of their influence. Do these factors explain the authorities' failure to devalue early and avert the 1998 currency crisis? One can hardly blame economic ignorance for this since leading macroeconomists in the West—as well as the International Monetary Fund (IMF)—also thought devaluation could be avoided.[5] Nor can one blame institutional conflict since all the relevant authorities were united against devaluation. As for oligarch capture, the oligarchs' interests on this were in fact closely aligned with those of the general public, which renders the question which had greater influence somewhat immaterial. Both stood to lose from a devaluation, and hoped to avoid one completely.[6] Finally, if these three explanatory factors determined exchange rate policy, one would expect policy to change when the three factors change. Since 1998, the influence of the oligarchs has been perceived as in decline. Previous institutional and political conflicts have been restrained by the president's popularity and electoral mandate. But the monetary authorities have stuck to an exchange rate policy very similar to that adopted in 1995–1998. The ruble has appreciated in real terms during this period to a level now approaching that of 1998. If this is seen as less threatening than in 1995–1998, it is more because of changed circumstances (high oil prices, large currency reserves) than changed policy.

Overall, the analysis casts doubt on arguments that problems of governance explain why Russia's exchange rate performance was disappointing in the 1990s. Poor performance had more to do with the extreme challenges that decision makers faced in the 1990s than with the ignorance, disorganization, or cooptation of such officials. Of course, this does not mean that failures of governance were not important in other spheres—other chapters in this volume make strong arguments to the contrary. And it does not guarantee that institutional incoherence, cronyism, or decision maker errors will not hamper Russian currency management in the future. But it cautions against attributing disappointing outcomes too readily to failures of political decision making and "weak" institutions without explicitly considering the challenges faced and the feasible alternatives.

RUSSIA'S TROUBLED RUBLE

The Facts

The ruble's exchange rate has been determined since the early 1990s primarily at currency auctions on the Moscow Interbank Currency Exchange (MICEX), where banks trade currencies among themselves. The Central Bank intervenes on this market, selling or buying currency to affect the rate. Although the

Central Bank is legally independent of the government, and determines operational interventions by itself, the basic parameters of exchange rate policy are generally decided in collaboration with the Ministry of Finance. The bank is accountable to the Duma, which can fire its chairman. In practice, presidents have been able on many occasions to persuade Central Bank chairmen to resign (see below).

Russian exchange rate management since 1992 falls naturally into three periods (see figures 7.1 and 7.2).[7] The first, from 1992 to around April 1995, coincided with the struggle to prevent hyperinflation. During this period, the exchange rate was allowed to float freely.[8] Price liberalization in January 1992 prompted a sharp jump in the price level, and subsequent large increases in the money supply fueled very high inflation. The nominal exchange rate fell sharply as the ruble supply expanded. In mid-1994, the Central Bank began intervening to slow the nominal depreciation. But it quickly ran through its reserves, and on October 11, 1994, which came to be known as "Black Tuesday," the ruble dropped 30 percent against the dollar in one day, before jumping back. The decline in the nominal exchange rate was not as fast as the rise in prices during this period, and so the real exchange rate appreciated rapidly (see figure 7.2).[9]

The second period began around April 1995, with the achievement of macroeconomic stabilization and the introduction of a "currency corridor." From July 1995 to January 1996, the monetary authorities committed themselves to keeping the rate between 4,300 and 4,900 rubles per dollar. In January 1996, the permitted range shifted to 4,550 to 5,150. It was adjusted upward again in July 1996, and again in December 1996. From July 1996, the government guaranteed in addition to keep the value within a narrow crawling band that would not move more than 1.5 percent in a day. The real value of the ruble reached a plateau around the beginning of 1996.[10]

The third phase began with the crisis of August 1998, during which the authorities let the ruble depreciate sharply. Its value fell from 6.27 R/$ at the end of July to 10.36 R/$ at the end of August and 16.05 R/$ at the end of September.[11] After that, the currency floated without any preannounced limits, although the Central Bank continued to intervene to prevent large changes. From early 1999 to early 2003, the ruble depreciated gradually, without major turbulence, while the real exchange rate appreciated moderately. As of late 2003, the real rate was about 75 percent above its postcrisis low.

Common Criticisms

The exchange rate fluctuations visible in figures 7.1 and 7.2 have prompted various criticisms of the authorities' management. First, the nominal exchange

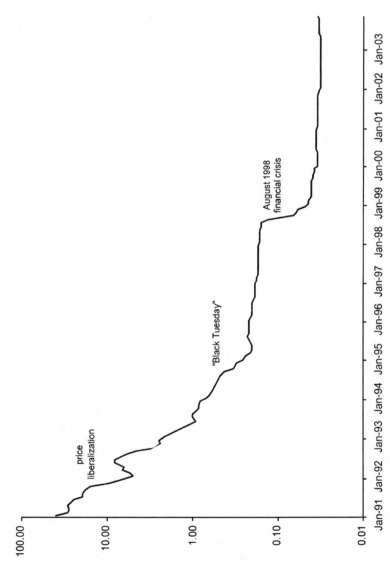

Figure 7.1. Nominal Exchange Rate (\$/R), Russia 1991–2003. *Source:* Russian Economic Trends database, Central Bank of Russia, *Bulletin of Banking Statistics,* December 2003.

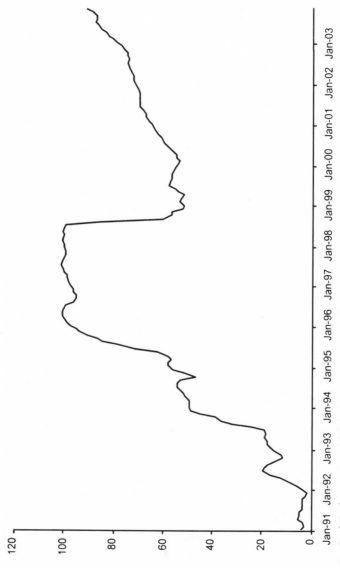

Figure 7.2. Real Exchange Rate, Russia 1991–2003. *Source:* Russian Economic Trends database, Central Bank of Russia, *Bulletin of Banking Statistics,* December 2003. *Note:* Exchange rate ($/R) deflated by CPI, December 1997 = 100.

rate has been extremely unstable. The ruble's dollar value dropped more than 99 percent between 1991 and 2001, mostly during the first phase (January 1991 to April 1995) and the months immediately following August 1998. Instability of a currency's nominal value makes calculating real future profits difficult, discourages long-term investments, and depresses growth. Changes in the nominal exchange rate have also been quite unpredictable, rendering financial planning even more complicated and investment riskier. A regular, steady decline in a currency's value can be factored into calculations; volatile fluctuations cannot. The dramatic collapse of August 1998 shocked investors and temporarily shook their confidence in the Russian market.

Second, some have argued that the authorities let the real exchange rate appreciate too much in the early 1990s. A higher real exchange rate reduces the domestic price of imports and benefits consumers. But it also reduces demand for exports (by increasing dollar export prices) and increases price competition for domestic producers. These effects are often thought to depress growth and lead to recession.[12] An "overvalued" real exchange rate is also thought to provoke speculative crises in which the currency's value suddenly crashes. Especially when the government runs large fiscal deficits and relies on foreign investors to fund these, real exchange rate overvaluation is considered dangerous. Several Russian economists argued vigorously from early 1997 that the real exchange rate had appreciated to an unsustainable level and that a moderate devaluation was vital to restore competitiveness and avoid a crisis.[13]

Third, the Russian authorities have been criticized for a variety of other policies that increased the likelihood of crisis or exacerbated its effects. Illarionov accuses the Central Bank of irresponsibly failing to build up sufficient currency reserves, despite large inflows of dollars in the years preceding 1998. Some also faulted the Central Bank for poor prudential regulation of the commercial banks that were engaged in international transactions. Months before the 1998 crisis, the Central Bank stopped requiring domestic banks selling dollar forward contracts to foreign investors to hedge their risk with it. The authorities also removed capital controls at a particularly dangerous time. Throughout 1997, the Central Bank was relaxing conditions for foreign investors to repatriate profits from the treasury bill market, making a sudden exodus easier. Just weeks before the ruble floated, the bank attempted to swap outstanding ruble-denominated treasury bills (GKOs) for longer-duration hard currency bonds. These obligations were that much harder to finance after the ruble's value crashed. Many observers also blamed the 1998 crisis on the government's "fiscal irresponsibility" in continuing to run large deficits.[14]

Comparative Context

Before evaluating the individual criticisms, some comparative context is useful. Was nominal exchange rate depreciation in Russia in the 1990s unusually large compared to exchange rate movements in other postcommunist and developing countries? Did other countries experience crises comparable to August 1998? Was the real appreciation of the ruble unusual?

The total drop in Russia's exchange rate does appear unusually large, although by no means unprecedented. The IMF provides data on exchange rates for 145 countries during the period from December 1991 to December 2001.[15] Five countries—Angola, Moldova, Brazil, Suriname, and Turkey—had currencies that depreciated faster than the ruble during this period. Another six countries—Armenia, Ukraine, Turkmenistan, Tajikistan, Zaire, and Belarus—also performed worse than Russia, suffering a larger drop in an even shorter period (1992–2001, 1993–2001, or 1992–2001; data were not available for these countries for the full decade). Some other countries for which the IMF did not publish complete data—such as Macedonia and Croatia—had depreciations equally large (calculated with supplementary information from their central banks or the European Bank for Reconstruction and Development—EBRD). In the 1980s, currency depreciations of this magnitude were more common. Depreciations even larger than Russia's occurred during that decade in Peru, Argentina, Bolivia, Brazil, Israel, Nicaragua, Uganda, Vietnam, Lebanon, Zaire, and even Poland, one of the success stories of macroeconomic stabilization in the 1990s. Thus, the depreciation of the ruble was an extreme event, but far from unique. Table 7.1 shows the total depreciation in Russia, compared to that in the eight countries with per capita income right above Russia's in this period and the eight with income right below Russia's.[16]

Still, the size of the total nominal depreciation may not be a good measure of the harm done by exchange rate volatility. If depreciation proceeds at a regular and predictable rate, the damage to trade and investment can be limited. One relatively simple way to measure the volatility of exchange rates is to calculate the size of the residuals from a linear regression of the exchange rate on its time trend. The residuals measure, in a sense, how wrong one would be if one tried to predict the exchange rate with a simple linear model. In table 7.1, column 2, I show the average (absolute value) residuals from regressions of the monthly exchange rate on the time trend, for Russia and the countries with per capita income right above and below Russia's. The regressions are run for the period January 1992 to December 2001. To normalize, I divide the average residual by the average exchange rate for the country during that period. In this group of countries, Russia's exchange rate was relatively unpredictable—although

Table 7.1. **Exchange Rate Indicators for Middle Income Countries with PPP GDP per Capita Close to Russia's**

Country	Total drop in value of currency, December 1991 to December 2001 (%)	Unpredictability of exchange rate,[a] January 1992 to December 2001
Belarus	100.00[b]	1.01
Brazil	99.98	0.15
Croatia	99.76[c]	n.a.
Macedonia	99.71[c]	n.a.
Russia	*99.44*	*0.34*
Bulgaria	99.02	0.30
Venezuela	91.93	0.11
Lithuania	80.55	0.11
Namibia	77.38	0.09
Poland	72.51	0.05
Botswana	70.32	0.05
Colombia	69.28	0.13
Mexico	66.41	0.12
Gabon	65.20	0.08
Trinidad and Tobago	32.43	0.06
Malaysia	28.32	0.09
Latvia	21.63	0.07

Sources: IMF *International Financial Statistics*, April 2002, EBRD *Transition Report* 1997, National Bank of the Republic of Macedonia, *Quarterly Bulletin* 11, 2003.

Notes: Table contains data for the eight countries with GDP per capita right above Russia's and the eight with GDP per capita right below (averages for 1991–2001, in PPP terms, as estimated by UN GDP International Comparisons Project, reported in World Bank, *World Development Indicators* 2003). In 1980–1990, Peru, Argentina, Bolivia, Brazil, Israel, Nicaragua, Uganda, Vietnam, Lebanon, Zaire, and Poland all had depreciations greater than 99.44 percent.

[a]Mean of absolute value of residuals from linear regression of country's exchange rate on time trend, normalized by mean exchange rate.

[b]January 1992 to November 2001.

[c]Annual average 1991 to annual average 2001.

it was less unpredictable than that of Belarus, and lack of data precluded comparisons with Macedonia and Croatia. Various other emerging market economies—such as Turkey, Ecuador, and Romania—had even more unpredictable exchange rates during the same years.

Russia's 1998 financial crisis was perceived by many observers at the time in apocalyptic terms. However, such crises are not unusual among developing countries. In Russia between July and September 1998, the exchange rate fell by 61 percent. During the decade from January 1992 to December 2001, the IMF's statistics contain thirty-four cases of two-month currency collapses at least this large, in a total of twenty countries.[17] Among countries undergoing transitions to democracy in the 1980s and 1990s, currency crises were relatively common. Figure 7.3 shows the path of the nominal exchange rate in several

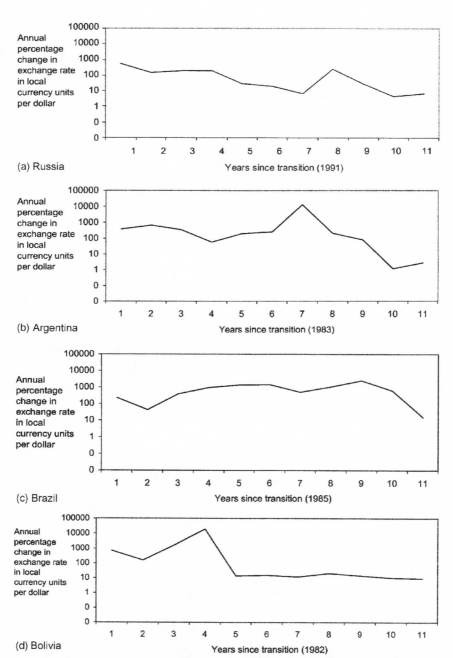

Figure 7.3. Exchange Rates and Democratization in Developing Countries.

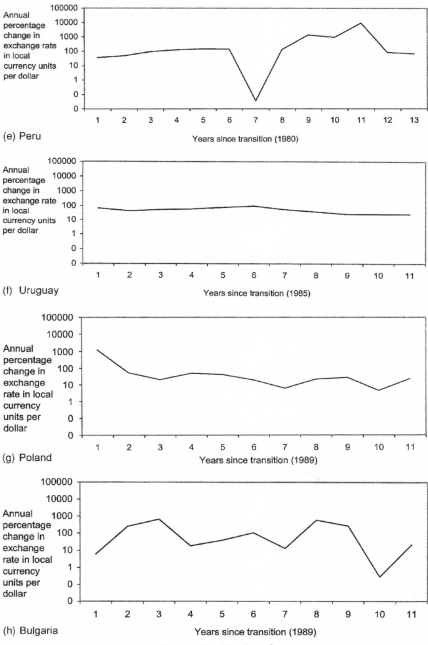

(e) Peru

(f) Uruguay

(g) Poland

(h) Bulgaria

Figure 7.3. *Continued*

new Latin American democracies, as well as in Poland and Bulgaria. In each case, I plot the annual percentage change in the nominal exchange rate against the number of years since the start of transition.[18] All these countries suffered years of exchange rate volatility, often with more than one upward spike along the way. By far the worst experiences were in Bolivia in 1985, Argentina in 1989, Peru in 1990, and Brazil in 1993. The twelve-fold increase in Poland's nominal (zloty/$) exchange rate in 1989 was more than twice the largest one-year depreciation in Russia's ruble.

Not only were currency crises quite common in developing—and democratizing—countries that were integrated with world markets, the type of crisis that occurred in Russia in 1998 bears a strong resemblance to other recent cases. In a common scenario, a temporary inflow of capital enables the government to finance relatively large budget deficits. Often, domestic banks act as intermediaries, borrowing dollars on international markets and investing in high-interest-rate government bonds. A fixed or insufficiently flexible exchange rate, introduced to create credibility in fighting inflation, leads to gradual real exchange rate appreciation, depressing growth and tax revenues. At a certain point, international investors start worrying about a devaluation—in part because of the high real exchange rate, in part because of accumulating public debt and weak revenue performance—and start withdrawing capital. Unless the IMF at this point helps with major support—and sometimes even if it does—fears turn to panic and a mass outflow, forcing the government to devalue. Although no two currency crises are identical, something resembling this occurred in Turkey in 2000–2001, Brazil in 1998–1999, Argentina in 2001—and Russia in 1998.[19]

From the perspective of 2004, the more extreme statements about the consequences of August 1998 seem overblown. In terms of output and low inflation, the country did not lose "ten years"—it lost about one.[20] If 1998 witnessed Russia's "total economic collapse," the next couple of years saw its total economic revival. While the crisis may have increased discontent with the way democracy was being implemented, it did not discredit the concept. Between 1996 and 1999, the proportion of respondents to one survey who said they were dissatisfied with how democracy was developing in Russia rose from 57 to 80 percent. Nevertheless, 64 percent of respondents in 1999–2000 still said they supported the idea of democracy, and 60 percent thought that it would be a "good way for governing Russia."[21] As for attitudes toward market reform, by July 2000 the percentage of survey respondents saying market reforms should be continued had increased from 29 percent in July 1998 *before* the crisis to 35 percent.[22]

What about the overvaluation of the real exchange rate? Theory provides few clues about what a country's real exchange rate should be. Real exchange rates in many transition economies appreciated sharply in early years, but probably remained substantially below purchasing power parity, as is common in developing countries.[23] Economists' opinions differ on whether or not the ruble was substantially "overvalued"—and even over exactly what that would mean.[24] Without resolving this question, a few other points are worth noting.

First, it is not entirely clear what role the real exchange rate played in the stagnation of the mid-1990s and growth of 1999–2000. Real appreciation is supposed to depress growth by stifling exports and exacerbating import competition. But throughout the early 1990s, as the real exchange rate was appreciating sharply, Russian exports were increasing and the trade surplus was expanding. Appreciation did not lead—as in some other countries—to a drop in exports and an unsustainable trade deficit.[25] Second, some economists believe that the rapid growth in 1999–2000 was caused by the resurgence of world oil and gas prices more than by the effect of devaluation.[26] After the 1998 crisis, the real exchange rate fell only to the level of early 1995. Since that exchange rate had not stimulated growth in 1995, it is not obvious how it would have done so in 1999.

Even if the real exchange rate's relationship to growth in Russia is open to question, rapid appreciation may still have increased investors' anxiety. What goes up does often come down. According to Goldfajn and Valdés, there were no cases between 1960 and 1994 in which real exchange rate appreciations of more than 35 percent were not followed by a devaluation.[27] However, in Russia the real exchange rate had peaked by early 1996—before the large inflow of international capital. So if investors were scared away by its overvaluation in 1998, it is odd that they were not also scared away in 1996.[28]

In short, Russia's unstable and rapidly depreciating currency—and the crisis the authorities drifted into in 1998—reflected failures common to many developing country governments. Russia's experience of exchange rate volatility was not unusual. While the circumstantial evidence suggests that currency overvaluation depressed growth and increased the risk of financial crisis in the mid-1990s, even this cannot be asserted unequivocally. That Russia's exchange rate problems were not unusual does not make it less important to explain their causes. But it suggests these causes may lie in factors common to other developing and democratizing countries, rather than in those unique to Russia.

EXPLAINING RUSSIA'S PERFORMANCE

Common Arguments

Why was Russia's currency so unstable in the 1990s? Why was the real exchange rate allowed to appreciate so much between 1994 and 1998? Why did the authorities fail to avert the 1998 financial crisis? Previous attempts to answer these questions have generally placed responsibility at one of three levels.

A first type of account locates the blame straightforwardly with individual monetary officials. Russia's currency gyrated and fell, in this view, because of the errors or economic illiteracy of the decision makers in the Central Bank and Ministry of Finance. The economic bureaucrats who staffed most ministries were certainly new to the task of managing a market economy. Boris Fyodorov, who served as finance minister in 1993 and head of the State Tax Service in 1998, blamed the August crisis in part on the "monstrous incompetence" of his colleagues in the Central Bank and Ministry of Finance.[29] Critics point to a number of specific "mistakes" of both the government and Central Bank. Some relate to the particular exchange rate policies pursued in different periods; others concern associated types of "incompetence," such as inadequate prudential regulation of the commercial banks' international operations or fiscal irresponsibility.[30]

A second common argument blames the institutional setup within which these officials operated. Dysfunctional outcomes resulted from the fragmented and incoherent organization of the state. In this view, disagreements and power struggles between different state actors undermined the effectiveness and rationality of policy. These conflicts occurred at several levels. Some attributed poor macroeconomic policy to a chronic standoff between the Central Bank and the Ministry of Finance.[31] Other observers pointed to the frequent confrontations between government and parliament. Many blamed the Duma's refusal to authorize most of the government's emergency fiscal package in July 1998 for triggering the crisis that followed.[32] In the early 1990s, disagreements between parliament and government over monetary policy and the budget led to large deficits and bursts of cash emission. Timothy Frye has shown that greater executive–legislature polarization correlates in the postcommunist countries with poorer economic performance.[33] In the "institutional division" view, the disorganization of political institutions and the polarized interests of their leaders generated contradictory and volatile exchange rate policies.[34]

Third, some observers attribute the ruble's instability and depreciation to "capture" of the state by powerful business groups and their leaders, the so-called "oligarchs." According to Charles Fairbanks: "The [Russian] state is weak because it has privatized away crucial powers to businessmen like the Moscow bankers."[35] Belief in the pernicious effects of state capture was widespread both in Russia and the West in the 1990s. Among Russian businessmen surveyed in the summer of 1999, 35 percent thought their business had been significantly harmed by the sale of parliamentary votes to private interests, and 32 percent said the same about the sale of presidential decrees.[36] In the "state capture" view, the ruble zigged, zagged, appreciated, and crashed in Russia in the 1990s because the powerful interests that pulled the strings of government stood to benefit from such movements.[37]

These views have different implications for how to improve macroeconomic management. If state capture caused Russia's exchange rate mismanagement, the solution would be to expose and constrain such illicit influence, and to insulate policy makers from special interests. If the problem was institutional conflict, then centralizing economic authority and streamlining decision making should help. If the real culprit was ignorance or mistakes, leaders would need to be taught more macroeconomics. (Of course, the three explanations might all be partly correct: Russia might suffer from ignorant policy makers, incoherent institutions, *and* oligarchical capture.) I now explore the extent to which these three sets of factors can explain the perceived failures of exchange rate management in the three phases of policy identified earlier: 1992–1995, 1995–1998, and 1998–2003.

1992–1995

In the first three years of Yeltsin's economic reforms, the nominal exchange rate was crashing while the real rate was rapidly appreciating. Both the nominal fall and the real rise have been seen as major policy failures. The former arguably scared away investors. The latter rendered Russian exports less competitive and prepared the way for the 1998 crisis.

One problem with these criticisms is that they are mutually inconsistent. The real appreciation occurred because the nominal rate did not depreciate *fast enough* to match the rise in Russian prices. The only way the central authorities could have resisted—temporarily—the rise in the real exchange rate would have been to throw even more rubles onto the currency market, driving the nominal exchange rate down even faster. This would have had at best a temporary effect, since the additional rubles exchanged for dollars would have driven up domestic prices when spent, eroding the initial effect on the real exchange rate.

The underlying causes of the real appreciation are unclear. As mentioned already, real appreciation occurred in almost all postcommunist countries in the early years of transition. Sometimes, such appreciations reflect anti-inflationary policies of the monetary authorities, who intervene by selling dollars. This cannot be true for Russia in this period, since the authorities started out with almost no dollars to sell. When the Central Bank did begin intervening significantly in mid-1994, its efforts were dramatically defeated on "Black Tuesday."[38] Real appreciation might reflect increased demand for—and an increase in the relative price of—nontradable goods.[39] However, there is no evidence of this. In fact, the price index for services rose more slowly than the consumer price index (CPI), while the price indexes for some of the main tradable commodities such as crude oil rose faster than the CPI. Alternatively, real appreciation might reflect increased productivity in the tradables sector (the Balassa-Samuelson effect), or increased capital inflows.[40] Neither of these seems very likely in Russia in 1992–1995.

Why did the monetary authorities not attempt to hold down this real appreciation by selling more rubles on the currency market? The answer to this seems too obvious to need much emphasis. In 1992, the country had suffered a burst of hyperinflation, and high inflation continued to disrupt economic activity. Thus, the opposite criticism seems more plausible. Why, given this extreme inflation, did the authorities not try harder to slow the nominal depreciation (at the cost of temporarily increasing real appreciation)?

After the initial burst of inflation associated with price liberalization, the proximate cause of this nominal depreciation was the Central Bank's large, periodic credit emissions. These went to finance the federal budget, as well as to provide earmarked credits to favored economic sectors. Thus, explaining the ruble's nominal fall in this period requires explaining the rapid money growth.[41]

Economic errors, interest group pressures, and conflicts between institutions may all have played a part. There were some in Russia around this time who argued that large increases in the money supply were not inflationary. However, such views were not dominant. And economic reformers in key positions in the finance ministry and Central Bank were quite familiar with the quantity theory of money. In fact, the government did cut spending dramatically, reducing the need for deficit financing. And the Central Bank even under its Soviet-style chairman Viktor Gerashchenko sharply reduced money emission in 1993–1994—albeit not as rapidly as critics would have liked.

Interest group pressures certainly contributed to slowing macroeconomic stabilization. The Central Bank's money creation generated enormous gains for some groups and losses for others. The main beneficiaries were the enterprises, farms, and budget-funded organizations that received government aid or cheap Central Bank credits. At the same time, commercial banks earned huge profits by converting their depositors' money into dollars and later repaying depositors in depreciated rubles. The main losers were the owners of low-interest-rate bank deposits—the public and enterprises (although some were compensated with budget or Central Bank aid), who suffered from soaring inflation. Estimates of the net gain for the commercial banks in 1992–1993 are on the order of 8 percent of gross domestic product (GDP).[42]

However, it is hard to view the movement of opposition to tight money in 1992–1993 as a real case of "state capture." Besides the commercial banks clamoring for loose money and the industrial managers and collective farm bosses lobbying for credits, labor unions and rank-and-file workers were also agitating for state aid to pay wages. Acting in concert, these groups constituted a powerful political force that could undermine government attempts to control inflation. But it had more the character of a vast coalition of special interests than a narrow group of state captors.

The argument that institutional divisions undermined exchange rate stability in these years is also subject to some obvious problems. First, as already noted (fn. 34), many economists actually contend that strict divisions between state agencies are *good* for macroeconomic policy. Central Bank independence has become a mantra among macroeconomists, but this is just such an institutional division. Similarly, some argue that dividing control over budgetary decision making in a certain way between parliament and government can increase fiscal discipline.[43]

Second, even if one believes that institutional divisions are bad for macroeconomic performance, it is not clear how great the institutional divisions in Russia—at least those between Central Bank and government—actually were. A law on the Central Bank of 1995 sought to make the Central Bank's chairperson more independent of politics. But in practice, such chairpersons were far from independent all through the decade. One was unceremoniously forced to resign before his term ended by the speaker of parliament in 1992. A second was forced out by the president in 1994. A third "acting" chairperson was also dismissed by the president in 1995. Yet another was fired by the president in 1998, with the second reinstated.[44] He too was fired before the end of his term by Putin in 2002. Of these five central bankers, not one left office at the end of his or her term. Despite the formal accountability of the Central Bank to parliament, it was the president who—in effect—dismissed four of the five.

The divisions between the government and parliament were much clearer, and did seem to add to macroeconomic pressures. But if these explain rapid nominal depreciation in 1992–1995, they make the success of stabilization from 1995 all the more puzzling. Money creation slowed substantially during that year, along with nominal depreciation. Yet the institutional and political divisions remained as intense as ever. There was no constitutional change at that time in the relationship between president and parliament. The Central Bank chair in 1995 was a close associate of Gerashchenko (who had been dismissed after "Black Tuesday"), and the government was itself an incoherent collection of mutually opposed sectoral lobbyists, old apparatchiks, and the odd economic liberal. Parliament and government remained generally at loggerheads. Clearly, fragmentation and institutional conflict were compatible with good outcomes as well as bad.

In short, errors and ignorance may have played a part, but probably not a decisive one. Institutional divisions and interest group lobbying were also elements of the story, but neither can explain why stabilization succeeded in 1995 but failed in earlier years. The most convincing explanation for the sinking nominal exchange rate and soaring real rate in the early 1990s would combine purely economic factors (which seemed to require real appreciation) and the competing pressures of *many* economic groups, which led to high—but not unlimited—money emission. This changed in 1995 when the government found a political strategy to overcome resistance to stabilization from key interest groups and their representatives in parliament and the Central Bank.[45] By that time, certain tactically useful tools—in particular a government bond market—had been created. But a major improvement in policy and outcomes occurred without any significant improvement in governance.

1995–1998

By late 1995, the nominal exchange rate had been stabilized within its corridor, and the real exchange rate had reached a plateau. Three sets of questions might be raised about exchange rate policy in this period. First, why did the authorities not devalue in 1997, as some economists recommended? Second, why did they make a series of decisions that in retrospect seem to have increased the odds of crisis or increased its severity in the event? Third, why did they not reduce budget deficits more in order to lower their dependence on hot international money?

Why No Early Devaluation?

By 1997, certain economists were warning that the ruble was substantially overvalued. The real exchange rate had not risen much since late 1995. However, the prices of oil and many of Russia's other major export commodities had plunged, rendering a high real exchange rate more costly. And, although a little positive growth was recorded in 1997, much of industry remained stagnant. In retrospect, Anatoly Chubais blames himself for not realizing the dangers in late 1997: "In the summer and autumn of 1997, I, working in the government, should have evaluated the situation more strictly and foreseen the risks. The year 1997 was very successful economically—it was the first year of economic growth in Russia—then was the time to correct policy, particularly on the currency."[46]

The Central Bank and government seriously considered a moderate devaluation in November 1997, after weathering a first blow from the Asian financial crisis, at the cost of several billion dollars in Central Bank reserves. According to Sergei Dubinin:

> The real decision to reject a devaluation was taken in the fall of 1997. Then we had
> a basis for conducting a devaluation quickly following the improvement on the

currency market, on the wave of the Asian crisis. But then a decision on principle was taken to try to avoid this, to oppose it with all force. Both the government and CB were committed to this.[47]

Why did they reject this option? Capture by the oligarchs is certainly one possibility. It is clear that by late 1997 most of the large commercial banks had come to fear a devaluation. By then, many had accumulated debt in dollars and had sold forward contracts on the dollar to foreign investors that would be harder to repay after a devaluation. As of December 1995, the banks' foreign liabilities came to $6.5 billion, and they had a surplus on foreign operations of about $3.4 billion. By 1997, foreign liabilities had risen to $17.4 billion, and the surplus had turned into a deficit of some $5.2 billion.[48] By January 1998, the Central Bank had even removed the requirement that commercial banks hedge their dollar forward contracts with it. For many of the banks, a serious devaluation meant bankruptcy. This explains the feverish lobbying of major bankers in the Russian White House the weekend of August 15.

Officials from both the government and Central Bank were certainly concerned about the health of the country's leading banks if the ruble were to fall. However, the image of "capture" does not quite fit the situation. First, the oligarchs' interest in avoiding devaluation was an interest the government itself had created. It would be truer to say that, in this regard, the oligarchs had been captured by the government. By making it easy for Russian banks to borrow in dollars and invest in fixed-rate government bonds, the government had given them an interest in low inflation and a stable ruble. Such tactics worked precisely by increasing the banks' exposure to currency risk. At the same time, by involving the main banks in privatization on highly lucrative terms, the government had created hostages to stable money. Most of the oligarchs hoped to resell their stakes to foreign investors, who would be scared away by financial crisis.[49] Thus, the government caused the oligarchs to support exchange rate stability, rather than the other way around.

The oligarchs were certainly not the only group opposed to devaluation as of late 1997. The main potential victim of a sharp drop in the ruble was the public. A falling ruble would devalue the population's ruble-denominated bank accounts. If, in addition, banks went bankrupt, depositors could lose their entire savings. Not only that, a general bank failure would threaten the system by which payments—including wages and salaries—were made. Decision makers at the time do appear to have been very concerned with public opinion. Yeltsin, while deflecting blame for August 1998 onto others, saw in the Kiriyenko government's reluctance to devalue early the quite accurate fear of losing public support.[50]

A third source of pressure against devaluation was the IMF. The fund was clear and forceful in its opposition. John Odling-Smee, director of the IMF's European II department, announced on May 29 that "The IMF management and staff believe that . . . a devaluation of the ruble can and should be avoided." As late as August 1998, the Fund reiterated its support for the "existing exchange rate and monetary policy strategy."[51] In fact, there was no lobby for a lower exchange rate at the time. As one Central Bank staffer put it: "The lobby was Illarionov."[52]

Nor does institutional conflict explain why the authorities did not devalue early on. In fact, all institutions—the Central Bank, government, and parliament—appear to have been united against such a devaluation.[53] Some observers hint that the Central Bank might even have wanted to provoke a crisis, and point out that Sberbank—which the Central Bank controls—did not roll over all its treasury bonds in July 1998. But since the outcome of the crisis was disastrous for the Central Bank leadership, it is not clear why they would have wished for this.[54] The mutual suspicion between different state bodies probably did not help. The October 1994 "Black Tuesday" crisis had prompted calls for the security services to investigate corruption at the Central Bank. Dubinin's deputy Sergei Alexashenko reported that any subsequent attempts to let the exchange rate slide a little led to alarming phone calls from the Security Council and FSB.[55] But this would not have been a problem had a devaluation been agreed upon in advance with the government.

Was refusing to devalue early simply a "mistake"? Some suspect that this would only have hastened the crisis, rather than reducing its force. When the Central Bank did try to let the ruble slide slightly faster in early 1998, interest rates on GKOs jumped; investors extrapolated the drop in the dollar value of their profits and demanded a higher rate to compensate. Given the government's dependence on foreign capital to finance the budget deficit, an earlier devaluation might merely have prompted an immediate budget crisis.[56] A second reason for doubting that an early devaluation would have helped was the country's large dollar-denominated debt. With foreign investors fleeing even faster, it might quickly have become necessary to default.[57]

Some also argue that the banks would have been even more vulnerable had a devaluation come in 1997. According to Dubinin, "There is a Russian saying: The sooner you go to jail, the sooner you'll get out. We could have started the crisis earlier. But it would have been as serious, may be more serious because banks then were less prepared."[58] If the aim was to buy the banking system time, it was surprisingly ineffective. The aggregate foreign liabilities of credit institutions on July 31, 1998, were almost exactly what they were on December 31, 1997.[59] Others argue that delaying increased the severity of the crisis.[60]

Particular "Mistakes"

Certain actions of the Central Bank and government seem puzzling in retrospect. Some would seem to have made crisis more likely, while others increased the costs when crisis came.

First, the Central Bank is accused of lax regulation of the commercial banks' international activities. In particular, the decision to remove the requirement that domestic banks hedge their risk on foreign currency forward contracts with the Central Bank seems odd. This increased the exposure of these banks to foreign currency risk. Why did the bank do this? According to the Central Bank's 1997 annual report, the IMF demanded this step. Eliminating the requirement for such hedging with the Central Bank was necessary, according to the report, to meet the conditions of Article 8 of the IMF Articles of Agreement, which Russia signed in August 1996.[61] The IMF's reasons made sense theoretically: the Central Bank was completely insuring foreign and domestic banks for currency risk, creating moral hazard. Perhaps a useful policy might have been to increase the required foreign currency reserves that commercial banks had to hold against such currency forwards. This would have both made forwards more costly (to the domestic banks) and slowed the inflow of foreign capital.

Second, throughout 1997 the Central Bank was reducing the barriers to repatriation of foreign investors' profits on the government bond markets. Why? Again, according to the bank, the IMF insisted on this.[62] According to one junior Central Bank official, the leadership also hoped that reducing barriers would help to attract desperately needed capital. Judging by the statistics, it did. The share of nonresidents on the GKO markets increased in the first half of 1998, and especially in July 1998 after news of the IMF credit was announced, at which point there was a strong inflow of nonresident capital. It was domestic investors who were fleeing the market most vigorously in 1998.[63]

Third, Illarionov faulted the Central Bank for failing to build up sufficient currency reserves in the years preceding the 1998 crisis, despite large inflows of dollars. I simply lack the detailed financial data to judge whether or not this is a fair criticism. The key issue is what share of the hard currency that flowed directly through the Central Bank was in fact used to support the ruble's value during the period of the corridor, and what share frittered away or misappropriated in the way Illarionov implies. The Central Bank does not publish accounts that reveal the size of its interventions on the currency markets. It is certainly true that the bank devoted enormous resources to staff, salaries, and benefits. The reason it was able to do so was—primarily—Central Bank independence. The law permitted the Central Bank to dispose of its "profits" autonomously. Even so, the government—together with the parliament—insisted that the bank make a large additional contribution to the budget out of its profits in the summer of 1998.

Fourth, many have criticized the decision of the authorities in August 1998 not just to devalue but also to declare a moratorium on international debt payments by the domestic banks.[64] This was a lifeline thrown to the banks, which may not have helped them survive but did enable some to hide assets from creditors. According to those involved, the moratorium aimed simply to avoid a crash of the entire banking system caused by the government's freeze of the GKO market, which was itself necessitated by the simple lack of cash to make the payments due. As Chubais put it: "For our banking system, not to receive the planned income from GKOs would be close to a fatal blow."[65] Another concern of the government was that the moratorium would reduce the pressure on the ruble by reducing the mass of dollars that domestic banks would have to buy to make debt payments.[66]

A final "mistake" was the government's attempted debt swap in July 1998. Under this program, also introduced on the IMF's recommendation, holders of ruble-denominated, short-term GKOs were allowed to trade them for dollar-denominated seven- or twenty-year bonds with guaranteed 14 percent yields.[67] Such debt swaps risk merely revealing the government's desperation, and so hasten the crisis. If they fail to avert collapse, the hard currency obligations are harder for the government to repay after devaluation. Some previous debt swaps of this kind had failed, as in Mexico in 1994, and some economists viewed the Russian attempt as foolish and dangerous.[68] The reason for this measure does not appear to have been capture—most of the oligarchs did not take up the offer. Rather, the motivation was pressure from the IMF and the hope that it might actually reduce the short-term debt problem that the government faced.

Fiscal Irresponsibility?

Almost all observers agree that a fundamental cause of the August 1998 crisis was large fiscal deficits and growing public debt. According to Chubais, who was brought in at the peak of crisis to negotiate with the international institutions, "On August 17 we paid for six years of irresponsible budget policy."[69] Poor fiscal policy is often explained as the result of a combination of interest group capture—the inability of parliament and government to stand up to scores of special interests—and institutional incoherence. Representatives of the government blame parliament for repeatedly passing unrealistic budgets containing unsustainable expenditures. They also blame the Duma for refusing to pass key parts of the government's emergency fiscal program in July 1998.[70]

Fiscal policy was actually improving in some respects in the years that preceded August 1998. The federal budget deficit fell sharply from the fourth quarter of 1996 (9.2 percent of GDP) to the third quarter of 1998 (3.0 percent of GDP). In the first half of 1998, the federal budget even had a primary surplus of 0.3 percent of GDP. However, these figures looked good in part because a large share of tax revenues was paid in noncash forms during this period. Debt service absorbed about 47 percent of cash tax revenues in 1997.[71]

In general, the evidence that poor fiscal policy lies at the heart of financial crises is not unequivocal. Fiscal imbalances often precede currency crises, but not always (Mexico in 1994, Chile 1978–1982, Finland 1988–1992 are counterexamples).[72] And many cases of fiscal imbalance do not lead to currency crises. Nor is there a threshold level of the budget deficit at which crisis is triggered. Sachs, Tornell, and Velasco examined how twenty emerging market economies were affected by the Mexican Tequila crisis of 1994.[73] They found that "fiscal policy stances during the period 1990–94, in and of themselves, do not explain why some countries experienced greater financial crises than others in the aftermath of the December 1994 devaluation."

In Russia, the markets do not appear to have been responding primarily to fiscal deficits. In fact, the interest rate that the government had to pay on its bond correlates *negatively* over time with the size of the deficit—the smaller the deficit, the more reluctant were investors to lend (see figure 7.4). This was particularly true in the period leading up to August 1998. From 1997 Q3 to 1998 Q3, the federal budget deficit fell from 6.3 to 3.0 percent of GDP. The average yield on government bonds rose during this period from 19 to 98.8 percent.[74] It is not clear, in any case, that sharp expenditure cuts would have created confidence in the markets since investors might well simply have believed that such temporary fiscal restraint was not politically sustainable.[75]

Conclusion

The monetary authorities decided not to devalue in late 1997 because even a moderate devaluation would have been extremely costly for Russian banks and the public. The IMF supported them in this stance. Policy makers hoped that it might be possible to scrape through without a crisis. While this might seem foolish in retrospect, it was not so obviously wrong at the time. Fiscal performance, although weak, was improving rapidly—and, in any case, market perceptions did not seem to be closely related to the actual fiscal data. External pressures, beginning in Asia, certainly played an important part in scaring away investors, as did the fall in the international oil price, which accelerated sharply in early 1998. The currency crisis of August 1998 resulted not so much from capture, institutional conflict, or simple mistakes as from a high-risk

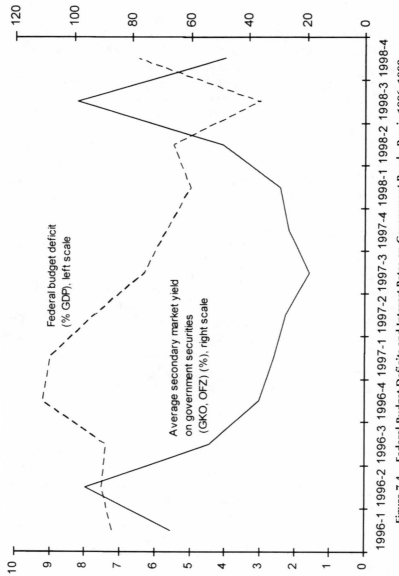

Figure 7.4. Federal Budget Deficits and Interest Rates on Government Bonds, Russia 1996–1998.

gamble—probably the best of the unattractive policy alternatives available at the time—that the government lost.

After 1996, Russia opened its capital markets to foreign investors at a pace that in retrospect seems foolish. One reason for this was pressure from the IMF. However, the spike in interest rates that occurred in the 1996 presidential campaign had left the government with GKO debt that would have been extremely hard to service without foreign capital. IMF officials were not always sure that liberalizing access for foreigners to the government bond market was a good idea. Yegor Gaidar recalls a conversation with Stanley Fischer of the IMF in late 1996, during which Fischer expressed doubts that the Russians should open up the government security market to foreigners. Gaidar recalls telling him that there was no alternative: "Without serious inflows of foreign money, it was absolutely impossible to see how we could cope with the problem of the GKOs and reduce interest rates."[76]

In sum, although the oligarchs and their banks certainly made their opinions known to the monetary authorities during this period, their interests were actually aligned with those of the general public: both desperately wanted to avoid a devaluation. Given the choice between provoking a crisis for sure in late 1997 and risking a potentially larger one in 1998, the government gambled.[77] The monetary authorities may have erred in liberalizing capital markets too fast, but the alternatives were also highly unappealing. Most of the failures of this period look more like consequences of difficult economic conditions than failures of government per se.

1998–2003

After the spurt of inflation that followed the devaluation, inflation returned to moderate levels quite quickly. The nominal exchange rate stabilized at around twenty-four rubles/$, and then began a gradual decline. Over the course of the next few years, the real exchange rate rose gradually. Exchange rate management during this period has not been subjected to serious criticism. However, certain features deserve comment.

First, the experience of this period casts doubt—again—on the role that political fragmentation and institutional conflict, as well as oligarch capture, played in previous failures. After Putin's rise to power in 1999–2000, political conflict appeared to diminish sharply. The 1999 election secured the government a stable majority in the Duma for the first time since 1992, and confrontations between government and parliament became rare. There was also very little evident disagreement between the Central Bank and the government. The oligarchs appeared, at least temporarily, weakened by their 1998 losses and on the defensive.

Yet exchange rate policy was extremely similar to that pursued between 1995 and precrisis 1998. Although the authorities no longer announced a corridor, the Central Bank still intervened to support a gradual nominal depreciation along with gradual real appreciation. While in June 1995–June 1998 the ruble's nominal value fell by 24 percent, in June 1999–June 2002 it fell by 22 percent. And whereas in June 1995–June 1998 the real exchange rate appreciated by 39 percent, in June 1999–June 2002, it appreciated by 33 percent.[78] As figure 7.1 shows, by the end of 2003, the real exchange rate was close to its precrisis peak.

What did change in this period was fiscal performance. Budget deficits turned into surpluses. The government began paying down, rather than accumulating, debt, while the Central Bank built up large currency reserves. This change in fiscal performance seems to have had more to do—at least initially— with changes in external conditions than with changes in government policies. A soaring international oil price and rapid economic growth were as salutary for the economy and state budget as the sinking oil price and stagnation of 1995–1998 had been harmful. They enabled the Central Bank to accumulate large currency reserves and the government to reduce its borrowing. As a result, despite a large real appreciation, the ruble is viewed today as much less vulnerable than in the mid-1990s.

That monetary authorities chose similar exchange rate policies in periods when (a) the oligarchs were at their strongest and (b) the oligarchs were perceived as far weaker suggests that oligarchical capture may not have had much to do with the choice of policies. That authorities chose similar policies in periods when (a) the state was perceived as seriously fragmented and factionalized and (b) conflicts and fragmentation had been muted by Putin's popularity and electoral mandate suggests, in turn, that such factors may not have been as influential as people thought at the time. The reduction in political fragmentation did not require any institutional changes. It resulted directly from Putin's soaring popularity.

Second, while the long-run trend in the ruble's value was quite clear and predictable, the short-run path was less smooth. In fact, the gradual nominal depreciation was punctuated by frequent small reversals. The reason for such a pattern was not entirely clear even to those working in the bank, where it was known as "Cherepanov's Staircase" after a former head of the bank's foreign operations department who set the daily level of Central Bank intervention (see figure 7.5).[79] If such small irregularities were deliberately generated by the bank, they are somewhat puzzling. The only benefit I can see in unpredictable movements is to create inside information in the hands of those who decide them.

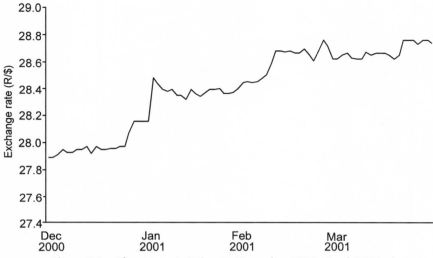

Figure 7.5. Cherepanov's Staircase, December 2000–March 2001.

CONCLUSION

Russia suffered very rapid and volatile nominal exchange rate depreciation in the 1990s, alongside sharp real appreciation in the first half of the decade. In August 1998, the Central Bank gave up trying to defend the previous currency corridor, and the ruble crashed. In the subsequent period, the currency depreciated slowly in nominal terms and rose gradually in real terms. The Russian authorities have been criticized harshly for their failure to provide nominal and real exchange rate stability, and this has been viewed as a symptom of a more general failure of governance. The country's currency instability has been variously attributed to capture of the state by big business, conflict between different state actors, and straightforward ignorance or policy mistakes.

The analysis of this chapter suggests a rather different view. First, comparison with other postcommunist and developing countries shows that Russia's macroeconomic difficulties were not unusual. Many middle-income and developing countries suffer from similar turbulence. The exchange rate problems of Argentina, Brazil, and Poland in the 1980s were more severe than those of Russia in the 1990s. There was nothing uniquely Russian—or even postcommunist—in the combination of inflation, exchange rate instability, loose budgeting, and speculative crisis that the country experienced.

Second, while lobbying oligarchs, institutional conflict, and economic mis-conceptions helped define the context in which policy was made, these factors do not convincingly explain the pattern of choices made by policy makers. They also do a poor job of explaining why exchange rate management was much more successful in some periods than in others. Policy—and performance—changed dramatically in 1995 without any significant change in institutions or in the degree of conflict among state actors, and at a time when oligarch influence was rising. When overt political conflict did subside under Putin, exchange rate policy remained very similar to that in the previous period. Although fiscal performance did improve after 1999, this reflected changed economic conditions—high oil prices, economic growth—rather than a funda-mentally different policy or new institutions. It is easy in retrospect to identify "mistakes" of economic policy makers, some of which do seem like manifes-tations of incompetence or corruption. But most of the so-called "mistakes" were not caused by ignorance or misunderstanding of economic theory. Rather, they resulted from ultimately unsuccessful but understandable attempts to ma-neuver between different dangers, making risky tradeoffs in the gray areas of science.

Nor does the common contention that Russian policy makers are unrespon-sive and that the force of electoral accountability is too weak to work as an explanation for this perceived failure of governance. Russia's political lead-ers are often accused of ignoring the wishes of voters in order to favor their cronies. However, a simple analysis of who stood to gain and who to lose from particular exchange rate policies at key points suggests that it was precisely the voters' interests that were prioritized at the expense of economic elites. Al-though economic insiders were favored in many ways by government policies in the 1990s, exchange rate policy does not seem to have been a major source of such favors. The problem—especially around the time of elections—may have been more a populist *excess* of responsiveness.

The government tolerated a high real exchange rate in the mid-1990s as part of a strategy to slow inflation and keep imports cheap for consumers. Business elites at the time had systems in place to profit from inflation and could have sold oil more competitively under a lower exchange rate. The urgency of policy makers' desire to beat inflation in 1995 was fueled precisely by the conviction that without this Yeltsin could not be reelected in 1996. The same hope of attracting voters from Zyuganov led to the bursts of pre-election spending, funded at high interest rates. It was to deal with the resulting debt that authorities later chose to relax capital controls. The decision not to attempt an early devaluation in 1997 was motivated at least in part by the fear that, after the experience of 1992, voters would not forgive reformers for inflicting another dose of such medicine.[80] In fact, had the state been more effectively captured by the energy sector oligarchs, Russia might well have continued with a floating exchange rate and protected domestic financial markets, avoiding the 1998 crash. In the longer run, the public suffered greatly from the 1998 devaluation. But there was an unavoidable tradeoff in 1995–1998 between low inflation and a low risk of financial crisis. In this case, the very competitiveness and historical significance of Russia's elections meant that pleasing the voters in the short run took precedence over their longer-run interests.

So what does account for the vagaries of Russian exchange rate policy and performance in the 1990s? The most convincing explanation has little to do with the incoherence or cooptation of state institutions, or with the unresponsiveness, ignorance, or corruption of officials. The main reason why Russia—and just about all middle-income countries like it—experience macroeconomic instability more frequently than developed countries is that the former face much greater economic challenges from a financially weaker position.

Developing market economies that are integrated—or integrating—into the world economy are particularly vulnerable to shifts in international market conditions. Their exports tend to be less diversified, rendering them sensitive to price shifts. Their currency and gold reserves are usually small. Their domestic financial markets tend to be shallow and subject to manipulation by small numbers of large investors. They rely on foreign capital for major infrastructure investments. But they are treated by international financial markets with alternating manic excitement and exaggerated reserve.

Russia had to struggle against all these factors. As of 1992, it had no currency or gold reserves to speak of, and no experience issuing government bonds. Its export and tax revenues were closely linked to world commodity prices, which plunged and then rose in the mid- to late 1990s. Financial markets were not just small; they had to be built from scratch. At the same time, the tasks of economic transformation that confronted Russia—and most other postcommunist states—were far greater than anything the advanced, capitalist countries had contemplated since 1945. Russia inherited a large monetary overhang, distorted relative prices, an obsolete capital stock, and a ballooning budget deficit. Lacking a large stabilization fund like that provided to Poland, any country with these problems was doomed to an extended period of macroeconomic turbulence. If, as President Yeltsin admitted in 1997, the Russian government tended to act as a "fire brigade" rather than implementing a strategic plan, this was not without reason. In many senses, both economic and political, Russia was on fire.[81]

What caused the—at least temporary—stabilization of 1999–2003 was the burst of economic growth, stimulated in part by the 1998 devaluation, in part by the resurgence of oil prices, which improved Russia's fiscal accounts and permitted accumulation of a very large currency reserve. By early 2003, the

Central Bank had over $50 billion in gross international reserves ($41.5 bn
in net reserves), equivalent to almost 90 percent of 2002 imports.[82] These
reserves, more than anything else, will buffer the economy from future swings
in international prices and investor sentiment. Like the earlier problems, the
recent improvement owes more to changes in economic conditions than to any
change in institutions or policy.

While economic conditions define the evolving challenges and constraints
within which policy makers maneuver, the policies themselves obviously
affect performance. The most notable improvement in Russian policy came
in 1995 with the stabilization program and introduction of the currency corridor. I argued that pro-reform politicians were motivated at this time by the
urgent desire to provide voters with one visible reform success before the presidential election. But the desire does not explain the implementation. Later,
in the summer of 1998, a reformist government failed to persuade parliament
to adopt a fiscal emergency package that might have forestalled the panic on
currency markets. Why success in one case and failure in the other?

I do not believe this pattern of outcomes was predetermined by any general
logic. One can show in retrospect why the political strategy of reformers in
1995 succeeded in breaking the opposition of elites, while that adopted in
1998 did not. In the first case, benefits were provided to co-opt the leading
commercial banks and the Central Bank, while implicit energy subsidies served
to demobilize and disorganize opposition from the industrial sector. In the
second, the Kiriyenko government simultaneously attacked the interests of all
major political actors—the oil barons, regional governors, and parliamentary
opposition—who then united to oppose it.[83] Why reformers chose a more
effective strategy to deflect political opposition in 1995 than in 1998 may have
as much to do with the individuals involved as the political context.

What does all this suggest about Russia's broader problems of governance?
One should clearly be cautious in generalizing. That Russia's exchange rate
troubles seem to have little to do with characteristics of its state or defects of
its governance does not mean that such factors are unimportant in explaining
other perceived government failures. In other areas, institutional incoherence
or oligarchical capture may indeed have interfered with policymaking. But
two general points do emerge. First, as several other chapters in this volume
attest, the effectiveness or capacity of a given country's government can only
be evaluated by comparing it to those of other countries rather than to an ideal-
ized vision of how governments operate elsewhere in the world. Second, such
comparisons must take into account the vastly different challenges that governments in different countries face and the different conditions that confront
them. Such differences in external factors may fully explain what appear at
first to be differences in the quality of institutions.

Both these points would seem banal, except that they are so often ignored in journalistic and academic analyses of Russia. Some critics of the country's economic and political performance in the 1990s seemed to be comparing Russia—implicitly or explicitly—to long-established, capitalist democracies that faced far milder challenges. Yet were an American president obliged to simultaneously cut the public budget by 50 percent, reduce all tariffs, reform the banking system, and run for reelection against a credible Communist candidate, the United States too would surely see some turbulence. No matter how well-oiled and flexible a state's institutions, if it faces fickle international investors with a depressed economy and minimal currency reserves, it is in for a rough ride. This is not to deny the many imperfections of Russian state institutions. But it is to argue against faulty comparisons that strengthen complacency about the political institutions of the West while obfuscating the causes of the problems afflicting postcommunist societies.

NOTES

I thank Tim Colton, Sergei Dubinin, Oksana Dynnikova, Yegor Gaidar, Leonid Grigoriev, Stephen Holmes, Victoria Kotova, Vladimir Mau, Aleksandr Morozov, Konstantin Yanovsky, Sergei Zhavoronkov, and other participants in the working group for helpful comments or conversations.

1. Boris Yeltsin, *Midnight Diaries* (New York: PublicAffairs, 2000), 165.

2. Andrei Illarionov, "The Roots of the Economic Crisis," *Journal of Democracy* 10, no. 2 (1999): 68–82, at 68–69.

3. See U.S. House of Representatives, Speaker's Advisory Group on Russia, *Russia's Road to Corruption: How the Clinton Administration Exported Government Instead of Free Enterprise and Failed the Russian People* (Washington, DC: U.S. House of Representatives, 2000), chap. 8. It was an odd conclusion given that by that time Russia's real GDP had far surpassed its level immediately preceding the crisis.

4. Quoted in Jonathan Kirshner, "The Inescapable Politics of Money," in *Monetary Orders: Ambiguous Economics, Ubiquitous Politics*, ed. Jonathan Kirshner (Ithaca, NY: Cornell University Press, 2003), 15.

5. As late as August 13, 1998, Rudiger Dornbusch of MIT, perhaps the world authority on exchange rate economics, thought the Russian government could limit itself to a debt restructuring and avoid devaluation completely. In a radio interview, he announced that "Devaluation is out" (National Public Radio, *All Things Considered*, August 13, 1998).

6. There were conflicts of interest over how the losses associated with the 1998 crash were distributed among bank owners and depositors, but these had more to do with banking regulation than exchange rate policy per se.

7. This periodization is based on macroeconomic factors, not on politics. Thus, the final period starts after the August 1998 devaluation rather than at the beginning of the Putin administration.

8. Adopting a floating exchange rate initially was dictated by two factors. First, the authorities had no idea—and could not have any idea—what a sustainable exchange rate for the ruble would be until the huge relative price changes associated with price liberalization had occurred. Second, they had no currency reserves to speak of that could have been used to defend a particular parity.

9. Appreciation of the ruble's real exchange rate occurs when the purchasing power of the ruble on world markets increases relative to its purchasing power on Russian markets. Imports become cheaper for Russians, and Russian exports more expensive for foreign buyers. The real exchange rate is the nominal exchange rate (in local currency units per dollar) times the ratio of world to local price levels: $\varepsilon_{R/\$} = e_{R/\$} \times P_\$/P_R$, where $\varepsilon_{R/\$}$ is the real exchange rate, $e_{R/\$}$ is the nominal exchange rate in rubles per dollar, $P_\$$ is the world price level (in dollars), and P_R is the local price level (in rubles). The estimate shown in figure 2 is simply deflated by the CPI, with no weighting of commodities by their trade volumes or allowance for dollar inflation. However, the pattern would look similar no matter how the rate is calculated.

10. OECD, *Economic Surveys: Russian Federation* (Paris: OECD, 1997).

11. MICEX end of month rate, Russian Economic Trends database.

12. See, for example, Rudiger Dornbusch, Ilan Goldfajn, and Rodrigo O. Valdés, "Currency Crises and Collapses," *Brookings Papers on Economic Activity*, no. 2 (1995), 219–93.

13. For instance, Andrei Illarionov and Vladimir Popov.

14. See Illarionov, "The Roots of the Economic Crisis," 70–71: "It was not only necessary but possible to balance the Russian federal budget through further reductions in non-interest expenditures. The authorities, however, chose instead to pursue the less responsible (but more politically palatable) policy of raising domestic and international debt." Central bank officials also tended to emphasize irresponsible fiscal policy to explain the crisis—a convenient position since the bank had no role in fiscal management. According to Sergei Alexashenko: "In our view, undoubtedly, the roots of the crisis lie mainly in the Chernomyrdin government's weakness and inconsistency in strengthening budget revenue and implementing structural adjustments" (quoted in Illarionov, "The Roots of the Economic Crisis," 70–71).

15. IMF, *International Financial Statistics* (April 2002).

16. By per capita income, I mean GDP per capita at purchasing power parity, as estimated by the UN International Comparisons Project, averaged for 1991–2001. The range in these seventeen countries was from Venezuela ($5,606) to Poland ($7,331). Russia's average for these years was $6,350.

17. These were Afghanistan, Angola, Armenia, Belarus, Bulgaria, Zaire, Indonesia, Iran, Kazakhstan, Liberia, Moldova, Mongolia, Nigeria, Rwanda, Sudan, Suriname, Tajikistan, Turkmenistan, Ukraine, Yemen.

18. I date the start of transition as 1983 for Argentina, 1985 for Brazil, 1982 for Bolivia, 1980 for Peru, 1985 for Uruguay, 1991 for Russia, 1989 for Poland, 1989 for

Bulgaria. These generally correspond to sharp increases in Freedom House's political rights scores.

19. On Turkey's crisis, see Alexandra Bibbee, "Turkey's Crisis," *OECD Observer*, May 3, 2001.

20. By about August 1999, the inflation rate had settled back around 20–30 percent a year. By the end of 1999, real GDP had risen above the level of December 1997.

21. Timothy J. Colton and Michael McFaul, "Are Russians Undemocratic?" (Washington, DC: Carnegie Endowment for International Peace, 2001).

22. Data from VCIOM, at www.russiavotes.org. Twenty-seven percent thought market reforms should be stopped in July 1998, and 24 percent did in July 2000. Forty-four and 41 percent respectively said they did not know.

23. For a comparative discussion, see Padma Desai, "Macroeconomic Fragility and Exchange Rate Vulnerability: A Cautionary Record of Transition Economies," *Journal of Comparative Economics* 26 (1998): 621–41.

24. Popov and Illarionov considered it significantly overvalued by 1997. László Halpern and Charles Wyplosz ("Equilibrium Exchange Rates in Transition Economies," *IMF Staff Papers* 44, no. 4 [1997]: 430–61) suggested it was only slightly overvalued. As noted earlier, Rudiger Dornbusch thought devaluation could be avoided completely as late as August 13, 1998 (see fn. 5).

25. Nevertheless, Dornbusch, Goldfajn, and Valdés ("Currency Crises and Compromises") argue that in countries introducing reforms that reduce labor demand (through trade liberalization, budget cutting, and restructuring), it is not enough for the real exchange rate not to impede exports; it must fall sufficiently to stimulate domestic industry to absorb the freed labor. This did not occur in Russia in the mid-1990s or in Argentina in the late 1990s.

26. O. V. Dynnikova, "Makroekonomicheskie perspektivy ukrepleniya rublya i valutnaya politika," in *Ekonomicheskaya Ekspertnaya Gruppa, Instrumenty makroekonomicheskoi politiki dlya Rossii* (Moscow: TEIS, 2001), 108–32.

27. Ilan Goldfajn and Rodrigo O. Valdés, "The Aftermath of Appreciations" (Working Paper No. 5650, Boston: National Bureau for Economic Research, 1996).

28. The country may have faced a greater short-term debt rollover problem in 1998, but budget deficits were lower than in earlier years. The federal government budget deficit was 5.1 percent of GDP in the first half of 1998 (with a primary surplus of 0.3 percent of GDP), compared to a deficit of 6.8 percent in 1997, and 7.8 percent in 1996 (OECD, *Economic Surveys: Russian Federation* [Paris: OECD, 1997] and OECD, *Economic Surveys: Russian Federation* [Paris: OECD, 2000]).

29. Boris Fyodorov, *10 bezumnykh let* (Moscow: Sovershenno Sekretno, 1999), 210. A. Aganbegyan ("*O prichinakh finansovogo krizisa v Rossii,*" in Institute for the Economy in Transition, *Finansovy krizis: prichiny i posledstvia* [Moscow: IET, 2000]) also attributes the crisis to "economic policy mistakes in the period October 1997–September 1998, not only of the government but of all authorities including the Central Bank and State Duma" as well as to "an inadequate, incorrect reaction to the financial crisis in South-East Asia."

30. It might seem mysterious that Russia's economic officials would have known *anything* about the economics of exchange rates in the early 1990s, given their schooling in Marxist economics and previous quarantine from the capitalist world economy. But there were oases, even under late communism, where such matters were studied quite seriously. One of these was the Main Currency-Economic Administration of the USSR Central Bank (Glavnoe valyutno-ekonomicheskoe upravlenie pravlenia Gosbanka SSSR), where Boris Fyodorov himself got his professional start in the early 1980s. There, Fyodorov reports, he received only lightly censored issues of the *Financial Times* and *The Banker*, as well as dozens of financial journals. He recounts that his "economic views were formed to a considerable extent under the influence of the Bank of England's quarterly bulletin," which he studied in great detail (see Fyodorov, *10 bezumnykh let*).

31. For instance, Illarionov blames the 1998 crisis in part on a "financial war waged against the federal government in the summer of 1998 by the CBR's leadership" (Illarionov, "The Roots of the Economic Crisis," 75).

32. For instance, Anders Aslund, "The Problem of Fiscal Federalism," *Journal of Democracy* 10, no. 2 (1999): 83–86.

33. Timothy Frye, "The Perils of Polarization: Economic Performance in the Postcommunist World," *World Politics* 54, no. 3 (2002).

34. There is no agreement in the literature on Western countries about the relationship between institutional and political divisions and macroeconomic outcomes. Some authors have found that political or institutional fragmentation impairs macroeconomic performance, while others have found that such divisions restrain overspending. Nouriel Roubini and Jeffrey Sachs ("Government Spending and Budget Deficits in the Industrialized Countries," *Economic Policy* 8 [1989]: 700–32) found that coalition governments in the OECD countries tended to have higher budget deficits than single-party governments. Torsten Persson, Gerard Roland, and Guido Tabellini ("Separation of Powers and Political Accountability," *Quarterly Journal of Economics* [November 1997]: 1163–1202) argue that a specific separation of powers between parliament and executive can restrain fiscal excess. Jürgen Von Hagen and Ian Harden ("Budget Processes and Commitment to Fiscal Discipline" [Working Paper WP/96/78, Washington, DC: IMF, 1996]) argue that a more streamlined, centralized budgetary process leads to lower deficits and inflation. I found evidence that greater vertical division of powers in a decentralized state tends to entrench existing patterns of macroeconomic policy, whether good or bad (Daniel Treisman, "Decentralization and Inflation: Commitment, Collective Action, or Continuity?" *American Political Science Review* 94, no. 4 [December 2000]: 837–57). Clearly, what matters may be not just the *amount* of division but also the *type* of divisions.

35. Charles H. Fairbanks Jr., "The Feudalization of the State," *Journal of Democracy* 10, no. 2 (1999): 47–53, at 47.

36. See Joel S. Hellman, Geraint Jones, and Daniel Kaufmann, "Seize the State, Seize the Day: State Capture, Corruption, and Influence in Transition" (Policy Research Working Paper 2444, Washington, DC: World Bank, 2000), 8–9. The same survey

found that 47 percent thought they had been significantly affected by Central Bank mishandling of funds.

37. One rather odd version of this argument is Joseph Stiglitz's claim that the Russian oligarchs engineered the real appreciation of the ruble in the mid-1990s in order to render "their Chanel handbags" more affordable (see Joseph E. Stiglitz, *Globalization and Its Discontents* [New York: Norton, 2000]). In fact, real exchange rates appreciated in almost all postcommunist countries, with or without powerful oligarchs. The oligarchs had far more to lose from real appreciation (which reduced the competitiveness of their oil exports) than to gain from lower prices in the Moscow luxury stores. Needless to say, since they earned much of their profit in dollars and their wives shopped in New York and Paris, the ruble exchange rate was quite irrelevant to their ability to purchase fashion accessories.

38. Russia's net international reserves were about $540 million as of March 1992, only enough to finance about five days worth of imports at current rates. Net reserves rose and fell during subsequent years, peaking at about $11 billion in July 1997, before turning highly negative in 1998. It was only during the Putin administration that they increased to a more comfortable level—$25 billion in December 2001 and $45 billion in December 2002 (see Russian Economic Trends database).

39. The real exchange rate, as in the analysis of Rudiger Dornbusch ("Money Devaluations and Non-Traded Goods," *American Economic Review* 63, no. 1 [1973]: 871–80), can be treated as the ratio of the price of nontradables to the price of tradables.

40. For a discussion, see Panagiotis Liargovas, "An Assessment of Real Exchange Rate Movements in the Transition Economies of Central and Eastern Europe," *Post-Communist Economies* 11, no. 3 (1999): 299–318.

41. The following section draws on Daniel Treisman, "Fighting Inflation in a Transitional Order: Russia's Anomalous Stabilization," *World Politics* (January 1998), and Andrei Shleifer and Daniel Treisman, *Without a Map: Political Tactics and Economic Reform in Russia* (Cambridge, MA: MIT Press, 2000).

42. William Easterly and Paulo Vieira da Cunha, "Financing the Storm: Macroeconomic Crisis in Russia," *Economics of Transition* 2 (1994). My argument is that the commercial banks lobbied hard against government or Central Bank attempts to tighten the money supply in 1992–1994, and—when joined by industrial lobby groups—succeeded in pressuring the authorities to back off. I do not mean to argue—as one reader of my earlier work understood—that the banks had a "grand design" to engineer inflation, just that they helped block several attempts to reduce it.

43. Persson, Roland, and Tabellini, "Separation of Powers and Political Accountability." One might counter that the alleged positive effects of institutional divisions relate to "orderly" divisions, whereas the scrambled chains of authority and bureaucratic fragmentation evident in Russia constitute a kind of "disorderly pluralism" that does not enhance policy credibility. But this just shows the need to focus on how institutions work in practice rather than on their formal structure. In macroeconomic governance, the formal institutions in Russia were not so different from those in many other countries with superior macroeconomic performance. And improvements

in performance occurred in Russia without major changes in the formal institutions (see below).

44. Yeltsin's own account of the firing of Dubinin in 1998 is revealing: "After August 17 I made the decision to dismiss Dubinin, the chair of the Central Bank. I thought it was absolutely natural that the chief banker of a country should resign following the collapse of the national currency exchange rate. At my request Yumashev invited Dubinin to the Kremlin and asked him to write a letter of resignation" (Yeltsin, *Midnight Diaries*, 175). Yeltsin does not appear to have been aware that under the 1995 central banking law he did not have authority to do this. The "asking" Dubinin to write a letter of resignation finesses the constitutional issue.

45. See Shleifer and Treisman, *Without a Map*.

46. *Moskovskie Novosti*, July 23–29, 2002, 1–3.

47. Author's interview with Sergei Dubinin, Moscow, December 14, 1999.

48. Figures are from the Central Bank of Russia's website, www.cbr.ru. In addition, commercial banks may have had some $6 billion worth of liabilities for forward contracts that were kept off balance sheet (OECD, *Economic Surveys: Russian Federation* [Paris: OECD, 2000], 39).

49. Much as in Argentina in the 1990s under Menem, the government managed to entrench exchange rate stability *too well*. By creating vested interests in a stable exchange rate, it rendered its commitment to tight monetary policy credible. The flip side was that this reduced the government's flexibility when looser monetary policy might have preempted serious crisis.

50. Yeltsin, *Midnight Diaries*, 168. Clearly, such considerations should be strongest around the time of elections. But intense public opposition makes it difficult to accomplish any policy objectives. And with Yeltsin due to retire in two years, no young politician with ambition would want to be publicly associated with a painful devaluation.

51. International Monetary Fund, *IMF Survey*, August 3, 1998, 238.

52. Author's interview with one junior Central Bank official, Moscow, August 8, 2001.

53. Author's interview with Sergei Dubinin, Moscow, December 14, 1999.

54. Illarionov suggests that the Central Bank leaders were trying to save their jobs by "forcing the government to default on its debt before it devalued the ruble" (Illarionov, "The Roots of the Economic Crisis," 75).

55. Vladimir Mau, *"Politekonomia finansovogo krizisa v Rossii,"* in Institute for the Economy in Transition, *Finansovy krizis: Prichiny i posledstvia* (Moscow: IET, 2000).

56. Sergei Sinelnikov-Murilev, *"Faktory i etapy finansovogo krizisa v Rossii,"* in Institute for the Economy in Transition, *Finansovy krizis: Prichiny i posledstvia* (Moscow: IET, 2000).

57. Arkady Dvorkovich, *"Upravlennie gosudarstvennym dolgom v usloviakh ottoka kapitala: Vozmozhnosti preodolenia dolgovogo krizisa,"* in Institute for the Economy in Transition, *Finansovy krizis: Prichiny i posledstvia* (Moscow: IET, 2000).

58. Author's interview with Sergei Dubinin, Moscow, December 14, 1999.

59. Information from Russian Central Bank, at www.cbr.ru. It is possible that their exposure to forward contracts, not shown on balance sheet, decreased.

60. Yevgeny Yasin, *"Vneshnie i vnutrennie faktory finansovogo krizisa,"* in Institute for the Economy in Transition, *Finansovy krizis: Prichiny i posledstvia* (Moscow: IET, 2000).

61. See Central Bank of the Russian Federation, *Annual Report, 1997* (Moscow: Central Bank of the Russian Federation, 1998), 134.

62. Central Bank of the Russian Federation, *Annual Report, 1997*.

63. Author's interview with one junior Central Bank official, Moscow, August 8, 2001.

64. E.g., Fyodorov, *10 bezumnykh let*, 216–17.

65. Anatoly Chubais, *"Posle krizisa: 17 avgusta—plata za bezotvetstvennost,"* in *Privatizatsiya po-rossiiskii*, ed. Anatoly Chubais (Moscow: Vagrius, 1999), 344.

66. Author's interview with Oksana Dynnikova and Viktoria Kotova of the Economic Experts Group.

67. William Tompson, "The Bank of Russia and the 1998 Rouble Crisis," in *Anatomy of the 1998 Russian Crisis*, ed. Vladimir Tikhomirov (Melbourne, Australia: University of Melbourne), 108–44, at 123.

68. Nadezhda Ivanova and Charles Wyplosz, "Who Lost Russia in 1998?" (Paris: manuscript, 2000), 32.

69. Chubais, *Posle krizisa*, 347.

70. See also Aganbegyan, *"O prichinakh."*

71. *Russian Economic Trends* 2 (1998): 34.

72. Sebastian Edwards, *Real Exchange Rates, Devaluation, and Adjustment: Exchange Rate Policy in Developing Countries* (Cambridge, MA: MIT Press, 1989).

73. Jeffrey Sachs, Aaron Tornell, and Andrés Velasco, "Financial Crises in Emerging Markets: The Lessons from 1995," *Brookings Papers on Economic Activity* 1 (1996): 147–215, at 193.

74. What created the dangerous fiscal situation was not so much the level of the budget deficit or the debt as its very short-term structure. This was, in turn, caused by the lack of investor confidence, which was fueled by the Asian financial crisis and by perceptions of political instability in Russia more than by current fiscal policy, and—as in all financial meltdowns—fed on itself.

75. Yegor Gaidar, presentation at UCLA, June 14, 2002.

76. Gaidar, presentation.

77. Since the perceived interests of the oligarchs and the public were aligned against a devaluation, it is hard to know the relative weight that each received in the authorities' calculations.

78. Calculations from *Russian Economic Trends* database and monthly updates. Real exchange rate is monthly average rate against dollar deflated by CPI.

79. Author's interview with one junior Central Bank official, Moscow, August 8, 2001.

80. If devaluing in 1997 offered a higher expected value than gambling on avoiding a crisis, then the public should—if fully informed—have preferred this option. However,

it was not fully informed. And it was not clear that the expected value of such an early devaluation was higher.

81. See Colton and Holmes "Introduction." Perhaps a more valid criticism would be that the "fire engine" did not do a better job of putting out the fires. However, given the real (although small) possibilities of territorial disintegration and Yugoslavia-style civil war in the early 1990s, the fire station was not without its successes.

82. *Russian Economic Trends*, monthly update (March 2003), table 22.

83. These arguments are spelled out in more detail in Shleifer and Treisman, *Without a Map*.

Chapter Eight

The Paradox of Energy Sector Reform

Erika Weinthal and Pauline Jones Luong

> Monstrously mismanaged, unaccountable to shareholders and politically well connected, Gazprom remains a challenge to the integrity of Russia's free-market economy.
>
> —*Washington Post*, June 23, 2002

> In Russia, nothing happens in legislation unless it is driven by the oil companies.
>
> —Russian financial analyst, name withheld[1]

With few exceptions, scholars and policy makers alike have been very pessimistic about Russia's prospects for economic reform.[2] Many have also attributed the stagnation or absence of economic reform in Russia to the evils of "insider privatization" and the efforts of these "early winners" to prevent further reforms in order to protect their own economic gains from the initial reforms that took place in the early 1990s.[3]

These fears seemed well founded for most of the 1990s while Boris Yeltsin was president. During the Yeltsin era, Russia followed a similar trajectory to other resource-rich states that have failed to build viable institutions that are crucial for fostering state capacity and long-term economic growth. Rather, economic elites relied on personal networks and informal bargains to derail the government's efforts at market reform. The results were disastrous for the

Russian economy on the whole, which did not record positive investment rates or economic growth for most of the decade.

Yet, economic reform in Russia began to change course in 2000. In particular, significant reforms in Russia's energy sector and the taxation regime during Vladimir Putin's first term in office challenge both of these prevalent views. The energy sector is clearly Russia's leading economic sector because it accounts for approximately 20 percent of Russia's gross domestic product (GDP), 55 percent of export revenue, and 40 percent of its fiscal revenue.[4] It is also the most notorious for the way in which its industrial leaders acquired private ownership through a pure "asset grab" followed by a "loans for shares" deal.[5] By the end of 1998, however, the majority of the oil industry was privatized to multiple owners, substantially deregulated, and had undergone significant internal restructuring (see table 8.2). Although the gas sector essentially remained under state control and has undergone significantly less reform under the Yeltsin administration, private oil companies, together with minority shareholders and independent producers in the gas sector, have been at the forefront of efforts to fundamentally restructure Gazprom and other natural monopolies in the energy sector (e.g., Transneft) under Putin.

Moreover, the Russian government has adopted (1998–2000) and enacted (1999–2002) a new tax code that by most accounts exceeds Western standards—not only because it sets lower tax rates than the Organization for Economic Cooperation and Development (OECD) recommends but also because it is much simpler and clearer than the previous one. It has also won the praise of foreign and domestic financial and political analysts for its potential to have a positive impact on the Russian economy as a whole.[6] The initial results indicate that tax collection rates have increased since the new code was put into effect.[7] That revenue collection rates jumped from 50 to 60 percent in 1999 to 95–96 percent in the third quarter of 2003 while the amount of noncash tax payments decreased from 40 percent in December 1999 to 10–15 percent in 2002 to almost zero at the beginning of 2004 provides a vivid illustration.[8] Moreover, in the first half of 2004 alone, for example, the Russian government recorded a 19.7 percent annual increase in dues and taxes.[9]

These significant reforms in Russia's energy sector and taxation regime over the past few years challenge the prevailing view that Russia would fall prey to the resource curse and fail to build the necessary institutions to promote economic growth. In this chapter, we demonstrate that Russia's highly controversial privatization of the oil sector to domestic capitalists has in fact encouraged, rather than discouraged, broad-based institutional reform—especially with regard to fiscal and regulatory policy. While the conventional wisdom is either that the Putin administration is driving policymaking or that the oligarchs have captured the policymaking process, we argue that the Russian government is

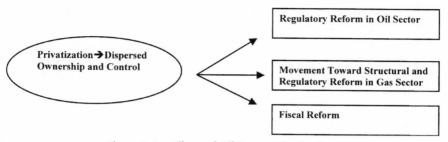

Figure 8.1. Effects of Oil Sector Privatization.

engaged in a long-term and sometimes contentious bargaining process with key economic actors over the formal rules of the game. This is possible because the privatization of the oil sector has created economic actors whose power can rival that of the state. More specifically, we argue that privatization has fostered dispersed ownership and control of the oil sector that, in turn, has led not only to greater regulatory reform in the oil sector but also movement toward the dispersion of ownership and regulatory reform in the gas sector. The desire of private actors in the oil sector for formal guarantees following the 1998 financial crisis has also led to broad-based fiscal reform.[10] These causal relationships are summarized in figure 8.1.

Furthermore, we conclude that the pessimism concerning Russia's future is unfounded in light of Russia's prospects for avoiding the "resource curse" to which the majority of its mineral-rich counterparts in the developing world have fallen prey. We argue instead that this pessimism stems both from the failure to take contentious politics seriously in Russia and to view clashes between state leaders and economic actors within a much broader context of state building. Given Russia's communist past, a large part of the state-building process has undeniably been about defining (and redefining) the nature of business–state relations. As the Putin administration's assault against what was once Russia's largest and most profitable oil company (Yukos) and its former chief executive officer (CEO), Mikhail Khodorkovsky, attests, this process is not a linear one; rather, it is mired in the political priorities of the moment, which can often temporarily derail economic ones.

SOURCES OF PESSIMISM IN THE 1990s: PRIVATIZATION AS "ASSET GRAB"[11]

Russia's controversial privatization program in the 1990s has fueled the pessimism regarding Russia's prospects for economic reform largely because it resulted in "insiders" gaining control over the state's most important strategic resources. In the Soviet Union, the energy sector was part of a large state-owned conglomerate in which the state effectively held the authority to control oil and gas exploration and production and reap the profits from their export directly. When the Soviet Union collapsed in 1991, this authority was transferred to the new Russian state. Within a few years, the Yeltsin government dramatically restructured the oil sector, ultimately transforming its structure of ownership from state to private ownership and breaking up this natural monopoly. In contrast, the gas sector has both remained under state ownership and retained its monopoly structure. In both cases, however, insiders were the primary beneficiaries of the nontransparent process through which the Russian government relinquished its hold on these valuable resources to commercial bankers and enterprise managers in the oil and gas sectors, respectively. As a result, many assumed that these "early winners" would "take all." In other words, they would exploit their privileged positions to prevent any real reform from taking place—either within or outside of the energy sector—that might also be beneficial for the economy on the whole.

Soon after Russia launched its official privatization program for large state enterprises, a presidential decree in November 1992 called for the breakup of the Soviet oil monopoly and the creation of several holding companies.[12] Specifically, this first stage of energy sector reform entailed breaking up the Soviet oil monopoly along geographical lines in which regional oil production associations were recombined with refineries and product distributors, resulting in the formation of vertically integrated joint-stock companies.[13] Initially, three vertically integrated companies (VICs) were established in 1993— Lukoil, Surgutneftegaz, and Yukos.[14] Subsequently, a large state holding company for oil—Rosneft—was constituted to direct this process and to manage in the interim the remaining state enterprises and shares.[15] From the onset, the government planned to retain some control over the oil industry through maintaining substantial ownership of stocks in the holding companies (i.e., at least 38 percent of total shares or 51 percent of voting shares) for a period of three years.[16]

Similar to the privatization of state enterprises that took place throughout the economy, during the first stage of energy sector privatization, shares were offered only to company employees and to Russian citizens. This initial phase of privatization (i.e., voucher privatization), however, enabled a small number of individuals (many of whom were tied closely to the state—i.e., Communist Party officials and factory directors) to buy up the majority of shares in Russia's oil companies at a nominal price rather than through competitive bidding.[17] Thus, from its inception, the first stage of privatization in the Russian oil industry has been harshly criticized for the way in which "insiders" were able to consolidate their hold over state assets—much of which they had previously seized through semilegal means.[18] Indeed, this process mirrored the "spontaneous" or unofficial privatization (a.k.a. "stealing the state") that took place throughout the entire economy.[19]

Shortly afterward, in order to reduce its growing budget deficit and cut inflation, the Russian government found itself forced to borrow money from the newly formed commercial banks that had emerged in the early 1990s.[20] Through its controversial "shares for loans" program in 1994–1995, the government put up for collateral its controlling shares in the integrated oil companies in exchange for commercial bank loans. Thus, when the government failed to repay these loans, these shares were transferred directly to the banks, allowing these commercial bankers to acquire some of Russia's largest and most valuable enterprises. These included Russia's main producer of nickel, Norilsk Nickel, and three of Russia's most lucrative newly formed vertically integrated oil companies—Sidanco (Oneksimbank), Yukos (Menatep Bank), and Sibneft (Boris Berezovsky's National Oil Company with the help of Menatep and Stolichnyi Bank).[21] According to critics[22] of the "shares for loans" program, the result was that these commercial bankers acted as "roving bandits," pursuing their own short-term economic interests by divvying up Russia's strategic oil resources through highly dubious means at the expense of Russia's economic recovery.[23]

Although the Russian government seriously considered privatizing the gas sector in tandem with its privatization program in the oil sector, by the middle of the 1990s it was clear that the former gas monopoly remained firmly under state control and ownership. In February 1993 the Soviet gas monopoly (i.e., the former Soviet Ministry of the Gas Industry), rather than being dismantled, was simply reconfigured into a state-owned holding company called Gazprom, which, like Rosneft, was set up in order to manage the enterprises that comprised gas production, gas transportation, and processing.[24] Unlike the oil sector in which the trunk pipelines do not belong to the oil companies, Gazprom is fully integrated, as it also controls its own pipeline network, which has enabled it to fortify its monopoly position in the gas market and restrict entry.[25]

During the first stage of voucher privatization in the energy sector, Gazprom shares (about 35 percent) were also divided up among workers and Russian citizens while others were auctioned cheaply to inhabitants of oblasts and republics in proportion to the value of Gazprom's assets on their territories.[26] Gazprom itself purchased 10 percent of the shares. Thus, only a small portion of Russia's citizens elsewhere could bid on these minority shares. Because there was a consensus among the Yeltsin government, parliamentary deputies, regional leaders, and the energy sector as a whole against any form of foreign direct investment, foreign ownership was restricted to 9 percent.[27] Moreover, similar to the first stage of oil sector privatization, the government retained a controlling interest in the holding company (i.e., 40 percent), yet unlike the "shares for loans" deals that ensued in the oil sector, the government avoided any subsequent privatization auctions for its controlling interest in Gazprom.

The main result of voucher privatization in the gas sector was, in effect, the nominal privatization of Gazprom as a single entity.[28] In other words, Gazprom's monopoly structure and the state's formal control over the gas sector remained virtually unreformed by the end of the 1990s. Yet, this did not prevent the same accusations from being levied against the early mass voucher privatization program for enabling insiders to steal state assets and capture key management positions in Gazprom.[29] The most blatant example is that Gazprom remained under the firm control of its former top managers, facilitated by the fact that its former head, Viktor Chernomyrdin, served as prime minister for most of this period (1992–1998).[30] Throughout the Yeltsin period, Gazprom's managers used their powerful positions to continue to steal from the state through authorizing the sale of shares and transfer Gazprom's assets to board members and relatives.[31] In particular, accusations have been levied against them for carrying out insider deals wherein Stroytransgaz received a contract to lay pipelines in Russia's regions, and Itera, a foreign-based gas trading company, received substantial gas reserves at below market prices.[32]

EXPLAINING REFORM: PRIVATE INTERESTS AND POLITICAL PRESSURE

Thus, in the minds of scholars and policy makers alike, the reform of the oil and gas sector in the 1990s amounted to nothing more than an asset grab. As a result, the vast majority have been very pessimistic about Russia's prospects for economic reform.[33] In particular, they have attributed the failure of economic reform in Russia to "insider privatization" because it created "early winners" who have exploited their privileged position to prevent further reforms that would threaten their economic gains.[34]

Yet, despite the notorious misdeeds of "insider privatization" and contrary to the pessimism it fostered, the reality is that energy sector privatization has brought about greater reforms—not only within the oil sector itself but also in the energy sector as a whole and for the Russian economy. By the end of 1998, the oil industry was largely privatized, substantially deregulated, and had undergone significant internal restructuring. (See table 8.1 for details.) Moreover, despite widespread expectations to the contrary, these reforms have not been reversed since Vladimir Putin assumed the presidency in March 2000.

Table 8.1. Stages of Reform in the Russian Energy Sector, 1992–1998

	Stage I (1992–1993)	Stage II (1995–1996)	Stage III (1997–1998)
Brief Description	Ownership Restructuring into Combination of Holding Companies and Subsidiaries (VICs); Some Privatization with Strict Regulation	More Privatization ("Loans for Shares") and Partial Deregulation	Full Privatization and Full Deregulation; Internal Restructuring
Ownership Structure	**State Ownership Maintained** • Ownership rights in Holding Companies (50+% shares) and majority interest (38%) in VICs. **Foreign Ownership Restricted** • Limited to between 5 and 15%	**State Ownership Reduced** • Largest banks acquire state shares as collateral for loans • HC Rosneft partially privatized and shares in several VICs sold • BUT several companies still protected from full privatization **Foreign Ownership Restricted** • Limited to between 5 and 15%	**State Ownership Relinquished** • In 1997, the government relinquished ownership rights in a large number of companies; held majority shares in less than half and no shares in almost one-third. • Transneft partially privatized **Foreign Ownership Opened** • Federal/Official limit abolished • Duma adopts PSA law in 1998
Regulation	**Strict Price Controls** • Oil prices set at 5% of world level **Strict Export Controls** • Quota and licensing system—some designated "state needs" exporters • Greater restrictions of JVs **Domestic Requirements** • Delivery despite nonpayments • Internal restructuring limited discussed	**Price Controls Eliminated** • Domestic and international prices near parity by mid-1995 **Export Controls Relaxed** • Export quotas abolished • Export duties reduced in 1995, then abolished in mid-1996 • BUT "state needs" program remained **Domestic Requirements** • Delivery despite nonpayments • Internal restructuring limited	**Export Controls Eliminated** • "State needs" export program greatly scaled back, then eliminated **Domestic Requirements Relaxed** • Shut-offs increasingly common • Workforce reduced, investment curtailed, and mergers

Table 8.2.   **Percentage of Government Stake in Russian Oil Companies**

Company	Year Formed	1994	1995	1996	1997	1998	1999	2000	2001	2002
Sidanco[a]	5/94	—	100	85	51	0	0	0	0	0
Sibneft	9/95	—	—	100	51.1	0	0	0	0	0
TNK	8/95	—	—	100	91	51	49.8	0	0	0
SNG	3/93	100	40.1	40.1	40.1	0.8	0.8	0.8	0	0
Onaco[b]	6/94	—	100	85	85	85	85	85	0	0
Komitek[c]	6/94	—	100	100	92	1.1	1.1	1.1	1.1	0
Yukos	4/93	100	86	53	0.1	0.1	0.1	0.1	0.1	0.1
VSNK[d]	4/94	—	100	85	38	1.0	1.0	1.0	1.0	1.0
Lukoil	4/93	90.8	80	54.9	33.1	26.9	26.6	23.7	14.1	7.6
Tatneft	1/94	—	46.6	46.6	30.3	30.3	30.3	30.3	30.3	30.3
VNK[e]	5/94	—	100	85	85	36.8	36.8	36.8	36.8	36.8
Slavneft	6/94	—	93.5	92	90	85.8	85.8	85.8	85.8	85.8
Rosneft	9/95	—	100	100	100	100	100	100	100	100

Source: Eugene Khartukov, *Oil and Gas Journal*, 2002
Notes: a. Actually controlled by TNK since mid-2001.
b. Controlled by TNK since September 2000.
c. Controlled by Lukoil since mid-1999.
d. Controlled by Sibneft (since March 1997 until November 1999) and by Yukos (since February 2001).
e. Controlled by Yukos since December 1997.
SNG—Surgutneftegaz
TNK—Tyumenskaia Neftianaia Kompaaniia
VSNK—Vostochno-Sibirskaia Neftianaia Kompaniia

In September 2000, for example, the government sold its 85 percent stake in Onaco,[35] leaving it with controlling shares in only two companies—Slavneft and Rosneft (see table 8.2). Thus, as of 2002, the oil sector comprised approximately a dozen privately owned vertically integrated oil companies, including Eastern Oil Company, Lukoil, Onaco, Sibneft, Sidanco, Surgutneftegas, Tyumen Oil Company, and Yukos, Bashneft, Komitek, Tatneft.[36]

In contrast, under Putin, the state has steadfastly consolidated ownership and regained control over Gazprom by both recouping its lost assets[37] and replacing its CEO Rem Vyakhirev—who was a former gas ministry insider—with Aleksei Miller in 2001.[38] As of 2002, government-controlled stakes in Gazprom have increased to 51 percent (see tables 8.3 and 8.4) through a combination of its effective voting control over the existing treasury stocks, which the Yeltsin government yielded to Vyakhirev while he ran Gazprom, and its own shares.

At the same time, in the spring of 2001 the Putin administration launched a new initiative to restructure the gas industry.[39] This initiative includes introducing stricter financial controls to prevent further asset losses; planning to break up Gazprom's monopoly, beginning with splitting the company into

Table 8.3. Government Controlled Stakes in Gazprom

Direct State Ownership	38.4%
Rosgazifikatsiya	0.9%
Treasury Shares	11.3%
Total	50.6%

separate pipeline and supply companies and allowing independent producers access to pipelines; and liberalizing the share market by removing "the ring-fence between local and foreign shares."[40] Beyond reforms in the energy sector, the Russian government has adopted (1998–2000) and enacted (1999–2002) a new tax code that is already having a positive impact on tax collection rates and has the potential to contribute to long-term economic growth.[41]

What explains this apparent puzzle of reform? How is far-reaching economic reform possible when early winners dominate the most important sector? We argue that the primary actors driving these reforms are the very actors that were created by the extensive privatization of the oil sector and partial privatization of the gas sector—the Russian oil companies (ROCs) and Gazprom's minority shareholders, respectively. These actors have increasingly put pressure on the Russian government, not only to support reforms within the energy sector itself but also to develop institutions outside the energy sector to promote greater transparency and fiscal stability. Perhaps most surprising is our finding that, although they have clearly had more success to date in reforming the oil sector, the ROCs in particular are leading the charge not only to liberalize the gas sector but also to break up Transneft's monopoly over pipeline access. Together with Gazprom's minority shareholders, they are one of the driving forces behind the Putin administration's efforts to reform Russia's natural monopolies.

Ownership Structure and Prospects for Reform

The key difference between Russia's oil sector and gas sector is ownership structure[42]—that is, the ownership and control over the former has been

Table 8.4. Ownership Structure in Gazprom

	1996	1997	1998	1999	2000	2001	2002
Russian government	40.9%	40.9%	38.4%	38.4%	38.4%	38.4%	38.4%
Russian corporate owners	26.8%	35.3%	36.3%	31.5%	33.6%	34.1%	35.1%
Russian private investors	30.3%	21.9%	20.8%	19.8%	17.7%	16.1%	15.1%
Foreign investors	2.0%	2.0%	4.5%	10.3%	10.3%	11.5%	11.5%

dispersed whereas it remains highly concentrated in the latter. Indeed, our contention is that their divergent ownership structure is also the primary reason that we find both greater reform in the oil sector than the gas sector overall and a greater role for private oil companies in influencing the degree and nature of energy sector reform narrowly and economic reform more broadly.

There are several reasons why we might expect concentrated and dispersed ownership structures to foster contrary incentives for institutional development and economic reform. Most importantly, they create two very different sets of primary actors, who are not only likely to have divergent preferences over institutional outcomes, such as regulatory and fiscal institutions, but also are likely to use different means to exert influence on these institutional outcomes. Concentrated ownership and control of energy reserves leads to the concentration of proceeds from their production and export and "state capture" by managers or bureaucrats who prefer to maintain or increase their discretionary power over both the generation and use of these proceeds. Thus, they have little incentive to support the development of formal institutions—particularly regulatory and fiscal institutions. In contrast, private ownership is more likely to result in the dispersion of proceeds and the creation of actors outside the state who desire formal guarantees (such as property rights and a stable tax regime) in order to maximize their profits and to secure their investments. As a result, they have a greater incentive to lobby government officials to develop the appropriate regulatory and fiscal institutions.

The nature of the relationship between the state and the energy sector therefore differs considerably under these two scenarios. Where ownership and control are concentrated within the state, there is no clearly identifiable principal.[43] In other words, there is effectively no separation between the owners and those who are responsible for regulating and taxing the mineral sector. For example, in the case of Gazprom, which was nominally privatized—at least partially— but nonetheless retained its essence as a natural monopoly and operated as an extension of the government, it is difficult to distinguish the management from the government. For most of the 1990s, Gazprom's president and board of directors not only controlled their own shares but also were entrusted with the government's shares—much like bureaucrats are authorized to manage energy reserves on behalf of the state where the sector is state owned, though perhaps even more explicitly.[44] Thus, they openly ran the company as if they owned it. Then, as now, the Gazprom CEO is a presidential appointee and Gazprom's managers and government representatives form a majority on the board of directors. As a result, some have suggested that it has been hard to determine where "Gazprom ends and the Russian state begins."[45]

This blurred boundary between the state and Gazprom has benefited both sides. On the one hand, it has empowered the gas sector to operate with very little internal or external scrutiny over its transactions. Despite an unsuccessful attempt by First Deputy Prime Minister Boris Nemtsov to request an audit of Gazprom,[46] for most of the 1990s the Russian Audit Chamber did not demand an official audit of Gazprom's finances.[47] This lack of oversight is evident in Gazprom's notorious mismanagement of investment funds and arbitrary transfer of assets detailed in the previous section, which occurred primarily during the Yeltsin era. Only in late 1999 in its efforts to reassert control over Gazprom did the Putin administration empower the Russian Audit Chamber to perform an "unprecedented" audit of Gazprom.[48]

In addition, this blurred boundary has enabled Gazprom to withstand domestic and international pressures for restructuring in both the Yeltsin and Putin eras.[49] Gazprom's managers have avoided such unwanted reforms either by using their control over the board of directors to stall the reform process indefinitely,[50] dominating commissions designed for this very purpose,[51] or insisting that it must protect the national interest in maintaining a secure domestic gas supply.[52] Gazprom's integrated structure also provides the company with a relatively costless and effortless way of hiding its profits, and thus, both lining its managers' pockets and lowering its tax burden. For example, as the sole regulator of the only pipeline system that distributes natural gas to domestic and foreign consumers, it is in a unique position to monitor the volume of gas that it actually sells on the internal versus external market.

On the other hand, this blurred boundary has enabled the Russian government—under both Yeltsin and Putin—to utilize its leverage as the ultimate "owner" to fulfill its domestic fiscal and spending requirements. The Russian government's political interests are often conflated with Gazprom's business interests, as the Russian government also can, and often does, utilize Gazprom as a foreign policy tool, whether to exert influence on the "near abroad" by supplying a cheap source of gas (e.g., Ukraine and Belarus) or the only viable pipeline for other gas producers (e.g., Turkmenistan). Gazprom remains subjected to price controls and delivery requirements for nonpaying domestic customers, which account for a large portion of its implicit tax burden. While Gazprom's representatives on the board have resisted other reforms and have rather pushed for regulatory barriers to entry (i.e., protectionism), price liberalization is not one of them; in this case, the official government representatives are the most adamant opponents. As a result, Gazprom is forced to sell most of the gas it produces (70 percent) on the domestic market for approximately 15 percent of the price it would receive on the global market. Combined with the high rate of tariff arrears in Russia among industrial and household consumers alike, therefore, it is not surprising that Gazprom operates at a loss.[53] Nonetheless, the government has refused to lower Gazprom's explicit tax burden, contributing further to its well-earned position as Russia's largest taxpayer.[54] The Yeltsin administration repeatedly threatened to break up the monopoly and seize its assets in order to force Gazprom to pay its taxes regardless of the heavy debt incurred by state-subsidized organizations.[55] This came closest to actually occurring in mid-1998 when Boris Nemtsov refused to renew Gazprom CEO Vyakhirev's management contract unless he agreed to a tax deal. Gazprom's explicit tax burden has actually increased following the August 1998 financial crisis and the adoption of a new tax code in 2000–2001 that tied export tariffs directly to the price of oil and introduced a new mineral extraction tax as a flat rate pegged to the price of oil. Meanwhile, its implicit tax burden has also steadily increased in the form of extrabudgetary funds. Under Putin, the government has often used Gazprom's budget to finance election campaigns and other pet projects such as taking over the national television station (NTV) and buying out Vladimir Gusinsky's remaining shares in Russian media companies.[56]

Many would argue, however, that the long-term costs of this blurred boundary outweigh the short-term benefits to each side. In sum, because it has created and reinforced an informal agreement whereby Gazprom's managers accept a high tax burden in exchange for the ability to line their own pockets and the government accepts less transparency and accountability for virtually unlimited access to Gazprom's coffers. This has resulted in a net economic loss for both Gazprom as a company and the Russian economy as a whole.

The costs to Gazprom have been primarily its financial health and reputation abroad. Gazprom managers not only have a greater opportunity to steal from the company but also a greater incentive to do so because, as de facto government employees, they are not compensated for performance.[57] Thus, managers can only reap direct benefits by stealing. In fact, this lack of connection to Gazprom's profitability (and hence desire to steal) was exacerbated by the new contract in 1998, which further reduced top managers' time horizons by decreasing their job security.[58] Furthermore, "years of asset stripping and lack of transparency" are responsible for the undercapitalization of Gazprom. As of the summer of 2002, "in spite of its size and importance, the market capitalization of Gazprom is so small that it's a national embarrassment. [Its] . . . market value . . . [is] less than that of smaller firms such as AT&T Wireless or Fox Entertainment."[59] The lack of external oversight has also created significant financial and accounting problems. Gazprom has amassed a substantial foreign debt by borrowing to fund new projects,[60] which has contributed to its acute financial and debt problems in 2002.[61] It has also been involved in an accounting scandal on par with Enron in the United States, which is likely to scare off already reluctant investors, and thereby lower its market valuation further. Specifically, minority investors suggest that Gazprom's stock has been undervalued owing to lax financial audits carried out by PricewaterhouseCoopers that deliberately "overlooked" the above-mentioned murky asset transfers.[62]

The resulting costs to the Russian economy are immense. It is not difficult to see why Gazprom's financial problems and damaged reputation translate directly into budgetary losses for the Russian government. In the past, for example, the government's attempts to fill holes in the budget by selling Gazprom shares have fallen short of their expectations. Although the Putin administration has reasserted greater control over the company and reclaimed many of its lost assets, the government has inherited Gazprom's debt and has had to expend a great deal of time and effort to repair its corrupt image.

Thus, concentrated ownership and control are more likely to foster a relationship between the state and bureaucrats (or managers) whereby neither side has an incentive to support the development of institutions that would create internal and external oversight mechanisms, increase transparency, or impose hard budget constraints. Rather, because both sides have direct access to the proceeds from the exploitation of the energy sector, they prefer greater discretionary power and informal agreements over the allocation and use of these proceeds. Conversely, dispersed ownership and control creates incentives for both the relevant actors—that is, the government and private owners—to support such institutions. Because their influence is relatively evenly balanced, moreover, policies and institutions are often the product of explicit bargaining and compromise between these two sets of actors.

Where ownership and control are dispersed, a clearer boundary emerges between those who are empowered to act as owners and those who are empowered to act as regulators and tax collectors. Both sets of actors have a legitimate claim to the proceeds from mineral production and export, yet the nature, and thus, means employed to realize this claim differ. Private owners have a direct claim to these proceeds and, as such, are more likely to have a vested interest in maximizing their profits and securing their investments. They are also more likely, therefore, to pressure the government to provide institutional guarantees—most importantly, property rights and a stable tax regime—as well as to promote a competitive marketplace. Because they have only an indirect claim to these proceeds, state actors also have an interest in developing reliable institutions—both for extracting revenue from private owners and for regulating anticompetitive behavior.

This clearer boundary fosters mutual incentives for institutional development in several ways. First, in contrast to bureaucrats or managers, private actors desire formal guarantees because it is both costlier to hide profits and less rational to steal. The ROCs, for example, incur higher transaction costs to avoid taxes by hiding their profits than Gazprom. For most of the 1990s, they devised several legal and semilegal schemes to reduce their profitability on paper that eventually proved too costly—not only because it required expending effort and finances on nonproductive activities but also because it earned them a lower stock market valuation.[63] Thus, it is often less costly for private actors to negotiate and pay a stable tax rate, even if the overall tax burden is slightly higher. As will become clear below, this calculation factored directly into the ROCs' support for the newly adopted tax code. In addition, because private owners can expect to reap the benefits of their respective company's performance in both the short and long term, they have a greater incentive to engage in profit seeking rather than purely rent seeking, and therefore to foster the institutions such as property rights, internal regulatory mechanisms, and a stable tax regime that would make profit seeking possible, for example, by reducing fiscal uncertainty, and thus, facilitating long-term investment. At the same time, the government's transaction costs for revenue extraction are much higher when it is forced to either confiscate revenue or to engage in continuous bargaining over revenue burdens—as was the case with the oil companies throughout the Yeltsin period. It is thus more likely to seek to reduce these costs through formal agreements that promote "quasi-voluntary compliance."[64]

Second, both private owners and state actors have an incentive to create oversight mechanisms because they encounter information asymmetries. The fact that private owners are more likely to have greater concern for profitability also suggests that they have greater incentives for establishing effective *internal* mechanisms for monitoring management decisions and the behavior of their employees. They will not tolerate the illicit deals that have characterized Gazprom's transfer of company assets, for example. And, owing to longer agency chains, doing so will require formal institutions.[65] Shareholders provide another independent line of defense against poor management in general and corruption in particular. Given each side's limited access to information about the behavior of the other, both sets of actors are also more inclined to demand mechanisms for *external* oversight. Because the state is an indirect recipient of monopoly rents through taxation on the profits, the government will demand independent audits of a company's economic performance to ensure that it is receiving its fair share. For example, in contrast to the absence of audits of Gazprom throughout the 1990s, the ROCs have been carrying out annual audits since the mid-1990s.

As the boundary between them becomes clearer, both sets of actors also have to develop a more formalized method for exerting influence on the other. For private owners, reduced or meditated access to government representatives often translates into a greater incentive to develop professional lobbying techniques as well as to support institutions (such as parliaments and political parties) that facilitate lobbying. Many experts agree, for example, that the ROCs have developed more sophisticated lobbying techniques over time—prompting one expert to claim that they are "looking more and more like the U.S. Congress."[66] Whereas simply bribing deputies was the common practice for most of the 1990s, since the 1999 parliamentary elections the norm has become supporting candidates (often former employees) for election to the single-mandate seats and organizing meetings regularly with deputies to discuss relevant legislation. Yukos CEO Mikhail Khodorkovsky went one step further by financing several of the opposition political parties (e.g., Union of Rightist Forces or SPS and Yabloko) in the December 2003 parliamentary elections that posed a direct challenge to the dominance of Putin's supporters in the current parliament.[67]

At the same time, however, the ROCs have not endeavored to pool their lobbying efforts or resources. Thus, contrary to the predominant assumption in the literature on natural monopolies and the "resource curse" that collusion and state capture are inevitable in sectors with a small number of large firms,[68] this is not necessarily the case when these firms are privately owned. Although they have similar interests, as direct competitors and possibly intense rivals, private owners are unlikely to rely on collusion to exert influence. In attempting to work together in order to pressure the government for favorable policies, even a small number of actors face a considerable collective action problem.[69] Thus, we do not either assume or find collusion among these private actors.[70]

The fact that dispersed ownership and control creates two separate sets of actors—private owners and state actors—who have a mutual interest in fostering the development of fiscal and regulatory institutions, however, is not sufficient to actually produce such institutions. Perhaps equally important is that these actors are relatively evenly balanced in terms of their potential influence on political and economic outcomes. For example, because the oil sector in Russia provides a significant portion—albeit, not the largest portion—of the state budget, its financial health and political support is of great concern to the government. At the same time, the ROCs' behavior is constrained by the possibility of state elites to revoke property rights in spite of the high political and economic costs from renationalization. As demonstrated below, private oil companies, along with minority shareholders and independent producers in the gas sector, are thus largely responsible for both previous regulatory reform in the oil sector under Yeltsin and efforts to restructure Gazprom and other natural monopolies (e.g., Transneft) under Putin. They are also responsible for the array of internal reforms within the oil sector that include increasing transparency and corporate governance. Newly created private owners have also influenced reform outside the energy sector in the form of a viable new tax code, which is the product of bargaining and compromise between the Russian government and the ROCs.

Private Owners, Internal Restructuring, and Regulatory Reform

The initial stage of reform in the oil sector consisted primarily of dismantling it through privatization. Since then, however, this sector has also undergone significant internal restructuring. The threat of bankruptcy has provided incentives for the ROCs to pursue internal reforms that have entailed improving corporate governance and restructuring their top management. Unlike Gazprom that can operate with soft-budget constraints, the ROCs must operate under hard-budget constraints. In fact, the 1998 financial crisis revealed how close many of the ROCs (e.g., Yukos, Sibneft, and TNK) were to bankruptcy due to non-transparent business practices during the early 1990s. Sibneft, as a result, was forced to shut down its operations for several months, and others were forced to radically downsize their operations and decrease expenditures.[71] The threat of bankruptcy and hence the desire to improve their profitability has impelled the ROCs to create oversight mechanisms for internal monitoring through the adoption of corporate governance measures and new international accounting procedures (i.e., generally accepted accounting principles [GAAP] standards). Because managers under private ownership are rewarded for performance, the ROCs have, furthermore, restructured their internal management structure through hiring international management. By 2001, approximately 25 percent of top-level management in Yukos were foreigners. This change in company strategy has signaled to both shareholders and potential strategic partners that the ROCs are concerned about improving their profitability and operating under hard-budget constraints.

In contrast to the gas sector, the oil sector has also been substantially deregulated. For example, price controls were eliminated in the mid-1990s and both export controls and domestic delivery requirements were lifted by the late-1990s. One might counter that because the private oil companies are the primary beneficiaries of deregulation, it is uncontroversial to argue that they have been behind these reforms. Yet, there have also been gains for the Russian economy as a whole. Domestic competition and more efficient production, for example, have yielded lower gasoline prices for consumers without the deadweight costs of subsidies.[72] Higher production levels and increasing domestic investment have also increased Russia's attractiveness to foreign investors across sectors and raised the possibility that Russia will become a viable alternative to OPEC.

Just as these reforms were beginning to yield results, the private oil companies had already turned their attention to the next, and perhaps most important, stage for regulatory reform in the energy sector—the breakup of the state-owned pipeline monopoly Transneft. The main issue behind the battle between the ROCs and Transneft is the latter's ability to block access to pipelines. Transneft's hold on the pipelines, which includes the regulation of export volumes and collection of transit fees, has restricted the flow of oil and flooded the low-priced domestic market.[73] The oil companies have sought to circumvent this problem by building private export pipelines, which Transneft has vehemently opposed because this would threaten its monopoly. In some cases, it has reacted by proposing to build its own pipeline. For example, when the government approved Yukos plans to build an eastern Siberian pipeline to China, Transneft proposed building its own pipeline that would serve Japan and other countries in the Far East as well.[74] Transneft has also resisted appeals from the oil companies to ship oil through Latvia's port of Ventspils.[75]

While this battle is far from over, it is also clear that the government has not yet taken a side.[76] Rather, it has sought to appease the oil companies while not fully relinquishing control over oil exports.[77] For example, the government under Prime Minister Kasanyov in November 2000 constituted a new commission for regulating export pipelines and domestic supply issues with the purpose of eliminating special treatment for certain favored oil companies and to create a level playing field.[78] Moreover, the government has not contested the existence of already private pipelines such as the Varandei export facility controlled by Lukoil.[79]

Similarly, reform efforts underway in the gas sector are clearly the result of increasing pressures from a variety of newly created private actors. The most significant of these are the domestic oil companies, which have been actively encouraging the government to undertake the same degree of reform in the gas sector that it has in the oil sector. Most importantly, they want liberalized gas prices and access to Gazprom's pipelines as well as more transparency in how this access is granted.[80] Their interest in these reforms is tied directly to their own prospective financial gains; currently, Gazprom's monopoly structure gives the private oil companies no other outlet to transport the gas they already produce as well as the gas they intend to extract from newly acquired fields and produce in newly acquired refineries.[81] Low gas tariffs also discourage investment in gas fields that are clearly aging. The fact that they are already "positioning themselves to become major players in a liberalized and restructured gas industry . . . [by acquiring] . . . gas processing facilities and buying . . . Gazprom shares in the secondary market," moreover, is a testament to their confidence that these reforms will be adopted.[82]

The drive for liberalization of the gas sector is also coming from private owners within this sector—in particular, independent producers and minority shareholders. Like the domestic oil companies, independent producers not only want greater access to Gazprom's pipelines but also a set of rules and procedures that will guarantee transparent regulation of this access.[83] These private domestic actors are neither numerous nor large, yet they are becoming increasingly important actors. In fact, "[d]uring the past two years... their ranks have swelled with the likes of LUKoil, Yukos, and other oil majors nudging their way into Russia's regulated gas market."[84] Alarmed by Gazprom's abysmal share price and market capitalization, undersold assets,[85] and low dividend payments,[86] minority shareholders are also pushing for greater transparency as well as more accountable and qualified management.[87] The specific reforms they have advocated to address these concerns include increasing the number of director seats to fifteen from eleven, giving independent directors at least four seats on Gazprom's Board of Directors, and liberalizing the share market. Moreover, Gazprom's minority shareholders—including former deputy prime minister Boris Fedorov and Hermitage Capital chief executive William Browder—have been at the forefront in pushing for an external audit of Gazprom's alleged asset stripping and dubious investment decisions.

Private Owners and Fiscal Reform

Private oil companies have also been instrumental in Russia's ability to achieve comprehensive fiscal reform. Between 1998 and 2002, the Russian government adopted (1998–2000) and enacted (1999–2002) a new tax code that by most accounts exceeds Western standards—not only because it sets lower tax rates than the OECD recommends but also because it is much simpler and clearer than the previous one.[88] For example, it introduced a 13 percent flat tax on personal income, capped corporate contributions to the social insurance fund, reduced the profits tax (a.k.a. corporate income tax) rate from 35 to 24 percent, abolished turnover taxes (as of 2003), tied export tariffs directly to the price of oil, and established new accounting procedures that are on par with GAAP.[89] In addition, a new mineral extraction tax was introduced in January 2002 (chapter 26, part II of the tax code) as a flat rate pegged to the price of oil.

Foreign and domestic financial and political analysts alike have also praised the new tax code for the inclusive nature of tax benefits, and thus, its potentially positive impact on the Russian economy as a whole.[90] The increased tax collection rates since the new code was put into effect support this optimism.[91] Between 2001 and 2004, for example, there was an almost 80 percent increase in real flat tax revenue owing to the increased compliance rate that has accompanied the introduction of the flat tax on personal income alone.[92] Moreover, by setting fixed tax rates and reducing incentives for the government to resort to coercive tactics to meet its revenue needs, the new tax code has the potential to offer more secure property rights for the ROCs[93] and thereby enable them to both increase their investments at home and attract foreign partners to expand their operations abroad.

Russia's new tax code is striking for two main reasons. First, it represents a significant departure from past practice. For most of the 1990s, tax policy in Russia can best be described as an informal bargaining process whereby economic elites presiding over the country's industrial enterprises as well as regional leaders engaged in ongoing negotiations with the government to determine their respective tax burdens.[94] Thus, the official tax rates for industry and revenue sharing for regions that existed on paper were rarely, if ever, observed in practice, and tax collection rates were abysmally low as a result.[95] As a result, the government was able to collect approximately half of its projected tax revenues and the ROCs could keep a substantial portion of their profits. For example, although the statutory tax rate for the oil companies was 53 percent of revenues, the Russian government only managed to collect between 33 and 35 percent of revenues.[96]

Second, it defies the overwhelming pessimism concerning Russia's prospects for economic reform in the absence of either a strong leader within or external pressures from outside the country. Many have attributed market failure in Russia throughout most of the 1990s to the weakness of either President Boris Yeltsin or central state institutions vis-à-vis powerful economic interests.[97] Thus, not surprisingly, Russia's hope for establishing the political order necessary to achieve market reform has often been placed in its seemingly more authoritarian leader, Vladimir Putin, who succeeded Yeltsin in March 2000.[98] Because he not only enjoyed a popular mandate but also faced a Duma that was less polarized, and therefore more pliable, after the 1999 elections Putin seemed poised to unilaterally redefine Russia's political climate and single-handedly push through his economic agenda.[99] Putin's former position as head of Russia's Federal Security Service (i.e., the FSB) from July 1998 to August 1999 bolstered the presumption that he would be a strong leader, capable of using force to impose his will.

Russia's new tax code, however, was not imposed by a strong central leader, mandated by international institutions, or the result of state capture by powerful economic interest groups. Rather, it is the product of a mutually beneficial exchange between the two most powerful actors in Russia—the Russian government and the ROCs—following an acute economic crisis.[100] The shock of the August financial crisis provided the impetus for institutional creation and economic policy change in the form of a new tax code because it generated widely shared perceptions among both sets of actors concerning the benefits of cooperation and the need for formal guarantees. These shared perceptions, however, were contingent upon both sets of actors feeling equally vulnerable to the effects of the crisis and recognizing that they depended on one another to recover from the crisis. Nor were shared perceptions alone sufficient to bring about institutional or economic policy change. Rather, the new tax code required that both sets of actors possessed common knowledge,[101] which was achieved through a series of incremental strategic moves.

The Yukos Affair

Since June 2003, what had only recently become the largest and most profitable Russian oil company, Yukos, has come under an increasingly fierce attack by various agencies within the government.[102] The assault began with the arrest of Yukos's Security Service Department chief, Aleksey Pichugin, and second largest shareholder, Platon Lebedev of Menatep Bank, in June 2003 and July 2003, respectively. It was followed by the arrest of now former CEO Khodorkovsky in October of that same year, after which the company was presented with the first of many excessive and unsubstantiated tax bills. It seems to have culminated in the forced sale of Yukos's most valuable subsidiary and covetable asset—Yuganskneftegaz—on December 19, 2004, allegedly to cover tax claims that exceeded the company's revenue, and Khodorkovsky's conviction in 2005 for tax evasion and embezzlement.[103] Most speculated that the end result for Yukos would be state takeover via Gazprom's winning bid for Yuganskneftegaz.[104] These speculations, at least for the short term, have proved incorrect. Gazprom was outbid at the eleventh hour by a mystery shell company—Baikal Finance Group—registered in Tver, which Rosneft then purchased almost immediately after the sale. To date, Gazprom has failed to acquire Yuganskneftegaz (and hence, a large portion of the oil industry).

Understandably, many have interpreted this assault against Yukos as a calculated first move toward eliminating the oligarchs as a class, and thus, private ownership of the oil sector—that is, as the continuation of the campaign that Putin began early in his tenure when he ousted two of the most notorious oligarchs, Vladimir Gusinsky and Boris Berezovsky, for their blatant attempts to influence Kremlin politics.[105] Yet, this conclusion is both premature and unsupported by the evidence.

First of all, the fate of Yukos's assets is still unknown. Although Khodorkovsky received a lengthy jail term, some have argued, Khodorkovsky "will get out someday, won't he?" And, when he does, "he will demand the return of his assets . . . [and] he will find plenty of people willing to listen."[106] Moreover, although the government carried off the auction of Yugansneftegaz, no concrete action had been taken against Yukos's other subsidiaries, Tomskneft and Samaraneftegaz. In fact, as of February 2006, Yukos has managed to maintain flat production levels of oil and gas condensate at these two production units.[107] If Yukos manages to retain these two subsidiaries, it "would be a little bigger than Sibneft," and hence, still worthy of attracting investment.[108] Furthermore, even if all its subsidiaries are sold off, this does not preclude a successful lawsuit by either Menatep Bank or the company's minority share-holders; at present, Yukos's minority shareholders have already filed a lawsuit in a U.S. district court in Washington, DC, against the government for illegally selling off Yugansk and four state-owned energy companies for conspiring to buy its production unit for a price that was below its market value.[109] In fact, there is already precedent for minority shareholders using foreign courts (in this case in the United States) to influence the turn of events in Russia. The fear of a lengthy (and high-profile) legal battle is, after all, what propelled a consortium of international banks to withdraw their financial support for Gazprom's bid and the Russian government to come up with an elaborate scheme to find another (albeit, temporary) Kremlin-friendly buyer for Yugansk.[110]

Secondly, there is no indication that the government intends to pursue other ROCs to the extent that it has Yukos. Rather, the assault on Yukos has thus far been unique, both in form and content. According to Edward Parker of Fitch Ratings, "In the case of other oil companies [(most notably, Sibneft)], these are tax bills they owe and are given scope to pay" such that their very existence is not in danger."[111] In contrast, Yukos's bank accounts and assets have been frozen such that it has been unable to pay excessive tax bills that it denies owing, thus justifying a forced government sell-off of its key assets. A large portion of these assets (i.e., Yugansneftegaz) will indeed fall under state ownership if Rosneft merges with Gazprom. Nonetheless, the events as they have unfolded thus far do not amount to the renationalization of the oil sector, but rather, the dismantling of Yukos. In fact, the government's decision to sell its remaining shares in the Lukoil Company in 2004 clearly demonstrated its commitment to privatization of the oil sector.[112] Nor was renationalization the inevitable outcome of the arrests of several Yukos executives, including Khodorkovsky's that began over a year ago. In contrast to Gusinsky and Berezovsky, Khodokovsky openly defied the government and refused to leave the country.[113] Had he been less bold, it is quite possible that the assault would have ended long ago and Yukos would have remained intact under new management.

Finally, and perhaps most important, is the closely related point that the overwhelming evidence suggests that the Putin administration's assault on Yukos is politically motivated.[114] This is suggested by the timing of the beginning of the assault on Yukos[115] and, in particular, the arrest of Khodokovsky, which coincided with the beginning of the 2003 elections campaign for the Duma in which Putin openly backed pro-government parties such as United Russia and, to a lesser degree, Motherland, while Khodokovsky provided financial support for the opposition parties, Union of Right Forces (SPS) and Yabloko. At the same time, it is clear that the government's primary interest in prosecuting Yukos executives is not recovering back taxes. Since the Putin administration presented Yukos with its first tax bill in December 2003, Yukos has sent an estimated fifty proposals to the government offering various ways to settle the debt, but has received no response.[116]

IMPLICATIONS FOR THE RUSSIAN STATE

In sum, we argue that private actors in the energy sector have influenced both the nature of energy sector reform and the structure of business–state relations in Russia. Contrary to most pessimistic accounts of Russian economic reform, the early winners created by Russia's insider privatization of the oil sector have not stymied subsequent reforms in the energy sector, but rather, have propelled the state to pursue broad-based institutional reforms—both within the energy sector and for the Russian economy on the whole. Precisely because privatization results in the creation of economically powerful actors outside the state who desire formal guarantees (such as property rights and a stable tax regime) from the state in exchange for revenue, both sides have a strong incentive to bargain explicitly over institutional outcomes—in particular, the development of regulatory and fiscal institutions.

This view contrasts sharply with the two opposing views that have dominated explanations of economic reform in Russia. The former suggests that reforms have occurred owing to Putin's vision and uncontested leadership while the latter concludes that self-serving oligarchs have derailed subsequent reforms by capturing the policymaking process. These opposing views also invoke dichotomous portrayals of the Russian state—that is, as strong and as weak vis-à-vis societal actors, respectively.

Thus, according to the former, Putin is at the forefront of efforts to restructure Gazprom and to recover assets that were brazenly stolen during the Yeltsin period.[117] These accounts contend, for example, that Putin's replacement of Vyakhirev with a close associate, Aleksei Miller, clearly demonstrates his ability to reassert state control over Gazprom's management,[118] and the board's subsequent decision to buy back Purgaz from Itera indicates a government commitment to recover stolen assets.[119]

Such efforts to reform Gazprom, however, have not resulted in its dismantlement. On the contrary, they have strengthened state ownership and control over the gas monopoly. In fact, Miller is de facto a presidential appointee and thus beholden to the Putin administration for his position. Following his appointment, Miller has confirmed the government's position that it is necessary to maintain Gazprom as a unified system.[120] Thus, the limited reform that has come to pass in the gas sector has been possible either because these reforms are advantageous to Gazprom or as a result of private pressure. For example, a new online system for electronic trading in natural gas (Mezhregiongaz) that seeks to liberalize the domestic gas market is clearly profitable to Gazprom, as it allows Gazprom to reduce its own domestic sales and instead to concentrate on the export market.[121] The government's decision to increase transparency—especially the government's decision to undertake an audit of Gazprom's relations with Itera—is also directly tied to minority shareholder pressure.[122] In short, the Putin government has not unilaterally directed efforts to reform Gazprom, but has been forced to respond to demands from private actors in the energy sector to introduce gas sector reforms. According to the latter perspective, the major oil companies have colluded to block any reform that would not benefit them personally. Thus, liberalization within the gas and pipeline sectors along with regulatory and fiscal reform only benefit a select group of actors that had profited from the insider privatization that took place in the early 1990s.

Yet this portrayal does not adequately account for why the oil companies would encourage corporate governance and endorse fiscal reforms that force them to fully disclose their profits, adopt international accounting procedures, and accept an overall increase in their tax burden. Moreover, it does not explain why the oil companies have pursued different policies vis-à-vis the government and each other, some of which have been openly confrontational with the government. For example, if the oil companies could easily capture state policy, there would be no need to invest in lobbying, including the formal support of opposition parties. If the ROCs were in collusion with one another to promote their collective economic gain, we should then expect them to engage in purely rent-seeking behavior rather than promoting competition by opening up gas markets and pipeline routes for export. Their support for fiscal and regulatory reform thus demonstrates that they are concerned with leveling the playing field rather than gaining privileged access for their collective special interests.

These overly pessimistic accounts of economic reform in Russia stem from their failure to place single, seemingly crucial, events within a much broader context. Instead, the onset of privatization during the Yeltsin era, Putin's showdown with a subset of the notorious oligarchs, and the sweeping fiscal and regulatory reforms in the late 1990s and early 2000s should be viewed in the broader context of building the Russian state. Given Russia's communist past, a large part of the state-building process has undeniably been defining the nature of business–state relations. Thus, the creation of private owners and the way in which they influence institutional outcomes have direct implications for state building within Russia and for mineral-rich states more broadly.

In contrast to the Soviet state, which was notorious for its overly interventionist role in all aspects of economic activity in which it served as both the sole owner and regulator, dispersed ownership and the resultant clear boundary between the state and private actors prevents the state from conflating these roles. The clear boundary between business and state actors not only promotes mutual incentives for building formal institutions, but also the explicit bargaining that serves to reinforce this boundary. For example, by pressuring the government to break up Transneft's monopoly over pipeline access, the ROCs are not only propelling further liberalization of the energy sector, but are also bargaining with the government to clarify its role as a regulator—in this case, regarding its ability to limit the volume of oil exports.[123] These private owners therefore do not eschew a role for the government in the economy. Rather, they seek clear regulations to ensure a level playing field and to promote competition.

As a result, the process of deregulating the energy sector is as much about learning not to intervene in the economy as it is learning what precisely it means to regulate economic activity. It is also about coming to the realization that the creation of a market economy does not merely require the creation of private actors, but also a state that is willing and able to regulate economic activity. In this regard, even the Putin administration's politically motivated assault against Yukos and its former CEO Mikhail Khodorkovsky should be seen as just another episode in the development of business–state relations— albeit, perhaps the most important one so far. For the Russian government, it is a matter of determining both the appropriate role of the state in the economy and of businessmen in politics. In short, it must decide whether it wants to serve primarily as a regulator or as an owner. For private businessmen, it is further evidence that they must be willing to incur high personal costs including the risk of jail, not only to push through economic reforms but also the political reforms necessary to solidify their economic gains.

The positive influence of private actors in Russia's reform process also suggests that privatization to domestic owners may provide a way for mineral-rich states to avoid the "resource curse." In particular, Russia's ability to negotiate a viable tax code challenges the existing literature, which posits a deterministic relationship between mineral wealth and an array of negative political and economic outcomes—including poor economic performance, weak states, and authoritarian regimes—because leaders in mineral-rich states are either too myopic or risk-averse to develop a strong taxation system.[124]

The variation in reform outcomes in Russia's oil and gas sectors provides overwhelming support for this premise. Both the significant reforms in the oil sector and Russia's new tax code can be attributed to the existence of private actors who could rival the state. As an indirect beneficiary of oil sector profits, the state not only relies on this sector for revenue but also has a strong incentive to invest in the institutions that will facilitate its ability to extract this revenue. In contrast, the gas sector has avoided substantial reform precisely because it remains under state ownership and control. Those reforms that have taken place, moreover, are the result of pressure from private actors in both the oil and gas sectors.

Finally, the positive influence of these private actors makes the prospects for renationalization of the oil sector all the more worrisome. If the Putin administration's intent is indeed to assume state ownership over the country's oil wealth, beginning with its largest and most efficient oil company (i.e., Yukos), then it will have succeeded in undermining property rights and, as a result, blurring the boundary that has thus far been so crucial in propelling economic reform forward. More importantly, it will have squandered an opportunity to strengthen the institutional capacity of the state, thus joining the ranks of the "cursed" resource-rich countries in the developing world.

NOTES

The authors share equal responsibility for the content and analysis herein. This article is part of a long-term joint project and we have chosen to rotate authorship on the articles we generate.

1. Authors' personal communication, Moscow, September 2001.

2. For a balanced evaluation of economic reform in Russia, see Andrei Shleifer and Daniel Treisman, *Without a Map: Political Tactics and Economic Reform in Russia* (Cambridge, MA: MIT Press, 2000).

3. Michael Alexeev, "The Effect of Privatization and the Distribution of Wealth in Russia," *Economics of Transition* 7, no. 2 (July 1999): 449–65; Bernard Black, Reinier Kraakman, and Anna Tarassova, "Russian Privatization and Corporate Governance: What Went Wrong?" *Stanford Law Review* 52 (2000): 1731–808; Joel Hellman, "Winners Take All: The Politics of Partial Reform in Post-Communist Transitions," *World Politics* 50, no. 2 (January 1998): 203–34; Konstantin Sonin, "Inequality, Property Rights, and Economic Growth in Transition Economies: Theory and Russian Evidence," *CEPR Discussion Paper 2300* (1999).

4. For more details, see www.eia.doe.gov/emeu/cabs/russia.html.

5. For details, see Juliet Johnson, "Russia's Emerging Financial-Industrial Groups," *Post-Soviet Affairs* 13, no. 4 (October–December 1997): 333–65 and Michael McFaul, "State Power, Institutional Change, and the Politics of Russian Privatization," *World Politics* 47 (January 1995): 210–43.

6. Authors' personal communications with domestic and foreign financial analysts, Moscow, September 2001 and June–July 2002.

7. See, e.g., *Pravda*, October 18, 2001; *Kommersant*, October 19, 2001; *Russia Journal*, July 18, 2002.

8. Keith Bush, *Russian Economic Survey 2005* (U.S.-Russia Business Council, 2005), 29.

9. *Russia Journal*, July 13, 2004.

10. Pauline Jones Luong and Erika Weinthal, "Contra Coercion: Russian Tax Reform, Exogenous Shocks, and Negotiated Institutional Change," *American Political Science Review* 98, no. 1 (2004): 139–52.

11. This section draws upon Pauline Jones Luong, "The Use and Abuse of Russia's Energy Resources: Implications for State Societal Relations," in *Building the Russian State: Institutional Crisis and the Quest for Democratic Governance*, ed. Valerie Sperling (Boulder, CO: Westview, 2000), 27–45.

12. Energy Information Administration, "Privatization and the Globalization of Energy Markets," Department of Energy, DOE/EIA-0609(96), 1996, www.eia.doe.gov/emeu/pgem/contents.html (May 17, 2005); Arild Moe and Valeriy Kryukov, "Observations on the Reorganization of the Russian Oil Industry," *Post-Soviet Geography* 35, no. 2 (1994): 89–101.

13. Energy Information Administration, "Privatization and the Globalization of Energy Markets," 1996; Matthew J. Sagers, Valeriy A. Kryukov, and Vladimir V. Shmat, "Resource Rent from the Oil and Gas Sector and the Russian Economy," *Post-Soviet Geography* 36, no. 7 (1995): 398.

14. In 1994, several additional VICs were carved out of Rosneft—including Slavneft, Sidanco, VNK, and Onaco. In August–September 1995, the number of enterprises remaining in Rosneft was reduced even further—two new VICs were formed—TNK and Sibneft. When the first phase of privatization ended on June 30, 1994, nine oil VICs existed along with state-owned Rosneft (*RPI*, July/August 1994, 16–17).

15. Catherine Locatelli, "The Reorganization of the Russian Hydrocarbons Industry," *Energy Policy* 23, no. 9 (1995): 813; Matthew J. Sagers, "Developments in Russian Crude Oil Production in 2000," *Post-Soviet Geography* 42, no. 3 (2001): 153–201. Nevertheless, on August 24, 1995, Yeltsin signed Presidential Decree No. 872, which nullified any plans for Rosneft to become the dominant player in the Russian oil industry in spite of the heavy lobbying of Prime Minister Chernomyrdin on Rosneft's behalf (*RPI*, October 1995, 11).

16. David Lane, ed., *The Political Economy of Russian Oil* (Lanham, MD: Rowman & Littlefield, 1999); Energy Information Administration, "Privatization and the Globalization of Energy Markets," 1996; Locatelli, "The Reorganization of the Russian Hydrocarbons Industry."

17. See, e.g., Leslie Dienes, *Corporate Russia: Privatization and Prospects in the Oil and Gas Sector* (The Henry M. Jackson School of International Studies, The University of Washington: The Donald W. Treadgold Papers, no. 5, 1996), 13.

18. See, e.g., Lane, *The Political Economy of Russian Oil*.

19. Steven L. Solnick, *Stealing the State: Control and Collapse in Soviet Institutions* (Cambridge, MA: Harvard University Press, 1998).

20. The government's decision stems not only from its dire need to reduce the budget deficit but also from its fear in 1995 that the Communists would return to power and reverse the course of privatization. In fact, Chubais declared that "[he would] sell everything, even for half a kopeck, before the Communists come to power" (*RPI*, November 1995, 13).

21. For more detail, see Virginie Coulloudon, "Privatization in Russia: Catalyst for the New Elite," *The Fletcher Forum of International Affairs* 22, no. 2 (Summer/Fall 1998): 43–56; Johnson, "Russia's Emerging Financial-Industrial Groups."

22. See, e.g., Dienes, *Corporate Russia.*

23. Ironically, many of these firms were often in compliance with Russian laws (Black, Kraakman, and Tarassova, "Russian Privatization and Corporate Governance").

24. Locatelli, "Russian Hydrocarbons Industry"; Energy Information Administration, "Privatization and the Globalization of Energy Markets."

25. Gazprom owns the world's largest gas pipeline network, totaling over 155,000 km (Johnson's Russia List, February 17, 2003), www.cdi.org/russia/johnson/.

26. Matthew J. Sagers, "The Russian Natural Gas Industry in the Mid-1990s," *Post-Soviet Geography* 36, no. 9 (1995): 521–64; Aleksandr Gorbachev, "Gazprom: Mid-Term Prospects," *New Energy* (April 10, 2003).

27. Pauline Jones Luong and Erika Weinthal, "Prelude to the Resource Curse: Explaining Energy Development Strategies in the Soviet Successor States and Beyond," *Comparative Political Studies* 34, no. 4 (2001): 367–99. Subsequently, in November 1998 Yeltsin issued a decree raising the limit to 14 percent. "Russia OKs Partial Gas Co. Sale," *The Associated Press*, November 2, 1998. A 1999 decree restricts foreign ownership to 20 percent but it is currently only at 11.5 percent—up from 2 percent in 1996. See e.g., New Energy Group, April 10, 2003.

28. Sagers, "The Russian Natural Gas Industry in the Mid-1990s."

29. See e.g., Dienes, *Corporate Russia.*

30. For example, Rem Vyakhirev, who Chernomyrdin selected to succeed him as Gazprom's chairman, was Chernomyrdin's first deputy.

31. See, e.g., *Business Week Online*, November 20, 2000.

32. *Johnson's Russia List*, March 22, 2002. Stroytransgaz's shareholders include family members of both Chernomyrdin and Vyakhirev. For details, see *Business Week Online*, November 20, 2000 and February 18, 2002.

33. See, e.g., Peter Reddaway and Dmitri Glinski, *The Tragedy of Russia's Reforms: Market Bolshevism against Democracy* (Washington, DC: U.S. Institute of Peace Press, 2001); Marshall I. Goldman, *Lost Opportunity: Why Economic Reforms in Russia Have Not Worked* (New York: Norton, 1994).

34. See, e.g., Michael Alexeev, "The Effect of Privatization and the Distribution of Wealth in Russia," *Economics of Transition* 7, no. 2 (July 1999): 449–65; Black, Kraakman, and Tarasova, "Russian Privatization and Corporate Governance"; Hellman, "Winners Take All"; Sonin, "Inequality, Property Rights, and Economic Growth in Transition Economies."

35. *RFE/RL*, September 20, 2000.

36. Eugene Khartukov, "Russia's Oil Majors: Engine for Radical Change," *Oil and Gas Journal* (May 27, 2002). Since the initial privatizations, several of these companies have further consolidated. For example, Menatep acquired controlling shares in the Eastern Oil Company (VNK), leading to the merger of VNK and Yukos when the state divested its shares of VNK in 1997. Lukoil also negotiated the acquisition of Komitek in 1999, buying 85 percent of Komitek shares from major shareholders.

37. For example, Gazprom bought back Purgaz from Itera (*NewsBase*, March 1, 2002).

38. See, e.g., *Moscow Times*, June 1, 2001, 1; *Russia Journal*, June 1, 2001.

39. *UFG Report*, May 30, 2002; Kent F. Moors, "Government Maps Plan to Restructure Gazprom End Its Gas Market Monopoly," *RPI* (February 2001): 57–60; Ben Aris, "More Details on Gazprom Reform Plan," *Alexander's Oil and Gas Connections* 7, no. 15 (17 July 2001).

40. *Moscow Times*, June 19, 2003. Currently, foreigners can buy only a small number of "ring-fenced" shares at a substantially higher price than shares available to Russian citizens. In September 2004, the Putin government pledged to lift all restrictions on foreign ownership; however, the government plans to retain a controlling stake (Guy Faulconbridge, "Zhukov: Gazprom Limits Will Go," *Moscow Times*, September 29, 2004, 1).

41. Jones Luong and Weinthal, "Contra Coercion."

42. By "ownership" we are not referring to the subsurface mineral resources themselves, which are (to our knowledge) state-owned in all mineral-rich countries, but rather, to ownership of the rights to develop mineral deposits and of production facilities.

43. See, e.g., Yair Aharoni, "State-Owned Enterprise: an Agent without a Principal," in *Public Enterprise in Less-Developed Countries*, ed. Leroy P. Jones (Cambridge: Cambridge University Press, 1982).

44. A 1993 agreement allowed Gazprom's director Vyakhirev to manage 35 percent of the government's 40 percent shares in trust. This agreement was so elusive that it was kept in a secret location to the extent that First Deputy Prime Minister Nemstov could not locate a copy (Peter Rutland, "Battle Rages over Russia's Natural Monopolies," *Transition Newsletter*, World Bank [May/June 1997]).

45. Peter Rutland, "Lost Opportunities: Energy and Politics in Russia," *NBR Analysis* 8, no. 5 (1997): 8.

46. Jamestown Foundation, April 14, 1997.

47. The Putin administration has sought to breathe life into the seemingly ineffectual Audit Chamber by making it directly responsible to the president rather than the state Duma. For details, see Michael Heath, "Putin to Increase Grip on 'New' Audit Chamber," *The Russia Journal*, June 29, 2001.

48. *RFE/RL*, November 1, 1999.

49. See, e.g., *RPI*, May 1997, 8; *RPI*, August 1998. Specifically, the IMF has been pushing the Russian government for years to break up Gazprom. See, e.g., *RFE/RL*, June 12, 1998.

50. See, e.g., *Johnson's Russia List*, February 17, 2003.

51. See, e.g., *Carnegie Meeting Report*, 3, no. 12 (April 18, 2001).

52. See, e.g., *Johnson's Russia List*, February 17, 2003.

53. See, e.g., *Observer*, February 9, 2003.

54. See, e.g., *Johnson's List*, February 17, 2003.

55. See, e.g., *Monitor* 7, no. 159 (August 31, 2001); *RFE/RL*, June 18, 1998.

56. See, e.g., *RFE/RL*, June 23, 2000; *Pravda*, July 11, 2002.

57. In other words, they have no claim to the residual (or profits). On "residual claimant" theory, see Arman A. Alchian and Harold Demsetz, "Production, Information Costs, and Economic Organization," *American Economic Review* 62 (December 1972): 777–95.

58. In the spring of 1998, Yeltsin forced Vyakhirev to sign a new contract, which not only had an expiration date (May 31, 2001), but also did not include stock options. For details, see *UFG*, May 30, 2002.

59. *Washington Post*, June 23, 2002.

60. *Special Report FBIS-SOC-98-112*, April 22, 1998.

61. Although one might be tempted to attribute this to lower gas prices, many argue this cannot be attributed to lower gas prices alone. See, e.g., *RFE Business Watch Report*, December 3, 2002.

62. See, e.g., *Business Week Online*, February 18, 2002; *Johnson's Russia List*, March 22, 2002.

63. For details, see Jones Luong and Weinthal, "Contra Coercion."

64. Margaret Levi, *Of Rule and Revenue* (Berkeley: University of California Press, 1988).

65. See, e.g., Joseph E. Stiglitz, "Whither Reform? Ten Years of the Transition" (Keynote Address, World Bank Annual Bank Conference on Development Economics, 1999).

66. Authors' personal communication with Boris Makarenko, deputy director general, Center for Political Technologies, Moscow, September 19, 2001.

67. *RFE/RL*, August 27, 2003.

68. See, e.g., Michael D. Shafer, *Winners and Losers: How Sectors Shape the Developmental Prospects of States* (Ithaca, NY: Cornell University Press, 1994).

69. Mancur Olson, *The Rise and Decline of Nations: Economic Growth, Stagflation, and Social Rigidities* (New Haven, CT: Yale University Press, 1982).

70. According to Olson, *The Rise and Decline of Nations*, collusion is also unlikely to occur in a fluid context such as Russia because it is found more often in stable societies with unchanged boundaries.

71. *RPI*, October 1998, 17.

72. As of May 2004, gasoline prices in Russia were among the lowest in the world, money.cnn.com/pf/features/lists/global_gasprices/price.html (May 24, 2005). With both the international price of oil rising dramatically in 2004 and export opportunities growing, of course, gasoline prices in Russia are also rising.

73. *RFE/RL*, January 29, 2003.

74. *RFE/RL*, January 31, 2003, and *The Russia Journal*, December 16, 2002.

75. *RFE/RL*, January 29, 2003.

76. *The Russia Journal*, February 7, 2003.

77. *RFE/RL*, January 31, 2003.

78. *RPI*, January 2001, 5.

79. Peter Lavelle, "Transneft's Crude Control of the Taps," *The Russia Journal*, February 7, 2003.

80. Authors' personal communications with Stephen O'Sullivan, United Financial Group, Moscow, July 2002. See also *Moscow Times*, June 28, 2002, 2.

81. Authors' personal communication with representatives of Russian oil companies, Moscow, September 2001 and June–July 2002. See also *Moscow Times*, February 17, 2002.

82. *UFG Report*, May 30, 2002.

83. Authors' personal communications with Stephen O'Sullivan. See also *Moscow Times*, June 28, 2002, 2.

84. *Moscow Times*, June 28, 2002, 2.

85. Minority shareholders voiced concern, for example, that shares to Ruhrgas were undersold in May 2003 (*Vedomosti*, June 6, 2003).

86. Hermitage has also complained, for example, that "the total of the gas monopolist's dividends makes only 9% of the company's net profit, whereas YUKOS and LUKoil pay more than 20% of net profits by way of dividends." See *hermitagefund.com*, May 22, 2003, and *Gazeta*, May 21, 2003.

87. See, e.g., *Focus on Gazprom*, June 16, 2003; *Shareholders Turn Screws on Gazprom*, June 13, 2003; *Moscow Times*, June 19, 2003.

88. The tax code consists of two parts. Part I was adopted in July 1998 and enacted in January 1999; it covers administrative and procedural matters, including the introduction of new taxes and the protection of taxpayers' rights. Part II was adopted in August 2000, amended in November and December 2001, and enacted in 2001 and 2002; it includes specifications on various taxes, including the value added tax (VAT), corporate profits tax, personal incomes tax, and the social tax. For an overview see, OECD, *The Investment Environment in the Russian Federation: Laws, Policies, and Issues* (Paris: OECD, 2001), 115–44.

89. Consider, for example, the fact that this 13 percent flat tax is even lower than the 17 percent advocated by Steve Forbes, and that the 24 percent profits tax is lower than the OECD rate.

90. Authors' personal communications with domestic and foreign financial analysts, Moscow, September 2001 and June–July 2002; see also, e.g., Arthur Anderson, *Doing Business in Russia* (Moscow: Arthur Anderson, 2002); Alvin Rabushka, "The Flat Tax at Work in Russia," *The Russian Economy*, Hoover Institution, Stanford University, February 21, 2002, www.russiaeconomy.org/comments/022102.html (May 25, 2005).

91. See, e.g., *Pravda*, October 18, 2001; *Kommersant*, October 19, 2001; *Russia Journal*, July 18, 2002. German Gref, minister of Economic Development and Trade, also boasted that "tax collection in the first six months of [2001] exceeded the projected level" (*RFE/RL*, August 2, 2001).

92. See, e.g., Alvin Rabushka, "The Flat Tax in Russia: Year Three." *The Russian Economy*, Hoover Institution Public Policy Inquiry, April 26, 2004, www.russianeconomy.org/comments/042604.html (March 4, 2006).

93. If property rights are understood as not merely control over an asset but also the proceeds from that asset, then the ROCs' ability to gain more control over their revenue stream clearly enhances their property rights.

94. For more detail, see Gerald Easter, "Politics of Revenue Extraction in Post-Communist States: Poland and Russia Compared," Politics and Society 30, no. 4 (December 2002): 599–627; Erika Weinthal and Pauline Jones Luong, "Energy Wealth and Tax Reform in Russia and Kazakhstan," *Resources Policy* 27, no. 4 (2001): 1–9.

95. See, e.g., Thane Gustafson, *Capitalism Russian-Style* (Cambridge: Cambridge University Press, 1999), chapter 9; Shleifer and Treisman, *Without a Map*, chapter 6. According to the IMF, even as of January 1, 2000, the value of unpaid taxes at the consolidated level (federal and local governments) was 8.3 percent of GDP (IMF, *Russian Federation: Selected Issues*, IMF Report 00/150 [Washington, DC: IMF, 15 November 2000]), 69, 71.

96. Authors' personal communication with Vitaly Yermakov, research associate, Cambridge Energy Research Associates (CERA), Moscow, June 2002 and with Dvorkovich.

97. See, e.g., McFaul, "State Power, Institutional Change, and the Politics of Russian Privatization"; Hellman, "Winners Take All"; Cynthia Robert and Thomas Sherlock, "Bringing the Russian State Back In: Explanations of the Derailed Transition to Market Economy," *Comparative Politics* 31, no. 4 (July 1999): 477–98; Reddaway and Glinski, *Tragedy of Russia's Reforms*.

98. Martin Nicholson, "Putin's Russia: Slowing the Pendulum without Stopping the Clock," *International Affairs* 77, no. 4 (October 2001): 867–84; Lilia Shevtsova, *Putin's Russia* (Washington, DC: Carnegie Endowment for International Peace, 2003). Putin was appointed as prime minister in August 1999 and then elected to the presidency in March 2000 with 52.94 percent of the vote (*RFE/RL Russian Election Report*, no. 5 [April 7, 2000], 13). The Duma elected in December 1999 contained a majority of his supporters, who appeared to form the first stable policy coalition in the Russian parliament (the Unity bloc). For details, see Timothy J. Colton, "Reinventing Russia's Party of Power: 'Unity' and the 1999 Duma Election," *Post-Soviet Affairs* 16, no. 3 (July–September 2000): 201–25; Regina Smyth, "Building State Capacity from the Inside Out: Parties of Power and the Success of the President's Reform Agenda in Russia," *Politics and Society* 30, no. 4 (December 2002): 555–78.

99. Thomas Remington, *The Russian Parliament: Institutional Evolution in a Transitional Regime, 1989–1999* (New Haven, CT: Yale University Press, 2001).

100. For details, see Jones Luong and Weinthal, *Contra-Coercion*.

101. Common knowledge refers to shared information among players concerning the parameters and payoffs of the game. In most game theoretic accounts, it is either assumed to exist or can be achieved without direct communication. See Sergio Ribiero Da Costa Werlang, "Common Knowledge," in *Game Theory*, ed. John Eatwell, Murray Milgrave, and Peter Newman (New York: Norton, 1989).

102. Yukos overtook Lukoil as Russia's number-one domestic producer in 2002. Some observers, particularly in the West, speculate that the *siloviki* (i.e., security faction or hard-liners) in the Kremlin are behind this attack on Yukos.

103. Yugansneftegaz accounts for two-thirds of Yukos' total oil production and approximately 11 percent of Russia's total oil production. As of December 2004,

the government claims that it alone owes more than $20 billion in outstanding taxes (Catherine Belton, "Yukos Accused of 'Filthy Theft,'" *Moscow Times*, December 14, 2004, 1).

104. Konstantin Sonin, "Yugansk Is Dead Meat," *Moscow Times*, December 14, 2004, 12.

105. See, e.g., Marshall I. Goldman, "Putin and the Oligarchs," *Foreign Affairs* 83, no. 6 (November/December 2004): 33–44.

106. Sonin, "Yugansk Is Dead Meat," 12.

107. "Yukos Sells London-Based Unit to Company," Associated Press, February 1, 2006.

108. Valeria Korchagina, "Kagalovsky Makes New Yukos Offer," *Moscow Times*, December 15, 2004, 1.

109. See, e.g., Guy Faulconbridge, "Yukos Unit Up for Sale at Discount Price," *Moscow Times*, October 13, 2004, 1, *RFE/RL* 2 November 2005.

110. See, e.g. Belton, "Yukos Accused of 'Filthy Theft,'" 1.

111. *New York Times*, 18 November 2004.

112. *RFE/RL*, September 29, 2004.

113. See, e.g., Rebrov, "Ne Dozhdetes" (Don't Wait), *Vremya*, October 7, 2003.

114. Indeed, our comprehensive survey of the Russian language press from June 2003 to August 2004, which we do not have the space to present here, indicates that this is the consensus among Russian analysts.

115. See, e.g., Denisov, Shvarev, and Gorelov, "Oligarkhi-Oborotni" (Oligarchs-Wizards), *Vremya*, July 3, 2003.

116. Valeria Korchagina, "Kagalovsky Makes New Yukos Offer," *Moscow Times*, December 15, 2004, 1.

117. See, e.g., *Moscow Times*, June 1, 2001, 1; *Russia Journal*, June 1, 2001; *Business Week Online*, November 20, 2000.

118. In addition, the government was able to force the resignation of Pyotr Rodionov, first deputy CEO (for finance and economics), which is seen as strengthening Miller's hold (i.e., the government's) on the company. Ben Aris, "Gazprom Reform on the Way," *Alexander's Gas and Oil Connections*, January 23, 2002.

119. Aris, "Gazprom Reform on the Way."

120. *Vedomosti*, August 30, 2001.

121. Sergei Glazkov, "Mezhregiongaz Launches Electronic Exchange for Trading in Natural Gas at Market Prices: Gazprom Benefits Still," *Russian Petroleum Investor* (2003): 54–59. Previously, all gas produced by Gazprom and sold in Russia was sold at prices set by the Federal Energy Commission. Independents were only allowed to sell gas under direct contracts with consumers.

122. Sophie Lambroschini, "Russia: Gazprom's Relations with Itera to be Audited," *Radio Free Europe/Radio Liberty*, January 29, 2001. This includes the government's decision to buy back Purgaz, which was not merely an attempt to recover stolen assets but a response to minority shareholders' demands to know where Gazprom's assets have vanished. See, e.g., Aris, "Gazprom Reform on the Way."

123. See, e.g., *The Russia Journal*, February 7, 2003.

124. See, e.g., Terry Lynn Karl, *The Paradox of Plenty: Oil Booms and Petro-states* (Berkeley: University of California Press, 1997).

WORKS CITED

Aharoni, Yair. "State-Owned Enterprise: An Agent without a Principal." In *Public Enterprise in Less-Developed Countries*, edited by Leroy P. Jones. Cambridge: Cambridge University Press, 1982.

Alchian, Arman A., and Harold Demsetz. "Production, Information Costs, and Economic Organization." *American Economic Review* 62 (December 1972): 777–95.

Alexeev, Michael. "The Effect of Privatization and the Distribution of Wealth in Russia." *Economics of Transition* 7, no. 2 (July 1999): 449–65.

Aris, Ben. "More Details on Gazprom Reform Plan." *Alexander's Oil and Gas Connections*, July 17, 2001.

———. "Gazprom Reform on the Way." *Alexander's Gas and Oil Connections*, January 23, 2002.

Arthur Anderson. *Doing Business in Russia*, 2002.

"Authorities Arrest Yukos Unit Manager." *New York Times*, November 18, 2004.

Belton, Catherine. "Yukos Accused of 'Filthy Theft.'" *Moscow Times*, December 14, 2004.

Black, Bernard, Reinier Kraakman, and Anna Tarassova. "Russian Privatization and Corporate Governance: What Went Wrong?" *Stanford Law Review* 52 (2000): 1731–808.

Carnegie Meeting Report 3, no. 12 (April 18, 2001).

Colton, Timothy J., and Michael McFaul. "Reinventing Russia's Party of Power: 'Unity' and the 1999 Duma Election." *Post-Soviet Affairs* 16, 3 (July–September 2000): 201–25.

Coulloudon, Virginie. "Privatization in Russia: Catalyst for the New Elite." *The Fletcher Forum of International Affairs* 22, no. 2 (Summer/Fall 1998): 43–56.

Denisov, Shvarev, and Gorelov. "Oligarkhi-Oborotni" (Oligarchs-Wizards). *Vremya*, July 3, 2003.

Dienes, Leslie. *Corporate Russia: Privatization and Prospects in the Oil and Gas Sector*. The Henry M. Jackson School of International Studies, the University of Washington: The Donald W. Treadgold Papers, no. 5 (1996).

Easter, Gerald. "Politics of Revenue Extraction in Post-Communist States: Poland and Russia Compared." *Politics and Society* 30, no. 4 (December 2002): 599–627.

Energy Information Administration. "Privatization and the Globalization of Energy Markets." Department of Energy, DOE/EIA-0609(96) (1996).

Faulconbridge, Guy. "Zhukov: Gazprom Limits Will Go." *Moscow Times*, September 29, 2004.

———. "Yukos Unit Up for Sale at Discount Price." *Moscow Times*, October 13, 2004.

"Gazprom: Russia's Enron?" *Business Week Online*, February 18, 2002.

Glazkov, Sergei. "Mezhregiongaz Launches Electronic Exchange for Trading in Natural Gas at Market Prices: Gazprom Benefits Still." *Russian Petroleum Investor* (2003): 54–59.

Goldman, Marshall I. *Lost Opportunity: Why Economic Reforms in Russia Have Not Worked*. New York: Norton, 1994.

———. "Putin and the Oligarchs." *Foreign Affairs* 83, no. 6 (November/December 2004): 33–44.

Gorbachev, Aleksandr. "Gazprom: Mid-Term Prospects." *New Energy*, April 10, 2003.

Gustafson, Thane. *Capitalism Russian-Style*. Cambridge: Cambridge University Press, 1999.

Heath, Michael. "Putin to Increase Grip on 'New' Audit Chamber." *The Russia Journal*, June 29, 2001.

Hellman, Joel. "Winners Take All: The Politics of Partial Reform in Post-Communist Transitions." *World Politics* 50, no. 2 (January 1998): 203–34.

International Monetary Fund. *Russian Federation: Selected Issues*. IMF Staff Country Report No. 00/150. Washington, DC, 2000.

Johnson, Juliet. "Russia's Emerging Financial-Industrial Groups." *Post-Soviet Affairs* 13, no. 4 (October–December 1997): 333–65.

Jones Luong, Pauline. "The Use and Abuse of Russia's Energy Resources: Implications for State Societal Relations." In *Building the Russian State: Institutional Crisis and the Quest for Democratic Governance*, edited by Valerie Sperling. Boulder, CO: Westview, 2000.

———, and Erika Weinthal. "Prelude to the Resource Curse: Explaining Energy Development Strategies in the Soviet Successor States and Beyond." *Comparative Political Studies* 34, no. 4 (2001): 367–99.

———. "Contra Coercion: Russian Tax Reform, Exogenous Shocks, and Negotiated Institutional Change." *American Political Science Review* 98, no. 1 (2004): 139–52.

Karl, Terry Lynn. *The Paradox of Plenty: Oil Booms and Petro-states*. Berkeley: University of California Press, 1997.

Khartukov, Eugene. "Russia's Oil Majors: Engine for Radical Change." *Oil and Gas Journal*, May 27, 2002.

———, and Ellen Starostina. "Russia's Oil Privatization Is More Greed Than Fear." *Oil and Gas Journal*, July 3, 2000.

Korchagina, Valeria. "Yukos Licenses Hang in the Balance." *Moscow Times*, September 28, 2004.

———. "Kagalovsky Makes New Yukos Offer." *Moscow Times*, December 15, 2004.

Lambroschini, Sophie. "Russia: Gazprom's Relations with Itera to be Audited." *Radio Free Europe/Radio Liberty*, January 29, 2001.

Lane, David, ed. *The Political Economy of Russian Oil*. Lanham, MD: Rowman & Littlefield, 1999.

Lavelle, Peter. "Transneft's Crude Control of the Taps." *The Russia Journal*, February 7, 2003.

Levi, Margaret. *Of Rule and Revenue*. Berkeley: University of California Press, 1988.

Locatelli, Catherine. "The Reorganization of the Russian Hydrocarbons Industry." *Energy Policy* 23, no. 9 (1995): 809–19.

McFaul, Michael. "State Power, Institutional Change, and the Politics of Russian Privatization." *World Politics* 47 (January 1995): 210–43.

Moe, Arild, and Valeriy Kryukov. "Observations on the Reorganization of the Russian Oil Industry." *Post-Soviet Geography* 35, no. 2 (1994): 89–101.

Moors, Kent F. "Government Maps Plan to Restructure Gazprom End its Gas Market Monopoly." *RPI* (February 2001): 57–60.

Nicholson, Martin. "Putin's Russia: Slowing the Pendulum without Stopping the Clock." *International Affairs* 77, no. 4 (October 2001): 867–84.

OECD. *The Investment Environment in the Russian Federation: Laws, Policies, and Issues*. Paris: OECD, 2001.

Olson, Mancur. *The Rise and Decline of Nations: Economic Growth, Stagflation, and Social Rigidities*. New Haven, CT: Yale University Press, 1982.

Rabushka, Alvin. "The Flat Tax at Work in Russia." *The Russian Economy*, Hoover Institution, Stanford University, February 21, 2002, www.russiaeconomy.org/comments/022102.html (May 25, 2005).

———. "The Flat Tax in Russia: Year Three." *The Russian Economy*, Hoover Institution, Stanford University, April 26, 2004, www.russianeconomy.org/comments/042604.html (March 4, 2006).

Rebrov. "Ne Dozhdetes" (Don't Wait). *Vremya*, October 7, 2003.

Reddaway, Peter, and Dmitri Glinski. *The Tragedy of Russia's Reforms: Market Bolshevism against Democracy*. Washington, DC: U.S. Institute of Peace Press, 2001.

Remington, Thomas. *The Russian Parliament: Institutional Evolution in a Transitional Regime, 1989–1999*. New Haven, CT: Yale University Press, 2001.

RFE/RL Russian Election Report, no. 5, April 7, 2000.

Robert, Cynthia, and Thomas Sherlock. "Bringing the Russian State Back In: Explanations of the Derailed Transition to Market Economy," *Comparative Politics* 31, no. 4 (July 1999): 477–98.

Rutland, Peter. "Lost Opportunities: Energy and Politics in Russia." *NBR Analysis* 8, no. 5 (1997).

———. "Battle Rages over Russia's Natural Monopolies." *Transition Newsletter*. The World Bank (May/June 1997).

Sagers, Matthew J. "The Russian Natural Gas Industry in the Mid-1990s." *Post-Soviet Geography* 36, no. 9 (1995): 521–64.

———. "Developments in Russian Crude Oil Production in 2000." *Post-Soviet Geography* 42, no. 3 (2001): 153–201.

———, Valeriy A. Kryukov, and Vladimir V. Shmat. "Resource Rent from the Oil and Gas Sector and the Russian Economy." *Post-Soviet Geography* 36, no. 7 (1995): 389–425.

Shafer, D. Michael. *Winners and Losers: How Sectors Shape the Developmental Prospects of States*. Ithaca, NY: Cornell University Press, 1994.

Shevtsova, Lilia. *Putin's Russia*. Washington, DC: Carnegie Endowment for International Peace, 2003.

Shleifer, Andrei, and Daniel Treisman. *Without a Map: Political Tactics and Economic Reform in Russia*. Cambridge: MIT Press, 2000.

Smyth, Regina. "Building State Capacity from the Inside Out: Parties of Power and the Success of the President's Reform Agenda in Russia." *Politics and Society* 30, no. 4 (December 2002): 555–78.

Solnick, Steven L. *Stealing the State: Control and Collapse in Soviet Institutions*. Cambridge, MA: Harvard University Press, 1998.

Sonin, Konstantin. "Inequality, Property Rights, and Economic Growth in Transition Economies: Theory and Russian Evidence." *CEPR Discussion Paper 2300* (1999).

———. "Yugansk Is Dead Meat." *Moscow Times*, December 14, 2004.

Stiglitz, Joseph E. "Whither Reform? Ten Years of the Transition" Keynote Address, World Bank Annual Bank Conference on Development Economics, 1999.

Weinthal, Erika, and Jones Luong, Pauline. "Energy Wealth and Tax Reform in Russia and Kazakhstan." Resources Policy 27, no. 4 (2001): 1–9.

Werlang, Sergio Ribiero Da Costa. "Common Knowledge." In Game Theory, edited by John Eatwell, Murray Milgrave, and Peter Newman. New York: Norton, 1989.

Chapter Nine

Democratization, Separation of Powers, and State Capacity

Thomas F. Remington

DEMOCRATIZATION AND GOVERNANCE

The institutional turn in political science and economics has had a powerful impact on our understanding of the determinants of long-term economic performance. The insight that the quality of a state's institutional environment can exert a cumulative influence on development, independently of regime type or policy choice, has challenged assumptions based on neoclassical theory.[1] For example, simply changing formal institutions from communism to democracy may do little to improve social well-being, and societies at a low level of development may remain stuck in a low-level equilibrium trap rather than catching up with the developed world. The new consensus is that "institutions" matter. But what do we mean when we say "institutions?" Although one strand of the literature identifies the institutional environment squarely with the degree to which property and contract rights are secure, many authors have expanded the concept much further, referring to it variously as institutional quality, state capacity, or governance.[2] Although some treatments distinguish governance or institutional quality from, on the one hand, formal institutions, and, on the other, policies, others join all three concepts into a broad composite concept. Dani Rodrik, for example, defines good governance as effective performance by five types of institutions: secure property rights; government regulation of markets; fiscal and monetary policy instruments to promote macroeconomic stability; social assistance programs that guarantee adequate living standards

261

to vulnerable groups of the population; and structures that can manage if not resolve conflicts among social groups.[3] Some of these institutions administer and enforce policy, but others make policy: they set tax rates, redistribute resources, allocate rights. Kaufmann and his World Bank associates have assembled a comprehensive set of measures of governance for all the world's countries in six domains, conceptually understood as representing separable (but highly intercorrelated) underlying dimensions of the quality of national institutions:[4]

1. voice and accountability
2. political stability
3. effectiveness of government
4. quality of regulation
5. rule of law
6. control of corruption

The dependent variable in institutional studies varies as well. In some it is measures of economic performance (such as growth or reduction of inequality). In some the prevalence of corruption is treated as an outcome,[5] in others a cause, of economic performance.[6] In some treatments, regime type (democracy vs. autocracy) is a control variable, while in others it is bundled in with the concept of institutional quality.[7] Clearly there is a good deal of imprecision in the concept as well as fuzziness about causal relations.

Nonetheless, there is now a substantial body of empirical results from large-N cross-national studies that show significant effects for *both* the quality of institutions *and* the structure of formal institutions on the performance of economies. Some of these studies explicitly postulate that the existence of formal legislative and judicial constraints on the executive is associated with better economic performance.[8] This raises questions about how formal institutions might affect the quality of governance. The empirical evidence from large-scale cross-national studies shows that democratization is associated with *both* higher growth *and* more equitable distribution, implying better governance.[9] Similarly, the cross-national studies of the postcommunist world consistently demonstrate that greater levels of openness, accountability, and inclusiveness of government are associated both with higher growth and greater equality of distribution and with lower levels of "capture" of government by powerful private interests.[10]

On the other hand, it is not immediately obvious why, holding other factors constant, democratization should improve governance. Indeed, research suggests that newly democratic states do a *worse* job than the average autocracy in protecting property and contract rights, although mature democracies perform better.[11] Is the improvement of institutional performance associated with mature democracy driven by the deepening of democracy, or are both themselves the product of other dynamic changes in economy, the society, or the international environment? Is the increase in checks and balances the cause of greater security of contract and property rights, or does it yield greater distributional costs as more interests must be accommodated?

Democratic transitions in times of severe economic crisis can stimulate a surge of demands for distributive policies that benefit particular groups at the expense of the public welfare, demands that weak new democratic governments are frequently unable to resist.[12] Their governing institutions are susceptible to capture by powerful organized interests, whether through direct control over policymaking structures, indirect influence, or outright corruption.[13] A strong party system, in which a relatively small number of competitive parties aggregate public interests across a broad range of particularistic interests and convert electoral programs into welfare-enhancing public policy, can overcome these dangers.[14] In many new democracies, however, party systems are weak and fragmented, and therefore ineffective at aggregating public demands. Both executive and legislative policymaking arenas fall prey to strong pressures from powerful particularistic interests.

In this chapter I examine the effect of democratization, defined here as the emergence of a system of separated powers from a fused, centralized system, on the quality of governance, taking Russia as a case study. The *quality of governance* in this chapter refers to the state's capacity to make and carry out policy producing Pareto-improving gains in public well-being. Conceiving democracy in terms of the separation of legislative from executive power needs some justification, however, since not all democracies are organized around the separation of powers principle. In the context of the postcommunist world, however, separation of powers has been a critical component of democratization in two respects. First, as many studies of institutions have emphasized, constraints on the executive are important in curbing rulers' appetites for appropriating and redistributing resources produced by others. In models emphasizing the incentive for credible self-restraint on the part of rulers, executives surrender part of their sovereign power to courts and parliaments precisely in order to encourage productive activity on the part of economic agents.[15] Moreover, democratization in Russia and other postcommunist countries broke the state monopoly on power and property. This monopoly was held by a constitutionally unitary system of political power: Soviet theory held not only that private productive property was prohibited, but that executive and legislative power were fused in a single source of authority, the soviets, themselves in turn controlled by the Communist Party. Dividing executive from legislative authority therefore created mutually restraining centers of initiative and veto power over the ownership of resources and the distribution of surpluses. The question for this chapter, therefore, is whether breaking the executive's monopoly on policymaking power makes policy makers more susceptible or less to the influence of powerful particularistic interests. Increasing the responsiveness of rulers and multiplying the number of access points to policymaking may create greater opportunity for well-positioned and well-organized social interests to exploit the larger society through rent-seeking, wasteful distributive policies, and corruption. Such a possibility would be consistent with the empirical finding that young democracies perform worse than most autocracies at protecting property and contractual rights.

Representative institutions such as parties and parliaments aggregate demands and preferences, providing some degree of accountability of decision makers to citizens where they compete for electoral support, and formulating policy alternatives. Inefficient aggregative institutions permit large welfare losses as the well-organized exploit society by concentrating distributional benefits for themselves while diffusing the costs to the larger society.[16] More efficient aggregative institutions facilitate decision making that internalizes the costs of distributive policy in order to realize maximum benefit from policies that increase society's productivity and welfare. But there has been a vigorous debate in the literature about the optimal institutional forms for raising the efficiency of aggregative institutions and increasing social welfare. A long line of thinkers have argued that insulating policy makers from the pressure of narrow, well-organized special interests by strengthening the autonomy of the executive can yield policies that are preferable for society as a whole. One standard argument is that institutions designed to maximize policy makers' responsiveness are more vulnerable to problems created by the time inconsistency of voter preferences than are more insulated institutions: where the short-term costs are acute and concentrated compared with the long-term benefits of a policy, as is frequently the case with stabilization and structural adjustment programs, autonomous bureaucracies and politically insulated technocrats may be more willing and able to formulate and enact them.[17] In support of this argument is a substantial literature showing that increasing the number of veto players whose consent is required for the adoption of decisions increases bargaining costs, which are typically paid in the form of distributive side payments, leading to oversized or even universal distributive coalitions that result in deadweight losses for society.[18] More broadly, much of the literature blaming Russia's poor economic performance on its "shock therapy" reforms and citing China's economic success as proof of the supposed virtues of "gradualism" under authoritarian rule assumes that Russian democratization under Gorbachev and Yeltsin undermined state regulatory and administrative capacities, whereas authoritarianism permitted China's state to maintain political and social stability as it introduced elements of a market economy.[19]

An opposing line of thought holds that making executives autonomous is no guarantee that they will be autonomous of demands from favored clients and sectors or will make decisions that increase social well-being. After all, a ruler strong enough to enforce property and contract rights is also strong enough to violate them.[20] Conceivably, increasing the number of actors participating in policymaking can *improve* the quality of aggregation by increasing the pool of information available to decision makers and reducing the scope for the arbitrary exercise of power and for socially costly rents and corruption. Therefore, parliamentary systems and programmatic party systems are preferable to presidential systems and clientelistic party systems because they are superior mechanisms for aggregating society's interests. When the aggregation of social interests through parties or other electoral institutions works effectively, a democratically elected legislature can curb tendencies for administrators to use their discretion for wasteful, corrupt, or abusive purposes. Separation of executive, legislative, and judicial powers was argued to be desirable precisely for this reason by James Madison in the *Federalist Papers* and by many authors since.[21]

In the context of the postcommunist world, the more open and flexible parliamentary systems have tended to perform better in overcoming the pressure of "early winners" and other rent-seekers than have the systems with more autonomous presidential executives.[22] Timothy Frye has shown evidence that it is precisely the oligarchic beneficiaries of partial reform who have sought to lock in their advantages by colluding in strengthening the presidencies of the postcommunist world.[23] It would be hard to argue therefore that autonomous executives necessarily aggregate social interests any more efficiently than can parliamentary systems. If increasing the number of veto points in the system increases the number of actors whose consent must be obtained through distributive side payments, then institutions such as separation of powers and proportional representation surely contribute to making policy more socially costly. On the other hand, the open give-and-take of legislative debate is often held to check the propensity of rulers to prefer redistributive to efficiency-enhancing policies. Therefore to the extent that the separation of powers increases accountability, transparency, information, and deliberation, it should produce better governance. The Russian case may help to reveal the mechanisms at work linking formal institutions with the quality of governance.

ASSESSING GOVERNANCE IN RUSSIA

Russia is a particularly interesting case for studying the effect of institutional change on performance because of the extraordinary changes in the state's institutional environment in the late 1980s to the 1990s. In the short span of a half dozen years, Russian political institutions were entirely rebuilt, and the very definition of the state itself changed. Constitutionally, Russia was transformed from a communist system where executive and legislative power were fused into a nominally democratic system with separately and freely elected parliament and president. To what degree did the new formal institutions established in the 1993 constitution improve the quality of deliberation, decision making, and policy implementation?

Ideally we would be able to assess governance in different eras of Soviet political history with a common yardstick, and therefore to measure the effects of institutional change on performance directly. Lacking exact measures, however, about the only statement we can make with some confidence is that, by comparison with the period of the Civil War or that of the early 1990s, the Soviet state in the late Brezhnev era was a model of efficient governance. Yet as many serious studies made clear, and as the outpouring of popular complaints under glasnost confirmed, the late Soviet state suffered from very poor governance. Moreover, most analysts would agree that by the end of the Soviet era, the Soviet mobilizational model of state building had exhausted its ability to increase state capacity.[24] This was certainly Mikhail Gorbachev's view. One of the principal aims of democratization was to revitalize the capacity of the state to make and implement policy and reverse the "stagnation" and "braking mechanisms" that had resulted in a poor standard of living for the Soviet population.[25] Among the institutional reforms he advocated, as we know, were broadened political participation, elections, and a "law-governed state."

The idea that separation of powers was an indispensable component of democracy arose as reformers pushed Gorbachev to embrace more radical ideas than simply broader participation in soviet elections under enlightened Communist Party rule. Boris Kurashvili, of the Institute for State and Law, boldly proposed introducing a system of functional checks and balances into the Soviet state in an article in *Kommunist* in May 1988, where he defined separation of powers "as a mechanism for complementing and balancing the powers of one state organ (which has taken a decision) with the powers of another organ, in order to achieve the adoption of a more well-founded decision, its annulment or correction." A constitutional court, for instance, might be empowered to nullify an act of the government.[26]

But not until Gorbachev and Yeltsin introduced presidencies in 1990 and 1991 in the USSR and Russian Soviet Federated Socialist Republic (RSFSR), respectively, was the formal principle of separation of powers established constitutionally. Even then, it coexisted with the old Soviet doctrine that state power was unitary and fused. In the amended Russian Republic constitution of 1991, for instance, Articles 1 and 3 provided that legislative and executive power were separate, while Article 2 retained the old language that the soviets retained supreme power over all matters affecting the state. This constitutional ambiguity only reinforced the intense struggle over control over resources that was breaking out as the union fell apart and the control of assets began to be redistributed.[27]

Although Soviet and post-Soviet reformers regarded the separation of powers as fundamental to democratization, they were much less attentive to the question of how broad social interests would be aggregated and mobilized against well-organized, narrow special interests. As studies by Herbert Kitschelt, Richard Rose, and others have argued, in postcommunist and other societies, where democratization occurs before a competent, professional public administration has developed, politicians have every reason to colonize the bureaucracy to maintain themselves in power by delivering privatized benefits to particular sets of clients rather than universalistic public policy.[28] In such systems, linkage mechanisms between state and society are based on clientelism, and policy makers specialize in supplying particularistic benefits at the public's expense. Certainly this has been the case in Russia. Even among postcommunist countries, Russia ranks high in the extent to which the state was captured by powerful interests in the 1990s.[29] Conceivably, constitutional changes that disperse agenda and veto power to new institutions, without the development of corresponding means for building support for broad programs of public policy, might only shift the location of political access for well-organized private interests rather than increasing the capacity of the state to improve society's overall well-being.

Still, some improvement in Russia's state capacity in the 1990s is evident. For example, Kaufmann and his World Bank associates find that in the six areas of governance in which they estimate performance, Russia has increased between 2000 and 2002 in five of them. Only in the area of "voice and accountability" (tapping observance of civil and political rights) has Russia's performance declined.[30] Our question, therefore, is: How, if at all, has the constitutional separation of powers in Russia affected trends in governance? Is it indeed anything more than a constitutional fiction? And if not, did it contribute to the breakdown in state capacity in the early 1990s or to the apparent growth in state capacity since then?

SEPARATION OF POWERS AND GOVERNANCE IN RUSSIA

Scholars identify three general ways in which a legislature may control the bureaucracy in a separation of powers system: oversight, legislation, and budget making.[31] For these to work, some conditions must be met: there needs to be a certain degree of cooperation between the branches in policymaking (each side must be willing to bargain and compromise in order to get some policy benefits), the legislature must have some capacity to monitor the executive, and the executive needs to be willing to comply with legislative enactments. Certainly these conditions have not always applied in Russia. Especially in the early 1990s, when President Yeltsin was fighting parliament for a greater share of a dwindling pool of state power, much policy was made in the form of executive acts, such as government regulations and presidential decrees, rather than being submitted to the open process of deliberation and mutual compromise. Yet there has been a considerable amount of interbranch cooperation in law making, even in periods of intense interbranch conflict. Since 1993, both sides have regularly preferred to compromise than to press a confrontation to the limit.[32] There has been a zone of shared agreement on policy goals between parliament and executive even when the two branches are at odds on many issues. For example, the communists and the reformers were able to agree on legislation governing the federal judiciary and federal elections in the mid-1990s. And even though the 1993 constitution removed any direct reference to a right of legislative oversight—"*kontrol'* "—over the executive, forms of legislative oversight have existed in such institutions as parliamentary hearings, interpellations, investigations, and government hour. Let us examine the exercise of each of these three categories of powers by the Russian Federal Assembly as it affects institutional performance.

Oversight

The power of oversight is equivalent to the Russian term, *kontrol'*. The history of *kontrol'* institutions in the Russian state is long and revealing, because, since *kontrol'* was always understood as an instrument of political control over the bureaucracy, the Soviet state set up a number of different types of structures for monitoring the compliance of the state bureaucracy with policy makers' goals.[33] These were instruments by which one branch of the bureaucracy checked others, however; the history of legislative oversight is far shorter. Institutionally, however, legislative *kontrol'* over the bureaucracy is analogous to congressional oversight of the executive in the American context, where it was defined by a U.S. Senate committee as "a wide range of congressional efforts to review and control policy implementation."[34]

Although Russia's parliament lacks a *formal* right of *kontrol'* under the 1993 constitution, de facto oversight is exercised through several mechanisms. One is the Audit Chamber, which has a staff of around five hundred people who conduct audits of state organizations. Parliament names its chair and gives it specific assignments. The Audit Chamber has investigated an extremely wide range of government organizations and state enterprises and worked assiduously to expand its powers. Under its ambitious chairman Sergei Stepashin, it has created a network of regional branch offices, which it has been trying to build into a centralized hierarchy.[35] In the 1995–2000 period, it conducted some three thousand investigations.[36] Much of the time, its reports have had little apparent effect on the bureaucracy, although often its findings are reported in the Russian press. Its 1997 investigation of the trust auctions (the "loans for shares" scheme) of 1995 found serious legal irregularities but the Procuracy refused to act. It has regularly clashed with the government and with the Ministry of Finance in particular over its right to conduct audits. It regularly complains that the government ignores its findings. It does not have the power to bring legal charges and its reports have only advisory force. But its power to expose abuses and corruption contributes to parliament's (and the president's) ability to generate political pressure on high-ranking government officials. In the spring of 2003, a series of well-publicized disclosures about the misuse of federal funds in the preparations for St. Petersburg's three hundredth anniversary undoubtedly weakened governor Yakovlev's political position and led to his removal as governor in June. By itself the Audit Chamber has little power to improve governance, but when elements of the executive branch are receptive to its recommendations, it becomes another instrument at the disposal of parliament for political influence.[37]

Parliament also has the power to hold legislative hearings and to invite ministers to appear and answer questions before the Duma during "government hour." Hearings do not need to be specifically associated with pieces of legislation; most Duma hearings in fact are not related to individual bills. Each year, Duma committees hold close to one hundred hearings. These give committee chairs and members the opportunity to publicize problems, advertise their policy positions, attract press attention to their legislative agenda, and put pressure on the executive branch to act on particular issues. Committees also conduct seminars and roundtable discussions for similar purposes. Government hour is another opportunity to focus the spotlight on particular government officials and to publicize parliament's watchdog role.

Members of parliament also have the right to submit interpellations (*zaprosy*) to the government (any deputy may propose one, but the motion to submit one requires majority support), to contact government officials directly, and to question government officials in the course of question hour. Often these powers are used for particularistic purposes—indeed, like other legislative powers, often they are used for corrupt purposes. In other cases the Duma uses interpellations as a way of demonstrating that it is playing its proper role as the guardian of the public interest, as when the Duma unanimously passed a motion calling for an interpellation to Procurator-General Ustinov demanding that he check into press reports of corruption in the Interior Ministry.[38] The net effect of these powers is a considerable increase in the flow of information from the executive to the legislative branch and greater pressure on the executive branch to fight corruption and inefficiency.

Parliament also has an implied, although again not formal, power to conduct investigations. It does this by forming special-purpose commissions to conduct wide-ranging inquiries, including, in the present convocation, a commission devoted to fighting corruption. An example is the Duma's investigation of the activity of former Atomic Energy minister Evgenii Adamov. The Duma's anticorruption commission reported at the beginning of March 2001 that Adamov had skimmed off huge sums from contracts with the ministry and created numerous commercial firms with them. At the end of the same month, Putin dismissed Adamov.[39] Pressure from the commission was also undoubtedly a factor leading to the fall of the powerful minister for railroads, Nikolai Aksenenko, at the beginning of 2002. In both cases, dismissal was the outcome of a lengthy subterranean bureaucratic war, in which pressure from the Duma was only one of many contributing reasons for the eventual outcome. The difference between these episodes and similar bureaucratic wars in the Soviet era is that now legislators, with an eye to the public and electoral consequences of taking sides, are opening them to public debate.

Thus parliament's de facto oversight powers have expanded the flow of open information, often of a scandalous nature, but they have not greatly strengthened parliament's capacity to check abuses in the executive or hold the executive accountable. This is because the executive usually acts in response to parliamentary pressure only when it is prepared to do so. Parliamentary hearings, investigations, and reports operate as another arena in which bureaucratic and social interests compete for influence.

Law-Making versus Presidential Decrees

The role of policymaking by legislation (*zakony*, or statutes) in promoting effective governance depends on how well laws deter the arbitrary use of bureaucratic power and promote the public welfare over particularistic interests. Above we noted two lines of thought in the literature about law making as opposed to decree making in this respect. One possibility is that, all else being equal, the legislative path to policy enactments may make policymaking more transparent and policy decisions more stable, and may prevent particularism or abuse of authority by the executive. The alternative possibility is that legislative procedures open policymaking to higher distributive costs than executive acts because more interests must be satisfied in order to build majorities. The Russian case, with its rich history of executive decree making and recent history of parliamentarism, invites us to test these competing arguments.

Historically, rather few policy decisions have been made by statute in Russia, either in the prerevolutionary or Soviet eras. Edicts (*ukazy*), decrees (*postanovleniia*), and sub-legal administrative rule making (through regulations, rules, and instructions [*rasporiazheniia, instruktsii*, etc.]) have far outnumbered statutes (*zakony*) for most of Russian history. The Presidium of the Supreme Soviet issued edicts in the Soviet period and continued to do so extensively into 1993. The Soviet system also relied heavily on *postanovleniia*, adopted by the CPSU by itself or jointly with the government and/or the trade unions. Strikingly few laws were passed (only about fifteen per year in the 1960s).

Law making is a critical feature of democratic governance because it requires open deliberation on policy and majority consent to decisions. In Russia, the post-1993 parliament has devised a number of institutional means to debate and decide policy in a range of policy areas. These include factions, committees, working groups, and agreement (*soglasitel'nye*) commissions. In turn, these institutional features of the Federal Assembly have enabled it to engage extensively in deliberation on legislation with the executive branch, both in the years when the policy distance between executive and legislative branches was high, and still more under Putin.

Indeed, the Federal Assembly since 1993 has greatly restricted the use of decree making. In the USSR and RSFSR Supreme Soviets of 1989–1991 and 1990–1993, decree making by the Presidium was a heavily used practice, and often used specifically to create lucrative privileges for special interests. In the period when Yeltsin and Khasbulatov were chairs of the RSFSR Supreme Soviet, and thus chaired the Presidium, they had wide latitude to issue orders and decrees on their own authority or that of the Presidium. Many of these acts were grants of special benefits, such as authorizations to create "free economic zones" in particular regions or licenses to particular organizations to import desirable goods such as liquor and cigarettes on a duty-free basis, or tax exemptions for particular regions or firms. These parliamentary-executive decrees and orders far outnumbered laws. For example, from May to November 1992, the Supreme Soviet produced over one thousand official acts, but only fifty-three of these were laws. Over six hundred were orders and decrees of the Presidium and its chairman.[40]

Moreover, in the face of dire social and economic crisis and unable to aggregate policy demands themselves, both the USSR Congress of People's Deputies (in 1990) and the RSFSR Congress of People's Deputies (one year later), delegated sweeping decree powers to Gorbachev and Yeltsin, respectively. Yeltsin then subsequently refused to relinquish the emergency decree powers he had been granted. Yeltsin's use of decree power reached a peak before and after the crisis of September 1993. For example, in the month following his famous decree of September 21, 1993, dissolving parliament and calling new elections, he issued some two hundred decrees.[41] In 1992–1993 and still later, in 1994–1995, President Yeltsin used his decree power to set policy in some of the most critical areas of economic reform. Often he used his decree power strategically, in order to pressure parliament into acting or to push a law in a direction favorable to his interests. As in other cases of presidential decree power, however, some of Yeltsin's high-handed exercise of his decree power reflected parliament's inability to assemble a coherent majority around a legislative program as least as much as it did arbitrary rule by decree on Yeltsin's part. Privatization policy in 1993–1994 is a case in point. Much of the polarization between the branches over privatization policy before and after the adoption of the 1993 constitution was less a matter of generalized ideology than it was a nakedly distributive war over the privatization of state assets—a new *chernyi peredel.*[42] The competition between laws and decrees as policy instruments in the sphere of privatization policy in the early 1990s gives us a direct comparison of each branch's capacity to formulate policies that resist particularistic demands for preferential treatment and costly distributive coalitions, and adopt policies that improve aggregate social welfare by creating secure property rights.

Regional bosses wanted to control the allocation of property rights to enterprises in their territories. Directors of state industrial firms wanted to acquire property stakes in their enterprises. As the Chubais team readily acknowledged, policy makers' desire to ensure the cooperation of regional and enterprise level elites in privatization against the opposition of the communists and ministerial-level officials induced them to design the voucher privatization program so as to favor them.[43] The concessions they made to managerial and regional interests undermined their stated policy goals and resulted in the concentration of enormous shares of state assets in the hands of several dozen financial-industrial groups. The privatization issue thus pitted a coalition of interests headed by the president's lead policy maker for privatization—Anatoly Chubais, as head of the State Property Committee—against an array of communist, bureaucratic, regional, and managerial interests. The vast wealth at stake in this fight strongly influenced the president's choice of policy instruments because of the urgency with which Chubais and his associates sought to create and transfer property rights quickly before their opponents could stop them.[44] President and parliament fought for the right to determine what enterprises would be subject to privatization after July 1, 1994, and in both, policy makers aggregated demands as they sought to build winning coalitions. Chubais adroitly used both legislative and decree instruments to preserve control over policy and maintain his coalition. On the one hand, he pressed the Duma to pass a law approving a program of privatization for the next phase that would give the government wide discretion to control privatization. If the deputies failed to give him the law he wanted, he warned, the president would simply set the terms of privatization by decree.[45] In July 1994, a group of centrist deputies from the economic policy committee and the privatization committee proposed a compromise bill following intensive bargaining with Chubais, but it fell thirteen votes short of a majority on the floor on the next-to-last day of the Duma's spring term. Yeltsin issued his decree on privatization the next day. The failure of the legislation was a defeat for the coalition of moderate forces in the Duma that wanted to gain legislative control over privatization and an immediate victory for Yeltsin and Chubais. (Chubais, reportedly, was not displeased by the defeat of the bill in the Duma because it left him free to use presidential decree power to set policy.)[46] Chubais used the threat of the presidential decree to force concessions from parliament on the legislation. The narrow margin by which the bill failed indicates how close parliament came to capturing control of privatization policy. Its failure, however, led to the arbitrary use of presidential decree power for privatization policy until parliament finally passed a law on privatization in 1997. Passage of the legislation might conceivably have left policy in this area just as susceptible to the play of particularism as did the president's retention of full autonomy, but it might also have made privatization more transparent and equitable.

The fight over the privatization of state television is another example where the president used his decree power to win control of a strategic asset for political purposes. In November 1994 President Yeltsin issued a decree, reportedly at Boris Berezovsky's behest, creating a new television company called ORT (Russian Public Television). ORT, formed from the state-owned broadcast company, Ostankino, was to be a joint stock company, with 49 percent of the shares sold to investors and 51 percent retained by the state.[47] Ostankino itself was the successor of the first program of Soviet television and reached nearly every home in Russia; it was thus an important asset both politically and economically. Yeltsin's decree, according to Scott Parrish, was part of his strategy to increase his own political control over the station and to deny it to his opponents. Under the decree, the state's shares in the new company would be managed by Chubais's GKI, while the private shares were sold to interests sympathetic to Yeltsin (one of the major investors was Boris Berezovsky).

The appearance of the decree stimulated action by parliament. A bill proposed by Vladimir Zhirinovsky to renationalize ORT received 199 votes. A bill suspending the transformation of ORT until a law was passed that would regulate the process passed with 275 votes the following April.[48] The Federation Council passed the bill by a wide margin in May. Yeltsin then vetoed the bill in June, but parliament was unable to override the veto. In November of 1995, Yeltsin issued another decree transforming additional radio and television companies into stock companies subject to partial privatization, and the Duma responded with another bill that required that any privatization of media properties be conducted according to rules set by legislation and providing that any acts of privatization adopted prior to passage of such a law were illegal. Like its predecessor, this bill was approved by the Federation Council but vetoed by the president. The Duma appealed Yeltsin's actions to the Constitutional Court as well, but the court refused to hear the case on the grounds that the president had the authority "to issue decrees of this nature."[49] Yeltsin's decrees effectively blocked parliamentary efforts to countermand his actions.

Policy on financial-industrial groups is another instance in which powerful interests lobbied both in the presidential decree-making arena and in parliament. As early as 1993 the presidential administration and government began to formulate policy on the formation of vertically integrated holding companies linking financial and industrial enterprises, called "financial-industrial groups" (FIGs). Some formed in the early 1990s: some at the initiative of banks, others at the initiative of industrial enterprises. Yeltsin's reformers were not opposed to their creation in principle but wanted them to improve competitiveness in their industries rather than to protect monopoly rents. There was intense competition within the government over the direction of policy in this area. Initially, the Industrial Policy Committee of the government—sympathetic to the old state industrial bureaucracy—began drafting a decree in consultation with representatives of the ministries, industries, banks, and experts. Its proposal was published as a draft decree in the summer. Chubais then fought to take over control of policy, gradually expanding his participation in the working group, and ultimately succeeded in taking control of the development of the policy. In December 1993, the president promulgated a decree reflecting the Chubais position.

The FIGs and government officials who were dissatisfied with the decree began working with parliament to draft a law on the subject that would shift policy back toward their position (i.e., toward guarantees of tax exemptions and other forms of state support). The law eventually passed the Duma in the summer of 1995 and was signed by Yeltsin on November 30, 1995. By this time, electoral concerns were becoming urgent: Duma elections were imminent, and the president's reelection campaign was to begin early in 1996. Yeltsin shifted from support for budget austerity toward support for more liberal distributive policies. Taking advantage of this political opening, a number of FIGs and their banking partners pressed for another presidential decree to supplement the legislation in order to procure control of the most promising investment projects. Chubais attempted to oppose them and did succeed in removing some of the provisions they opposed, but was unable to prevent a decree favorable to the FIGs from being adopted in April 1996, two months before the first round of the presidential election.[50] Undoubtedly electoral considerations expedited the adoption of a decree that Chubais would have managed to block at another time.[51]

Probably the most notorious episode in the use of presidential decree power in the post-1993 period was the decree of August 31, 1995, launching the "loans for shares" scheme. There are now several reliable journalistic accounts of this decree's history.[52] They make it clear that the small group of tycoons who won the president's consent to the plan exploited the government's desperate need for operating revenues as the parliamentary election campaign season was approaching, and seized control of the very process of writing the decree and obtaining clearance for it from the government. The scheme was also a way of removing the recalcitrant old-guard management from the firms. Again, Chubais appears to have made a deliberate calculation to use the decree instrument to benefit a narrow group of private interests, perhaps reasoning that the long-term benefits would outweigh the immediate political costs, or perhaps because he was unable to resist them. The case should be taken as evidence that where strong parties or other encompassing institutions are absent, a small group of well-organized, well-connected agents can capture the policymaking process for their own benefit, even where the executive is formally strong and autonomous. In the early 1990s this occurred *both* in legislative and executive decision-making arenas, often because of the competition between branches to win over powerful allies. They are motivated by the competitive struggle for power. In such cases, separation of powers, like a potlatch, encourages a wasteful race to supply public largesse to private interests. In a state as porous and corrupt as Russia's was in much of the 1990s, giving the president powerful decree-making power is no guarantee that policy will be insulated from the powerful tug of particularistic interests seeking special exemptions, funding for pet projects, exclusive import-export licenses, or privileged ownership rights.

Accounts of the decree-making process under Yeltsin agree that however firmly successive heads of the presidential administration attempted to enforce an orderly system of consultation and sign-offs (*soglasovaniia*) among affected executive offices before a decree was presented to the president, sometimes decrees were thrust before Yeltsin and signed despite not having been cleared

Table 9.1. Published Normative Presidential Edicts, 1994–2003

Year	No. of Edicts
1994	201
1995	240
1996	458
1997	190
1998	210
1999	143
2000	202
2001	146
2002	155
2003	132

with all the relevant departments. In 1994, a well-connected entrepreneur from the Caucasus persuaded Yeltsin to issue a decree setting up an "off-shore zone" in Ingushetia, which soon became a vast conduit for the diversion of state resources into private hands.[53] A particularly notable instance was the November 27, 1995, decree, when in the extraordinary space of three days, Boris Berezovsky induced Al'fred Kokh to draft and clear through the presidential administration the presidential decree creating Sibneft' and letting Berezovsky acquire it through the loans for shares scheme.[54] In other cases, of course, draft decrees got quietly sidetracked by officials who wanted to bury them. President Yeltsin's impulsiveness, coupled with political expediency and the inherent secrecy of executive rule making, meant that policymaking by *ukaz* easily served particularistic interests—whether Yeltsin's, oligarchs', ministerial, or other. By my count, nearly 30 percent of Yeltsin's 458 decrees in 1996 were distributive in content. In contrast, in 2001 Putin issued fewer than 150 decrees (published, normative decrees, that is), and only around 10 percent could be classified as distributive.

Yeltsin also used the decree power lavishly when his reelection was at stake. In 1996, a large proportion of his decrees were acts of distributive largesse. The unpredictability of policymaking by decree was very dramatically illustrated when Yeltsin issued a decree in August 1996 rescinding at one stroke some fifty of the distributive decrees he had enacted during the election campaign.[55] Since 1996, however, the use of decrees to make policy has diminished sharply both in quantitative and qualitative terms. As table 9.1 shows, the number of presidential decrees has declined since the late 1990s, under both Yeltsin and Putin. And an examination of the decrees suggests that almost none of them in the last three years have concerned significant policy decisions. Law making, meantime, has settled into a much more regular rhythm. As table 9.2 shows,

Table 9.2. Legislative Production of Russian Parliaments, 1937 to Present

Time Period	No. of Terms (sessii)	No. of Statutes Passed	Mean No. of Laws Per Term (approx.)
Stalin Era			
Nov. 1937–Feb. 1946	12	64	13
Feb. 1946–Mar. 1950	5	30	6
Mar. 1950–Mar. 1954	5	26	5
Post-Stalin Era			
Mar. 1954–Mar. 1958	9	51	6
Mar. 1958–Mar. 1962	7	72	10
Mar. 1962–Jun. 1966	7	51	7
Gorbachev-Era USSR Supreme Soviet			
June 1989–Nov. 1990	4	62	15.5
Jan. 1991–July 1991	1	50	50
RSFSR Supreme Soviet			
June 1990–July 1991	3	69	23
Apr. 1992–Nov. 1992	2	53	26
Jan. 1993–July 1993	1	98	98
Russian Federation State Duma*			
Jan. 1994–Dec. 1995	4	464	116
Jan. 1996–Dec. 1999	8	1045	130
Jan. 2000–Dec. 2003	8	781	98

*Figures refer to federal and constitutional laws, including treaty ratifications, passed by State Duma in third reading.
Source: Table 7.18 in Thomas F. Remington, *The Russian Parliament* (229–30); sessional reports of State Duma website, www.duma.gov.ru/.

the Duma now passes between 200 and 250 laws per year (three quarters of them were signed by the president in the 1994–1995 and 1996–1999 periods; nearly 93 percent were signed in the two years of Putin's presidency).

Yeltsin's advisors have written that they recognized the limitations of the decree as an instrument of policymaking. Because it could so easily be superseded by a subsequent decree, bureaucratic officials and third parties such as investors could ignore a decree with more impunity than they could a law.[56] Decrees, everyone understood, were used as temporary "quick fix" solutions to immediate problems, but unless someone in the bureaucracy or private sector had a stake in seeing to it that the decree was carried out, they were often dead letters.[57] Decrees not only tended to have shorter shelf lives, but they had lower legal status than laws, since decrees, according to the constitution, could not contradict legislation.[58]

When the executive apparatus itself is weak, these case histories suggest, decree-making power is no proof against capture by bureaucratic or private interests, just as when interest aggregating institutions are weak, parliaments can readily be captured by powerful private interests. For example, a recent study tallied the number of pieces of regional legislation in Russia that granted preferential treatment to specific enterprises on their territories, among them tax exemptions, investment credits, direct and indirect subsidies, budget guarantees, grants of state assets, and creations of "special economic zones" on the territories of particular enterprises. The largest firms received a disproportionate share of such benefits, at the expense of small business. The study found that such breaks gave firms significant short-term economic advantages, but at the cost of lower tax payments to the federal and regional government, and lower labor productivity.[59]

Similarly, the Federal Assembly has granted numerous costly favors to individual firms and organizations. Often, the weakness of parties has required that oversized distributive coalitions be built around individual pieces of legislation. One way this came about in the Yeltsin period was by increasing spending and widening budget deficits by agreeing to fund the projects and programs favored by special interests in parliament (despite the fact that the huge gap between revenues and expenditures meant that many spending commitments went unmet).[60] Another was by stripping enactments of specific language and increasing the scope of discretion for executive departments in implementing them. This practice allows state officials to use administration rules to reward or punish particular players. Many legislative acts in Russia have been so vague that the bureaucracy has been able to eviscerate, reinterpret, or ignore them freely using sub-legal administrative acts (agency-issued rules and instructions). Some laws have invited brazen, widespread law breaking because they have set impossibly high standards for behavior, which could only be upheld if they were backed by a strong public consensus reinforced by effective, honest law enforcement. All such legislative acts—special grants of preferential treatment, vague laws that allow the bureaucracy to interpret them according to political interest, and broad statements of good intentions—reflect the parliament's low capacity for aggregating support for efficiency-enhancing public policy.

Over time, however, there is some reason to think that the Federal Assembly increased in its ability to build majorities around ever more coherent, more specific, and less distributive legislative acts, at least through the Third Duma (2000–2003). This is the result of two trends. First, the coalescence of a cohesive four-faction progovernment majority for legislation in the Third Duma meant that the government needed to make fewer concessions in order to win 226 votes. Second, business associations such as the Russian Union of Industrialists and Entrepreneurs (RUIE) and Trade-Industrial Chamber (TPP)

Table 9.3. Factional Strength and Composition by Electoral Mandate Type, July 2003

Faction	Total faction membership	% SMD	% Party list
Independents	19	53	47
Russia's Regions	47	85	15
CPRF	83	41	59
People's Deputy	54	98	2
Unity	82	21	79
Yabloko	15	13	87
Union of Right Forces (SPS)	31	15	85
Fatherland-All Russia (OVR)	54	37	63
Agro-Industrial Group (APG)	43	52	48
Liberal Democratic Party of Russia (LDPR)	13	0	100

Source: State Duma website, www.duma.gov.ru/.

became effective, authoritative, and skilled in representing the interests of big business. Let us examine both points more specifically.

Building Legislative Majorities

In the Third Duma, the government consolidated its majority in parliament by concentrating its efforts on four factions, Unity, People's Deputy (PD), Russia's Regions (RR), and Fatherland-All Russia (OVR). As table 9.3 indicates, People's Deputy and Russia's Regions were made up of single-member district deputies. Groups made up of single-member district deputies tended to be less cohesive in voting than factions based on list parties.[61] Nevertheless, the RR and PD were nearly as cohesive as Unity and the OVR in voting, allowing the four factions to deliver majorities for government and presidential bills. The four factions contributing the basis of the government's majority represented a minimum winning coalition in the Duma (237 members of 450), in that without requiring the participation of any other faction, they could carry an absolute majority on any nonconstitutional issue. Other factions often jumped on their bandwagon, especially the Liberal Democratic Party of Russia (LDPR) and the Union of Right Forces (SPS), which tended to depend more on the government than the government on them. Therefore by bargaining before major issues came to the floor with the coalition of the four, the government could assemble a majority for its position, and in turn induce other factions to support it as well.

The greater efficiency with which majorities were built is reflected in the data in tables 9.4a and 9.4b, which show the declining trend over time in the

Table 9.4a. Vote Margins in the State Duma: All Contested Votes (Average Number of Affirmative Votes per Period on Items Where at Least 100 but Not More than 350 Affirmative Votes Were Cast)

	N	Mean	Median	Std. Dev.
1996–1997	5896	264.36	273	56.9
1998–1999	6422	258.91	268	57.89
2000				
Jan.–June	1102	269.5	285	61.25
June–Feb. 01	1386	253.04	264	66.83
2001				
Feb.–June	1094	250.9	253	64.62
June–Sept.	924	226.76	231	69.03
Oct.–Feb. 02	1604	228.56	235	68.278
2002				
Feb.–June	1368	233.29	239	64.1
June–July	243	235.47	244	65.23
Sept.–Oct.	620	226.1	231	68
Nov.–Dec.	689	235.45	245	68.15
2003				
Jan.–Feb.	373	219.42	217	60.78
Mar.–Apr.	576	230.72	234	60.76
May–June	564	233.02	243	66.81

Table 9.4b. Vote Margins in State Duma: Passing Votes (Average Number of Affirmative Votes per Period on Items Where at Least 225 but Not More than 350 Affirmative Votes Were Cast)

	N	Mean	Median	Std. Dev.
1996–1997	4536	288.94	290	33.67
1998–1999	4795	286.16	286	33.23
2000				
Jan.–June	861	296.26	299	33.59
June–Feb. 01	936	292.65	297	35.11
2001				
Feb.–June	721	289.13	290	37.67
June–Sept.	491	281.4	275	37.66
Oct.–Feb. 02	870	281.89	276	35.34
2002				
Feb.–June	788	279.18	272	34.679
June–July	153	277.7	273	33.78
Sept.–Oct.	326	281.32	276	36.63
Nov.–Dec.	401	284.94	281	35.21
2003				
Jan.–Feb.	172	275.36	263	33.51
Mar.–Apr.	315	276.43	268	35.73
May–June	340	279.51	273.5	34.56

number of affirmative votes cast for motions in the Duma. The data are noisy because they contain votes on procedural motions as well as laws (but they eliminate acclamation votes where items are rejected or passed by overwhelming margins). But, assuming that the mixture of votes is relatively similar from one time period to another, the data show a clear tendency for margins to narrow over time, whether we examine all contested votes, or just those that cleared 225. This finding supports the supposition that majorities were composed of narrower coalitions as the government was able to count on its backers in the Duma to deliver majorities. In turn, this allowed the government to target its sticks and carrots more narrowly on the four friendly factions.

We can also observe the government's alliance with its Duma friends in the cases of several highly contentious issues that arose in the spring term of 2003. These included a package of bills launching the reorganization of the electric power monopoly in preparation for the privatization of the industry. The first four bills in the government program came up for a vote in second reading on February 14, 2003, and the progovernment factions provided the basis for the majority. On March 21 the Duma approved in second reading an extremely contentious bill providing for the breakup of the state monopoly in housing and communal services. The bill passed with 227 votes only on the fourth attempt. Another controversial bill was the government's proposal for the reform of local self-government, which among other things provides that bankrupt local governments can be taken over by the federal government. Finally, a bill eliminating the excise tax on natural gas but raising the tax on the extraction of oil and gas—a bill that had also been long debated by the government and the large oil and gas companies—passed as well on June 11 in first reading. Table 9.5 shows the breakdowns of voting by factions on these bills.

Overall, it is probably fair to say that in the 2000–2003 period, not only did policy come to be made almost entirely through legislative bargaining among interest groups, government, and parliament, but the distributive content of legislation was much lower than in the Yeltsin period. Privatization policy then, as we saw, was strongly influenced by the Yeltsin administration's conscious decision to favor political allies at the expense of opponents and the tendency for government and parliament to pass budgets with enormous gaps between spending and revenue targets has ended. Policymaking became far more fiscally disciplined in the early 2000s. The aggregation of social interests was much more efficient, in the sense that it required fewer side payments to powerful private actors, than it was under Yeltsin.

But although policymaking has grown in efficiency since 1999, most of the change reflects the dominance of the Putin presidency in policymaking rather than the strengthening of political parties. This very dominance, in turn,

Table 9.5. Voting by Faction on Contentious Issues, Spring 2003 (% of Faction Voting Yea)

Vote	Elec Pwr1 (2nd rdg)	Elec Pwr2 (2nd rdg)	Elec Pwr3 (2nd rdg)	Elec Pwr4 (2nd rdg)	Housing-Utilities (2nd rdg)	Local Govt (2nd rdg)	Oil & Gas Tax (1st rdg)
Date	Feb. 14	Feb. 14	Feb. 14	Feb. 14	Mar. 21	June 11	June 11
Indep.	58	58	58	58	26	53	26
RR	70	68	68	68	62	70	87
CPRF	1	2	2	1	1	0	0
PD	87	85	87	89	80	98	83
Unity	96	96	98	93	96	98	95
Yabloko	0	0	0	0	0	7	80
SPS	96	97	97	97	13	13	100
OVR	78	78	94	85	94	69	96
APG	0	0	0	0	0	0	0
LDPR	100	100	100	100	100	100	100
Total yea	260	259	270	261	227	231	278

undercuts any incentive for parliamentarians to challenge the president and government through oversight. The first Putin term more closely resembles the dominance of executive over legislature that a strong majority party has in a Westminster-style setting than it does a U.S.-style system of separated powers. But the weakness of independent partisan or other linkage mechanisms that might give parliamentarians autonomous resources with which to hold the executive accountable means that the relationship between executive and legislative branches is far more one-sided than in the Westminster system. Certainly the more routinized process for developing policy in the presidential administration and the government, together with more intensive consultation with large umbrella organizations outside government, such as the Russian Union of Industrialists and Entrepreneurs, has allowed the Putin administration to develop and pass its legislative agenda much more efficiently than did Yeltsin. Putin seems to have constructed centers for policy development that negotiate effectively with bureaucratic, oligarchic, and regional interests. Absent from the aggregation process are political parties. The presidential administration's control over both chambers of parliament ensures the passage of legislation that has been developed in such sites as Gref's Center for Strategic Planning and other think tanks, the Ministry for Economic Development and Trade, Dmitrii Kozak's special commissions, and other bodies answering to Putin's staff. The nature of control differs sharply between the two chambers: in the Duma, the coalition of factions oriented around Unity could command a reliable majority on most issues in the Third Duma, and the United Russia faction gained total control over the Fourth Duma, while in the post-2001 Federation Council, a universal coalition of appointed senators provides near-unanimous majorities on nearly every vote.[62] Parliament lacks the power to convert an electoral mandate into a party government.[63] Still, it is notable that the president and government are devoting all of their policymaking effort to developing and passing major legislation as opposed to decrees.

Sectoral associations have also become skilled at representing the interests of their members in the policymaking process. The RUIE and TPP are widely considered to be the most authoritative and influential business associations. The focus of their activity has also increasingly come to include lobbying with the legislature, not only with the executive branch. A survey of business associations in the mid-1990s found that at that time they tended to prefer dealing with the executive branch rather than the legislature because, as one representative of the Russian Computer Association put it, "it is easier to work with the executive branch than the legislative branch.... Often issues [in the Duma] are resolved jointly by several committees, committees operate separately, it's almost impossible to catch deputies."[64] This situation has changed considerably. Now the RUIE's working groups develop policy positions on a range of legislative issues, sending experts to working groups made up of representatives of the government, the presidential administration, and the Duma to work out differences on legislation. As one business association staff official put it in an interview, "we all send our experts [to legislative working groups], and the strongest experts carry the day." To be sure, business associations exert influence only on issues where they hold a united position; on many issues, of course, business itself is divided. Still, the RUIE and TPP have gained influence in the policy process in recent years as a consequence of having overcome the old split between the statist, protectionist "red directors" and the interests of the "new entrepreneurs." There are some indications that the RUIE's members themselves have become more interested in improving the business environment for Russia generally, rather than in capturing industry-specific privileges.[65] Both the RUIE and TPP have developed legislative liaison offices to reinforce their own capacity to participate in policymaking. On a wide range of issues such as land reform; tax law; pension policy, bankruptcy legislation; reform of the natural gas, energy and railroad monopolies; regulation of the securities market; and the terms of Russia's entry to the World Trade Organization, the RUIE and, to a lesser extent, the TPP and other business groups have been influential in shaping policy.

The weakness of electoral parties and the dependence of most members of both chambers of parliament on the government and presidential administration for career benefits means that in the bargaining between government and parliament over legislation, the government holds the upper hand. Therefore the shift in the political interests of the powerful private actors, together with the stronger aggregative capacity of policy makers in the executive branch, are stronger explanations for the declining distributive content of policy under Putin, the drastic reductions in the levels of special exemptions and privileges in tax policy, and lower levels of regulatory intervention in the economy, than is the change in the capacity of parliament itself. Nonetheless, by comparison with the early 1990s, the accumulation of expertise, authority, and institutional resources in parliament has modestly increased parliament's ability to exercise influence over policymaking through legislation. At the same time, the dominance of the executive branch in aggregating interests, formulating coherent policy, and mobilizing reliable legislative majorities in parliament undermines parliament's interest in checking the executive's power. Following the 2003 parliamentary election, when United Russia took control of two thirds of the seats in the Duma, executive dominance of parliament became almost total.

Budget Control

The power of the purse is a vital domain of legislative control over the executive. The evidence suggests that in Russia, parliamentary influence over the budget grew substantially through the Third Duma. For example, the level of detail of the state budget law has increased every year as the government has shared more information about state revenues and expenditures with the Duma. If sheer length of the budget law is any indication at all of increased legislative capacity to monitor the state budget, then surely it is worth noting that the 2002 budget law was fifty times longer than the 1992 budget (see table 9.6). The budget law is now regularly signed each year before the budget year begins, rather than partway through it. The law also includes a far greater level of detail for individual line items. And this is not the product of large distributive coalitions in support of deficit spending, since the budget has been in balance since 2000.

In the Yeltsin period, passage of the annual budget law was a parody of responsible budgeting: as everyone knew they would, budget revenues invariably fell far short of projections, while planned outlays incorporated far more commitments than could ever have been honored. As Georgii Satarov and his associates observed, Yeltsin never vetoed the budget, despite the fact that powerful pressures from within and outside the government invariably managed to bypass the Ministry of Finance and to win concessions from the parliament and the presidential administration.[66] The government always succeeded in persuading the Duma and Federation Council to pass the budget law by accepting some of parliament's demands for increases in spending on politically

Table 9.6. Federal Budget Laws

Budget Year	Date Signed	No. of Articles	No. of Pages
1992	July 17, 1992	18	8
1993	May 14, 1993	27	19
1994	July 1, 1994	39	28
1995	March 31, 1995	62	67
1996	Dec. 31, 1995	71	33
1997	Feb. 26, 1997	99	119
1998	March 26, 1998	120	115
1999	Feb. 22, 1999	141	59
2000	Dec. 31. 1999	163	243
2001	Dec. 27, 2000	139	340
2002	Dec. 30, 2001	147	423

Note: Number of pages refers to pages in official publication of law in Sobranie zakonodatel'stva Rossiiskoi Federatsii. Budgets for 1992 and 1993 are from Vedomosti S"ezda Narodnykh deputatov RSFSR i Verkhovnogo Soveta RSFSR.

influential groups and interests, despite the fact that these changes widened the projected deficits—never mind the actual deficits.

Nonetheless, over the course of the Yeltsin period, parliament increased its ability to enforce budget discipline. As a result of the Budget Code, signed into law in 1998, parliament significantly restricted the discretion of executive agencies at all levels of the state to use budget resources arbitrarily. It introduced a treasury system for the first time, requiring that all budget revenues be held in the state treasury. It closely regulated the use of incomes and revenues by state organizations and restricted the right of administrative authorities to deviate from spending the amounts specified by the budget law, and provided substantial penalties for violations. Moreover, it ended the right of regional and local governments to form their own off-budget funds and required them to cut back on spending in proportion to shortfalls in revenue.[67] The budget code was tightened further in 2000, when the Duma adopted amendments proposed by the government that eliminated regions' right to borrow money in foreign capital markets and ended the practice of mutual write-offs of budget obligations.

Even more significant is the fact that parliament has also expanded its control over *extra*budgetary funds, after the period in the early 1990s when both executive and legislative acts created nonbudget funds freely. When Khasbulatov and his supporters in the Russian Congress of People's Deputies were fighting for supremacy with Yeltsin, Khasbulatov frequently signed decrees creating special-purpose off-budget funds under government agencies, specifying that only he could control the use of funds from them.[68] The practice continued into the mid-1990s under the new constitution. Typically, by law or executive action, an administrative body would be created and given the right to form its own extrabudgetary account to receive and spend revenues. These revenues, in turn, would be exempt from taxation. In some cases they would include the right to conduct import and export operations without paying customs duties.[69] For instance, the press minister tried to persuade parliament to create a "fund for support of the press"—which he would control—as part of the law on state support for the media (the provision was dropped from the final version of the law). An LDPR deputy introduced a bill "on the preservation and development of Slavic traditions," which would create a tax-exempt fund. Another deputy proposed a bill creating special purpose off-budget fund for development of the Far North, another for treatment of solid wastes. Industries formed their own extrabudgetary funds authorized by the government and funded through contributions from individual enterprises (treated as part of production costs). In 1994, Gazprom's off-budget fund took in about ten trillion rubles in revenues, or close to $3 billion. Railroads Minister Aksenenko was accused of creating six off-budget funds, including the "fund for supporting educational institutions of the ministry," "the fund for health care," the "financial reserve fund," and the "fund for investment programs of the ministry." Only in December 2001 did a new law on the Procuracy-General eliminate the procuracy's right to maintain its own off-budget "development" funds. These funds may have been legal, but they created an enormous opportunity for corrupt diversion of resources for other purposes.[70]

The use of off-budget funds by local and regional governments, ministries and other state organizations, and enterprises proliferated. The volume of resources flowing through them was staggering. By the mid-1990s the money in off-budget funds totaled close to two-thirds of the state budget.[71] But off-budget funds were not subject to budget control, often were free from tax, and (until the introduction of the treasury system in 1998) often were managed in commercial banks. At a time when the economic system was shifting from one based on the administrative control of physical resources to one in which money became a financial resource, off-budget funds enabled public entities to act as if they were private interests outside of any public accountability and to provide elected officials with politically useful slush funds. Granting the right to form off-budget funds became yet another of the ways in which the executive and legislative branches competed for support during the early 1990s. Both parliamentarians and executive branch officials benefited from control of large slush funds outside any budgetary control. They deadlocked over policy measures designed to bring off-budget funds under budgetary control. A bill requiring that extrabudget funds be subject to budget oversight and regular audits, and maintained in the state treasury, died following heated debate in the Duma in summer 1995. Many deputies wanted to bring the Pension Fund and other social funds under the Duma's budgetary control but the Pension Fund itself and deputies sympathetic to it argued that doing so would only increase the likelihood that pension resources would be diverted to other uses.[72] Meantime, the Audit Chamber and the government's own auditors constantly discovered massive abuses in the use of off-budget funds, including the highway fund, the Pension Fund, and other social funds, often by regional authorities.

Over time, parliament has imposed tighter budget controls over these funds. A 1999 law established a general framework for social insurance funds, separating them from budgetary social assistance programs. The law on the single social tax passed in 2000 unified contributions into the four funds (pensions, medical, and the two social funds) and lowered the aggregate rate. This did represent a significant step toward placing all the social funds under budgetary control. The next step was to increase the Pension Fund's control over pension spending by restricting governors' ability to treat pension funds as part of general budget resources (Putin issued a decree to this effect in September 2000, which the Constitutional Court upheld). In the future, the Pension Fund's control over pension contributions will be reduced through the shift away from social insurance (though a component of social insurance will remain) to a contributions and investment system consisting both of the state's pension system and private funds. Over time, therefore, parliament increased its control both over the state budget and over extrabudgetary flows of resources.

The government's ability to pass balanced budgets through parliament owes to several changes since 1998 in the political and economic environment; it is certainly not only or even mainly the consequence of increased parliamentary efficiency. The more favorable exchange rate for the ruble, higher oil and gas prices on world markets, and higher tax collections, as well as the government's ability to command a majority in the Duma that requires fewer spending concessions than in the past, all play a part. In the Third Duma, the formation of a coalition of four factions that commanded a stable majority provided a more efficient institutional mechanism for aggregating policy interests than did the old system of building ad hoc cross-factional coalitions for every individual piece of legislation. Bargaining between the government and its allied factions allowed the government to win over a secure majority for the budget bill without having to spread benefits across the Duma too widely. The government's practice was to enter into negotiations with the "coalition of four" even before submitting the budget bill to the Duma.[73] For example, the finance ministry consulted with the leaders of the four allied factions in the summer of 2003 over the shape of the 2004 budget. Sensitive to the deputies' electoral interests, the government relaxed budget discipline somewhat and gave each of the four friendly factions the right to raise spending in one or two issue areas. For example, Unity,

Table 9.7.   Factional Voting on 2003 Budget (% of Each
Faction Voting Yea)

	1st rdg Sept. 25	2nd rdg Oct. 18	3rd rdg Nov. 22	4th rdg Dec. 11
Indep	58	53	68	58
RR	87	72	77	79
CPRF	1	1	2	2
PD	94	98	100	93
Unity	96	95	96	90
Yabloko	60	60	67	60
SPS	97	93	97	61
OVR	98	96	96	96
APG	23	21	30	16
LDPR	100	100	100	100
Total yea votes	302	292	309	279

the Duma arm of United Russia, sought to identify itself with the cause of
greater defense procurement. The faction People's Deputy, which formed the
People's Party, pushed the government for greater spending on budget sector
employees in the regions. The OVR (which originated as the Duma faction
of the Fatherland-All Russia party, then subsequently merged into the United
Russia party) demanded more funding for agricultural producers. The Russia's Regions group sought more spending on transportation and housing.
Sympathetic to their interests, the government reportedly developed a budget
with optimistic estimates for revenues in order to accommodate the deputies'
interests; experts estimated that the deputies' wish list was filled by about
85 percent.[74]

Voting on the budget demonstrates the effectiveness of the government's
alliance with its factional allies in the Third Duma. Table 9.7 illustrates the
breakdown of voting by faction on the 2003 budget, votes which took place in
the fall of 2002.

As the table shows, the progovernment factions voted rather cohesively, even
those that were made up of single-member district deputies, and the budget
passed easily. Close coordination between the government and its supporters
in the Duma made it possible for the government to ensure solid majorities at
each stage of the budget process, something that did not occur in the Yeltsin era.
Budget and tax policy remain subject to distributive bargains, but with fewer
costly side payments because the government can concentrate its largesse on
the interests of a smaller and more cohesive set of factions.

In the Fourth Duma, which convened in December 2003, the government
scarcely needed to bargain with its Duma allies at all over the budget—United

Russia's complete dominance of the Duma coupled with its total dependence on the Kremlin for political backing meant that the government did not need to forge cross-factional alliances to build majorities for its budget bills but could simply dictate its preferences to its parliamentary allies.

CONCLUSION

Studies of governance often emphasize the contradictory qualities expected of institutions. Democratic institutions must be responsive but also decisive.[75] Policy makers must be able to respond to public demands and urgent policy needs, but they must also be able to maintain commitments to policy in the face of resistance. Effective governance may require imposing losses on some groups in favor of benefits for the larger public good.[76] Democratization does not necessarily improve institutional capacity; it can allow a broader range of interests to be taken into consideration in making policy and prevent special interests from capturing state power for private benefit, but does not necessarily do so. A weakened state undergoing democracy during a time of economic crisis is particularly vulnerable to capture and corruption by powerful interests that seek concentrated particularistic benefits at the public's expense. In the absence of strong, effective aggregating institutions, such as parties, opening the system to competitive elections and separation of powers may simply compound the problem of fragmented authority and multiply the arenas where organized interests can capture particularistic benefits. Giving a president in a weakened state decree-making authority allows him to buy off key players by granting them special benefits.

Considering the magnitude of Russia's state crisis in the early 1990s, the growth in institutional capacity is substantial. By contrast with the early 1990s, policymaking has become much more efficient. Nearly all significant policy now is made by legislation rather than decree. Legislation passed in the late 1990s and under Putin has significantly increased budget control and reduced the level of loopholes, concessions, and grants of unaccountable power in fiscal policy. Public confidence in central institutions has risen. The system of parliamentary political factions and bicameralism have enabled parliament to overcome its own collective dilemmas, as it was unable to do in the two interim systems of 1989–1991 and 1990–1993. With greater capacity to deliberate and reach decisions has come greater capacity for oversight, law making, and budget control.

The record of success that President Putin and his government have enjoyed in passing their legislative agenda through parliament is partly the result of the growth of expertise and efficient institutions in parliament (such as the emergence of a stable majority coalition of four factions in the Third Duma and the domination of the Fourth Duma by United Russia). But it is even more due to the greater policymaking capacity in the executive, as well-coordinated networks of officials and experts based in the presidential administration, government, and policy research centers have taken charge of policy development. And while parliament has grown more efficient at passing legislation, members' incentive to jeopardize their electoral and career prospects by challenging the executive's dominance through a vigorous exercise of the oversight power has fallen considerably since the Yeltsin period. The improved institutional performance of the 2000–2003 period, compared with the 1994–1999 period, also owes something to the growth in the capacity of major business associations to aggregate the interests of their members—and perhaps also a greater concern on the part of big business with the social consequences of public policy. So far, Russia has not developed a system of programmatic parties offering voters ideologically based choices over government formation and government policy. We may conclude that the key to effective governance is less the formal separation of powers than the existence of linkage mechanisms that aggregate social interests as broadly as possible and allow policy decisions to be made with as few side payments to affected private interests as possible. In democratic polities, systems of competitive parties, tied with national interest groups and mass media, perform this role. Russia remains far from establishing such institutions.

NOTES

I am grateful for the support of the Carnegie Corporation of New York through the Project on Governance in Russia directed by Stephen Holmes and Timothy J. Colton, and for the stimulating discussions at the conferences held under the auspices of the project.

1. Douglass C. North, *Institutions, Institutional Change and Economic Performance* (Cambridge: Cambridge University Press, 1990); Stephen Knack, ed. *Democracy, Governance, and Growth* (Ann Arbor: University of Michigan Press, 2003).

2. For example, see the World Bank's annual World Development Reports. Beginning with the 1997 volume—*The State in a Changing World*—and continuing through the 2002 report *Building Institutions for Markets*, the Bank has emphasized that unless institutions, defined as the "rules, enforcement mechanisms, and organizations supporting market transactions," make economic markets work effectively, market-oriented reform policies will not promote growth or mitigate inequality. World Bank, *World Development Report 1997: The State in a Changing World* (New York: Oxford University

Press, 1997); World Bank, *World Development Report 2002: Building Institutions for Markets* (New York: Oxford University Press, 2002).

A more forceful argument of the same nature—demonstrating that many policy prescriptions proposed by development economists for growth in poor countries were dismal failures owing to the poor quality of the institutional environment in which they were attempted—is offered by William Easterly, *The Elusive Quest for Growth: Economists' Adventures and Misadventures in the Tropics* (Cambridge, MA: MIT Press, 2002).

3. Dani Rodrik, "Institutions for High-Quality Growth: What They Are and How to Acquire Them," *Studies in Comparative International Development* 35, no. 3 (Fall 2000): 3–31; Rodrik, "Development Strategies for the Next Century" (paper presented at Annual World Bank Conference on Development Economics 2000, April 2001).

4. Daniel Kaufmann, Aart Kraay and Pablo Zoido-Lobaton, "Governance Matters II: Updated Indicators for 2000/2001" (World Bank Working Paper, Washington, DC, January 2002); Daniel Kaufmann, Aart Kraay, and Massimo Mastruzzi, "Governance Matters III: Governance Indicators for 1996–2002" (World Bank Working Paper, Washington, DC, 2003).

5. Daniel Lederman, Norman Loayza, and Rodrigo Reis Soares, "Accountability and Corruption: Political Institutions Matter" (World Bank Working Paper, Washington, DC, November 2001).

6. Lederman, Loayza, and Reis Soares, "Accountability and Corruption"; Susan Rose-Ackerman, *Corruption and Government: Causes, Consequences, and Reform* (Cambridge: Cambridge University Press, 1999).

7. Stephen Knack and Philip Keefer, "Why Don't Poor Countries Catch Up? A Cross-National Test of an Institutional Explanation," *Economic Inquiry* 35, no. 3 (July 1997): 590–602; Kaufmann, Kraay, and Zoido-Lobaton, "Governance Matters II."

8. Roumeen Islam and Claudio E. Montenegro, *What Determines the Quality of Institutions?* Background paper for the *World Development Report 2002: Building Institutions for Markets* (Washington, DC: World Bank, January 2002).

9. John F. Helliwell, "Empirical Linkages between Democracy and Economic Growth." *British Journal of Political Science* 24, no. 2 (April 1994): 225–48; Rodrik, "Institutions for High-Quality Growth."

10. Anders Aslund, *Building Capitalism: The Transformation of the Former Soviet Bloc* (Cambridge: Cambridge University Press, 2002); Joel S. Hellman, "Winners Take All: The Politics of Partial Reform in Postcommunist Transitions," *World Politics* 50, no. 1 (January 1998): 203–34; Joel S. Hellman, Geraint Jones, and Daniel Kaufmann, "'Seize the State, Seize the Day': State Capture, Corruption, and Influence in Transition," Washington, DC: World Bank Institute, 2000.

11. Christopher Clague, Philip Keefer, Stephen Knack, and Mancur Olson, "Property and Contract Rights in Autocracies and Democracies," in *Democracy, Governance, and Growth*, ed. Stephen Knack (Ann Arbor: University of Michigan Press, 2003), 157.

12. Stephan Haggard and Robert R. Kaufman, *The Political Economy of Democratic Transitions* (Princeton, NJ: Princeton University Press, 1995).

13. Hellman, Jones, and Kaufmann, "'Seize the State, Seize the Day.'"

14. Compare Matthew S. Shugart and John M. Carey, *Presidents and Assemblies: Constitutional Design and Electoral Dynamics* (Cambridge: Cambridge University Press, 1992); Stephan Haggard and Mathew D. McCubbins, eds., *Presidents, Parliaments, and Policy* (Cambridge, Cambridge University Press, 2001); Herbert Kitschelt, Zdenka Mansfeldova, Radoslaw Markowski, and Gabor Toka, *Post-Communist Party Systems: Competition, Representation, and Inter-Party Cooperation* (Cambridge: Cambridge University Press, 1999).

15. Douglass C. North and Barry R. Weingast, "Constitutions and Commitment: The Evolution of Institutions Governing Public Choice in Seventeenth-Century England," *Journal of Economic History* 49, no. 4 (1989): 803–32; Barry R. Weingast "Constitutions as Governance Structures: The Political Foundations of Secure Markets," *Journal of Institutional and Theoretical Economics* 149, no. 1 (1993): 286–311.

16. Mancur Olson, *The Rise and Decline of Nations* (New Haven, CT: Yale University Press, 1982); Gary W. Cox and Matthew D. McCubbins, "The Institutional Determinants of Economic Policy Outcomes," in *Presidents, Parliaments, and Policy*, ed. Stephan Haggard and Mathew D. McCubbins (Cambridge: Cambridge University Press, 2001): 21–63.

17. Stephan Haggard and Robert R. Kaufman, "Introduction," in *The Politics of Economic Adjustment*, ed. Stephan Haggard and Robert R. Kaufman (Princeton, NJ: Princeton University Press, 1992); Haggard and Kaufman, *The Political Economy of Democratic Transitions* (Princeton, NJ: Princeton University Press, 1995); Hellman, "Winners Take All," 208.

18. Nouriel Roubini and Jeffrey D. Sachs, "Political and Economic Determinants of Budget Deficits in the Industrial Democracies," *European Economic Review* 33, no. 5 (May 1989): 903–38; George Tsebelis, "Decision Making in Political Systems: Veto Players in Presidentialism, Parliamentarism, Multicameralism and Multipartyism," *British Journal of Political Science* 25, no. 3 (1995): 289–325; George Tsebelis, "Veto Players and Institutional Analysis," *Governance* 13, no. 4 (2000): 441–74.

19. Characteristic treatments include Peter Nolan, *China's Rise, Russia's Fall: Politics, Economics, and Planning in the Transition from Stalinism* (New York: St. Martin's, 1995); and Joseph E. Stiglitz, *Globalization and Its Discontents* (New York: Norton, 2002).

20. North, *Institutions, Institutional Change and Economic Performance*, 35; Weingast, "Constitutions as Governance Structures," 287.

21. As Madison put it, the possibility that the legislature will aggrandize its powers at the expense of popular liberty means that the power of both branches needs to be checked by the independence of the executive and judicial branches. Each branch must have, as Madison put it, "a constitutional control over the others" (*Federalist* No. 48).

More recently, Lederman, Loayza, and Reis Soares have argued that parliamentary systems are superior to presidential ones from the standpoint of the effectiveness of checks and balances, surely a paradoxical line of reasoning from the standpoint of

American constitutional theory, and they argue that political stability in and of itself improves checks and balances, although it is more plausible that stability in authoritarian systems reduces them (Lederman, Loayza and Reis Soares, "Accountability and Corruption").

22. Joel Hellman, "Constitutions and Economic Reform in the Postcommunist Transitions," *East European Constitutional Review* 5 (Winter 1996): 46–56; Hellman "Winners Take All," 203–34.

23. Timothy Frye, "Presidents, Parliaments, and Democracy: Insights from the Post-Communist World," in *The Architecture of Democracy: Constitutional Design, Conflict Management, and Democracy*, ed. Andrew Reynolds (New York: Oxford University Press, 2002): 81–103.

24. A sampling of works on these issues includes Philip G. Roeder, *Red Sunset: The Failure of Soviet Politics* (Princeton, NJ: Princeton University Press, 1993); Thane Gustafson, *Reform in Soviet Politics: Lessons of Recent Policies on Land and Water* (Cambridge: Cambridge University Press, 1981); Michael Voslensky, *Nomenklatura: The Soviet Ruling Class: An Insider's Report* (Garden City, NY: Doubleday, 1984); Zbigniew Brzezinski, "The Soviet Political System: Transformation or Degeneration?" *Problems of Communism* 15, no. 1 (1966); John P. Willerton, *Patronage and Politics in the USSR* (Cambridge: Cambridge University Press, 1992); Seweryn Bialer, *Stalin's Successors: Leadership, Stability, and Change in the Soviet Union* (Cambridge: Cambridge University Press, 1980); Timothy J. Colton, *The Dilemma of Reform in the Soviet Union* (New York: Council on Foreign Relations, 1986); Anders Aslund, *Gorbachev's Struggle for Economic Reform* (Ithaca, NY: Cornell University Press, 1989); Edward A. Hewett, *Reforming the Soviet Economy: Equality versus Efficiency* (Washington, DC: Brookings, 1988); Mark Beissinger, *Nationalist Mobilization and the Collapse of the Soviet State* (Cambridge: Cambridge University Press, 2002); Valerie Bunce, *Subversive Institutions: The Design and the Destruction of Socialism and the State* (Cambridge: Cambridge University Press, 1999); Philip G. Roeder, "Soviet Federalism and Ethnic Mobilization," *World Politics* 23, no. 2 (1991): 196–233; Ronald Grigor Suny, *The Revenge of the Past: Nationalism, Revolution, and the Collapse of the Soviet Union* (Stanford, CA: Stanford University Press, 1993); Gail Warshofsky Lapidus "Ethnonationalism and Political Stability: The Soviet Case," *World Politics* 36, no. 4 (1984): 355–80; Gregory Gleason, *Federalism and Nationalism: The Struggle for Republican Rights in the USSR* (Boulder, CO: Westview, 1990).

25. Stephen White, *Gorbachev and After* (Cambridge: Cambridge University Press, 1991), 24–27.

26. B. Kurashvili, "K polnovlastiiu sovetov," *Kommunist*, no. 8 (1988), 31–32, cited in Thomas Remington, "A Socialist Pluralism of Opinions: Glasnost and Policy-Making under Gorbachev," *The Russian Review* 48, no. 3 (July 1989), 281.

27. Thomas F. Remington, "Menage a Trois: The End of Soviet Parliamentarism," in *Democratization in Russia: The Development of Legislative Institutions*, ed. Jeffrey W. Hahn (Armonk, NY: Sharpe, 1996), 111–12.

28. Herbert Kitschelt, "Linkages between Citizens and Politicians in Democratic Polities," *Comparative Political Studies* 33, no. 6/7 (2000): 845–79; Kitschelt et al., *Post-Communist Party Systems*; Richard Rose and Doh Chull Shin, "Democratization Backwards: The Problem of Third-Wave Democracies," *British Journal of Political Science* 31, no. 2 (April 2001): 331–54.

29. Hellman, Jones, and Kaufmann, "'Seize the State, Seize the Day'"; Timothy Frye, "Presidents, Parliaments, and Democracy."

30. Kaufmann, Kraay, and Mastruzzi, "Governance Matters III."

31. John D. Huber, Charles R. Shipan, and Madelaine Pfahler, "Legislatures and Statutory Control of Bureaucracy," *American Journal of Political Science* 45, no. 2 (2001): 330–45.

32. Thomas F. Remington, "The Evolution of Executive-Legislative Relations in Russia since 1993," *Slavic Review* 59, no. 3 (2000): 499–520; Remington, *The Russian Parliament: Institutional Evolution in a Transitional Regime, 1989–1999* (New Haven, CT: Yale University Press, 2001); Paul Chaisty, "Legislative Politics in Russia," in *Contemporary Russian Politics: A Reader*, ed. Archie Brown (New York: Oxford University Press, 2001), 103–20; Michael McFaul, *Russia's Unfinished Revolution: Political Change from Gorbachev to Putin* (Ithaca, NY: Cornell University Press, 2001); Tiffany A. Troxel, *Parliamentary Power in Russia, 1994–2001: President vs. Parliament* (New York: Palgrave Macmillan, 2003).

33. For early Bolshevik efforts to reconcile "workers' control" with "state control," see Thomas F. Remington, "The Rationalization of State Kontrol'," in Party and Society in the Russian Civil War: Explorations in Social History, ed. William Rosenberg, Ronald Suny, and Diane Koenker (Bloomington: Indiana University Press, 1989); Remington, "Institution Building in Bolshevik Russia: The Case of State Kontrol'," Slavic Review, 41, no. 1 (Spring 1982): 91–103.

34. As cited in Mathew D. McCubbins and Thomas Schwartz, "Congressional Oversight Overlooked: Police Patrols versus Fire Alarms," *American Journal of Political Science* 28, no. 1 (February 1984): 170.

35. Polit.ru, May 16, 2001.

36. Polit.ru, September 15, 2000.

37. Stepashin has sought to put the Audit Chamber under the direct authority of the president and to reduce the Duma's ability to demand investigations. In the spring of 2002, Stepashin pressed for a law that would make the body subordinate to *both* president and parliament, while in summer 2003 he called for a change in rules that would require a vote by a majority of the Duma (rather than merely ninety votes) in order to begin an investigation. Stepashin has repeatedly expressed frustration that the government and the procuracy do not respond to Audit Chamber reports, and argues that placing the chamber under the presidential administration would increase its bureaucratic clout. The Ministry of Finance has opposed Stepashin's empire-building efforts, and the legislation incorporating some of Stepashin's proposals has languished in parliament for want of support. See Polit.ru, April 23, 2003; RFE/RL Newsline, August 1, 2003.

38. Polit.ru, October 18, 2001.

39. *Segodnia*, March 3, 2001.

40. Remington, *The Russian Parliament*, 130.

41. Vladimir Rimskii, "Biurokraticheskie mekhanizmy preobrazovanii v Rossii v period prezidentstva Boris El'tsina," in *Effektivnost' osushchestvleniia gosudarstvennogo upravleniia v Rossii (period prezidentstva El'tsina): rabochie materialy* (Moscow: Institut prava i publichnoi politiki, 2002): 62.

42. Andrew Barnes, "Property, Power, and the Presidency: Ownership Policy Reform and Russian Executive-Legislative Relations, 1990–1999," *Communist and Post-Communist Studies* 34, no. 1 (2001): 39–61; see also Thomas F. Remington, Steven S. Smith, and Moshe Haspel, "Decrees, Laws, and Inter-Branch Relations in the Russian Federation," *Post-Soviet Affairs* 14, no. 4 (1998): 287–322; and Thomas F. Remington, Steven S. Smith, and Olga Shvetsova, "Decrees, Laws, and Presidential-Parliamentary Bargaining in Russia," unpublished paper.

43. Maxim Boycko, Andrei Shleifer, and Robert Vishny, *Privatizing Russia* (Cambridge, MA: MIT Press, 1995).

44. On the privatization policy, see Anders Aslund, *Building Capitalism*; Boycko, Shleifer, and Vishny, *Privatizing Russia*; Andrei Shleifer and Daniel Treisman, *Without a Map: Political Tactics and Economic Reform in Russia* (Cambridge, MA: MIT Press, 2000); Anatoly B. Chubais, ed., *Privatizatsiia po-rossiiski* (Moscow: Vagrius, 1999).

45. *Segodnia*, July 8, 1994.

46. Georgii Satarov et al., *Epokha El'tsina* (Moscow: Vagrius, 2001), 419.

47. Scott Parrish, "Presidential Decree Authority in Russia," in *Executive Decree Authority*, ed. John M. Carey and Matthew Soberg Shugart (Cambridge: Cambridge University Press, 1998): 87–88. This account is based on Parrish and an interview with a senior government official in February 1997.

48. Parrish, "Presidential Decree Authority in Russia," 88.

49. Parrish, "Presidential Decree Authority in Russia," 89; OMRI Daily Digest, April 6, June 8, and November 6, 1995, and May 16, 1996.

50. The decree provided that the federal budget would subsidize any FIGs involved in federal economic programs, and called for transferring federally owned shares of company stock to them. See *Segodnia*, April 2, 1996.

51. Account based on interviews with two officials who participated in drafting these decrees, March 1997.

52. Chrystia Freeland, *Sale of the Century: Russia's Wild Ride from Communism to Capitalism* (New York: Crown Business, 2000); David E. Hoffman, *The Oligarchs: Wealth and Power in the New Russia* (New York: PublicAffairs, 2002): 297–320; Rose Brady, *Kapitalizm: Russia's Struggle to Free Its Economy* (New Haven, CT: Yale University Press, 1999): 135–43.

53. Freeland, *Sale of the Century*, 99–110.

54. Freeland, *Sale of the Century*, 187–88.

55. Remington, Smith, and Haspel, "Decrees, Laws, and Inter-Branch Relations."

56. Satarov et al., *Epokha El'tsina*, 426.

57. Satarov et al., *Epokha El'tsina*, 426. For instance, Chubais often prepared a decree, persuaded Yeltsin to sign it, then ensured that it was carried out. The same was

true of decrees where a particular business magnate such as Berezovsky persuaded Yeltsin to sign a decree, and then captured the benefits that it conferred.

58. Chubais, *Privatizatsiia po-rossiiski*, 154.

59. Irina Slinko, Evgeny Yakovlev, and Ekaterina Zhuravskaya, "Institutional Subversion: Evidence from Russian Regions" (CEFIR Working Paper, 2nd draft, 2003). They cite a characteristic example. The Volgograd regional Duma passed a law in 1998 called "On the special economic zone on the territory of the Volgograd Tractor Plant." The law exempted any firm from paying regional and local taxes for ten years so long as it operated on the territory of the plant and was at least 30 percent owned by the plant.

60. Satarov et al., *Epokha El'tsina*, 413.

61. Thomas F. Remington, "Putin, the Duma, and Political Parties," in *Putin's Russia: Past Imperfect, Future Uncertain*, ed. Dale Herspring (Boulder, CO: Rowman & Littlefield, 2002), 39–59.

62. Thomas F. Remington, "Majorities without Mandates: The Federation Council since 2000," *Europe-Asia Studies* 55, no. 5 (July 2003): 667–91.

63. Thomas F. Remington, "Putin and the Duma," *Post-Soviet Affairs* 17, no. 4 (2001): 285–308; Remington, "Putin, the Duma, and Political Parties."

64. Quoted in I. M. Bunin et al., *Sistema predstavitel'stva rossiiskogo biznesa: Formy kollektivnogo deistviia* (Moscow: Center for Political Technologies, 1997), 63.

65. The degree to which big business is satisfied with the current distribution of ownership over major assets and thus is interested in greater security of contract and property rights is a controversial point. Peter Boone and Denis Rodionov of Brunswick UBS Warburg argue that Russia's tycoons, having achieved extremely high concentrations of ownership in the companies controlled by their financial-industrial groups, now want the greater protection of their property interests that the impersonal rule of law can provide. Compare Peter Boone and Denis Rodionov, "Rent seeking in Russia and the CIS," Paper prepared for EBRD tenth anniversary conference in London, December 2001.

An opposing view—for which the campaign to break up Yukos provides some evidence—is that neither the powerful bureaucratic clans nor big business interests are seriously committed to expanding the sphere in which the rule of law prevails. For a strong statement along these lines, see Andrew Barnes, "Russia's New Business Groups and State Power," *Post-Soviet Affairs* 19, no. 2 (2003): 154–86.

66. Satarov et al., *Epokha El'tsina*, 440–42.

67. *Segodnia*, April 15, 1998.

68. Satarov et al., *Epokha El'tsina*.

69. *Izvestiia*, June 6, 1995.

70. Polit.ru, October 24, 2001.

71. *Izvestiia*, June 6, 1995.

72. *Segodnia*, June 8, 1995.

73. The Federation Council now participates informally but regularly in these "zero reading" consultations between government and Duma on a number of pieces of legislation, which in turn allows its members' interests to be accommodated before and

during the passage of bills through the Duma. This is one reason that nearly all legislation reaching the Federation Council from the Duma passes.

74. Ivan Preobrazhenskii, "Pravitel'stvo naidet deneg dlia vsekh," from the website of the Center for Political Technologies, Politkom.ru, as of August 7, 2003.

75. Haggard and McCubbins, *Presidents, Parliaments, and Policy.*

76. R. Kent Weaver and Bert A. Rockman, eds., *Do Institutions Matter? Government Capabilities in the United States and Abroad* (Washington, DC: Brookings, 1993).

Chapter Ten

Conclusion: The State of the State in Putin's Russia

Stephen Holmes

By enriching our understanding of the capacities and debilities of the postcommunist Russian state, this book naturally raises the question of trajectory. How have the contours of the Russian state changed since Vladimir Putin acceded to power? And what kind of a state are Putin and his circle trying to create? By drawing attention to the complex maze of relations *inside* the federal executive, our authors have opened a little explored but promising path toward addressing such questions. Putin has dramatically diminished the noisy conflicts, raging in Yeltsin's Russia, between the federal executive and rival centers of power, namely, the Duma and Federation Council, the gubernatorial bureaucracies (such as Moscow city government), the so-called oligarchs (including the media barons), the regional industrialists, and the natural monopolies. Today's surface calm may not signify that all conflicts have been resolved, however. It is more likely to signal a *relocation* of conflicts inside the federal executive where they have become frustratingly harder to study. By looking inside the federal executive, therefore, this volume, besides explaining the past, should help shed important light on poorly understood present trends.

THE YELTSIN LEGACY

For outsiders, the most dramatic feature of the 1991 collapse of the Soviet state was territorial amputation. Moscow lost control over vast swaths of land and

299

population to the south and west. An equally dramatic breakup occurred inside the political apparatus, namely the overnight disappearance of the Communist Party (CP). Dashed together with the party hierarchy was the principal instrument for supervising and coordinating the various specialized bureaucracies that made up the Soviet state. Under the old regime, ministries and other executive agencies (such as the Procuracy) had, with varying degrees of loyalty and resistance, served the CP. In 1991, they were suddenly "orphaned." They were thrown back on their own resources, left scrambling to find a new mission and perhaps a new master.

Yeltsin's Kremlin entourage no doubt dreamed that all Russian ministries would someday work in tandem and defer to orders delivered from above. But executive authority, during his incumbency, remained essentially fragmented or dispersed among squabbling agencies, unable to agree on a common agenda. As we have seen, the left hand often did not know what the right hand was doing. Ministerial staffs were confused by overlapping jurisdictions and unclear chains of command. They concealed useful information from their counterparts in rival agencies. They worked at cross purposes, lobbied for clashing interests, vied for scarce resources, and pursued disparate policies, while paying only occasional lip service to the ostensibly common purposes weakly articulated by the Kremlin.

Executive agencies and ministries that habitually conceal essential information from each other and work at cross-purposes tend to produce incoherent and self-defeating policies. They also tend to seize up in periodic deadlocks and to react slowly to unexpected crises. That Yeltsin's ministries did not always sing from the same songbook was clear from tensions between the Central Bank and the Ministry of Finance. Rivalries among the Ministry of Justice, the Procuracy, and the judiciary, and conflicts among the Ministry of Defense, the Foreign Ministry, and the General Staff were also serious and sometimes virulent.

Admittedly, all modern states suffer from some failures of interagency coordination. (This should be especially clear to American analysts who have recently witnessed two highly dysfunctional intra-executive conflicts between the Pentagon and the State Department and between the FBI and the CIA.) But there is good reason to believe that pluralism inside the postcommunist Russian executive, 1991–2000, was particularly disorderly and dysfunctional, to the point, as several contributors have remarked, where different ministries, under Yeltsin, negotiated with each other as if they were foreign countries.

The disappearance of the Communist Party was not the only factor encouraging turf warfare among the disjointed bits and pieces of the post-1991 Russian state. Russia's immense natural resource riches presented an almost irresistible temptation to nomenklatura-criminal networks. It is very unlikely that any political system could have maintained its inner coherence—that is, could have kept its agents focused on common national purposes—within grasping distance of such beckoning treasures. Russia's abundant natural resources, therefore, bear a good deal of responsibility for the pathological incoherence of the Russian state in the 1990s. The scramble for windfall wealth helped wrench the already weakened state apparatus apart and drew various fragments of the disintegrating political system into the sordid machinations of rival predatory clans.

Striking about this disorderly situation, as several contributors to this volume have pointed out, was the promiscuous blurring of political power and economic wealth. The example of Gazprom immediately leaps to mind. The Russian economy, under Yeltsin, was neither a free-market economy nor a command economy nor a mixed economy. It was, instead, an unevenly politicized (and to some extent criminalized) economy. In this system, as we have learned, the state was both a player and a regulator. Russia's corporate elite was created by state action and the umbilical cord was never cut. A typical example was the $100 million tax break that, in 1996, First Deputy Prime Minister Vladimir Potanin granted to Norilsk Nikel, a company that he owned. The concept of "state capture" is too anodyne to capture this extraordinary commingling of power wielders and profit seekers.

PUTIN'S RESPONSE

Formally, Putin's powers under the 1993 constitution remain more or less the same as Yeltsin's. But the way he exercises those powers and the informal networks he uses to rule are different. The principal differences between Yeltsin and Putin can be summarized by the latter's commitment to the "consolidation of vertical power." One of Putin's most striking accomplishments is the transformation of the obstreperous Duma of the 1990s into a docile and submissive body, thereby effectively reuniting legislative and executive power, Soviet-style, in the Kremlin's hands. By strengthening the presidential administration in this and other ways, he is, or says he is, trying both to overcome the bureaucratic fragmentation and duplication just described and to increase the government's bargaining power vis-à-vis oligarchic capitalism.

During the preliminary phase of post-Yeltsin state building, the Kremlin set out to bring to heel rival centers of power outside the federal executive. As a result, a state has now emerged that looks more coercive than participatory, perhaps more monarchical than democratic, with a severe and mysterious tsar at the pinnacle of power. The *vybory bez vybora* (elections without a choice) of March 2004 showcased the Kremlin's ability to work its will without any serious resistance from elected legislators, hostile political parties, the media, or civil society.

Immediately after the 2004 presidential election, moreover, Putin launched a major initiative at administrative reform, with the ostensible goal of rationalizing and streamlining the federal bureaucracy. We may consider this the beginning of the second phase of Putin's state-building project. The question is, how should we interpret it?

Before answering this question, we need to acknowledge how difficult it has become to understand the inner workings of the Kremlin under Putin. If an insider as clever and well-informed as Mikhail Khodorkovsky could so grossly misunderstand the nature of Russian *vlast'*, then outside commentators should offer their observations with considerable modesty. Neither the press nor the foreign diplomatic core has the same access today as they did under Yeltsin. This is reason enough for skepticism about the much touted consolidation of vertical power. The Kremlin can dispirit adversaries and rally supporters by spreading false rumors of its own irresistible power. In fact, it sometimes seems less interested in capacity building than in incapacity hiding. But a press blackout is not a sign of increased state power. It may, on the contrary, be a sign of anxiety. It may indicate fear of disclosing weakness and incompetence, for example. Everything we say about Putin's state-building aspirations or plans, as a result, must remain highly tentative.

We are nevertheless on fairly safe ground when we assert that Putin is trying to overcome some troubling features of the Yeltsin legacy by subordinating all federal ministries and executive agencies, including the office of the prime minister, to the will of the Kremlin. The Russian state under Putin will no doubt be more of a unified actor than it was under Yeltsin. But we can be forgiven for asking if this new bureaucratic "harmony," wrought by strong-arm tactics, will necessarily serve the greater good of ordinary Russians.

So how has Putin set about introducing a measure of coherence into the federal executive? To answer this question we need to look first at the new political dominance of the Federal Security Service or FSB. In order to call the shots at the Central Bank, Minatom, the General Staff, the Procuracy, or any other executive agency or ministry, the Kremlin must be able to replace holdover personnel with new cadres unswervingly loyal to the presidential administration. To consolidate vertical power, the Kremlin needs a reliable staff as well as extensive oversight capacities to keep operational officers steadily in line. This is the proper context in which to view Putin's recent administrative reform initiative. His aim is apparently to purge the remaining Yeltsin-era officials and replenish the federal bureaucracy with compliant personnel drawn from the FSB and other clandestine services.

The FSB seems to be the most successful "orphan" of the deceased Communist Party of the USSR. Its cadres may well have proven more loyal than those of any other Soviet-era bureaucracy. Not only did 1991 release the FSB from CP supervision. The subsequent years of government insolvency and disorientation also led to the nearly total collapse of one of its principal rivals, namely the Russian military. Thus, when the Kremlin managed to pluck from obscurity a minor FSB officer and stage-manage his election to the presidency, few observers doubted that the *spetzsluzhba* itself had some role in the process. Their behind-the-scenes role seems to have grown larger over time. As a result, we cannot even state with confidence that the Russian presidency has become fully institutionalized, with powers that would pass to a properly elected successor who happened not to be backed by the FSB.

AN AUTHORITARIAN STATE?

Reflecting on the influence of the FSB, pessimistic commentators argue that Putin is basically an authoritarian ruler who would have already shed his liberal clothing if he did not need to deceive the eyes of Western observers. They regard him, not altogether implausibly, as a KGB master of disguises. He may have rented a few liberal advisers as trompe l'oeil cabinet dressing; but he is obsessed with secrecy and bristles at the slightest criticism, even when justified and constructive. He has eliminated the independent monitoring of government agencies, subordinating oversight bodies to the ministries they oversee. He uses the Audit Chamber to harass political rivals rather than to expose government waste. He has shut down independent television, so that news programs now lead with the president's daily schedule. He has attempted to fill the space evacuated by genuine civil society organizations with cardboard replicas that do the bidding of the Kremlin. And he has orchestrated his own unopposed reelection to the presidency, not hesitating to violate freedom of speech and freedom of assembly in the process.

This is all dismaying, especially to those who expected some grand historical teleology to sweep Russia irresistibly toward Western-style democracy. But to understand the basic political dynamic in Putin's Russia, it is essential to grasp that authoritarianism is just as difficult to consolidate as democracy. There is no evidence, in fact, that Putin is attempting to create an authoritarian state on the Soviet model. This is true, even though the Kremlin faces no organized resistance from below. Political parties supporting democratic freedoms are anemic and exhausted and the citizenry remains apathetic, passive, poorly organized, and without political influence. But the absence of a political opposition is neither proof of state capacity nor an indicator that Putin is reviving a Soviet-style authoritarian state.

The Kremlin can certainly hurt individuals. But we cannot infer from isolated abuses of police powers that the institutional framework within which they occur is evolving toward despotism. It is very difficult to estimate the authoritarian potential of a state, for one thing, in a situation where the irritants that it combats and occasionally eliminates are intrinsically weak and defenseless, where the plants that it plucks out have embarrassingly shallow roots. It does not take much force to rip out a rootless flower, such as the "civil society" artificially planted in Russia by Western nongovernmental organizations (NGOs). Breaking Khodorkovsky was not especially difficult. Jailing or exiling ruthless tycoons, who are happy to sell each other to the tax police or the Procuracy, does not evince massive power. We should therefore not confuse the absence of a noisy opposition with the capacity to solve difficult problems or impose authoritarian discipline on an unruly society.

True, Putin has been able to balance the budget and take care of salary and pension arrears, thanks in part to sky-high world oil prices. He has also decreased and stabilized incomes taxes and profit taxes, to universal acclaim. But his record probably displays more grim failures than luminous successes. For one thing, he has not been able to end the bloodletting in Chechnya. His troops have spectacularly failed to assert control over the country's own territory, so that Russian soldiers in Grozny are as likely to be shot as American soldiers in Baghdad. The military's power is largely negative, it seems. It can destabilize the near abroad, but cannot govern it. Similarly, Putin has proven unable to reduce crime rates or address the country's demographic or health catastrophes. He has not been able to reform the educational system, the legal system, or the military, nor has he been able to respond intelligently to a series of emergencies from the Kursk to Nord-Ost. His government has not dealt effectively with the leaks from decommissioned nuclear submarines in the North Sea, nor has it improved security at plutonium storage sites. It has not been able to provide such elementary public goods as a nontoxic environment, books in elementary schools, X-ray film in public hospitals, dignified veterans' benefits, a nationwide highway system, railroad maintenance, and potable water. And so forth.

More than any other factor, the failure to invest collective resources into the Russian military reveals the distance separating Putin's Russia from the USSR and the absence of ambition, in the Kremlin, to turn back the clock. A genuine restoration of Soviet-style rule, it should be said, would require a re-sealing of the borders or at least a drastic scaling back of unshielded contacts with the West. There are admittedly some signs that such a trend is underway. But a serious reversion to autarky is unlikely. Not only would it strike directly at material interests of influential individuals in the Russian establishment, but it would also leave Russia alone with problems (such as maintaining what is left of the country's territorial integrity despite a militarily exposed southern flank) that cannot be confronted without Western help over the long haul.

State building in Russia also faces another obstacle, namely the disproportion between the country's daunting problems and the modest tools and resources available to the Kremlin. By the vastness of problems, I mean something that innumerable observers and experts have described in shocking detail, namely a massive crisis of deferred maintenance in eleven time zones—the crisis of demodernization that ranges from a public health disaster to rivers choked by pollution and includes a seemingly unstoppable rotting away of the transportation infrastructure, the educational system, and other basic public services, and the basic nonviability of Soviet-era rust belt industries that became clear once Russia was opened up to the modern global economy. By the weakness of tools, I mean lack of adequate funds and the poor quality of federal bureaucracies, the result of many years of hemorrhaging talent, low pay, collapsing morale, blurred chains of command and so forth. This disproportion naturally generates a tendency in the Kremlin to wash the central government's hands of unsolvable problems, off-loading them onto hapless regional and local officials. This delegation downward of thankless responsibilities was endemic under Yeltsin and has not ceased under Putin. Why claim to be all-powerful in a country where catastrophes occur with increasing frequency? Governors who preserve some degree of independence can be more plausibly blamed for poverty in their regions. Putin clearly recognizes the usefulness of burden shifting. His need for deniability may even explain why he has not done more to increase the power of his "super-governors," originally created to increase Moscow's grip on the provinces, but now widely viewed as only modestly effective.

BUILDING AN ILLIBERAL STATE

As a tightly knit and hierarchically organized corporate group, the FSB has collective habits as well as corporate interests. Its culture was shaped in a "fortress state" that was cut off from a supposedly hostile world. Surveillance, secrecy, and intimidation come as second nature to its officers. They are driven to eliminate all opposing forces, even when these rivals are fundamentally weak and pose no real threat. This is because their mind-set classifies negotiation as a sign of weakness. They are said to prefer ruling over a desert to dealing tactfully with independent forces that could be helpful partners but that could also annoyingly refuse to comply with diktats from above.

This is the most powerful objection to those optimists who see Putin as a Russian Pinochet, using authoritarian means to achieve liberal goals. Since 80 percent of the Russian population lives in poverty and is shut out of consumer society, such optimists argue, any genuine market reformer would have to turn a deaf ear to the pleading of the popular majority. They acknowledge Putin's authoritarian side, in other words, but argue that he is an "autocratic reformer" who is struggling to establish new rules of the game, balance the budget, stanch capital flight, reduce foreign borrowing, knock some sense into the predatory elite, introduce political stability and legal certainty, shield ordinary citizens from racketeers and bribe-taking officials, and encourage investments.

Some important evidence can be adduced to support such a rosy claim. The problem with this diagnosis, however, is that economic liberalism requires a liberal-minded ruling group. The *siloviki* currently in power sometimes cultivate a liberal image to assuage the suspicions of Western businessmen, bankers, and statesmen. But they also have very strong incentives to prevent the emergence of a genuinely liberal political system. For instance, the power ministries do not want their off-budget slush funds to become visible to the Ministry of Finance or the treasury. To this ingrained hostility to transparency, which is an economic, not merely democratic virtue, we need to add a deep resistance to predictability.

The elemental illiberalism of the FSB should not be in question. Its main strategy for ruling is to inject uncertainty into people's lives. Fomenting uncertainty, keeping people off balance, is one way it maintains its domination. That is how it governs. The Khodorkovsky episode strongly suggests that this is a highly self-conscious approach. CEOs can be brought into line by decreasing the security of their jobs, assets, citizenship, and bodily liberty. People who feel secure are harder to control than people who feel insecure. Indeed, if a property holder feels secure in his property, he may employ that property as a platform from which to attack the government. He may use it as a staging area from which to expose the Kremlin's stupidities and even crimes. He may create an NTV.

However eloquently the Kremlin speaks about the need to stabilize property rights, its ability to follow through and render property holders secure remains dubious. Can the Kremlin reliably stabilize property rights while repeatedly destabilizing its critics and potential critics? Its capacity to target insecurity so accurately, to deliver uncertainty so selectively, is questionable, to say the least. And therefore the Kremlin's real, rather than merely rhetorical, commitment to liberalism remains highly dubious, whatever its defenders and apologists say.

INSECURE PARTNERS FOR AN INSECURE STATE

Liberal state building does not depend only on the intentions and mental habits of ruling groups. It also depends on the way power is distributed in society. A liberal state is very unlikely to emerge unless a large number of well-organized and independent social groups induce the government, by threats and negotiation, to make its behavior predictable. But where, in today's Russia, might Putin find a well-organized and politically powerful constituency to support the creation of a liberal state, dedicated to transparency and the rule of law? What profit seekers in Putin's Russia have a strong motive to stop asking for ad hoc exemptions and special help and to start asking for rules that will be reliably enforced by independent courts? How many legally minded profit seekers, who seek no unfair advantage over business rivals, exist in Russia today? Will Russia's rich begin to view Russia's court system in the amiable way in which other privileged groups around the world view their national courts, that is, as more or less effective debt collection agencies, designed to help the wealthy keep their money?

Putin, it should be said, has done relatively little to clarify the blurred boundaries between the regulatory state and the regulated economy. He has reasserted direct and indirect control over some parts of the formerly state-owned economy that had escaped Kremlin control during the 1990s. And he has made sure that the most important private actors, namely the vertically integrated oil companies, have understood that their CEOs could be imprisoned and their assets allocated to rivals if the Kremlin so wished. Thus, Russia's remaining oligarchs, holding onto their assets at the sufferance of the Kremlin, have been chastened by the examples of Gusinsky, Berezovsky, and Khodorkovsky.

Attentive to foreign opinion, the oilmen, in particular, have also publicly proclaimed their eagerness to embrace the rule of law. But talk is cheap. Why should we believe them if we know they have an interest in deceiving us? Remember that most if not all of the truly wealthy Russians have accumulated their wealth under murky and shifting rules that have been fairly easy to evade. They have good reasons to believe that their own rude skills of acquisition would lose value in a system where clear rules were reliably enforced by independent agencies. And they would not be wrong to fear that, under such a system, the skills of foreigners, perfectly at ease in rule-of-law environments, would gain in relative value. So why would most Russian businessmen support the introduction of the rule of law, rather than merely paying lip service to the idea?

For a liberal state to emerge, two conditions must coincide: power wielders must have an incentive to make their own power predictable and profit seekers must have an incentive to ask for general rules rather than special deals. If this generalization has any merit, then what is the chance that a liberal state is being created in Putin's Russia? If the FSB cannot renounce unpredictability and the remaining oligarchs cannot renounce special deals, then how will Putin cobble together a political coalition favoring the rule of law? Where will he find support for this aspect of his consolidation of vertical power?

When private wealth is as heavily concentrated as it is in Russia, it becomes temptingly easy for the lethally armed government to work its will by a *nyet-cheloveka-nyet-problemy* approach. This may be why liberal state building has historically depended upon a wide dispersal of wealth—much wider that what we observe in Russia today—making it less attractive for the government to use force and more attractive for it to enter into negotiated exchanges with its tax base. What students of Putinism need to ask is: Where, inside Russia, could the Kremlin locate political support for a liberal state, assuming (implausibly) that it would view such a state as desirable? Liberalism obviously has no constituency among the vast majority of Russians who own no property, lack the means to enjoy freedom of travel, and have no interest in freedom of the press.

The remaining oil barons are often mentioned in this regard. But they are too vulnerable and there are too few of them to exert the requisite pressure on governing authorities. True, they still retain significant bargaining power, because the country's cash flow depends to a considerable extent on their management skills. They cannot all be replaced, at least not in the short run, by members of the FSB. But they no longer imagine themselves as economic powers that can rival the state. Their position has become insecure. They continue to negotiate with the state, often quite successfully, but they now know that their bargaining partner has a cocked gun under the table.

Despite his efforts so far, Putin has failed to improve the investment climate to the degree wished for and promised. This is probably because his loyalty to, and reliance on, the FSB has compelled him to accept citizen uncertainty as the price for establishing and maintaining order. Pervasive insecurity will continue to make long-term investment unattractive, effectively undermining efforts at stabilization periodically undertaken, perhaps with the best of intentions, in other domains.

To be sure, Yeltsinism and Putinism are not entirely discontinuous. To bring the continuities into focus we need only examine state/society relations, that is, the connection between the country's ruling elite and its general public. Despite all the talk about democracy, freedom of the press, and civil society, Yeltsin did little to reduce the Soviet-era gap between government and the public. Under Yeltsin, too, power was in the hands of a "hovercraft elite." To say that its ruling and profiteering groups were democratically unaccountable is to put it mildly. The total absence of legislative control over privatization is well known. The Yeltsin-era elite, such as it was, staged democratic rituals, but it had little interest in consulting with civil society. And under Putin, despite the serious changes under way, a very similar pattern prevails. In Yeltsin's Russia, an incoherent state was tenuously connected to a demoralized society. In Putin's Russia, by contrast, a somewhat more coherent state is tenuously connected to a demoralized society. This is the essence of the change.

Ordinary Russians are therefore not deluded when they continue to associate *vlast'* with the power and privileges of an indifferent few or when they describe politics as an insider's game serving insider interests. Repressive elites are now proudly back in the saddle, while the extractive elites of the 1990s have scampered ignominiously under the carpet. But the powerful remain essentially detached from the population and are still, presumably, focused on their own well-being. Relations may shift again in unpredictable ways. But experience suggests that, however the identity of power wielders changes, we are not going to witness anytime soon the emergence of a ruling group in any way accountable to ordinary citizens. The state will remain detached and nonresponsive to society. Its officers will continue to look after themselves, first of all. This disinterest in the commonweal will continue even if the entire executive bureaucracy is brought to heel by the Kremlin.

The total lack of accountability of the (incoherent or coherent) Russian state to Russian society appears to be the one steady point in a turning world. Yeltsin's Russia was marked by the fragmentation and decentralization of unaccountable power. Putin's state-building project, if we want to call it that, is focused on recentralizing this unaccountable and unrepresentative power, not making it more accountable. We may eventually get to the point where the Procuracy, Goskomstat, the Central Bank, and so forth all work exclusively for the Kremlin, rather than serving a diversified clientele on an ad hoc basis. We are not there yet, but that appears to be where we are headed. But if recentralization goes so far, it will do nothing to increase transparency and accountability.

For what purpose is the Kremlin trying to recentralize unaccountable power in this way? It seems fair to assume that it does not wish to impose an iron discipline on all of Russian society. It is no doubt less interested in governing Russia's poor and downtrodden masses than in inflicting pain on a few noxious enemies and securing control of Russia's natural resource wealth. To understand what sort of state is being built, therefore, we will need to keep track of future budgetary allocations. Expenditures can resoundingly falsify the analysis tentatively offered above. We will know that the FSB has less power than it now seems, for example, if the Yukos fortune is channeled toward rebuilding the decomposed military, a traditional rival of the FSB. And we will discover that the Kremlin is honestly focused on national problems, rather than taking care of the corporate interests of the ruling clique, if it channels collective resources toward refurbishing the decayed health, education, and transportation systems. If resources are channeled this way, we will have learned something unexpected and revealing. If not, our unpleasant suspicions will have been to some extent confirmed.

Whatever kind of state Putin is trying to build, it is not a state that will voluntarily explain itself or its decisions to its citizens. It will probably be dominated by a few executive agencies, capped by the FSB, survivors from the militarized wing of the Soviet bureaucracy. We may think of this as "state capture" by a subunit of the state. The ruling group will continue to be closed, its devotion to secrecy intense. Its plots and machinations will be difficult to follow. The consequences of its dominance are still unknown, although the emergence of some sort of "*silovik* capitalism" seems highly probable. All that we can predict with confidence is that Putin's Russia will not develop a political system where the folly and selfishness of governing circles will be easy to observe or combat.

Index

Alfa-Bank, 168–69
appreciation. *See* real appreciation
ARKO, 168
Aslund, Anders: on pension spending, 139

banks: bridge, 168; budget balance and governance of, 169–71; budget deficits' effect on, 160, 181n20; budget deficits as leverage for policy by, 156; capital accumulation in Russian, 162–63; CBR governing, 157; commercial, 205; criteria for, 173; cross-country analysis of governance's quality on, *161*, 161–62; in currency crisis as intermediaries, 198; currency risk of, 205; declining political polarizations' effect on governance of, 171–75; deposit insurance from, 165, 173, 182n50, 185n95; devaluation as feared by commercial, 205; after financial crash, 168–69; fiscal irresponsibility of commercial, 200; foreign, 169; frailty in postcommunist Russian state of, 155; incentives for stronger regulations for institutions, 170–71; Mamut plan for, 171; moratorium on international debt payments by domestic, 208; neocommunist/anticommunist elites' political conflict led to weak state, 160–61, 178, 181n24; oligarchic, 159; opacity of, 167, 173; ownership structures of, 173; pocket, 157, 176, 185n86; policymaking by, 163; policy uncertainty and, 156; political polarization and governance of, 162, 165–66; private, 164; private versus state, 166; quality of governance in sector of, 156–58; reform for, 172; risks of lending, 170; in Russia from 1990–1999, 162–68; in Russia from 2000–2004, 168–77; Russian government's stance on foreign, 173–74; shares for loans program between Russian and, 229, 250n20; spetz, 157, 167; state council

311

About the Contributors

Timothy J. Colton is professor of government and director of the Davis Center for Russian and Eurasian Studies at Harvard University. He is author of *The Dilemma of Reform in the Soviet Union* (1986), *Moscow: Governing the Socialist Metropolis* (1995), *Transitional Citizens: Voters and What Influences Them in the New Russia* (2000), and other books. His study *Not in One Leap: A Political Biography of Boris Yeltsin* is forthcoming in 2007.

Linda J. Cook is professor of political science at Brown University and an associate at the Davis Center of Russian and Eurasian Studies at Harvard University as well as the Watson Center for International Studies at Brown. Her main research interests are in the politics of Russia, the former Soviet Union, and Eastern Europe and in domestic and international influences on welfare states. She authored *The Soviet Social Contract and Why It Failed* (1993), and is currently revising a book manuscript, *Postcommunist Welfare States: Negotiating Change in Russia, Eastern Europe, and the CIS*, for publication.

Gerald Easter is associate professor of political science at Boston College. He specializes in the comparative politics of Russia and Eastern Europe. He is author of *Reconstructing the State: Personal Networks and Elite Identity in Soviet Russia* (2000) and of *Capital, Coercion, and Postcommunist States* (forthcoming).

Timothy Frye is professor of political science at Columbia University. He is author of *Brokers and Bureaucrats: Building Market Institutions in Russia* (2000) and of articles on property rights and the rule of law in Russia and trade liberalization in the postcommunist world. He is currently writing a book on the politics of economic reform in postcommunist countries titled *Partisan Politics in Transition Economies.*

Yoshiko M. Herrera is John L. Loeb Associate Professor of the Social Sciences in the Department of Government at Harvard University. Her research interests include politics in Russia and the former Soviet states, social identities, norms and institutional change, and constructivist political economy. She is author of *Imagined Economies: The Sources of Russian Regionalism* (2005) and of *Transforming Bureaucracy: Conditional Norms and the International Standardization of Statistics in Russia* (forthcoming).

Stephen Holmes is Walter E. Meyer Professor of Law at New York University School of Law. He previously taught at the University of Chicago and Princeton University and was a Carnegie Scholar in 2003. His interests include the history of liberalism, the disappointments of democratization after communism, and the difficulty of combating terrorism within the limits of liberal constitutionalism. He is author of *Benjamin Constant and the Making of Modern Liberalism* (1984), *The Anatomy of Antiliberalism* (1993), and *Passions and Constraint: On the Theory of Liberal Democracy* (1995) and the coauthor (with Cass Sunstein) of *The Cost of Rights: Why Liberty Depends on Taxes* (1999).

Pauline Jones Luong is associate professor of political science at Brown University. Her research interests include institutional development, identity and conflict, and the political economy of market reform. Her books include *Institutional Change and Political Continuity in Post-Soviet Central Asia: Power, Perceptions, and Pacts* (2002) and an edited volume, *The Transformation of Central Asia: States and Societies from Soviet Rule to Independence* (2003). She is currently finishing a coauthored book manuscript (with Erika Weinthal) titled *Enriching the State: Resource Wealth, Ownership Structure, and Institutional Capacity.*

Thomas F. Remington is professor of political science and chair of the political science department at Emory University. Among his publications are two books on the Russian parliament: *The Russian Parliament: Institutional Evolution in a Transitional Regime, 1989–1999* (2001) and *The Politics of Institutional Choice: Formation of the Russian State Duma* (coauthored with

Steven S. Smith, 2001). Other books include *Politics in Russia*, 4th ed. (2006), *Parliaments in Transition* (1994), and *The Truth of Authority: Ideology and Communication in the Soviet Union* (1988). His research focuses on the development of representative institutions in postcommunist Russia, particularly the legislative branch and legislative-executive relations, and on problems of governance in postcommunist states.

Kathryn Stoner-Weiss is associate director of research and senior research scholar at the Center on Democracy, Development, and Rule of Law at the Freeman Spogli Institute for International Studies at Stanford University. She was previously on the faculty at Princeton University, jointly appointed to the Department of Politics and the Woodrow Wilson School for International and Public Affairs. In addition to many articles and book chapters on contemporary Russia, she is author of *Local Heroes: The Political Economy of Russian Regional Governance* (1997) and *Resisting the State: Reform and Retrenchment in Post-Soviet Russia* (2006). She is also coeditor (with Michael McFaul) of *After the Collapse of Communism: Comparative Lessons of Transition* (2004).

Daniel Treisman is professor of political science at the University of California, Los Angeles. He is author of *After the Deluge: Regional Crises and Political Consolidation in Russia* (1999), *Without a Map: Political Tactics and Economic Reform in Russia* (coauthored with Andrei Shleifer, 2000), and of articles on a variety of topics related to Russian politics and comparative political economy. He is currently working on a book about the consequences of political decentralization. He has received fellowships from the Guggenheim Foundation, the German Marshall Fund of the United States, the Smith Richardson Foundation, and the Hoover Institution.

Erika Weinthal is associate professor of environmental policy at the Nicholas School of the Environment and Earth Sciences at Duke University. Her research focuses on environmental and natural resources policy. She is author of *State Making and Environmental Cooperation: Linking Domestic and International Politics in Central Asia* (2002). Her current book project (with Pauline Jones Luong) is entitled *Enriching the State: Resource Wealth, Ownership Structure, and Institutional Capacity.*